"THE HIGHER CHRISTIAN LIFE"

SOURCES FOR THE STUDY OF THE HOLINESS, PENTECOSTAL, AND KESWICK MOVEMENTS

*A forty-eight-volume
facsimile series reprinting
extremely rare documents for the study of
nineteenth-century religious and social history,
the rise of feminism, and the history of the
Pentecostal and Charismatic movements*

Edited by
Donald W. Dayton
Northern Baptist Theological Seminary

Advisory Editors
D. William Faupel, *Asbury Theological Seminary*
Cecil M. Robeck, Jr., *Fuller Theological Seminary*
Gerald T. Sheppard, *Union Theological Seminary*

A GARLAND SERIES

THREE EARLY PENTECOSTAL TRACTS

with a Preface by
Donald W. Dayton
Northern Baptist
Theological Seminary

Garland Publishing, Inc.
New York & London
1985

For a complete list of the titles in this series
see the final pages of this volume.

The facsimiles of *The Spirit and the Bride* has been made
from a copy in the library of Emmanuel College.

Library of Congress Cataloging-in-Publication Data
Main entry under title:

THREE EARLY PENTECOSTAL TRACTS.

("The Higher Christian life")
Reprint (1st work). Originally published: Chicago,
Ill., U.S.A. : Evangel Pub. House, 1910.
Reprint (2nd work). Originally published: 1907?
Reprint (3rd work). Originally published: St. Louis,
Mo. : Gospel Pub. House, © 1916.
Contents: The latter rain convenant and Pentecostal
power / D. Wesley Myland — The spirit and the bride /
G.F. Taylor — The apostolic faith restored / B.F.
Lawrence.
1. Pentecostalism—Addresses, essays, lectures.
I. Myland, D. Welsey, 1858–1943. Latter rain covenant
and Pentecostal power. 1985 II. Taylor, George
Floyd, 1881–1934. Spirit and the bride. 1985.
III. Lawrence, Bennett Freeman, 1890–   . Apostolic
faith restored. 1985 IV. Series.
BR1644.T48 1985   230'.99   85-20734
ISBN 0-8240-6415-1 (alk. paper)

The volumes in this series are printed on
acid-free, 250-year-life paper.

Printed in the United States of America

CONTENTS

PREFACE

This volume brings together three of the earliest and most important tracts of the Pentecostal movement during its first decade or so of existence. They illustrate the varieties of approach developed in offering an apologetic for the new movement and reveal something of the regional differences within the movement.

The earliest of these, *The Spirit and the Bride* (apparently published in 1907) originated in the holiness-oriented southern Pentecostal denomination that became the Pentecostal Holiness Church. George Floyd Taylor (1881–1934), whose life is the best documented of the authors represented in this volume, was born near Magnolia, North Carolina, and labored all his life under the burden of a congenital physical handicap. His roots were apparently in the Methodist Episcopal Church, South, but in 1902 he fell under the influence of the holiness movement and joined the Holiness Church, the major antecedent of the present-day Pentecostal Holiness Church. Much of his life was centered around the leadership of schools that he founded: Bethel Holiness School (near Rose Hill, North Carolina), 1903; Falcon Holiness School (Falcon, North Carolina), 1907; and Franklin Springs Institute (Franklin Springs, Georgia, now Emmanuel College), 1919, which he served until his early death. Taylor served in a variety of denominational offices, as well, becoming perhaps the determinitive figure in the emerging denomination as founder and editor of the *Pentecostal Holiness Advocate*, founder of the Advocate Press (including starting the denominational program of Sunday School literature), and holder of denominational offices (Conference Superintendent, General Treasurer, and General Superintendent). He was also

PREFACE

author of a number of books and tracts, of which the most widely circulated was *The Second Coming of Christ* (1916).

The Spirit and the Bride was written in 1907, the year that Taylor was "baptized in the Spirit" and was incorporated into the Pentecostal movement. Chapters V and VIII especially reveal the struggle of the Pentecostal movement in articulating a distinctive stance against the holiness movement which had identified the "baptism of the Holy Ghost" with the experience of "entire sanctification" or "Christian perfection" as it had been understood in the traditions of Methodism stemming from the work of John Wesley. In these chapters we see an early statement of the three "blessings" or "works of grace" that characterize (and perhaps define) the large branch of Pentecostalism in the holiness tradition. This tradition of Pentecostalism accepted the "second blessing" of the holiness movement but refused to identify this experience with the "baptism of the Spirit." This "baptism" was understood to be a third experience evidenced, as also indicated in chapter V, by "speaking in tongues."

Chapter IX illustrates the Pentecostal claim to be the "latter rain" of spiritual blessing and restoration of spiritual gifts of which Pentecost was understood to be the prototype or "early rain." This very distinctive argument—the source of one of the most important names of the early Pentecostal movement—made the nonexistence of such gifts in most of the history of mainstream Christianity an argument for the validity of Pentecostalism and part of the apologetic for the new movement. This argument led to a self-understanding of the historical lineage of Pentecostalism expressed at the end of Chapter X, which also serves as an excellent summary of Pentecostal theology. The "latter rain" argument also shows the close linkage between the restoration of the gifts and the announcement of the imminence of the return of Christ which was so characteristic of early Pentecostalism that many thought that its distinctive message was about the end of the age.

This "latter rain" apologetic for Pentecostalism was given its definitive articulation a few years later by D. Wesley Myland (1858–1943). Myland was born in Ontario, Canada, and his early denominational identification was with the Methodist Episcopal

Church. He apparently, as indicated in the last chapter of his tract here reprinted, moved toward the holiness tradition primarily through the healing movement, a theme emphasized by the Christian and Missionary Alliance (see G. P. Pardington, *Twenty-five Wonderful Years*, reprinted as volume 34 in this series) and the World's Faith Missionary Association, groups with which Myland was identified before the turn of the century. Myland came into the Pentecostal experience in 1907 and was involved awhile with the Gibeah Bible School (Plainfield, Indiana, near Indianapolis) and the Association of Christian Assemblies centered there before moving on into the emerging Assemblies of God, the largest American white Pentecostal denomination. Myland was variously an evangelist, an evangelistic singer and author of gospel songs, a bible school principal and author.

His major work, reprinted here, was *The Latter Rain Covenant and Pentecostal Power*, for the most part originally given as a series of lectures at the Stone Church in Chicago at a Pentecostal convention in the spring of 1909. These lectures were first published in *The Latter Rain Evangel*, edited by William Hamner Piper, the pastor of the Stone Church, and then issued in book form out of the *Evangel* offices in Chicago. Significantly this book is already introduced by Alexander Boddy, a Church of England clergyman who by this time had had his own Pentecostal experience.

This tract is the definitive articulation of the "latter rain" apologetic for Pentecostalism. This edition contains an interesting appendix in which the patterns of physical rainfall in Palestine are used as an argument for the coming of the "end times" and the return of Christ. The volume is also noteworthy for the theme of divine healing in the last chapter, which contains a narrative of the author's involvement in the healing movement and provides interesting documentation about the spread of the healing movement in the late nineteenth century.

The third tract in this volume is by Bennett Freeman Lawrence (1890–?), whose denominational roots were in the Christian Catholic Church of Alexander Dowie of Zion, Illinois. He along with other founders of the Assemblies of God briefly held credentials in the predominantly black Church of God in Christ.

PREFACE

Lawrence was active in the founding of the Assemblies of God and served awhile as a denominational official before being "rebaptized" in the "Jesus Only" wing of Pentecostalism (represented in volume 13 in this series of reprints).

The Apostolic Faith Restored is a very useful volume in that it collects early reports of the spread of the Pentecostal movement by participants in the events. It also stands in striking contrast to the apologetic of the other two "latter rain" arguments reprinted in this volume. Here the emphasis is on the "restoration" of the "apostolic faith" and the authenticity of the movement is grounded not in the "latter rain" argument but in the suggestion that there has been a tradition of Pentecostal-like piety down through the history of the church. Particularly interesting are the reports of speaking in tongues and other gifts in the late nineteenth century before the Pentecostal theology was clearly articulated and the movement had gained its own identity.

Donald W. Dayton
Northern Baptist
Theological Seminary

The
Latter Rain Covenant

and

Pentecostal Power

With Testimony of
Healings and Baptism

By
Rev. D. Wesley Myland

THE EVANGEL PUBLISHING HOUSE
CHICAGO, ILLINOIS, U. S. A.
1910

TABLE OF CONTENTS.

Prefatory

AT various times in the history of the Church God
has emphasized certain great scriptural truths—
Justification under Luther, Sanctification under Wesley, etc.

We are living in the time when the Latter Rain
truths are due, and hence God is giving them through
Spirit baptized Teachers.

"The Latter Rain Covenant!" Who ever heard
of it before? Of course we have read in Deuteronomy about "The Days of Heaven upon the Earth,"
but who has seen that those days were to be introduced through the spiritual outworkings of this Covenant? What a Wonderful God!

No man could have *thought* these lectures out;
they bear the imprint of heaven's teaching. How
marvelous the Book! Its treasures are deep and lie
hidden, except to the "mind of the Spirit," who reveals them to whomsoever He will.

Our studies in Exegesis have revealed nothing which
in uniqueness and originality equals this exposition
of the blessed Latter Rain truths. "How our hearts
burned within us" as we listened to their unfolding.

Those prejudiced against the Baptism in the Holy
Spirit; speaking in other tongues and the manifesta-

tions of the Spirit generally, we are persuaded will find nothing that will open their minds and hearts so much to these truths as this exposition of the Word, because of its great sweep of truth, covering, as it does, both the Old and New Testaments.

This treatise ought to be a required part of the curriculum of every really Pentecostal School.

Incorporated with the Latter Rain lectures is Brother Myland's striking exposition of the twenty-ninth Psalm, which is on the same general subject of the Latter Rain and Pentecost. The chapter entitled "In Deaths Oft" is a detailed account of his seven-fold miraculous escape from death through Divine Healing.

We have made a close study of all Pentecostal literature that has appeared during the past three or four years, and have been in close touch with the subject and work of Divine Healing for the last fifteen years, and in all this time we have not seen any scriptural exposition, nor have we seen or heard of any aggregation of healings in the life of one individual, equal to that which appears in this book. Prayer, as well as reading, will be necessary to a clear, spiritual understanding of these lectures. Language fails to express the blessing they have been to me.

WM. HAMNER PIPER, Pastor.

February 1910.   The Stone Church.
Chicago U. S. A.

Introduction

THE Victorious Cross of Calvary has been made very real to many of us through the out-pouring of the Latter Rain in these last three years, and the ever precious blood of the Son of God has proved in these times powerful in an extraordinary degree, both for cleansing and for keeping clean. This blessed baptism in the Holy Spirit with its Pentecostal sign of "tongues" is the blood-bought right of Christ's redeemed ones, and many such around the world are rejoicing today in the fact that the Lord has immersed them in Himself.

Not only in Chicago and Sunderland, not only in Los Angeles and London, but throughout the United States and Canada, throughout Great Britain and Germany; throughout Holland, Scandinavia, Africa, Asia and Australia, the Lord has graciously kindled Pentecostal fires which no man can extinguish.

The author of the remarkable book, "The Latter Rain Pentecost," shows among other things the significant fact that simultaneously the Jews are returning to their native land; the literal latter rain is falling upon Palestine, and the spiritual latter rain is falling upon God's expectant people.

There has been much literature issued of late in connection with the Baptism in the Holy Spirit, but nothing more scriptural or more satisfying has been printed than this remarkable book by Pastor D. Wesley Myland, which I now warmly commend to God's people everywhere. The author has been equipped for the work by the Holy Ghost Himself.

Some of us on this side the Atlantic are very thankful to Pastor Wm. Hamner Piper of Chicago for printing the articles in his most valuable paper, The Latter Rain Evangel, and now issuing them in book form.

This Pentecostal out-pouring of the Holy Spirit brings into touch many of the Lord's earnest followers, for which we have reason indeed to thank Him.

It was my great privilege last summer to meet many children of God in Pentecostal Camp Meetings in Canada and in the United States, who testified to the arrival of the spiritual "Latter Rain." So also in Amsterdam, Hamburg, Christiania, Zurich, London, Edinburgh and Sunderland, the writer has experienced a blessed fellowship with those who are looking for and hastening the coming of the Lord.

May this book, "The Latter Rain Pentecost," be found in every Pentecostal home. It is an invaluable work of reference on the all-important subject of the Baptism in the Holy Spirit.

ALEXANDER A. BODDY, Vicar.

Sunderland, England, December, 1909.

CHAPTER I.

The Latter Rain Covenant

OUR first study will be somewhat introductory and preparatory, but I am sure there will be enough of vital, practical truth in it to keep you busy with your own heart and with the Lord for a long time.

The present, and, we may say, mightier movement and manifestation of the Holy Spirit has been called, quite generally, "The Latter Rain," doubtless from the fact that it is at least the spiritual aspect of the outworking of God's great Latter Rain Covenant. If it is remembered that the climate of Palestine consisted of two seasons, the wet and the dry, and that the wet season was made up of the early and the latter rain, it will help you to understand this Covenant and the present workings of God's Spirit. For just as the literal early and latter rain was poured out upon Palestine, so upon the church of the First Century was poured out the spiritual early rain, and upon us today is being poured out the spiritual latter rain.

1

THE LATTER RAIN PENTECOST.

So we must approach this great discussion carefully, soberly, meditatively, if we want to cover the ground scripturally, and thoroughly, and get our experiences and lives to harmonize therewith; then we shall be so safe, so sound, and so happy in it all, that coming out into God's own purpose we shall realize the consummation of all His great plan for us and the world.

Now this great Latter Rain Covenant is found in the eleventh chapter of the Book of Deuteronomy, from the tenth to the twenty-first verses inclusive; twelve verses, typical, as someone has said, of the twelve tribes of Israel, to whom it was given, and also of the twelve patriarchs and the twelve apostles of the Lamb that form the great foundations of the city of God and the entrance thereto. Revelation 21: 12-14.

This movement is also called Pentecostal, and you hear that word perhaps more often than the other. Pentecost is simply the spiritual aspect of this Covenant, and means the fulness of the Spirit; that is to say, it is the display of God's power and glory as it was manifested first under the law at Mount Sinai; clouds, darkness, fire, glory, personal manifestation at the time of the inauguration and institution of the Israelitish people as a nation, and then its anti-type of Pentecost in the "Upper-Room" ten days after the ascension of our Lord, with the display of God's power, manifestations and glory in another body, greater than the Israelitish nation, the inauguration and organization of the body called the Christian Assembly, which stands as the highest order of God's work and to the highest praise of His glory of anything in His universe, even the very body of Christ.

Now we get a better idea of Pentecost if we hold these two things together, one under law and the other under grace. Turn with me to your New Testament II Corinthians 3:7-11, and let us look a little there, because I have been making a remark or two that needs to be buttressed with scripture. If I make any remark in all these addresses that is not supported and buttressed by scripture I will thank anybody to call my attention to it. If I preach anything but the Word of God, God bless the man or woman that will help me to get right. Let us look a moment at II Corinthians 3:7-11, for this scripture will substantiate the remark I just made concerning the double aspect of Pentecost at Sinai and in the Upper Room. "But if the ministration of death, written and engraven in stones, was glorious, so that the children of Israel could not steadfastly behold the face of Moses for the glory of his countenance; which glory was to be done away: How shall not the ministration of the spirit be rather (or more) glorious? For if the ministration of condemnation (under the law) be glorious, much more doth the ministration of righteousness (under grace) exceed in glory. For even that which was made glorious (under the law) had no glory in this respect, by reason of the glory that excelleth. For if that which was done away was glorious, much more that which remaineth is glorious. Seeing then that we have such hope, we use great plainness of speech"—concerning Pentecostal things. I wish people would get cured of their hesitancy about Pentecost. Therefore we use great plainness of speech, we approach these things with great confidence. We approach the mount of grace from which the glory of grace is manifested, with greater confidence than Moses approached the mount that shook and quaked with fire, for he had to go "into the thick darkness where God was"; but we come through the glorious Gospel to the face of Jesus Christ, our Elder Brother, and yet we hesitate. And if the law condemned people on this lesser ground, shall not we be more condemned if we neglect the great light of the closing days of this dispensation of grace, for if they were judged who received the law by the disposition of angels, "how shall we escape if we neglect so great a salvation" which was spoken by the Lord Himself and was confirmed unto us by the apostles who heard Him. Hebrews 2:1-3. I want you to get this comparison, Pentecost under law and Pentecost under grace; these spiritual aspects of the Latter Rain Covenant.

The Latter Rain Covenant that I am going to read in a moment, may be said to rank third among the seven great covenants of the Bible. No man or woman can ever comprehend God's purposes and the full compass of the teachings of His Word until he has learned something about these covenants.

Now let us read this blessed Covenant:

"For the land, whither thou goest in to possess it, is not as the land of Egypt, from whence ye came out, where thou sowest thy seed and waterest it with thy foot as a garden of herbs.

"But the land, whither ye go to possess it, is a land of hills and valleys, and drinketh water of the rain of heaven.

"A land which the Lord thy God careth for; the eyes of the Lord thy God are always upon it from the beginning of the year even unto the end of the year.

"And it shall come to pass, if ye shall hearken diligently unto my commandments which I command you this day, to love the Lord your God, and to serve Him with all your heart and with all your soul.

"That I will give you the rain of your land in His due season, the first rain and the latter rain that thou mayst gather in thy corn and thy wine and thine oil.

THE LATTER RAIN PENTECOST.

"And I will send grass in thy fields for thy cattle, that thou mayst eat and be full.

"Take heed to yourselves that your heart be not deceived, and ye turn aside and serve other gods and worship them.

"And then the Lord's wrath be kindled against you and He shut up the heaven, that there be no rain, and that the land yield not her fruit; and lest ye perish quickly from off the good land which the Lord giveth you.

"Therefore, shall ye lay up these, My words, in your heart and in your soul, and bind them for a sign upon your hand, that they may be as frontlets between your eyes.

"And ye shall teach them, your children, speaking of them when thou sittest in thine house, and when thou walkest by the way, when thou liest down and when thou risest up.

"And thou shalt write them upon the door posts of thine house and upon thy gates.

"That your days may be multiplied, and the days of your children, in the land which the Lord sware unto your fathers to give them, as the days of heaven upon the earth."

Let us now analyze this Covenant and thereby lay a basis for our future unfolding of it. In all my thirty years eating of the Word of God I had not discovered this Covenant, but when I was baptized in the Holy Spirit, God revealed it to me in its seven aspects. I then took my Bible-index and ran through, and I saw there were just seven places in the Bible where this word was mentioned after this Covenant was given, six in the Old Testament and once in the New. Seven; no more and no less. Perhaps a little confusion may arise here in tracing it out in the English translation, but when we go back to the original, we are saved from that. And so I just took my Hebrew concordance and ran through it, and this word in the Hebrew for Latter Rain Covenant is found only seven times besides the Covenant itself, and it is along these seven lines I propose to trace it in these lectures.

Let us go back and look at this Covenant a moment that you may get some real spiritual bread out of it, for though it is a matter of history as to literal Israel, it is also typical as to God's spiritual people, and it is also prophetical and therefore dispensational under the great plan of God for the ages. It is along these three lines, historical or literal as it applies to God's ancient people and land, typical and spiritual as it applies to God's people, the church, and prophetical as to its dispensational aspect in the unfolding of God's plan in the ages, and bringing in the eternal kingdom of our Lord Jesus Christ.

THE LATTER RAIN PENTECOST.

This term "Latter Rain" Hebrew, *mal-koshe,*
signifies "the rain of the latter or second growth; the
harvest rain, the rain of the after crop." This term
is used seven times in the Old Testament and once
in the New Testament. The Greek word is a com-
pound, *op-si-mos* and signifies "late in the day rain,
rain at close of day, at evening; in the end of a time
or dispensation; rain needed to get the last crop or
fruit."

The seven sections of this Covenant are Contrast,
Condition, Promise, Warning, Exhortation, Duty and
Purpose.

I. THE CONTRAST.

The first section of this Covenant is therefore a
contrast between the land they came out of and the
land they came into, as is seen in the tenth, eleventh,
and twelfth verses, and in this contrast there are three
or four things said about it. It shows the superiority
of the land of Canaan, the land of Promise, over the
land of Egypt from which Israel had been delivered,
which was a land watered by *foot-power.* They had
to irrigate from the Nile; dig little ditches just as they
do in the arid lands of the western part of these United
States. But that is laborious, and expensive, you
know. It is much better to have land that is watered
by rain from heaven, and watered at the right time.
There is no uncertainty about that. Think of it!

THE LATTER RAIN COVENANT.

Wouldn't you like to have your soul watered by heaven? Haven't you obtained what water you had for your soul by foot-power? that is, by a good deal of hard work? Well now take heaven's way and just open up the land of your life—your soul, and receive your Pentecost by letting the rain from heaven on it. That is the way to apply it spiritually, and so I want you to see it here in this little lesson on irrigation.

This comparison shows the excellence of the land of Canaan in three particulars. First, it is a land *"watered by God."* God, you know, is moving around in the heavens with the great sprinkling-can of His goodness and pouring out a shower on you when you need it. God has His watering-can, yet His little garden is dry; the garden of your heart and your life. God will come around and water your land if you will take down your umbrella and let Him.

I am reading about the old Latter Rain Covenant *historically,* but I want to make it literal and typical to your heart. Are you still down in Egypt? God bless you! Move up into the land of Promise—the "Promise of the Father." You won't have to irrigate any more; no more foot-power. You won't be sore; no backache from digging ditches, trying to get a little water in this way or that. God will rain His grace upon your soul and make you fat and flourishing; a garden of the Lord. Yes watered by God. It "drinketh water of the rain of heaven." It *drinketh*. Why this land knows more than the people that live on it, because when God rains, it drinks. Now go over into the New Testament, Matthew 5:6, "Blessed are they which do hunger and thirst after righteousness; for they shall be filled." What do thirsty people do, generally? Drink, don't they? They do unless they have lost their minds. This land knows enough to drink the rain of heaven. Oh soul, if you are hungry and thirsty, will you drink in the Pentecostal rain of heaven, the Holy Spirit, and receive your Pentecost tonight? "Open wide thy mouth and I will fill it." It is sometimes a little hard to get people to open their mouths, but many are getting a little more limber-jawed; they are losing that stiffness about the mouth, and God will get into their poor hearts that are crying out. Spurgeon, and I think Martin Luther also, used to render that verse: "Open wide thy mouth and I will fill it *to thy heart.*" It is the heart He is after; that is what needs to be filled.

"It drinketh the rain of heaven," eleventh verse. It's a land watered by God, and when the land is watered it knows enough to drink. You see God is watering people these days. We are in the Latter Rain Belt, the Latter Rain time. We are in the

10

midst of a cloud-burst. It would be a shame, wouldn't it, if nobody drank when God is watering?

But here is a *second* item. It is "a land *desired by God*." "The land which the Lord thy God careth for"; looketh after, seeketh after with great desires. He loves that land, so you can depend on it, God will stay by that land; He wouldn't take the trouble to water it if He didn't love it. God watering His land, going to all that trouble; don't you think He loves to see it blossom and bear fruit? Why God takes more concern about that than you do, a thousand times. Why don't you drop into His blessed sovereign will and get the best there is, the fulness of the Covenant, "the days of heaven on the earth"?

Third, it is a land *watched by God*. "The eyes of the Lord thy God are always upon it." God's eyes are on Palestine tonight. The usurper has tramped over it; Mohammedans have overrun it, the Sultan of Turkey has ravished it, and he is paying a part of the judgment now, for God's eyes are on it. Even this week negotiations are in progress for the purchase of Mesopotamia, which will finally eventuate in the ancient people of God entering into the Holy Land by way of Mesopotamia. This is the fulfilment of prophecy and shows the hastening of the end. They will go just as they did originally, the hardest way, for God's people shall return, but not in His way. Isa. 54:15, Hosea 7:16. They will go up just as Abraham did from Mesopotamia.

"The eyes of the Lord thy God are always upon it." He continually looks after His interest and cares for it and keeps it, so you see it is better a thousand times than the land of Egypt.

II. THE CONDITION.

Since there is such a contrast in favor of God's land, are you not willing for God to lay down a few conditions? Would you be willing to meet just a few simple conditions so that we may get adjusted to the thing properly? I am so glad God has made it that way.

Verse thirteen: "And it shall come to pass, if ye shall hearken diligently unto my commandments which I command you this day to love the Lord your God, and to serve Him with all your heart"—some people *love* God with their heart, but they do not like to *serve* Him with their heart. We have a good deal more of *professed heart love* than we have of practiced *heart service* If you say, "I love God with my heart" I want to see you serve Him heartily. Many love God and shout when the meeting is on, and talk about the "latter rain" and all that, but fail to give out to other souls the heavenly manna through heart service. Some people serve God with their heart or affection (spirit) but they do not serve

12

Him with their soul (mind, psychical). God differentiates between the spiritual and the psychical, between your affections and your intellect, with its imagination, reason, perception. judgment and will, and He says, "I want the body to have spirit and soul back of it, for that makes the whole man." Oh, there is so much divorcement between spirit and soul. We either serve God in a psychical. that is intellectual, way, without the spiritual, or we serve Him in the spiritual and forget the psychical, and go beyond all bounds of reason and judgment. If our service is only in the spiritual, it leads to fanaticism; if in the psychical only, the result is formalism. God save us from either one of these awful extremes and enable us to worship Him with both the heart and the mind.

Anything done in the psychical never gets into the spiritual, whether it is prayer, song, testimony or sermon, because it is done in the intellect and never reaches down into the spiritual in another. It may be done twice as well to the ear, to the eye, but it won't reach the spot, because it is kind that produces kind; it is like that begets like, the world over. Let us get an understanding of this matter. "The natural (psychical) man receiveth not the things of God;" "they are spiritually discerned;" discerned only by the *pneumatos*, the spiritual man. So few people understand the workings of Pentecost because they are trying to work it out intellectually, but spiritual things are to be discerned by the *spirit.*

So these are the conditions for receiving the "latter rain." They are *three-fold:* first, the *ears* are to be attentive to God, the material, the physical. You shall *harken,* and this is the means by which God reaches the soul of mankind, through the ear-gate, and the voice of His Spirit or the voice of His Word through men chosen of God to expound His Word. You are hearing it tonight. You ought to thank God all your lives for ears (physical) to hear the words of the Spirit, and spiritual ears to hear the voice of the Spirit. As Jesus told John on the Isle of Patmos, "If any man hath an ear to hear, let him hear what the Spirit is saying to the churches." The trouble is not with God these days, but with the churches, for in nine cases out of ten, she has no longer an ear to hear what God is saying to her, and that is according to the prophetic word that by and by her ears would be deaf to God, and she would heap to herself teachers that would tickle the other kind of ears; but cursed is the man that goes around tickling ears; greater will be his condemnation.

God reaches the soul through the ear-gate, the physical nature, by the voice of the Spirit and the Word Then comes into the *heart,* the spiritual; the heart is to love Him. Heart stands for the heavenly

14

nature, the conscience; "to love the Lord your God, and to serve Him with all your *heart* and with all your *soul,*" because the psychical (soul) stands mid-way between the physical and the spiritual, binding them together; it is the great power of the man, the center of his being, where he either glorifies God, worships Him, serves Him in sanctification unto honor, or where he commits all his sins.

That is where the biggest trouble is, in the soul, the intellectual nature. All the false systems of religion, so-called, have their seat and development in the psychical; every one of them, and God in these days is putting Himself into the spiritual in such power and manifestation, through the psychical in physical manifestation, that He has challenged and answered all these things. These psychological writers are very busy; from Dan to Beersheba they are writing and filling the magazines, and there is more psychological literature now being put out from the printing press than any other kind of religious literature. A preacher said to me not long ago: "They will have to raise my salary; there is so much literature I have to keep up with and put in my library." I said I would not give five cents a ton for it. I find more in this Book I hold in my hand now, this Word of God, on all these subjects than there is in the whole University of Chicago. All there is good and sound about it they get out of this Book, and it is the only Book in the world that really differentiates, really shows the fine distinction between the physical, the psychical and the spiritual natures of man.

God wants the conscience purged; the affections purified, made holy and strong in everlasting fellowship with Him. Then He wants the soul,—"serve Him with all your soul;" every faculty and energy is to be employed for Him, to His glory. The great faculties of your soul are to be controlled by Him, your imagination purified, your perception clarified, your reason and judgment well balanced, and your will submissive to God. The spiritual faculties, and I mean by that your conscience and your affections, must be renewed and brought under the dominance of the Holy Spirit, so that these may move in a perfectly pure way upon the psychical. All things, speaking generally, begin in the affections and emotions but should not end there, and should not be exercised there. We are not to rest upon the emotions. What is the trouble with over-emotional Christians? They live in the spiritual alone, divorced from the soul, and that won't do. The spiritual nature must dominate the psychical, but the psychical must be allowed its divinely appointed place. The great affections of your being must be sanctified and then you will move on with God, the soul deeply seated in the spiritual realm.

THE LATTER RAIN COVENANT.

The world, although it is not spiritual, can shame lots of good, spiritual Christians on this line, because the world is living in that master place, the soul, though it is all for self, while the child of God is simply living in its conscience, sometimes, perhaps, over-scrupulous. Many are without good judgment, over-sensitive; we pastors have the most trouble with that kind of people, for they strain at gnats one day and swallow camels the next. Such people have great affections, strong emotional natures, and when everything is all right they are ecstatic, but when matters go wrong they think the devil has gotten everything. It is therefore hard for that class of people to live a straight life in the experience, for example, of divine healing, because the minute they have a little sickness they think it is all up with them. But it isn't. Just drink in some more of this "rain." Don't look at yourselves. Don't look in your mirror, but look away to Jesus.

When your will is subordinate to God's will and use, then the members of your body will be brought into subjection; your tongue, your eyes, your hands, and your feet, for these are all hinted at here, that what we say, what we see, what we do and where we go may be all to His honor and service. So this covenant includes the whole man, and that man will have a whole God. The only people that have a whole God are those who give God the whole man. There

17

are people trying to get a whole God into one part of their being, and you never can do that. God is a Trinity, a Triunity; One in Three; and Three in One. So also is man, and if you are to have a whole God, God must have a whole man, and when the Triune God, Father, Son and Holy Spirit comes into the spirit, soul and body of the triune man, then you have God manifested in the flesh, which is Pentecostal fulness, the "promise of the Father."

But when people tell us they never had any of the Spirit before they received Pentecost, they speak unscripturally, for no soul could ever come into the Pentecostal experience without the previous working of the Spirit in his life. What could ever bring it about? It is the Holy Spirit that convicts of sin, and imparts faith to enable one to become a child of God. How the devil does come along in his subtle way and lay right beside the most precious truths of God some deception or exaggeration, thereby taking from or adding to. He says, "Keep the old Book but let me add to it." Don't do it, for one little drop of poison will spoil a whole pitcher of cream, and it must then be labeled poison. One little point of error dropped into a chapter of scripture, poisons it, and that is what Satan is doing in these days.

I want you to understand about the Spirit. It is not only a question of having the Spirit, or the Spirit having you, but it is how much and what quality you have. Now it is useless to ask God for more of Himself until He gets more of you. You may not understand this, but those who teach must. God is sovereign, and when He sees your attitude is right He will give it to you whether you understand it or not. It will not do to take the extreme position of relying upon spiritual revelation alone. There must be an earnest study of the Word of God also, and to be a teacher I must have the understanding as well as the revelation. If one is to lead others to God he must know the Word and be apt to teach it. Therein we need to wait on God with our Bibles open.

So when you are asking God, "Give me more of Thyself," the real prayer should be, "Lord get me, I am yielding to Thee." We would like to get more of God while in our present position, but we cannot do that. God moves down to man only to show him how to move into God, but He will never change His will to accommodate us. This requires on our part the forsaking of all things that are not of God. It is a good thing to study well the conditions, because if we get the conditions right the work is done. God will attend to the rest when we meet His conditions.

THE LATTER RAIN PENTECOST.

III. THE PROMISE.

The *promise* of this Covenant is contained in the fourteenth and fifteenth verses, and if we meet the conditions the promise is sure. The promise is also three-fold, because the trinity runs through this seven-fold or complete Covenant. You cannot find per-fection without the trinity, and where you find the trinity, you find perfection, completeness. That is a law of scripture.

"I will give you the rain of your land in his due season;" you need never worry, beloved, about get-ting things from God in the right order at the right time, if you meet the conditions. We waste time on that side of the question. Let us be more careful and concerned that we meet the *conditions*.

In your study of the scriptures, keep your eye on the conditions, and the promises will be sure. The con-ditions are found, for the most part, in the command-ments; I find people will take a dozen promises to one commandment, but the commandments are more valu-able than the promises. I do not bother much about the promises any more, and haven't for twelve years. I saw this Latter Rain baptism was not only "the *promise* of the Father," but also the COMMAND of Jesus, Acts 1:4, and I set myself to obey the com-mand, and soon the promise was upon me.

So it will be with everyone. You may not have

understood it that way, but it is true. You either haven't met the conditions and commandments or else He has come. You haven't much trouble in pleading the promises when you obey the commandments. Of all the testimonies I have heard personally, the great trouble with everybody has been in the life of obedience. We are behind in our obedience. The great purpose of God's precious love is to teach His children in these important days, under these mixed conditions, how to know Him and obey Him, for everyone of us, teachers, preachers, laborers and people, all need to know how better to obey Him, that we may yield unquestioning obedience to His will.

"I will give the rain of *your* land;" not My land. It is *your* life. God has committed it to you, and it is the rain of *your* land. It belongs to you, and He will give it in its due season. There are some things you will never get in meetings, but when you are away out alone in the hard places, God will pour out the rain, and there is no rain so good as that which falls on the desert place, the hard place.

"That I will give you the rain of your land in his due season, the first rain and the latter rain, that thou mayst gather in thy corn, and thy wine, and thine oil"—three things. First, *corn* for sustenance, second, *wine* for joy and gladness, satisfaction and happiness; third, *oil* for beauty, dignity and glory. But you must be sustained first, and corn is better than wine for that purpose. If you must do without any, you can do without wine better than corn; and when you haven't any exuberant joy and any great two-bushel basketful of glory, you can settle down with your handful of corn on the top of the mountain, and the fruit thereof shall shake like Lebanon. You hold on to the corn, so that if the joy all seeps out after the meeting is over, you may go on with a few kernels of corn. You know you can make wine out of corn, but you cannot make corn out of wine. So the first thing we gather is corn, and we are getting some good old corn now. The Latter Rain Covenant has more in it along the great lines of scripture than any other covenant.

First, therefore, gather in the corn for food, for sustenance and strength; second, wine for joy and gladness, satisfaction and happiness; third, oil for beauty, dignity and glory. Some people think you have no beauty and say you are the ugliest Christian they ever did see, and that you don't have any dignity at all, or any glory. Never mind, keep on with the good old corn, the wine will come, the exuberance, the gladness, the happiness, and so will the dignity and the glory. God *puts* these on us; when we get low enough He gives us beauty for ashes; God begins to beautify the meek with His salvation. Do you want some of God's beauty? You know what to do now. Well this oil is for beauty, dignity, and glory; that is for sacred service—not to show off, but for sacrificial, sacred, holy service. I want to use three scriptures with reference to this corn, wine and oil. Look first at Psalm 104:15. I want you to see three great passages in the Word of God that we would not have but for the Latter Rain Covenant. We have to read the context a little and see how God works. "He watereth the hills from His chambers; the earth is satisfied with the fruit of thy works. He causeth the grass to grow for the cattle, and herb for the service of man; that He may bring forth food out of the earth; and *wine* that maketh glad the heart of man (spiritual nature), *oil* to make His face shine (physical nature), and *bread* which strengtheneth man's heart (original, *life* or soul nature)." So wine, oil and bread (or corn) are mentioned here also, in connection with God sending the "latter rain."

Now see Jeremiah 31:12, "Therefore they shall come and sing in the height of Zion, and shall flow together to the goodness of the Lord." When you seem to be slipping away from yourself and losing your bearing, just think, "I am flowing into the goodness of the Lord;" let yourself go; it is all right. Don't hold on to yourself, or examine yourself, or hold back for

23

fear you might slip somewhere; for you will "slip in," and underneath will be the everlasting arms.

It is so strange to see humanity hold on to itself, when the Lord God will hold His people, saying unto them, "Fear thou not; for I am with thee: be not dismayed; for I am thy God: I will strengthen thee; yea, I will help thee; yea, I will uphold thee with the right hand of my righteousness." When we get quiet enough to hear the whispers of God, confidence is borne in on our soul, and we say, "Lord, I am sorry, just take the whole thing; I am worn out like a fretful, tired child." He does it and you fall asleep as you used to do on mother's bosom, from sheer exhaustion, and like the mother He stands crooning to you all the time. We wear out before God does, for He says He never faints nor grows weary, and I am so glad for that. He waits until we get tired, but He is as fresh as ever. Isn't that precious?

"And shall flow together to the goodness of the Lord." You have to flow *together*, you cannot run by little individual streams and call that your own. God wants to bring all these little streams and babbling brooks into one great river. When we get a whole lot of people together, into unity, they just flow into the goodness of the Lord, and all their starch and stiffness disappears. Starch doesn't run; it's too stiff. So we begin to flow and come together, and the bigger the stream the greater the momentum, and the devil goes away and says, "I'll have to go somewhere else where they are not so much together; this 'together' business breaks me all up," and so it does.

"Flow together to the goodness of the Lord." What then? Why we come for wheat, sustenance and strength; we come for wine, gladness, joy and satisfaction; and we come for oil, for beauty, dignity and glory; power for service. It is all for us in the goodness of God, and we are flowing into it. Why didn't you flow before? You didn't let the Lord break you up. Some people stop when they are broken, but that won't do. You can take pig-iron and break it up into as small pieces as you please, but it is still pig-iron. You have to melt it, and by and by it comes out pure bessemer steel, and bears the weight of commerce; so God will make you. But it's not enough to be broken merely; for it is not simply the broken heart, but the broken and *contrite* heart. God will melt you in His mill and bring you out as sons and daughters. They won't stick you away any more as pig-iron. No sir; sons of God now!

We think a *covenant* is a hard thing, but this is not a hard thing. This flows. It is God liquidized; anybody can take that; babies and people that haven't any digestion at all; it is an aid to digestion. It will cure the worst case of spiritual or moral dyspepsia in the world. If I couldn't get enough salvation to make my face shine seven days in the week, thirty days in the month and twelve months in the year, I would go grubbing; I would look for roots of God's truth, and take spiritual sassafras tea.

But we are flowing into the goodness of the Lord. Human goodness isn't worth ten cents a ton, but a little of *God's* goodness just melts us up. It amazes me that we don't yield to Him. But many are yielding. Hearts all over the world are just saying, "God, You may break me and melt me into Your goodness." Dear old Jeremiah knew something about it down there in the dungeon. "For wine and for oil;" and what is it for? It is going to take care of the children. It is "for the young of the flock and of the herd; and their souls shall be as a watered garden; and they shall not sorrow any more." Well, did you ever hear the like of that?

Just turn over to Joel and see what he said, for there is a third place where it is given in a little different order. Let us see what Joel says in that great second chapter, twenty-third and twenty-fourth verses:

"Be glad, then, ye children of Zion, and rejoice in the Lord your God: for He hath given you the former rain moderately, and He will cause to come down for you the rain, the former rain and the latter rain as at the first." This is the latter rain coming ⸜upon Israel, and it has started on the church first. It has come upon the land contemporaneously, and will soon be on literal Israel. The former rain was "moderately," and this is going to be intensified immeasurably. And what about it? "And the floors shall be full of wheat (corn) and the fats shall overflow with wine and oil." We thought we would have to get along with just wheat and corn, and now He says, seeing you stayed by the corn so long, and got along on that, I will make the fats of wine and oil to OVERFLOW when the latter rain comes, and that is PENTECOSTAL FULNESS. It overflows with the wine and oil, with the joy of the Lord, the happiness, the exuberance; with the oil, the beauty, the glory and power of God.

Now we have had these three blessed passages. What for? Corn, wine and oil may be said, therefore, to be the type of the living God-head, the Triune God. Listen! The corn is a type of the divine manifestation in the life of Jesus, the great God-life; the corn, bruised for our life, for our sustenance, the very bread of heaven. The Holy Spirit is the wine, the joy of life, the happiness, the exuberance, the joy of the Lord; and the oil is the type of the Father, the manifestation of God in beauty, in dignity, in glory

27

and power; the Father coming down and taking possession of the body that He had created, manifesting His glory through it and doing His own witnessing through it while it lies yielded and quiet—receiving the "residue" of the "fulness of God."

We see, therefore, in this promise that this Latter Rain Covenant is the basis and condition of all man's supply from God.

It has a three-fold application also in its outworking and fulfilment; first, historical or literal, in reference to the Hebrews and their land, Palestine; second, typical as it applies to the Christian life, and third, prophetical or dispensational in the preparation of God's people in the different ages, thus bringing in the perfect age when there shall be what this Latter Rain Covenant eventuates in, the perfect millennial age, "the days of heaven on the earth." We have never had them since our first parents sinned in the garden; we are having an earnest of them now, but the time is coming when all the days shall be as the days of heaven on this earth. That is what I am living, serving, laboring for, to see those days, and to come back with Jesus to see them on this earth. God is working to that end, and will accomplish it.

IV. THE WARNING.

We now come to the fourth section of this Latter Rain Covenant. The sixteenth and seventeenth verses of this chapter contain the *warning*, and this occupies the central place in this Covenant. After we have met the conditions, the blessing of God has been poured out upon us, and His promise fulfilled in us; then the warning is needed, "Take heed to yourselves, that your heart be not deceived." Your heart is never in one-tenth the danger of being deceived under trial as it is under blessing. I have lived this life of faith thirty years, studied God's Word and loved it, and believe me, you are never, nine times out of ten, in as much danger of deception and of failure under trial as you are under blessing. How often have you had great blessing and been so ashamed a day or two afterward. What happened? The enemy touched you when you were in the great glow of blessed ecstasy, fervor and zeal, for perhaps you were not controlled by divine wisdom and knowledge.

Why does He say the "heart"? Because these blessings begin in the spiritual nature; the heart stands for the spiritual realm, and God intends you to move from that directly into the soul or mind (psuche) and have your imagination subdued, your reason adjusted, your perceptions clarified, and your judgment and will sanctified; otherwise you will be governed, not by knowledge, but by emotion and feeling. No other ground is so dangerous. This is where warning is needed, because the enemy everlastingly seeks to play all kinds of tunes on our emotions and feelings and then laughs at us while we try to dance to his "piping," but cannot.

So this warning begins in the spiritual life but it must go on into the soul, the intellect, and that must be well sanctified and preserved in Christ Jesus. This is well expressed in the epistle to the Colossians, where they had drifted into worshiping angels and familiar spirits, and Paul says, you must hold these holy things God has given you in all good judgment; that is sanctified judgment. I do not mean common sense; the world has that; business men have that. God never talks about common sense in the Bible. It is *good* sense, *good* judgment, the seat of which is in the great soul (psuche) nature. Here Jesus must be enthroned until we not only have the *Spirit of Christ in our hearts* (spiritual nature) but until we have also the *mind of Christ in our soul* (intellect). Then the devil cannot drift us into extremes of any kind. Therefore, "Take heed to yourselves, that your heart be not deceived, and ye turn aside, and serve other gods and worship them;" (and there are many seducing spirits and doctrines of demons) "and the Lord's wrath be kindled against you, and He shut up the heaven, that there be no rain, and that the land yield not her fruit; and lest ye perish quickly from off the good land which the Lord giveth you."

First, deception in the spiritual realm, the seat of the conscience, the affections and emotions; then false worship and service; then the heavens shut up; no latter rain. So, O literal Israel, if you had taken heed, the land would never have been cursed and barren. Take heed, then, O spiritual Israel that you do not lose out under the great Pentecostal latter rain blessings. Take heed to your heart, for many have been deceived through their emotional and demonstrative natures, and other spirits have slipped in. Oh, if they had only been prepared before!

After you are justified you must immediately proceed to sanctification and the crucified life, until Christ is enthroned in the judgment, the will, and in all the perceptive faculties, so that you may discern between the good and the bad, for we must interpret things aright.

V. THE EXHORTATION.

The *exhortation* is given in the eighteenth verse: "Therefore shall ye lay up these My words in your *heart;*" God's Word in the spiritual nature is the only corrective and preventive. "My words in your heart and in your soul"—the Holy Spirit is not given to tautology. He doesn't repeat things unnecessarily. He says you are to lay up His words first in the spiritual nature; that is where God begins, where

31

you are born, but these words must be laid up in the soul too. And that is not all, for God takes up at once the physical and says, "bind them for a sign upon your hand" which stands for the physical nature.

Now God has the whole man, and I have a whole God. Where is the possibility of deception coming now? Your body needs the protection of God's truth and Spirit. When God has subdued it unto Himself, then it shall not be exercised superficially or excessively, but only to the touch of the Master hand, under the Spirit, and when He is through, you will immediately return to rest and peace.

God can exercise us that way, but it is not intended our bodies, our human natures shall suffer at all because of any excessiveness in them, but rather it shall be for our additional comfort and joy. I am sorry for people that haven't come to a clear knowledge of these things. God doesn't work His vessels to destruction,—never, but to enjoyment and blessing. "Take heed." This is an exhortation, and you thought perhaps this would not mean much in Pentecostal things, but this old Covenant covers the point and scope of the whole question; takes in all the teaching of the New Testament, and therein lies the wonder of this Book. What man could ever breathe a thing like that! The Spirit of God did it, beyond man's power, for "they spake as they were moved by tne Holy Ghost," and as Peter tells us, they didn't even understand the things they wrote and spoke.

"Bind them for a sign upon your hand;" that is, keep the Bible in your hand and work and move according to the testimony. "That they may be as frontlets between your eyes;" so that you can see clearly where you are. Of course, I cannot see to read my Bible very well, nor you yours until we take it up in our hands, and that is "as frontlets between our two eyes" and our two eyes fixed in one light and one word. Jesus said, "When your eye is single your whole body will be full of light;" so also with the eye of the soul.

"Lay up these My words in your heart and in your soul, and bind them for a sign upon your hand;" that is spirit, soul and body again. The confusion and disobedience in these last days is because of the failure to lay up the words of the covenants of our God in the center of our spiritual, psychical and physical life. Let God fill the spiritual life, dominate the soul and control the body to the praise of His glory. Let us let Him for "He doeth all things well." "He worketh all things after the counsel of His will." The trouble is, things are not enough in His hands. When they are, all is well.

THE LATTER RAIN PENTECOST.

VI. THE DUTY.

The nineteenth and twentieth verses have something I want the parents to hear, especially in these days. I just read a report from the committee on "House Religion" of the Presbyterian General Assembly in the Denver convention. Most of the report was smothered by the committee; they were ashamed to bring it out before that great religious body. They had to report to that great assembly that "family worship, family prayers and the reading of God's Word, has been largely discontinued in the homes of our people. It is popular no longer, and is not considered essential." What is going to become of the next generation? They will be in the tribulation, and that is what has been the matter with the present generation. These things have been too much discontinued. In that home where there is no prayer, no reading of the scriptures before the children, how can you claim any covenant of God? The world, the flesh and the devil have first rights with those children, and last rights too. Oh, it is a painful thing. Hear the duty of this Covenant. There have been warning and exhortation, but this is duty; this is imperative.

"And ye shall teach them your children, speaking of them when thou sittest in thine house,"—in your social life; be careful how you talk to your neighbors and friends before your children; "and when thou walkest by the way;"—when you go out and come in; that is in your business life, when you are buying and selling, be sure to put in a little of the Word of God. It helps to make the bargain right; it helps to sanctify the relation, and you will be friends. There wouldn't be any enemies in business if you remembered the Word of God.

"And when thou liest down, and when thou risest up;"—in your domestic life, morning and evening worship. Life is pretty well protected when thus guarded in its social, business and domestic relations. The devil won't then have much chance to break up and interfere with this Latter Rain Covenant working out. "And thou shalt write them upon the doorposts of thine house, and upon thy gates." Bless God for the time when we shall hang up the mottoes on the doors, and put them out on the gates if we have a fence at the front of the house. I hung one out once in Cleveland and a poor woman came and knocked at the door; I supposed she had come for alms, perhaps. She looked at me and the tears were in her eyes, as she said, "I read that out there; if you please can I have it?" "Oh yes," I said, "take it right along, and I will hang out another, and you can get that too if you want it." That little motto was, "Great peace have they that love Thy law."

She never had that great peace and wanted it. I said to her, "It comes from loving His law, and nothing shall offend them;" nothing shall interrupt the peace. You cannot upset that peace no matter what you throw in the way.

VII. THE PURPOSE.

Last of all, the *purpose*, the design and end of the Latter Rain Covenant is to bring back perfection and perpetuity to this fallen world. Verse twenty-one, "That your days may be multiplied, and the days of your children, in the land which the Lord sware unto your fathers to give them, as the DAYS OF HEAVEN UPON THE EARTH." That is the highest perfection; man's greatest good and God's highest glory. God is working that out now.

"That thy days may be multiplied;" you get a thing right, or let God get it right, and you cannot get too much of it. All days can be multiplied just like the good old Ninety-first Psalm. The Ninetieth Psalm says a man's days should be three-score and ten, and if he should go on by reason of a good constitution, yet there will be labor and sorrow, and he is soon cut off. That is the Psalm of law and nature, but the Ninety-first Psalm doesn't end that way, because it is the Psalm of grace and of the Spirit. He says, "Because he hath set his love upon me, therefore will I deliver him: I will set him on

high because he hath known my name,"—I will take
him to a safe place. "With long life will I satisfy
him and show him My salvation." Get the days of
heaven on the earth. Many of us would be dead and
buried long ago if we didn't know God as our
Healer. I would have been dead twenty years ago.

"The days of heaven on the earth!" Where else
can you get that in the Bible? This is one of the
sweetest verses in the Word of God. Where can
you get that anywhere else but in connection with the
Latter Rain Covenant? What else could produce it
in its outworking and fulfilment? Nothing else. Take
its spiritual aspect in Pentecost, and when you get
that rain of the Spirit upon you, don't you begin the
days of heaven on the earth? You begin to get
heavenly tongues, heavenly songs, heavenly choirs,
heavenly interpretation, heavenly inspiration, heavenly
fellowship; you are in the heavenlies of Christ Jesus.
It is true, beloved. Look at that great arch, greater
than the rain-bow, spelled by these seven words,
this seven-fold covenant. "THE-DAYS-OF-HEAVEN-
UPON-THE-EARTH." We go up three steps and it is
all heaven; we come down again three steps from
heaven—seven words, forming a perfect arch, with
"heaven" as its keystone. What then must its bases
be but such days on the earth as are heavenly?

CHAPTER II.

How It May Be Restored

ONIGHT we want to take up the solid part of the scriptures on this subject, and see the second and third sections in the seven-fold division of this great subject; secondly, the cause and failure of the "latter rain," and, thirdly, how it may be restored.

As I said in the beginning, the Latter Rain Covenant not only has a literal bearing upon the land, but it applies typically to God's people, and also prophetically to God's plan of the ages. There are many scriptures that are not only double-barreled, but triple-barreled; they are literal, typical and prophetical; or putting it in other words, historical, spiritual and dispensational. A large portion of scripture, of course, is double-barreled, and we ought always to consider it that way; first, as a matter of history, an account of literal things and of a literal people, and also that it has a spiritual significance for us; but some scriptures like the Latter Rain Covenant have a third aspect— dispensational.

HOW IT MAY BE RESTORED.

I am proceeding to analyze the Word of God relative to this great Covenant as God gave it to me. As far as I know, God has given this to no other man, and I have communicated with many bible students upon this subject. God revealed it to me when He baptized me in the Holy Ghost and fire, the third of November, 1906. I then took up the Hebrew and Greek and found the word which stands for "latter rain" appears just seven times in addition to its appearance in the Latter Rain Covenant—six times in the Old Testament scriptures and once in the New.

It is remarkable that this word occurs just seven times after its use in the Covenant itself, and that the scriptures wherein it is used cover all the points and scope of the teaching on the "latter rain," and form, so to speak, a chalice made by the hand of God to contain the truth on this great subject.

The first scripture is Jeremiah 3:2-5, which gives the cause of the failure of the latter rain literally on the land, and its failure spiritually, on God's people or church.

"Lift up thine eyes unto the high places,"—that is the religious places, for here is where the trouble is. Do not blame the world for what belongs to the church. The trouble is not with the world today; the trouble is with the church. Judgment begins at the house of God. That is where Pentecost is work-

ing; that is one of the great purposes of God revealing Himself. The "high places" always mean in all
scripture, religious places, spiritual places, so-called.

"Lift up thine eyes unto the high places, and see
where thou hast been lien with. In the ways hast
thou sat for them, as the Arabian in the wilderness;"
get in the way to welcome, to go out to meet these
things, as the Arabian in the wilderness goes out to
meet the traders coming along; "thou hast polluted
the land with thy whoredoms and with thy wicked-
ness. *Therefore the showers have been withholden,
and there hath been no latter rain;* and thou hast a
whore's forehead, thou refusedst to be ashamed. Wilt
thou not from this time cry unto Me, my Father,
be Thou again my Guide as Thou wast in my youth?
Will He reserve His anger forever? Will He keep
it to the end? Behold thou hast spoken and done
evil things as thou couldst."

"Therefore"—the cause, characterized in modern
phraseology here set forth, is the great sin that breaks
all God's covenants; that shuts up heaven's blessings
for literal latter rain or spiritual—the awful sin of
self-love, manifested in *sensuality,* terminating in
shamelessness. Oh the self-love! Oh the self-love
that is keeping God's messengers back from India,
and China, and Africa, and the ends of the earth!
Oh the self-love that is eating the vitals out of the

church of the living God! Self-love! There is one prayer that we need to make and that is: God Almighty, by the eternal burnings of the fires of Thy Spirit, in Thy love, burn the self-love out of us, that we have no time any more to love ourselves or think of ourselves, but others! *others!!* OTHERS!! and God's love for a dying world! Oh I remember the night when it seemed about the last ounce of that old self-life died out in me—all the pulling and all the other separations from my life were nothing to that; and after that I felt so free, so empty and so ready to do anything God asked. If your Pentecostal baptism hasn't taken the last remains and residue of self-love out of you, you haven't had the whole of Pentecost.

But there are *two* causes; the other is in the fifth chapter of the same prophecy, for it seemed Jeremiah was the most suitable vessel, the one who set forth the deepest sins, the law of *self-denial* and *self-abnegation, crucifixion* and loathsomeness before God, of any of the Old Testament saints; he seemed to be the one to give these two causes for failure of the latter rain. I exhort you to read from the nineteenth verse to the end of the chapter, but will just characterize it by one or two verses here, twenty-third and twenty-fourth verses:

"But this people hath a revolting and a rebellious

41

heart; they are revolted and gone!" When you have a revolting and rebellious *heart* you will soon revolt in your *ways*. The trouble begins in the heart, as we saw in the "*warning*" of the Covenant. When the warning isn't heeded, the *exhortation* is passed by, the *duty* is neglected, and the latter rain stops. Here, God speaking through Jeremiah, is reminding them in those emphatic words concerning the warning, "Take heed to yourselves, that your heart be not deceived." Nobody gets away from God but by a deceptive, seducing spirit, and then by and by the way opens for demon possession. "Neither shall they say in their heart, Let us now fear the Lord our God, that giveth rain, both the former and the latter, in his season; he reserveth unto us the appointed weeks of the harvest."

Coupled with the spiritual and moral failure that begins in the heart, in *self-love*, which leads out into *sensuality* and results in *shamelessness*, is the literal trouble—drought in the *land;* all of which has come out of the revolting and rebellious heart. Now we have *self-will* and *indifference*. "Neither say they in their heart, Let us fear the Lord our God, that giveth rain, both the former and the latter rain in his season, and reserveth for us the appointed weeks of the harvest."

Self-love leads to self-will, and self-will leads to

sensuality. Self-will always leads to gross indifference, until nothing but the leanness of heaven and judgments of God can wake up such a people. Now these are strong scriptures and I am glad we have the bitter first, for we shall have some sweet before we get through.

> "The bud may have a bitter taste,
>   But sweet will be the flower;
> For God's purposes will ripen fast,
>   Unfolding every hour."

These are the causes of failure of the latter rain. I need not take time to amplify them at all, for they are so open, so patent to everybody. These sins were intensifying, they were growing upon the church before this Pentecostal movement began, and God put His people down on their faces for three yea..; worldwide intercession for a world-wide revival, and the result is showers of "latter rain."

Now we pass on to Isaiah, thirtieth chapter, and open up the higher and better theme: *How shall we get it restored?* Everybody knows the wrong, everybody comprehends it, and people are really confessing it, though they do not like to do so in public. They are talking about the spiritual dearth in every convention, assembly and conference. But what we are concerned about is the remedy; how to have it again restored. Now what is true of the physical latter rain is also true of the spiritual latter rain, the Pentecostal baptism, for the physical latter rain is being poured out coetaneously with the spiritual latter rain. This fact will be brought out more fully later on.

L. THE WORD OF GOD.

Now the way to get it restored is: *Back to the Word of God!* "Ask for the old paths and walk therein for the comfort of your soul." I am tracing this word through the scriptures. Now let us look at the thirtieth chapter of Isaiah; I would recommend you to read from the fifteenth to the twenty-sixth verse which contains the great paragraph on this subject, but I will just read two or three verses, beginning at the twentieth.

"And though the Lord give you the bread of adversity and the water of affliction,"—because you would not have the "latter rain," the water from heaven, you will get other water, the "water of affliction," and because you will not have the bread produced by the latter rain, you will get the "bread of adversity." Now you can take your choice, but you are going to have bread of some kind and water of some kind. You will not want to be fed long on the bread of adversity and water of affliction; many are feeding on these and they look like it. They do not look like God's people, they are a misnomer. God is

44

desirous of getting a people who will go forth producing in their lives and others what His Word provides for in this time of the latter rain. Remember, the "bread of adversity" and the "water of affliction" are not God's *directive* will; these are only God's *permissive* will. God acts permissively, but His best things come to us through His directive will.

"Yet shall not thy teachers be removed into a corner any more, but thine eyes shall see thy teachers;" and God shall start them out to teach His Word. You notice the Jewish teachers that have sprung up, who are teaching about Palestine and the Zionistic societies, that it is time to go back to Palestine? They do not know the meaning of it all, but it is according to the will of God, through the prophecies, and unwittingly they are doing it. God's sovereign arm is over every movement after all, keeping it from going to pieces; hence the stir at this time in all parts of the world over Palestine.

"And thine ears shall hear a word behind thee, saying, This is the way, walk ye in it, when ye turn to the right hand, and when ye turn to the left." Oh it is so blessed that God doesn't leave His children when they get off at the right side or the left; He stands and calls them back. You know a train that runs off at an open switch into a side-track must come on the main line from the point she left it; you cannot jump across from the side-track to the main line, but you must go back to the place you turned off. Now God doesn't throw any switches open to run us off the main track, but the devil does it every chance he gets, and if you don't keep a close eye on the main line of the Word of God, and get the light and revelation of the Spirit of God so you can see when the switch is open, you will come to a dead stop until such time as Satan is rebuked, and that switch closed; then you move on with God. "Resist the devil and he will flee from you." Close the switch and he is gone.

Twenty-third verse: "Then shall He give the rain of thy seed, that thou shalt sow the ground withal; and bread of the increase of the earth, and it shall be fat and plenteous"—enough for the heathen, glory be to God! Oh, I am praying God to make these meetings so fat they will be plenteous for India, for Africa, and for China, and that you shall give more than a little handful of an offering for the ends of the earth. For a good many years, whenever there is a missionary offering no matter where I am, I always contribute to it, even if it is the last cent I have. I did that once and went to the train without any money, and along the way a man gave me just double what I had given. I said, "There it is, increased again."

HOW IT MAY BE RESTORED.

"And it shall be fat and plenteous: in that day shall thy cattle feed in large pastures." . . . Moreover (when the day fully comes) the light of the moon shall be as the light of the sun, and the light of the sun shall be seven-fold, (perfection) as the light of seven days,"—in one day. It was like that the night God baptized me. It was like that when the Lord Jesus Christ revealed Himself to Saul in midday on the way to Damascus. Why it is the old Shekinah glory! I have been tracing it through the Bible recently; it is away beyond the light of the sun at mid-day. It is that glory that stood at the gates of Eden, that appeared to Moses in the burning bush; it is that glory that was in the pillar of cloud and at the door of the tabernacle; it is that which flashed before Isaiah and gave Ezekiel his vision, and that swept the gloomy isle of Patmos into a sea of glory, with Jesus in the midst of it, and John worshipping at His feet when the vision of the coming age was flashed upon Him. "The light of the moon shall be as the light of the sun, and the light of the sun shall be seven-fold, as the light of seven days, in the day that the Lord bindeth up the breach of His people, and healeth the stroke of their wounds." We haven't had that yet, but we are coming to it through the renewing of the Latter Rain Covenant.

47

THE LATTER RAIN PENTECOST.

II. PRAYER.

Now turn to Zachariah 10:1. The second step in restoring this latter rain is *prayer*, and prayer is of little use if you do not understand the Word of God, for unless you pray according to the Word of God, the answer will not come. You must ask according to the will of God, but how do you know His will? Do you learn it from tree-tops and rivers, oceans and sands? from mountains, hills and valleys? No, you may get the *thought* of God from them, but if you want His *will* you must get to where His will is revealed and that is in His word. Study His will to find out if there are any little codicils in it. I have found some blessed ones there. Then we can come and "ask of the Lord rain," but if the latter rain is due latter rain will come.

We wanted rain, and for three years prayed for a universal revival; we were not asking for "latter rain" and only a few people realized at all that it was time for the latter rain. I remember I got a letter from one of your Chicago men who is now in Shanghai, China, on a mission there. He was sending out his little prayer-slips, prayer calendars everywhere. I wrote back to him and said, "Brother N., do you know what this is going to mean? It will mean more than the people of God are ready for." I didn't know all it meant, but I knew it meant much, for

48

about that time God began to take me through the Bible on the fire and water line, and I learned many things.

The prayer went on. They were asking for "rain;" asking for a Revival, but they were asking for "*rain in the time of the latter rain*" and they got it. You may fail in asking because you know not the times or the season, but God gives what is *due*. Of course, if you ask for bread He will not give you a stone, but He may give you *Boston* bread. If you ask for an egg He will not give you a serpent, but He may give you a goose-egg, or even a golden one. If you ask for a fish He will not give you a scorpion; He may give you a whale as He did Jonah, even when he wasn't looking for it.

Do you apprehend what I am getting at? He, the God of Pentecost, has said in the third of Ephesians, He will do "exceedingly abundantly above what we can ask or think." The church was only praying for rain, ordinary rain, and God sent the latter rain, for it was time. His apostles were waiting in the upper room for rain and God sent more than they apprehended, for the early rain was a surprise even to Peter. The only way they came to understand it was, Peter went back and found the little old scroll of Joel's prophecy and as he stood that day and held it up before the flocking, scoffing, multitude, he said, "THIS IS THAT!" Where did he get his key? In the Word of God! In the scriptures! He had been down looking them over, looking for truth during that ten days, you may be sure. That's how I got Pentecost, studying my Bible on my knees; and if more of you would study your Bibles, you would get more from God. Back to the Word of God if you want to pray aright and want victory in your lives. God puts no premium on laziness. I'd rather go with less sleep than not know the Word of the living God.

"Ask ye of the Lord rain in the time of the latter rain; so the Lord shall make bright clouds," or *clouds of lightning;* that is, thunder showers, for latter rain is that kind; it is not a steady dribble, dribble, dribble, but it is lightning and thunder. The clouds split and burst; this is latter rain; "and give them showers of rain, to everyone grass in the field." Rain makes things grow. It takes the April showers to bring May flowers. Dribble, dribble, dribble, a long cold rain won't do it, but it is the warm, dashing shower that brings out vegetation; and only that kind will wipe out the church's self-love, self-will and indifference, and make it bud and blossom for God.

"For"—what is the trouble? "For the teraphims have spoken vanity, and the diviners have seen a lie, and have told false dreams; they comfort in vain: therefore they went their way as a flock." "Teraphims" mean false systems of religion. "The diviners have seen a lie." Christian Science, spiritualism, theosophy and psychical research have only discovered lies, and people do not get real comfort from them. The poor folks are going along sick, unregenerated, mixed and tangled up in sin. They don't get enough of the Gospel to discover the difference between the gnat and the camel. Here are these things in the record, right when God is sending the "latter rain." Indeed He had to send it for things were getting so desperate some special display of God was necessary to stem the tide of higher criticism which has been overrunning the whole church. "Therefore they went their way as a flock, they were troubled because there was no true shepherd." God sent the "latter rain" and He is raising up a multitude of shepherds, and this is disturbing the worldly church. May God bless and save her! He says, "Mine anger was kindled against the false shepherds, and I punished the goats; for the Lord of hosts hath visited His flock the house of Judah, and hath made them as His goodly horse in the day of battle."

III. RIGHT DESIRE.

The next step after prayer is *right desire*, and that is in perfect accord with Mark 11:24. That is not the passage to which I am now referring, but it is in harmony with that. You would think *desire* was the mother of *prayer*, "What things ye desire when ye pray," but here the desire comes after prayer; you do not know whether your desires are right until after you pray. There are lots of desires in our hearts but when we get into the prayer spirit before God, it is wonderful, sometimes, how few desires we have left. James says, first you don't get answers because you don't ask, and second, because you ask amiss, to consume it on self-love; therefore, God cannot hear us. As we really wait on God there are many things taken out of our hearts. I had only one desire and that was for God Himself, and He baptized me. I forgot even about gifts or anything else, and I said, "God, You Yourself; nothing else but You. I was like the poor Shunammite woman, "you needn't send Gehazi or the stick, or anything else, but you yourself;" and when Elisha came, that was more than Gehazi, rod and everything else, and the young lad was brought to life. "As the Lord liveth and as my soul liveth I will never leave thee;" that is Elisha when he is going out with Elijah, and it's the true grip of Pentecost. "As the Lord liveth and as my soul liveth, I will never leave thee"—that soul will surely be baptized.

Now let us come to the Sixty-fifth Psalm and see whether that is not in harmony with Mark 11:24. We put desire after prayer because it is created now;

right desire, and you see what the Lord does. This is the *third step* in getting the latter rain back. I will read from the ninth verse:

"Thou visitest the earth, and waterest it: thou greatly enrichest it with the river of God, which is full of water:" That is the kind of river we want, the river of God which is full of water. Where is the river of God? It is the one that flows down from heaven. Why more water comes through that river than the Mississippi or the Amazon. Do you know that they would run dry if it was not for the river of God, and it is a type of the "latter rain" here. Dr. Young translates it: "Thou visitest the earth after thou hast made it to *desire* the rain." God had to make it desire the rain. Now will you let God give you the desires of your heart? "He shall *give* you the *desires* of your heart." Don't you have any until He gives them. "Delight thyself also in the Lord and He shall give thee the desires of thy heart," doesn't mean that He will *gratify any desire*, but it means that if you delight yourself in the Lord you won't have any desires but what are from the Lord; only what He begets.

"Thou visitest the earth and waterest it," but not until He has made it *desire* the thing He wants to give. God is working with His people and so He said, "Blessed are they (already) that hunger and

53

thirst *according to* righteousness." Please take that translation. "Blessed are they that hunger and thirst" not simply after righteousness, but "*according to* righteousness," that is, in a right way; they are already blest. Because if righteousness was the object, there would be nothing added, but "Blessed are they that *hunger* and *thirst* according to righteousness, they shall be filled." Filled with what? Filled with God; they that hunger and thirst for Him, but you must hunger and thirst for Him in a right way. You know there is a great difference. You say, "I am hungry and thirsty for God." People that hunger and thirst in the right way eat and drink; that is as sure as you live. Poor dyspeptics are hungry but cannot eat; they are afraid to eat; dyspeptic souls, hungry and thirsty and cannot eat. Oh you must get cured of that first and then you will drink of the water of God.

"He visitest the earth and waterest it," and so He has, but He had to make it thirsty; it was no man-made or church-made affair, for most Pentecostal work has had to come into store-rooms, halls, barns and tents. God is taking the despised things and base things, and being glorified in them, and the meeting-house—the river of God—is full of water. "Thou preparest them corn;" there is the old covenant again with that corn in it. Stick to the corn even if the wine and oil lose out. Hang on to the corn. You can make wine and oil both out of corn, but you cannot make corn out of wine and oil. With corn you will always have sustenance and strength.

God prepares the corn "when thou hast so provided for it" by this watering through right desires, "Thou waterest the ridges thereof abundantly." It would be natural for the ridges to be dry. No, sir. He won't have even the ridges dry. He will water the top of your head, even your brain, your intellect, and it is the great mercy of God that He put the mouths of rivers, that is our eyes, in our heads, so that the rivers might flow out in weeping and thus bring relief. He knew that water would not ordinarily stay on ridges (head), but God can make water even there. He watered my brain. This poor brain was paralyzed one time, my tongue dumb, but now I can remember half a Bible in one day. Why God is the Creator; He is the only God that does wonderful things, I am the God that only does *wonders*." Everything else is common, but when God does anything it is wondrous.

Yes, He waters the ridges thereof, that's Pentecostal; then He "settlest the furrows thereof;" then your *heart* will stay right sure. You will have no trouble with the old places in your life then. "Thou makest it soft with showers;" Oh God, make our hard heads soft; some time give us softness of the brain!

That is a good disease in Pentecostal times. Hard-headed fellows cannot get it; we have to be "crucified at the place of a skull," and then have our heads put to soak. God said, "Your brain is all right, it is a wonderful piece of mechanism, but never amounted to much until I put it to soak." Put yourself to soak in God, and don't be looking around to see what A., B., C., and D. are doing. No! No! No! Get to God. Get to His face and see Him. When Thou hast made it "soft with showers, Thou blessest the springing thereof." When your soul begins to spring up to God He meets it with a great flood of "latter rain." Yes He does. But you must have gone down and gotten the right desire.

IV. WAITING WITH EXPECTATION.

Now the center of the seven steps is here, and the central one is the *waiting days*, but it is coupled with *expectation;* and after that there must be waiting coupled with *preparation*, and here it is in just a little short verse in Job 29:23. You didn't think there was any "latter rain" in Job, did you? Well, you read on to the end of his life and you will find he received it. But here is the prophecy of it out of Job's own mouth: "And they waited for me as for the rain;" I tell you when there is a long drought like there was last autumn, the people do wait for rain. There is a difference in the waiting then. Oh what a longing and a crying; real unbelievers and skeptics attended churches that had prayer-meetings for rain in many places, and in some places they had all-day meetings in their churches for prayer. I know one place in Kentucky where they went three days in succession, and some came all night; skeptics and unbelievers came in and sat in awed silence while the people prayed. The cattle were dying because there was no water, and God did send some special local showers in that section of the country and the rivulets broke out with water. God will do almost anything to help people seek His face. Many, many of these skeptics turned to the Lord.

V. FAITH IN APPROPRIATION.

"And they opened their mouth wide as for the latter rain." If it takes an *open* mouth to get ordinary rain, what kind does it take for "latter rain?" Why they opened their mouth *wide;* that is, down to the heart. I do not mean physically, exactly, but the idea is that your *whole heart* is opened up to God, and the cry goes out of the open mouth. There are two things there: *waiting,* and waiting with *great expectation;* and that is the way they waited in Jerusalem for the "early rain." They waited with great expectation, and so must you. There was acceptance too, of the whole proposition; there was a ready preparation of faith; so we have here two things, really, the *waiting* and the *receptivity*, and all the while faith is in course of preparation. We are now at the *fifth* point in this subject. This point is especially adapted to a number of people seeking the Pentecostal blessing, because the same steps and the same order that were pursued to get back the rain on Palestine literally must be observed to receive the latter rain spiritually—there is the literal and the spiritual; the type and the anti-type.

Get your faith fixed at the start, that you are believing for Pentecost now, and then wait until it comes. Some say there is no faith in it, that you are just to *wait;* but you cannot wait without faith: others say it is faith, and that is the only thing about it; each have a half truth. If you *believe* for a thing, then *wait* with patience until it comes. You must couple the two together. You cannot dictate to God. "Though the vision is for the appointed time, wait for it; it will come and it will not tarry." When it begins to come it frequently comes quickly, and you want to be right there with your mouth wide open; it may light right there. "He sent a word to Jacob and it lighted on Israel." So God is sending the latter rain and all the good people got it first, did they? the old Christians? No, He just poured it out upon the little sons and daughters, and servants and handmaidens, and people that were not before converted. Some of these made the mistake of thinking they at once had more than the others, and forgot to go on into the depths of a sanctified life, and some have lost their blessing. The one must have a great emptying out, subduing, before they get it; the other must have a great infilling to contain it afterwards. Here "the first shall be last, and the last shall be first," but they must all be brought up to the standard of God.

VI. GOD'S GRACE.

The *sixth* step is *mercy, grace.* Proverbs 16:15, "In the light of the king's countenance is life;"—life to any subject; because the king has the prerogative, the executive power, just as the governor of your state has pardoning power; therefore, "in the countenance of the king is life." In the countenance of our King, what is that? Oh you want to see His face and see it in righteousness, and when He lifts up the light of His countenance upon you He becomes the health of your countenance. "The light of the king's countenance is life, and his favor," that is his grace, his unmerited favor "is like a cloud of the latter rain." All of grace!

Now there is another place we will find this word, and it is the Sixty-eighth Psalm, and I am glad it is so. I was so glad when I discovered it. It helped me so much to have more confidence in this Movement and not to mind the false prophets who said that the thing would be over in a short time, and we would all be backslidden.

VII. GOD'S SOVEREIGNTY.

We have these six steps: by the *Word*, by *prayer*, by right *desire*, by *waiting*, by *faith*, by *grace*, but it is last of all by God's own *sovereignty*. Remember the Sixty-eighth Psalm is the Psalm of God's sovereignty. You read of God arising and leading Israel up out of Egypt with His outstretched arm, and working those sovereign acts of His to the astonishment of all the nations round about. Remember it is not God's grace simply that makes His people to be a power in this world and feared by even the devil, as well as the world; it is not God's grace simply that sends the money for these missionaries and the money for this or that great work of God, but His sovereignty. When we come into perfect faith with God in His sovereignty He makes a man say, "Don't you want money?" God's sovereignty works either in conjunction with or apart from His grace, but when He gets us *one with Him in grace*, then He works in a sovereign way for us, for the sovereignty that *follows* grace is much mightier in its display and more glorious than the sovereignty that works apart from grace; therefore the sovereignty of the New Testament time, that is, early and latter rain time, you may expect to be greater than any sovereignty of Old Testament time. Hence, Jesus could say, and on no other hypothesis could He say, "Greater works than these shall ye do because I go to My Father," because the *sovereignty* of *post-Calvary* and *post-Pentecost* is greater than any that preceded it, to the ends of the earth. What we call the Providence of God in missions is the sovereignty of God. See how He is moving! And that is what makes missionaries the greatest witnesses in the world, because with every missionary that goes out, even the weakest, though they go trembling and with fear, fully appreciating their own insignificance, more than grace goes with them. There is a special manifestation of God's sovereignty over them because they are the messengers of the cross especially, and they are following out literally the commission of Jesus, "Go ye into all the world, and preach the Gospel," and listen! There is a promise there that nobody else can claim, and that is the *sovereign* presence of Jesus Christ: "Lo, I am with you all the days, even unto the end." That is sovereign presence; otherwise He would say, "I am *in* you;" but He says, "I am *with you*, in *Providence*. I am *with* you in *sovereignty*." "*Ye in Me and I in you*," is grace, sanctifying relationship, but, "I AM WITH YOU," is sovereignty, and a statement of a fact because you are in that spiritual condition. It is the sovereignty of God, and we need to reverence it; we must take the shoes off our feet; we want to pause before God's sovereign will. He is revealing His sovereignty before He takes His people away, and before the tribulation and judgments are ushered in.

You could not get that passage in the Sixty-fifth Psalm for that is the Psalm of *grace*. The Sixty-eighth is the Psalm of *sovereignty*. Here in the ninth verse we take up the connection: "Thou, O God, didst shake out"—the *wise* preacher and teacher will come into the Pentecostal meetings and tell you, "This thing is all of the devil, God doesn't shake that way; grace doesn't work that way." "Well, I know, brother, that's true, but do you know when God works *sovereignly* things do shake?" They shook away back in the Garden of Eden; they shook on Mount Sinai; they shook on Calvary when the sovereign God was stretching out an arm to redeem a world and letting His Son go to death. The sovereignty of God is moving toward the great consummation of His purpose in all things. He shook out a "plentiful rain whereby thou didst confirm thine inheritance." When? "When it was weary," and therefore helpless. God's sovereign arm came and shook all that could be shaken. "I shake not only the earth but the heavens," He shook the earth under the law, but in this dispensation He shakes the

heavens and the earth; sovereignly—heavens *and*
earth.

"Thy congregation hath dwelt therein;" that is,
in the rain belt, and they like it, and don't like to see
the meetings stop. There is one congregation, bless
God, in this end of Chicago that likes the latter rain
belt. Some said, "No, I won't come anymore;" they
are back again smiling, heart open a little wider, God
working a little more. Beloved friends, you want to
move with God; be sure you don't miss that in these
days. Find out when God is moving and quickly
move with Him. "Thy congregation hath dwelt
therein." Yes, let us stay in this Latter Rain Movement; let us stay in this Pentecostal fulness of blessing and power for service, where self-love is dead,
and self-will obtains no more, and we are willing to
be anything and go anywhere He wants. Let us
dwell therein. Don't plan any cessations. Please
don't come with umbrella or rain-coat. Just step
right out in your common clothes in this latter rain,
and let it wet you to the skin; let it go through the
skin down into the bones and into the marrow. That
is what God wants.

"Thou, O God, hast prepared of Thy goodness
for the poor." These despised people, base things,
weak things, "things that are not, to bring to naught
things that are; that no flesh should glory in His

presence." He prepared of His goodness for the poor. I don't know what the poor can do, the church has little use for them; but God sent this latter rain to gather up all the poor and outcast, and make us love everybody: feeble ones, base ones, those that have just been cast out of human society; no one wants them, all the outcasts of India and China; these are what God sent the latter rain people to pick up. What is the end of it all? We go back to where it says, *"The Lord gave the Word,"*—like the creation— He just spoke and it was done. God gave the word and the "latter rain" started, glory be to His Name! "The Lord gave the word!" I tell you it is His sovereignty, after all, and it is due. We asked rain but it was the time of the "latter rain," and the rain-crows were crowing "rain," but God said, "latter rain;" it doesn't come the way you ask, it comes the way God says. I have known people to ask for a little bit of justification and get sanctified; I have known people to ask for a little bit of sanctification and get healed. God is sovereign when He gets a chance. "The Lord gave the word, great was the company of women that published it." That is the marginal reading, the literal version. "The Lord gave the word, and who started? Why the women, of course, *four to one.* Where would the church be today without the women. God bless them. Look at Ramabai! Look at these nine who consecrated themselves today for the foreign field, only one brother among them! God bless him, I hope he will get there first.

Now by these seven steps—the Word of God, Prayer, Right Desire, Waiting with Expectation, Faith in Appropriation, God's Grace and God's Sovereignty, we may have the Latter Rain, the fulness of the Spirit and power of the Gospel of Christ restored. This closes the *third* division of the subject: "How the Latter Rain may be restored," and may God lead many dear souls to take these seven steps and be *"filled with all the fulness of God."*

CHAPTER III.

Its Design and Operation

ET us harken to the reading of two passages from the prophecy of Isaiah, first in the thirty-second chapter, from the thirteenth to the eighteenth verses, inclusive: "Upon the land of my people shall come up thorns and briars; yea, upon all the houses of joy in the joyous city: because thy palaces shall be forsaken; the multitude of the city shall be left; the forts and towers shall be for dens forever, a joy of wild asses, a pasture of flocks; *until the Spirit shall be poured upon us from on high*, and the wilderness be a fruitful field, and the fruitful field be counted for a forest. Then judgment shall dwell in the wilderness, and righteousness remain in the fruitful field. And the work of righteousness shall be peace; and the effect of righteousness, quietness and assurance forever. And my people shall dwell in a peaceable habitation, and in sure dwellings and in quiet resting places."

Second, in chapter forty-four, the first eight verses: "Yet now hear, O Jacob My servant; and Israel whom I have chosen: Thus saith the Lord that made thee, and formed thee from the womb, which will help thee: Fear not, O Jacob My servant; and thou, Jeshurun, whom I have chosen. For I will pour water upon him that is thirsty, and floods upon the dry ground; I will pour My Spirit upon thy seed, and my blessing upon thine offspring; and they shall spring up (that is, the offspring) as among the grass, as willows by the water courses. One shall say, I am the Lord's; and another shall call himself by the name of Jacob; and another shall subscribe with his hand unto the Lord, and surname himself by the name of Israel. Thus saith the Lord the King of Israel, and His Redeemer (that is Jesus) the Lord of Hosts; I am the first and I am the last; and beside Me there is no God. And who, as I, shall call, and shall declare it, and set it in order for Me, since I appointed the ancient people? and the things that are coming and shall come, let them shew unto them. Fear ye not, neither be afraid: have not I told thee from that time, and have declared it? ye are even My *witnesses.* Is there a God beside Me? yea, there is no God; I know not any." That was the answer of the prophet, and he was trying to speak for the people: "There is no God; I know not any."

This brings us to the fourth in this series of expositions on the subject of the Latter Rain, and although the words "latter rain" are not found in these scriptures, yet they are so closely allied that they teach the same great truth; especially *the design and operation* of the *"latter rain"; that is, how it comes and what it does.*

BETHEL AND PENIEL.

"Yet now hear, O Jacob My servant; and Israel whom I have chosen": Here is God's *call* and God's *choice.* Here is the double idea of salvation and sanctification. God *calls* men to be saved, but He *chooses* them to be sanctified. They are both called and chosen. There is the *ekklesia*, those called out, and also the *eklektoi*, those called the second time, called out from the called ones, for the Hebrew word here rendered *"chosen"* is equivalent to the Greek word *eklektoi* of the New Testament. Notice, it is Jacob who is *called*, but Israel who is *chosen.* Jacob was called at Bethel, which means the house of God, but Israel was chosen at Peniel, the face of God. It is God in each case. Bethel—called in the house of God to get the bread of God, for that word means both. You can get the bread of God in the house of God, and so we come to God's house to get God's bread. There are many of God's houses, so called, where there is not much of God's bread; hence they are not worthy the name of God's house. I'd rather have a little old tumble-down mission-room packed full of God's good bread than I would have your high-steepled, high-spired churches, with an immense amount of money invested in them that ought to be scattered to the heathen world supporting missionaries; far better to have a little humble cottage full of the bread of God where souls might get something than these great empty houses where people starve to death.

"And Israel, whom I have chosen": that happened at Peniel. "Peniel" means the *face* of God; face to face with God where I shall see Him as He is and begin to be made like Him.

"Jacob My servant," but "Israel whom I have chosen." Now these two things are bound in one self-same individual. Jacob became Israel at Peniel, not at Bethel. There is a lot of strong meat at Peniel, and when you come to Israel you can talk about "latter rain" because the Latter Rain Covenant is renewed; you can talk about Pentecostal out-floodings and out-pourings; He will trust you. "Thus saith the Lord that made thee, and formed thee from the womb, I will help thee; Fear not," Pentecostal worker; fear not! God says He will help, and He can help you more than anyone else. He says He will help you "right early"; at the dawning of the morning. Sometimes it takes all night like as with Jacob before he became Israel, but when the morning dawned Jacob was changed to Israel.

THE GOD OF JESHURUN.

"Fear not, O Jacob My servant; and thou Jeshurun"; this latter term Jeshurun is Israel's *business* name, given him because he has gone out to do great things for God. It is God's business that is done now. Turn over to the thirty-third chapter of Deuteronomy, especially from the twenty-sixth verse on, and you get the unfolding of this name. It means a God who is prosperous in all His ways, and this makes us to see He is the sovereign God. Why, if you get the *business* name of God and move in His sovereign purpose, you are bound to succeed; all earth and hell cannot stop you. You want to link yourself right there with the God of Jeshurun. It means the God of grace, of power and uprightness. You do not find this word very often, but it is used in connection with the great outworking of God and the displays of His sovereign majesty through somebody whom He can trust. God can never trust us until we trust Him. When we have reposed one everlasting trust in God and yield unquestioning obedience to His will, then God can begin to trust us and can give us something to do and to say for Him; places to go and ministries to perform.

Are you complaining of a narrowed life? The trouble is with you. Lay it at your own door. When God can bring you where He can trust you, He will give you more than ten ordinary people can do, and then He will give you the strength of ten, for He has promised in His Word, "One shall chase a thousand and two shall put ten thousand to flight." Is your life circumscribed? It's your own fault. Get through to God. Lay your life open to Him; lay it out on His altar. Lay it out even though it has a dry night; lay it out again and it will be wet this time. Let God take you and know that He has you on both the dry side and the wet, for there will be a dry side sometimes. Some people seem to want to be dry; it is an excuse for lazy people to be released from service. They say, "I am dry." Why should they be dry when God has said, "I will pour water on him that is thirsty, and floods upon the dry ground; I will pour My Spirit upon the seed, and My blessing upon thine offspring"? I will cause them to spring up "as willows by the water brooks." "I will help thee, fear not."

THE LATTER RAIN PENTECOST.

"Give to the winds thy fears,
    Hope and be undismayed;
God hears thy sighs, God sees thy tears,
    God shall lift up thy head,"

and Pentecost will fill you. Fear not! He will
help you. Who doesn't want God's help? Who
won't go through with God's help? But He will
have unquestioning obedience.

"Fear not, O Jacob My servant; and thou Jeshurun, whom I have chosen." It is God's choice
when you get into the deeper life of the Spirit, and it
is God's choice again when you get into business
life. Now that doesn't mean preachers or missionaries only; it applies to you in your shop, to you in
your kitchen, to you in your store; it means you behind your desk if God has called you there. Take
Him as the God of Jeshurun, the God of all that is
good and righteous and prosperous. God needs many
good stewards to make money for Him whereby to
send missionaries to evangelize the world. God bless
them; they will get their reward; they have been
hands and feet for the Master. Have you read the
story of the two men that made one? One had a
good pair of hands, but had lost his limbs; the other
had a good pair of strong limbs, but had lost his
hands. The man with hands rode on the shoulders

of the one with feet, and thus they sowed their crop of rice. I have seen missionaries going out to the foreign countries carried by strong men and women at home who toil and bear the expense of the work in the foreign field. I'd be a missionary if I had to live in the back kitchen all my life.

This is the way God is going to work it: "I will pour water on him that is thirsty." Jacob, are you thirsty? Israel, are you thirsty? You may be thirsty in the beginning of your salvation as Jacob was, and God will give you the baptism right there. God is no respecter of persons; there are first that shall be last, and last that shall be first, and in these sovereign workings of God He will do a thing when you are ready for it; He will baptize even Jacob. Sometimes the Jacobs get it easier than the Israels. But are the Israels thirsty? He will give you thirst, and I say to you there is something more than the blessing of holiness, and something more than the doctrine of sanctification.

No matter how often you have said, "saved, sanctified and healed," you need Pentecost. I said, "Lord, I have had Thy Spirit; I have been preaching all these years." "Yes," He said, "don't you remember seventeen years ago how I met you in your library?" "Yes, Lord, what about that?" "I'd

like to finish what I did then." I didn't know
enough then, but I did receive the Spirit, and I went
out into what I called the Spirit-filled life. I had
been marvellously healed, and I said, "Lord, if that
was the beginning and I didn't get this residue, You
give me all there is now, and instruct me how to
teach it"—there were a multitude of questions coming to me, orally and by mail—"and heal my body
instantly"—I was at the point of death with blood-
poisoning from awful burns I had received from an
explosion in our chapel; the flesh was burned off my
hands and face, my eyes were blind for three days,
the blood-poison had gone clear up into my brain.
I said, "Lord, do this and I will give you just one
hour in which to settle with me," for I had become
desperate. I had been getting ready for a year;
God met me inside of that hour and it was all done.
God illuminated my mind until I saw more truth in
an hour than I saw in a year before. He took me
up and i joined the heavenly choir. I wanted to
stay there, but He wouldn't let me. He made me
come back, but He showed me where I would be by
and by. I had a wonderful time in heaven with
Jesus and the angels and all the saints. Oh, what
a wonderful time! I heard such glorious singing
there that I was ashamed of all the singing I had

ever heard on earth. I remember I went up to Jesus and said, "Jesus, I am so sorry we ever sung so poorly down there," and He said, "Never mind, My child, I am going to teach you better so that you shall make real spiritual melody in your heart to the Lord." While He was flooding my soul and baptizing me, a flood of truth came into my understanding, and I then began to write out the song I had just sung in a tongue and suddenly found I was healed, for I was writing with the hand from which the flesh had been burned and the arm which had been so swollen with blood poison.

Oh, I tell you it is blessed to have the water poured over you; to feel God inside and outside. I am always going along with the taste of it in my mouth. It is on my tongue to stay. "I will pour water on him that is thirsty." He will pour it on Israel, the sanctified; yes, and He will pour it on Jeshurun, one that is out busy in service. I was very busy the winter He poured it out on me; there was only one night in the week I had to myself, and that was Saturday night. My Bible-classes and other public ministries, my correspondence, writing and editing hymns just went right on. As I went to my Bible-class I seemed to be walking along the street looking for something. I went out to some summer meetings, went up to Beulah Park, expecting all the time; came back home and opened my Convention on the 13th day of October.

On that fatal day the magazine in our church exploded and threw me twenty feet up against the door, and filled me with burning gas until they saw it coming out of my mouth. They prayed for and anointed me, and took me home. I could not hold my hands down; my hands and face were bound and wrapped in medicated cotton. In this condition I caught cold and blood-poison set in, but God kept saying to me, "Twenty-one days." He took me back to Daniel; twenty-one days Daniel was down and he had become very uncomely, and I had, too. God showed me how Daniel was down on his knees and finally how he had no strength at all; again and again came to me, "twenty-one days, twenty-one days, twenty-one days." I didn't know what it meant, but by and by that Saturday night came, the third day of November, and after it was all over and I had written out the "latter rain" song and translated it into English, I realized it was just twenty-one days since the explosion on the 13th of October. Oh, such dealings with God, such shutting up to Him and emptying out of everything I had; not that I had to repudiate it, remember, but all had to be laid aside, all my experience and all my ministry, and when God baptized me, all there ever had been in my life worth anything was intensified and multiplied. You don't have to repudiate anything God has already done for you to get Pentecost, but you have to be emptied out as though you had nothing.

"I will pour water on him that is thirsty, and there shall be floods upon the dry ground." So, Jeshurun, get it. I got it. Oh, how busy! For eighteen years I was doing three men's work, leading people to God, teaching sanctification and divine healing, training missionaries and sending them out from our Bible-school. I had been doing a good work, but I had to lay it all aside and let God do what He wanted to do; and give me the bigger and better thing.

I want you to see there are three calls, because it is very important; a call to Jacob, a call to Israel and a call to Jeshurun, or, to express it in other words, a call to the saved, a call to the sanctified and a call to those already working for God. God will transform your work, too, my brother, and give you a new kind of ministry; at least He will make it more effective, for "I will pour water," that is, give it to the one that thirsts in order that there may be floods on the dry ground. The dry ground cannot get to God. You see the dry ground all around. The only way God can get to that barren land is through somebody that is thirsty, and He will pour water on that one until it will either run through or run off them on the dry ground. God reaches the people that are not directly in touch with Him through those whom He can immerse and submerge in His Pentecostal fulness.

That is the order in any Gospel ministry—somebody must have something of God to take to somebody else, but, oh, in this sense it means that He will put it on you so full it will run off naturally; that is, He will make you a great system of spiritual irrigation for the arid lands of needy souls. It is not for yourself; it is not to make *me* full of God; of course, one cannot help but be full of God, but that is not the design of it; it is to make you great pipe-lines of blessing through which to carry this water of salvation to others. "Ye shall be witnesses" then. "Ye are My witnesses, saith the Lord"; you have the same idea in Acts 1:8, so it is a Pentecostal message in every sense; witnesses to the great God— He pours Himself on us and through us to reach others. "And there shall be floods on the dry ground."

And then, more specifically He tells us what this

water is. It is just a drop of the Holy Spirit, for "I will pour My Spirit upon thy seed," so that there shall be "blessing upon thine offspring." You know we are to bring forth. The reason we haven't more offspring is because God's Spirit is not on our seed. What is the seed? The thing we sow. We plant the Word of God, our message, our ministry, the song, the prayer, the testimony, and the instrument that gives it out is the tongue—"I will pour My Spirit upon your seed." Pentecost is not simply for me, not merely to satisfy my feeling, but to get floods on the dry ground; to make me a medium, a transmitter. The real thirst for Pentecost should not, then, be a selfish thirst. I know the reason ten thousand more have not received Pentecost; they want it for themselves. But it is thirst for others that will bring me my Pentecost; thirst for others! "My God, I haven't the fulness and power sufficient to reach these people!" Pray that from the heart and God will pour the water on you until there will be floods on the dry ground.

"MY SPIRIT ON THY SEED."

"I will pour My Spirit on thy seed." Ah, it is different now from what it used to be. We used to talk about the Word of God, give testimony, sing, pray; no result. What was the matter? God's Spirit was not poured on the seed. Peter could talk a good deal before Pentecost, and perhaps could preach more eloquently and more self-assertively than he did after, but a little bit of a word after Pentecost cut them to the heart, pricked them in their conscience, and they said, "Men, brethren, what shall we do?" God's Spirit was on the seed. That is what Acts 1:8 means: "Ye shall receive the *dunamis* (the dynamite, the dynamics) of the Spirit coming upo_ you, and ye shall be witnesses unto Me," and when the power of the Holy Spirit falls on the witness, something is done; His Spirit is poured on the seed and the little message in song changes, the prayer changes, the little utterance of the tongue changes, the message from the Word changes, God's Word itself changes, because then it is both spirit and life.

When God's Spirit is poured on the seed it shall not return to Him void. You may hear it only once, but it will stay. We do not give it out like those that fight uncertainly or beat the air, any more. Oh, bless God, when He has taken hold of the deep places of your life, and when He has poured His Spirit on the seed, then there will be blessing on your offspring, and that kind of offspring will survive after birth. They will be born living and active, and there won't be one-half the trouble about backsliders that there used to be. What is the matter with the ministry that a few months after the revival is over the souls are gone? The Spirit was not poured out on the seed. Oh, give us souls that are born to live and love and move with God! You will have blessing on your offspring then, and you know the offspring is like the seed. Like begets like, and kind produces kind. God is getting some children out of this Pentecostal Movement, and He is getting them in a different way from the old way. We are not pulling and hauling them to the altar after the manner of men, but God is moving them by His Spirit. Another thing, God has a spiritual way of "borning" children, I will tell you, and it is through the Word, the incorruptible seed, the Word of God that lives and abides forever.

"And they shall spring up among the grass, as willows by the water courses." They will spring up before you know it. Why? Because the water courses carry life. If rivers of God are flowing through your life, offspring will be produced. "They shall spring up"—I have seen my father take out a whole handful of little twigs that looked dry and dead, and stick them in the ground along a little stream; the next year they were willow trees. Plant a little of the seed of God along the water courses

of the Holy Spirit, and suddenly they will spring up
without coaxing. They will spring up just like the
beautiful crocuses out in the front lawns in the early
spring, that bloom before the sun has hardly warmed
the earth—while the cold north winds are yet blowing; at the first opening of the spring up they jump,
and it looks as though somebody stuck them in the
lawn during the night. That flower seems to say:
"I am a heralder of spring, and I am not afraid of
a little frost or snow. I have been pushed out because that is the kind of life I have." It is not the
old way of holding a set service and seeing how
many souls we can get saved, but here and there,
around the corner, and while you are at work, a
new soul "springs up"—Pentecostal! It is a new
thing in my own ministry; every little while a soul
springs up. There is a crocus, here a willow by the
water course.

"WILLOWS BY THE WATER COURSES."

One sister told me how one sprang up one morning when she went to empty her garbage; she had
a neighbor with whom she was not on friendly terms.
This morning she went out under the Spirit of God,
praising the Lord, and suddenly she and the neighbor happened to come together at the garbage can.
She said, "Good morning; praise the Lord, isn't

this a lovely morning?" (She had received her Pentecost a few days before.) The neighbor looked up, and she said, "Oh, I feel so bad the way you and I have lived." The bad neighbor hardly knew what to make of it and tried to turn the conversation. The other said, "I feel so bad, and the worst of it is I hurt Jesus." The neighbor said, "Do you think Jesus is affected by these things? I thought no one was hurt but us." "Oh no," she said. "He is touched with a feeling of our infirmities; He was wounded for our transgressions," and she went on pleading Isaiah fifty-third chapter. The woman dropped her vessel and burst out crying, and leaning over the fence the two wept together; one told out all her troubles and the other told what the Lord had done for her; there she sprang up by the water courses, in the back yard, out by the alley.

"I will pour My blessing upon your offspring and they will spring up as willows by the water courses. God is saving souls now. In the old way? No, no. God is doing it in the direct spiritual way, because we had to get a new working. The devil had discovered everything the church had, but he can't keep up with Pentecost. And so we Pentecostal people are believing that mighty imperative "shall be"—"there *shall* be floods"—or did you get the little Pentecost to satisfy your own little thirst? Shame on you! I could not thirst that way. We must thirst for others—boys and girls, fathers and mothers; there shall be floods, and the neighbors and the enemies, and those who have gone into sin shall believe, for wherever the water flows it bubbles up. They will believe it; they will testify; they won't be struck dumb. I don't see how people are saved and are struck dumb the next minute. "One shall say, I am the Lord's. Glory to God, I'm saved!" That is how you will know it, for the witness of Pentecost will come. The baptism will produce a like result on these offspring, and you won't have to go around and say, "Are you saved?" They will jump up and say, "I am the Lord's;" they will give an account of it. Another shall say, "I call myself by the name of Jacob," and another shall subscribe his hand, if he is not in the meeting to testify. He will write you a letter saying, "I have it." I shall get a good many letters from this Convention; they will subscribe and say, "I am saved," "I am healed," "I have been baptized too, and I want to tell you all about it."

"Thus saith the Lord the King of Israel, and His Redeemer the Lord of hosts." The Father and the

Son are closely allied in this work. It is the larger work of the Spirit and not only manifests the Son, but also the Father in His sovereignty. "I am the first, and I am the last; and beside Me there is no God." "I am the Alpha and the Omega; I am the beginning and the end." This divine sovereignty is manifested in pouring out water on him that is thirsty, and also the manner in which God works with the souls that are born today. They are of a Pentecostal order. You know how it was on the Day of Pentecost. They didn't go around coaxing people, but the Holy Ghost was poured out and three thousand people came jumping up like willows by the water courses, and in a little while five thousand, and everywhere they went men and women were saved.

PENTECOSTAL MISSIONARIES.

Again God is making workers and landing them in the uttermost parts of the earth in about the same length of time that it requires an ordinary bible-school to examine them and enter them as students. I am not depreciating training, nor putting a premium on the short cut, but I do love to see the Lord cut the thing short in righteousness. I would rather see one person baptized in the Holy Ghost and fire, dead in love with God's Word, reading it day and night, and praying the heathen through to salvation than to see a score of missionaries go out with only an intellectual equipment. Some go out with just about enough grace to say, "Well, goodbye," with great tears and a long struggle, like the old cows that drew the ark of God back to Israel, "lowing as they went" for their calves they had left behind; they are getting along some way, reforming and educating the heathen, but God wants it done now like willows by the water courses. He wants to pour His Spirit on the seed and start the seed growing right away. The time is short. God has to do it that way. We are moving too slowly now. I have watched various methods of missionary activity and I will take God's way as I find it in His Word, manifested by His Spirit and confirmed by His Providence.

I have seen the missionaries sent out full of love and faith, trusting God not only with their souls but also with their bodies, and I tell you they have done more for God than those who go carrying with them a medicine chest. I am reluctant to help send missionaries that have to carry some *materia medica* with them. I do not turn them down; not at all. I pray for them every day, but God is giving us another class; God is giving us another kind. "Suppose they die," you say. Well, suppose they do die.

ITS DESIGN AND OPERATION.

I want to tell you this, that where one has died trusting God for healing, a half dozen have died who were trusting in medicine. The missionaries who have trusted God the fullest have come through the best. You say they cannot get through by trusting God, but they have, and they are going to do it again, hallelujah! God is greater than the earth He has made, and God is greater than the devil that tries to rule this earth, and if God has a purpose in a life over in Africa, He will keep that life until His work is done, if there is real trust. Let us pray for those who cannot fully trust God.

"I am the first, and the last; and beside Me there is no God. And who as I shall call,"—God's Pentecostal call. Who can call like God?—"and shall declare it, and set it in order for Me." If you get God's call you may rest assured you will see it declared clearly. God will decare it; He will make it so plain that "the way-faring man though a fool could not err therein." Then God will set it in order; then look out for a Providence confirming everything, everything in order; you will just go step by step—the money will be there, the tickets will be there at the right time, for God will set it in order, and you won't need to worry about it. Just use good, sanctified sense, obey God and it will be all right;

no undue enthusiasm about it; no hop, skip and jump business, but moving along on your knees in prayer. "And who, as I, shall call, and shall declare it, and set it in order for Me, since I appointed the ancient people? and the things that are coming,"—God appoints them—"and shall come." God has appointed the things that are coming, including the coming of Christ and all that that means; God has appointed it all. So "all things work together for good to those that love God, to them who are the called according to His purpose." "Who, as I, can call then declare it and make it plain to you, and set it in order with things that are coming. I appoint and they shall come," and nobody can stop them, glory be to God! Take your Pentecost that way; believe it and wait for it; accept it and trust God. Well, let anybody else show this kind of God. They cannot do it.

"Fear ye not, neither be afraid: have I not told thee from that time, and have declared it? Ye are even My witnesses. Is there a God beside Me? Yea, there is no God; I know not any." No such a God as the Pentecostal God! This is His *design* and *operation*. This is how it comes and how it works. What a God He is manifesting Himself to be today! People see a little of it, and say, "I do not understand that way." Of course not. Otherwise, you know First Corinthians, second chapter, would not be true, because that scripture says "they are spiritually discerned." "The Spirit searcheth all things, yea, the deep things of God." It is God, and some people, because they cannot understand it, actually attribute it to the devil, and repeat the Pharisees' mistake when they said, "This man doth not cast out demons, but by Beelzebub, the prince of demons."

Now I want to go back to the thirty-second chapter of Isaiah. He says matters will be so bad that "thorns and briars" and loathesome creatures will be in palaces where there ought to be beauty, peace and joy. All these destructive, unpleasant things will abound, showing the natural abasement of mankind "until the Spirit be poured out from on high." Oh, if you could have a vision tonight of Chicago or any of these great cities as I have had it years ago when I did rescue mission work! I have visited the slums in many of the large cities of this country in my earlier ministry, seeking to lead men and women to Jesus; the sin and degradation are indescribable. Sin and sensuality do not confine themselves to the slums but are found just in the same degree, but more under cover, in the palaces of what is called "high so-

ciety," rotten to the core. This thing that destroyed
the palaces of Israel in Jerusalem, in literal Israel,
is just as true in a spiritual and moral sense today,
and it shall be so "until His Spirit is poured out from
on high," and what then? "The wilderness" of
Palestine shall be changed, and before these things
can grow at all it will "become a fruitful field," and
you can count that fruitful field "for a forest," for a
thousand years hence. There will be great, majes-
tic oaks in that forest. In the same way you can
count in this Pentecost that when God pours out His
Spirit from on high, the old wilderness will be changed
into a fruitful field, and you can count on that fruitful field becoming a forest; indeed, there is no telling what it will make for God. There is no com-
puting it by any human system, because "One shall
chase a thousand and two shall put ten thousand to
flight." Oh, here is geometrical ratio of living faith
coupled with the out-poured sovereign Spirit from
the throne of God. There is no limit to the power.
But it is not that I may *feel* power; it is not that *you*
are to have power at all. "Ye shall receive power
from on high, the power of the Holy Ghost coming upon you to be a *witness.*" You are not to
realize that you have power; pity the worker that
has to feel a sense of power before he does any-

thing. What am I to feel? *Weakness*. What am I to have in my weakness? *The power of God.* When I am weak then am I the dynamics of God, then am I power. Why do I glory in my weakness? That the power of God may rest upon me. Who are they in the eleventh of Hebrews that are made the strength of God in the earth—"out of weakness were made strong"? Oh "the people are yet too strong for Me, saith the Lord." There is yet too much of human strength in God's work. Weakness! Weakness! As long as you feel you can do anything, I pity your doing, but when you feel as if you had no strength, God can do something. Oh God, I thank You that You said the "bruised reed" You would not break, the "smoking flax" You would not quench. I felt tonight just like a piece of flax nearly burned out, but God permits this that no flesh may glory in His presence; that the glory may be of God, and not of us. He "takes the *weak* things to confound the mighty." May we realize that "when I am weak then am I strong," for a little bit of weakness is worth a great deal more than a lot of human strength. "It is God that worketh in us both to will and to do of His own good pleasure." That is the *design* and the *operation* of Pentecost. "Not unto us! Not unto us oh God, not unto us, but unto Thy Name be all the glory." Pentecost has come to display and manifest God, and He is willing to take any kind of vessel. "I will pour out My Spirit," and "judgment shall dwell in the wilderness, and righteousness remain in the fruitful field." Judgment shall obtain in the wilderness; get right in that place and everything will be made right, and "righteousness shall remain in a fruitful field. And the work of righteousness shall be peace;" that is, righteousness works peaceably, "and the effect of righteousness"—when it has wrought its work in peace, shall be "quietness and assurance forever."

And oh, how you can move on in God. The effect is quietness and everlasting assurance. You needn't talk to me or sympathize with me about what God wants me to do, for anything else would kill me or crush me, but His will is the joy of my life and heart. "Who, for the joy that was set before Him endured the cross, despising the shame." He did not count it any hardship. And what was the end to Him? He is sitting at the right hand of the throne of God, and because He is exalted at the right-hand of God, He sheds out this to make us do the selfsame thing. Oh beloved people, let us sink down, sink down, and sink out, and let

ITS DESIGN AND OPERATION.

God be manifested; not for us, but for the offspring, for the dry ground, to reach others. We can afford to be nothing or anything if only God will reach somebody, save them, sanctify them, heal them, and "pour water on the thirsty till there shall be *floods on the dry ground.*"

"O I'm glad the promised Pentecost has come,
    And the 'latter rain' is falling now on some;
Pour it out in floods, Lord, on the parched ground
    Till it reaches all the earth around."

CHAPTER IV.

Its Fulness and Effects

 HIS afternoon's lecture brings us to the *fifth* division in the subject of the Latter Rain, *The Fulness and Effects of Pentecost* itself. When I left home God said to me on the train, "Tarry in Chicago until Pentecost." I had no idea then of giving these special addresses, but somehow in God's providence they were thrust upon me just at a time to bring us to this phase of the subject on this, the anniversary of the day of Pentecost. Nobody planned this, but all the Spirit's leadings, all my praying, and all God's communications to me have led up to this very point.

LITERAL AND SPIRITUAL LATTER RAIN.

The latter rain was once literally restored to Israel's land after the seventy years of captivity, but that rain largely ceased. God is bringing it back the second time to the land which is shown by the reports from the weather bureau in Jerusalem. Since 1860 the measurement of rain in Palestine has been recorded very accurately at Jerusalem, and shows a great increase, especially of the latter rain. It is a generally understood fact that for many centuries the rain-fall in Palestine was very small. During comparatively recent years the rain has been increasing. The official record of rain-fall, which was not kept until 1860, divides the time into ten-year periods, and the facts are that forty-three per cent more rain fell between the years 1890 and 1900 than fell from 1860 to 1870.*

Spiritually the latter rain is coming to the church of God at the same time it is coming literally upon the land, and it will never be taken away from her, but it will be upon her to unite and empower her, to cause her to aid in God's last work for this dispensation, to bring about the unity of the body, the consummation of the age, and the catching away of spiritual Israel, the Bride of Christ. God said He would bring back this latter rain "as at the first" and He is doing it. The *early* rain was for the sowing and the *latter* for the harvest; one for the beginning and the other for the end; one for the introduction and the other for the consummation of the dispensation.

Significant is it also that at this time Israel is turning back to her land; she seems to be hindered and divided in her purpose, but that is because she is not going back God's way; she is taking her

* See rain-chart at end of book.

own way, going back through Mesopotamia. Even since this Convention began the news has reached us that the Jews are in a serious way taking hold of Mesopotamia, going in there with their millions to irrigate that country and make a place for the ten million Jews who have been scattered up and down the earth through persecution. Nearly nine million of them are under persecution today; only the million in this land and the few scattered in other lands, principally in the British Isles, have any liberty. I mean the Jews—that part of Israel that has retained its identity, for they never can be mixed with any other people.

There was a different promise to the two tribes than to the ten. The ten are lost; many men think they know where they are, but they are lost. No man knows where they will be brought from; they are mixed up among all the nations of the earth. But the Jews have gone into every nation and yet are distinct from all other peoples and nations. They are buying Mesopotamia for these persecuted Jews, and it is according to God's Word that they will return, but not in His way. It also fulfils another prophecy, that they shall come up out of Mesopotamia, the land of their Father Abraham.

ITS FULNESS AND EFFECTS.

All of these are latter rain signs, and in the prophecy of Joel the two are linked together; the latter rain, both literal and spiritual, is falling; literal Israel and spiritual Israel are coming each to its own possessions.

Peter says: "This is that which was spoken by the prophet Joel; and it shall come to pass in the last days, saith God, I will pour out of My Spirit upon all flesh; and your sons and your daughters shall prophesy, and your young men shall see visions, and your old men shall dream dreams; and on My servants and on My handmaidens I will pour out in those days of My Spirit; and they shall prophesy." Acts 2: 16-18. Now the beginning and the end of the age are linked together in these verses, and then he said there would be signs in heaven and on earth, blood and fire and vapor of smoke; the sun shall be darkened, the moon shall be turned into blood, in the great and terrible day of the Lord. That is about all that Peter quotes, that which particularly refers to the *beginning* and *end* of this Gospel dispensation. But let us go back now to read the connections in Joel from the twenty-first verse to the end of the second chapter:

"Fear not, O land; be glad and rejoice: for the Lord will do great things." Great things, wondrous signs, miracles, stupendous manifestations, the dynamics of the Godhead! Oh, I wish you could conceive what these two Hebrew words "great things" mean. You read about them in the Acts, and we are seeing some of them today.

"Be not afraid, ye beasts of the field: for the pastures of the wilderness do spring, for the tree beareth her fruit, the fig tree and the vine do yield their strength." The animals that had gone away from Palestine on account of its barrenness are coming back again because the latter rain has returned, and there is food for them now. Travelers will tell you that for centuries the animal life of Palestine has been greatly changed from ancient times, but with the return of the latter rain not only are the people coming back, but also the animals. The land will have again all things that it contained in the days when it lived in obedience to the Lord.

"Be glad then, ye children of Zion, and rejoice in the Lord your God: for He hath given you the former rain moderately, and He will cause to come down for you the rain, the former rain and the latter rain as at the first. And the floors shall be full of wheat, and the fats shall overflow with wine and oil." That's Pentecost! always overflowing, more than anybody can contain. Somebody must get the effects of it, and if they don't you haven't your full Pentecost.

"And I will restore to you the years that the locust hath eaten, the cankerworm, and the caterpillar, and the palmerworm, my great army which I sent among you,"—"sent" in the sense of *allowed* to come upon you, God's permissive will. God does not let judgment fall on any individual or people or nation but for their good, and when He, through these judgments, has called back His people to obedience and unity with His purpose, He not only takes away that which He allowed to come, but actually wipes out their effects, and then gives *double*. You needn't be afraid of the trial, for when the trial is over God will obliterate even the marks of it.

"And ye shall eat in plenty, and be satisfied, and praise the Name of the Lord your God, that hath dealt wondrously with you: and My people shall never be ashamed." Glory to God for a Pentecost that takes the reproach of Egypt off of us forever, and removes the shame from our faces. Have you such a Pentecost? Oh, God, take the shame from us; remove our timidity and our shrinking! How quickly Pentecost wiped the shame off Peter's face, and with the face of a lion he stood before the multitude at Jerusalem and said: "His blood is on you, you crucified the Son of God!" A little while before that he was cowed by a young maid, and said in his heart, "I am ashamed of this Man; I am sorry I ever knew Him," and then swore to the maid he never did know Him. Oh when God pours His Spirit on young maidens, little babes and servants, His fulness has come; not riotousness, not lawlessness, not anything unseemly, but a fulness, a sweetness that is the very fulness of the Son of God!

"And it shall come to pass afterwards, that I will pour out My Spirit upon all flesh;" upon both Jew and Gentile, "and your sons and your daughters shall prophesy, your old men shall dream dreams, your young men shall see visions." That occurred at the first Pentecost which was Jewish only; that was upon the "sons and daughters" of the people; Joel was addressing the sons and daughters of the Jews—the Jewish Pentecost at Jerusalem. This same Pentecost ran over, by and by, into Samaria, then into Cæsarea and also at Ephesus, because God meant it to be in Judea, in Samaria, in the Roman world, and in the uttermost parts of the earth. It had to come to these four places in order that Acts 1:8 might be literally fulfilled; you could not have any less than four and no more than four, because it must reach the places Jesus Christ said it would. He is the one Man whose word shall never pass away. It is with Him I keep company; He is the man I stand with, and He it is who stands with me while I preach His Word, glory be to His holy Name!

Now here is where we are in the "latter rain" period, at the twenty-ninth verse of this prophecy of Joel, and there is a binder here like you see put on a load of hay; it is the word "*also.*" He is reaching down; "And *also* upon the servants and upon the handmaids in those days will I pour out My Spirit." That means upon us, for we are servants and handmaids compared with Israel—Gentiles always were looked upon as servants by the Jews. If one was to be a part of Israel he had to be taken as a servant, his ear bored through and he nailed to the door for a time. He had to bear the marks of a servant and so did the handmaidens.

Now we are in the Gentile Pentecost; the first Pentecost *started* the church, the body of Christ, and this, the second Pentecost, *unites* and *perfects* the church unto the coming of our Lord. While we are busy getting ready for His return the Jew is busy getting ready to go to the land of his people.

Get that clear: we are "servants and handmaids;" you cannot be anything more, even if you were once a bishop. And you know God's servant is very blind and deaf; he doesn't see much and doesn't hear much. That is where the servant of the Lord should be—shut away from the things of this world. Oh,

THE LATTER RAIN PENTECOST.

I love to dwell where nobody dwells but God, and
when I come out I come from the presence of the
Lord; I see and hear nobody but God. So we are
only servants and handmaidens. That is all God has
now. Nobody must think he is going to be a preacher
or anything like that. God cannot use anybody now
but servants and handmaidens. That is all! And if
He does use anybody else they will have to become
as servants and handmaidens. All your preaching
abilities, gifts and graces must be brought down into
the little servant. I am among you as one that
serves, for I am among you as one that ministers;
that is the Jesus life. "For the Son of Man came
not to be ministered unto but to minister," and after
He got through a greater ministry than any of us
can ever perform, He gave His life a ransom. The
best thing at the end of a ministry is to lay down your
life at the last, like the old Scotch collie, after he
had made three long hunts and had brought back
the three lost sheep to the fold, he went into his kennel,
laid down and panted out his life in the presence of
his master. Oh, if my life must go out on the earth
before Jesus comes, let it go out in ministry for others
—bringing back the lost sheep. Ah, yes, it's the
servant and the handmaid life!

Listen! "In those days will I pour out My Spirit."
Peter quotes most of this also, from the twenty-eighth

to the thirty-second verses. "And I will show wonders in the heavens and in the earth, blood, and fire, and pillars of smoke. The sun shall be turned into darkness and the moon into blood when the great and terrible day of the Lord comes," or "before" if you please, but it means *in that day.*

Now you see right following this outpouring of the Holy Spirit in this "latter rain" time, is the gathering of God's people, the quickening of His people, bringing them into unity for His last work, and immediately following that, comes the tribulation. Don't you see that the tribulation comes before "the great and terrible day of the Lord?" "The day of the Lord" is the *epiphany* when Christ comes back *with* His Bride, having already at the *parousia* come for her. The seven years that intervene between the *epiphany* and the *parousia* are the time of Jacob's trouble, the great tribulation, but the *day of the Lord* is the *epiphany,* the appearing of Jesus, when He introduces the millennium, for one of the Lord's days is a thousand years, according to II. Peter 3:8.

"And it shall come to pass," during this tribulation time, "that whosoever calleth on the Name of the Lord shall be saved." Here that word "*saved*" means "delivered"; it doesn't mean "converted." It is very doubtful whether many or any will be converted during the tribulation, but those that have been converted before and have not been sanctified and thus made members of the Bride of Christ may, by calling on the Name of the Lord, be delivered.

There are two great sections that are "delivered"; one mentioned in the seventh chapter of Revelation, and the other in the fourteenth; two sections of tribulation saints that come up. They cannot become members of the Bride, but they do receive places of privilege; one is the company of *harpers*, the great orchestra that plays for the Bride of the Lamb, and the other the *palm-bearers*, the victorious company who will march along in advance with the orchestra in the great procession; but the *Bride is with the Lamb.* You will find this in Revelation in connection with the one hundred and forty-four thousand literal Israelites that are saved on the earth at the time Antichrist is manifested. Never confuse the one hundred and forty-four thousand with the Bride; the Bride will number millions of souls. Make no mistake. Don't treat God as though He were a little two-penny whistle. Look at earth's teeming population! Look at the men and women who have fallen asleep in Christ! Look at the multitudes that have died in the redemption of the Lord Jesus! Don't talk to me about the one hundred and forty-four thousand constituting the Bride of Christ. Men were cured of that nonsense long ago. The one hundred and forty-four thousand literal Jews converted during the tribulation are made up of the "twelve thousand to a tribe." Dan is out because his is an apostate tribe, and the double tribe of Joseph is reckoned in, which makes twelve complete tribes. While the devil was stealing one tribe God made another, for He usually makes double to overtake the devil's intervention—*Where sin abounds, grace shall doubly abound.* During the tribulation many shall call on the Name of the Lord and shall be *delivered.*

Now we begin to understand this great prophecy: "I will pour out My Spirit"—literally on Israel, spiritually on God's church, dispensationally to bring in the consummation of the ages and open the millennium, the age of righteousness. To this great point we are converging, and we see enough now that ought to make anybody willing to go through life a continual sacrifice to help hasten that day. I am surprised at men and women who say they believe these things and then hold back their time, their talent, and their money. If the Lord should burst through the air to-day with the sound of the trump and the voice of the archangel, many who profess to believe these truths could not go up to meet Him because they are bound down by bank stocks, bonds, and real estate—these are weights upon them. Oh, you must be light; you must have laid aside the weights and the sin that doth so easily beset you—the sin that is so common among us, the sin of unbelief, of not being sharp and quick in our faith. Our questions, doubts, fears and misgivings—let us lay them aside.

> "Oh for a faith that will not shrink
> Though pressed by every foe,
> That will not tremble on the brink
> Of any earthly woe."

"God is able to make all grace abound toward us, that we always having all sufficiency in all things, may abound to every good work." Glory to His Name! If God has His way, men and women who have come up to these meetings will find new places in God's earth to serve Him and bring forth fruit. Beloved, will you take time to get a vision of the Almighty? Will you take time to let God project in you, through you and upon you the vision of His purpose for you? If you do, some will soon find themselves in the uttermost parts of the earth. Then there will be people living in Chicago united so closely with those God has sent to foreign lands that they will be living one life, one laboring here and one laboring there; one working here that the other might prosper there. This is the *intent* of Pentecost, that my heart might be bound with men and women in Africa, in Japan, in the fastnesses of Tibet; that my spirit might be bound with men and women in India and we are made one in working out the purposes of God. When we come up to meet Him it will be like one man, developed into the fulness of the stature of Christ, because we have come by the love of the Spirit, into the unity of the Spirit, through the wisdom of the Spirit, into the unity of the faith that works as one, believes as one, labors, and toils, and suffers as one.

FULNESS OF THE GODHEAD.

Pentecost then is *this,* and "this is *that.*" Jesus is at the right hand of the Father "shedding forth that which ye see and hear"; for He said, "I will ask the Father and He will give you another Comforter," and I will pour Him out upon you. It was well-pleasing to the Godhead that in Him should all the fulness dwell. Col. 1:19. He is made Head over all things, to the church which is His body, "the fulness of Him that filleth all in all." Eph. 1:23. He is Head over all principalities and powers. He can take care of the things that hinder. He is the Head; let Him have the body and He will take care that it shall be full of him. Fulness!

That is how I always like to see Pentecost. His fulness! Pentecostal fulness! If it is a tongue let it be the fulness of the tongue; if it is discernment let it be the fulness of discernment; if it is interpretation let it be in its fulness; if healing or faith, let them all be

in fulness; whatever the display, let it be in its *fulness.*
We must never stop short of that. But first, Pentecost
was the promise of the Father, foretold by Joel, and
reiterated by Christ. In Luke 24:49 Jesus said,
"Behold!" that is, look for the promise of the
Father, I am going to send Him upon you; "but
tarry ye in the city of Jerusalem, until ye be endued
with power from on high." He didn't say, "Behold,
I send the promise of the Father on you, but tarry ye
at Jerusalem until you speak in tongues!" Now I
am no modifier of tongues, please remember that,
nor am I a stickler about tongues; you never had any
too much tongues for me, but I will not, I cannot, and
I *shall* not magnify tongues out of its legitimate place,
its scriptural setting, and its value compared with cther
gifts of the Spirit. Tongues is the least of all the
gifts, and subordinate to other gifts, and when it is
not kept so, there is some trouble.

Now that is the strongest statement I have ever
made on this phase of the subject, but I say again, it
is the least of all the gifts and subordinate to the
others. And when it is not, there is sure to be trouble.
It is least because it is last, and because it is physical,
and because it is dependent upon other gifts. Three
of the gifts are spiritual, three in the psychical realm,
and three in the physical. Satan can manifest all
the three physical gifts. They are all gifts of God,

but I am talking about the region in which they operate: miracles, healings and tongues are physical, that is, they operate in the natural realm. Satan can imitate each of these three, but he cannot give you wisdom, nor can he give you intuitive knowledge. Satan cannot give you discernings of spirits nor true interpretation of tongues; nor can he give you true prophecy. Satan works from the physical, from the lower up. God works from the spiritual down. The spiritual must dominate the psychical and the psychical the physical; in other words, the spirit must control the soul and the soul the body.

Keep in consonance with all the Godhead and His revealed will and you will never have any trouble. Tongues is a great gift; I will never minimize it, never modify it, but I will give all the gifts their proper setting.

Do not think that all these displays are of the Spirit alone; the Father is there, the Son is there, and the Holy Spirit is there. Whenever God has come to anyone, the whole Godhead is manifested therein; it is the dynamics of the Godhead; the things of the Spirit are displayed in His sovereign working. This movement must be saved from saying that there is never any Spirit until there is Pentecostal fulness, and also after we get Pentecost, from saying it is the Spirit only. It is God! the Father, the Son and the

Holy Spirit. Read Christ's own words in the fourteenth chapter of St. John, twentieth verse: Ye shall know that I am in My Father, and ye in Me, and I in you." Twenty-third verse: "If a man love Me, he will keep My words: and My Father will love him, and We will come unto him and make Our abode with him." It is God now in the house, moving around as He pleases, through your eyes, your lips, your tongue, your hands, your feet; it is God dwelling in mortal flesh; "I will dwell in them and walk in them," and speak through them. It is God—Spirit, Son, Father, the fulness of the Godhead bodily.

THE PROMISE OF PENTECOST.

Now Pentecost is first a *promise.* He charged them that they should not leave Jerusalem, but "wait for the promise of the Father, which, said He, ye have heard from Me." Acts 1:4-5. "Ye have heard about it in My paschal sermon; ye shall be immersed, or submerged in the Holy Spirit and in fire not many days hence. Behold, I send the promise of the Father upon you."

PREPARATION FOR PENTECOST.

"But tarry ye in the city of Jerusalem until ye be endued with power from on high." Tarry! Wait! That is for preparation; that is not so much that God has a time and that He cannot give it before, but

110

you must tarry for your own *preparation.* Historically, there had to be a completion of the scriptures. The work had to be completed by Christ; He had to go to the Father and get the Godhead power put into Him. Peter comprehended it aright when he said, "being by the right hand of God exalted, and having received of the Father the promise of the Holy Ghost," (this great fulness of the Godhead) "He hath shed forth this which ye now see and hear." So we have the promise coupled with the demonstration in its realization. Seeing then that Pentecost results from the absolute oneness of the Godhead what oneness and unity ought it to produce in us who have received! It ought to make us as one body, and it will do it. I am one with everybody that is at all one with God. I simply cannot help it. The only thing that can keep me from being one with others is some work either of the flesh or of the devil. Will you throw away your little scruples and colorings and shades of opinion? When Christ pours out the Godhead fulness upon us, who are we, as Peter said, "that we should withstand God?" This preparation moves us on into one-accordness; and when it is complete through yieldedness, prayer, trust, obedience, and praise, He will flood you; yes, He will. The floods from above will meet the floods from beneath and there will be a blessed shower. Oh, it is wonderful! You will know it is real.

Then you will know it is "*upon* you." You are immersed into the Spirit. The Spirit is upon you. He has been "*with* you," and has been "*in* you," and now He is "*upon* you." You cannot eliminate from your New Testament these three prepositions, "with," "in," and "upon," and understand truth in its right relation regarding the Spirit. We have seen the *promise*, the *preparation*, now here is the *position*. He is "upon you," making you a witness, and thank God, you cannot escape. In this sense the witness is in the "witness-box." You do not fix up things any more, saying—I guess I will do this for the Lord, I guess I will pray, I guess I will give a testimony. The thing goes and it is God. You cannot help it. He has thrust you right out. Everybody sees it. Jerusalem found them with the goods on them: "They spake in *tongues* as the Spirit gave utterance." I wish we could catch more of them that way today. There are lots of people saying, "I have had my baptism," but one that He fully baptizes today shows the sign, and the best of it is, you cannot stop it. Tongues, in one sense, is the advance agent, the telltale of Pentecost. That is where it is valuable as a gift when nothing else will do. But you need a baptism of interpretation when you get a baptism of tongues, and some need a baptism of discernment, and some will need, especially the leaders, a baptism of wisdom, and you will have to have a baptism of knowledge and a great baptism of faith to lead this kind of life, or you will have a great deal of trouble. And so when we get all these ministries together we can make some sort of a complete assembly, but, like the Corinthians, we may get too much of the gift of tongues and not enough wisdom to balance it, and then it works weakness. We may have too much "caution" also, and so come to neglect even tongues. If we do we shall not see God display Himself in freshness and newness thus subduing the human. Every little while it requires the outburst of a tongue to subdue things and make us mind our business and look to God. We are too well acquainted with the old English tongue, and we can play fast and loose with that; but not when God begins to talk. The people begin to get near to God and say, "What meaneth this?" How we need perfect assemblies where all the gifts are in operation! I am praying day and night for this. The great deficiency in this movement is interpretation of tongues, and discernment of spirits, and these are the fundamental parts of Pentecost.

THE LATTER RAIN PENTECOST.

PROFUSION OF PENTECOST.

"*They were all filled*," overflowing. Everywhere you find that word in the New Testament it means the "*overflow.*" They were overflowing with the Holy Ghost. That is the first thing that is said about Pentecost, and the second was, "they began to speak in other tongues as the Spirit gave them utterance." It manifests itself through the organs of speech apart from any mentality—that is its profusion, its fulness. And so above everything else, we must look for *fulness, overflow of God in whatsoever manner He pleases.* We needn't know much about it; just enough to take the first step. No "yesterdays" and no "tomorrows," but moment by moment in His will, realizing His fulness.

God, as you read in the fourth chapter of Ephesians, is above all, through all and in you all. Don't forget that the God who is in you wants to go through you. He wants to diffuse Himself through all, and then He will be over all. He is *in you* to reveal Himself, He is *through you* to manifest Himself, and He is *over you* to control you. All these things God will do.

PENETRANCE OF PENTECOST.

Then there is that *penetrance* of God which every soul may have, which is mentioned in Acts 1:8: "Ye shall receive power"—*dunamis*, the dynamite, we like

114

to call it, for dynamite is both *explosive* and *expulsive;* it breaks into bits and throws the bits wherever it pleases. But it is also the *dynamics,* and that is the better word, for it is the divine display, heavenly theatricals. It is the *pneumatikos,* the *spirituals* of I. Corinthians 12:1, the *dynamics* of the Spirit. The word "gifts" is in italics, having been supplied by the translators. It might better read "spirituals," a word similar to our "victuals." In this chapter there are nine kinds of "spirituals," which means things of the Spirit, dynamics, outward displays of the Spirit. There are nine of them. Which will you have? Do not seek any more, just sit down at the table; the Head of the table, who is Christ, the Dispenser, the Baptizer, with the *pneumatikos*—"the things of the Spirit," will give you just what He wants you to have. I sat down at the table and He gave me just what I wanted. I took it and I am thankful for it, as He who distributed also worketh it according to His own will. Don't try to work your healing; don't try to work your faith; don't try to work your wisdom; don't try to work your tongue; don't try to work discerning or interpretation. Listen! Let it work you! Faith will put people to work, and faith works by love. Love is the atmosphere in which faith and work live, and if you do not give them a good, big, pure atmosphere, they will soon die, some by disease and some by suffocation; still others will die by perversion. Oh, it is love that is the life of every gift, and without this it dies.

PURPOSE OF PENTECOST.

I have shown you that the purpose of Pentecost is to make you witnesses. You cannot help it. Now look here: if one of the courts of Illinois sends down here for me by an officer of the court, and serves a subpœna on me saying that I am to be a witness in a certain case, I must go and witness in spite of myself. It is a very serious thing in this government to be found in contempt of court. It has cost men large sums of money sometimes to get their freedom, and when God wants us as witnesses and pours upon us the subpœna of the court of heaven, immerses us in the Holy Ghost, pours out the power of His penetrance on us, we are going to have a time if we try to get away from being a witness. There are many workers in contempt of court now everywhere because they try not to be witnesses. You had better throw up your hands and obey even if it takes you from Los Angeles to Chicago and back again.

Well, here you are, witnesses, and you cannot help it. What are you to do? "Take no thought what ye shall speak in that hour," for listen! It is a Christian's court. It is not a court of law, but the court of grace—for "it shall be given you in that

116

same hour what ye shall speak." Was that ever fulfilled? Oh, yes, ever since Pentecost was fulfilled in the apostles. Look how they opened their mouths and spoke boldly. Prisons were shaken and men feared. God worked with them in signs and wonders, and works of power, till men trembled in the places of legislative and executive power, and said, "We had better leave these men alone."

"Ye shall be witnesses unto Me." Peter said in Acts 5:32, "We are His witnesses of these things," and in the twentieth verse of the fourth chapter he said, "We cannot but speak the things which we have seen and heard." "With great power gave the apostles witness of the resurrection of the Lord Jesus: and great grace was upon them all." Acts 4:33. *Great grace!* You won't run out. There will be great grace on those who are called to witness. In Acts 5:32 we read: "And we are His witnesses of these things; and so is also the Holy Ghost whom God hath given to them that obey Him." There it is, the active verb, *obey Him.* In other words, God will keep Pentecost continuous with increasing fulness and power, *if we obey.* It would be a shame if I had not today an increase of the presence and power and fulness of Pentecost, with increased intensity and knowledge over what I had when He baptized me two years and a half ago. I cannot conceive of such

117

a thing as Pentecost running itself out and failing;
with me it is an increase of God. "He *must* increase,
but I decrease." It should be continually less of us
and more of God. You must look at it that way.
"We are witnesses, and so also is the Holy Ghost."
It means that we are joined together and as we obey,
the Holy Ghost witnesses in us and through us. We
are witnesses, not alone of something that *has* happened, but I am a witness now because the Holy
Ghost this minute is witnessing in me; a new thing
every day, every hour. The same thought is in
Ephesians 5:18, "Be filled with the Spirit," active
verb; *being* filled, keeping filled, being flooded, keeping flooded all the time for everything God wants
done—flood-tide. That is His purpose.

PERFORMANCE OF PENTECOST.

And God will give the *performance*. God will
perform the signs and wonders. We have nothing to
do with them. There are five words that we have for
miracles in the New Testament, among which are a
sign, a wonder, a work of power, etc., all of which
are translated "miracle." You have it stated in its
simplicity in John 9:4, "I must work the works of
Him that sent me." Any work of God is a work of
power; any work of God is a miracle, any work of
God is a sign; any work of God is a wonder; any
work of God is supernatural. "I am a God that only

doeth *wonders."* Anything God has already created may go on producing something that is natural, but when God Himself works it is supernatural, for it was supernatural for God to make the world in the beginning. "He spake and it was done." The devil cannot do *supernatural* work. I wish we would get cured of that idea. That is what has brought forth a lot of confusion in our present literature. Satan cannot do supernatural things; he dwells in the *preternatural* realm. There is only One who can do supernatural things, and that is Father, Son and Holy Ghost.

It is in the preternatural realm that we find spiritualism and all the occult beliefs. God is "*super,*" above and better, as well as superior to nature, with the great *goodness* of the Lord added. If the natural man cannot perceive the things of God, how can men and women who have given themselves into Satan's preternatural workings in all lying wonders and seducing spirits and doctrines of demons—how can they ever comprehend the doctrines of Deity? These demons must be cast out of such and the Holy Spirit must enlighten them. God is doing this very thing in these Pentecostal days. He is taking men and women from the lowest depths of preternatural conditions until nature is almost spent, and in a few hours or weeks making them to comprehend the great things of

THE LATTER RAIN PENTECOST.

God. That is the God of Pentecost. That is the God that says, "Fear not, O land, for I will do great things." Let us come to Him as children; let us bow down before the Lord our Maker; let us subject ourselves, yield ourselves, abandon ourselves into His loving arms. There is not one of you who does not need a manifestation of the supernatural God in some way every day. You need it with the children, and in all domestic life, to keep you preserved from the evil world that is pressing hard on every hand. Everybody needs this. HE IS THE SUPERNATURAL GOD OF PENTECOST. We must trust Him; we must obey Him. We will give ourselves in obedience to Him who is manifesting His power in these last days to make up His body, to gather the scattered members who are yet waiting over in the heathen darkness, to fill up the measure of the sufferings of Christ, to complete the body "until we all come into the unity of the faith" to the full stature of the perfected man in Christ Jesus our Lord.

> Let the fire fall while on Thee we call,
> Send us now the Pentecostal flame;
> Let the power fall, we are yielding all—
> O baptize us *now* in Jesus' Name!

CHAPTER V.

𝕴𝖙𝖘 𝕯𝖎𝖘𝖕𝖊𝖓𝖘𝖆𝖙𝖎𝖔𝖓𝖆𝖑 𝕾𝖊𝖙𝖙𝖎𝖓𝖌

I N this last lecture we take up the sixth and seventh divisions of this subject. In the sixth place, we shall deal with *the Return of God's Ancient People*—the Jews —*to their native land*, and the *Beginning of Christ's Millennial Reign*, and in the seventh place, the most important of all, we shall see that it is *The Evidence of Christ's near return and the preparation of His body, the Bride, for that event.*

ISRAEL'S RETURN TO PALESTINE.

I will read a passage in Isaiah 32:13-18, and although the *word* for latter rain is not there, yet it evidently refers to it:

"Upon the land of my people shall come up thorns and briers; yea, upon all the houses of joy in the joyous city: Because the palaces shall be forsaken; the multitude of the city shall be left; the forts and towers shall be for dens forever, a joy of wild asses, a pasture of flocks; until"—that's the saving word, "until,"

121

just as it is a saving word to say that sin abounds in
the heart *until* the grace of God comes in—"until the
Spirit be poured upon us from on high." Then what
will happen? "The wilderness shall be a fruitful
field, and the fruitful field be counted for a forest.
Then judgment shall dwell in the wilderness, and
righteousness remain in the fruitful field." "Remain,"
that is abide, continue without any interruption. "And
the work of righteousness shall be peace; and the
effect of righteousness"—when peace shall be established—"quietness and rest forever. And My people," that is Israel, "shall dwell in a peaceable habitation, and in sure dwellings," never be removed again,
"and in quiet resting places."

Again in Ezekiel thirty-fourth chapter, from the
twentieth verse to the end of the chapter, we read:

"Therefore thus saith the Lord God unto them:
Behold I, even I, will judge between the fat cattle
and between the lean cattle. Because ye have thrust
with side and with shoulder, and pushed all the diseased with your horns, till ye have scattered them
abroad; therefore will I save my flock, and they shall
no more be a prey; and I will judge between cattle
and cattle." God is speaking of the nations that have
pushed Israel aside and have persecuted and afflicted
them, until many who are God's "diseased" people have lived more like cattle than human beings, as

122

for example the Jews of Russia and Rumania. One of the saddest stories in history since the dark ages is the persecution of the Jews, who constitute the larger portion of Israel. I am speaking now of the Jews who are distinct among every other people—not the lost ten tribes. You cannot mix the Jews, according to the Word of the Lord. The ten tribes cannot be found, and the two tribes, Judah and Benjamin, cannot be lost, though they are scattered among every nation. That is one of the marvels of prophecy, and is sufficient in itself to make the Bible supernatural. Today Israel is a great credential to the supernaturalness of prophecy, a living witness in the earth.

God says, "I will set up one shepherd over them, and he shall feed them, even My servant David; he shall feed them, and he shall be their shepherd. And I the Lord will be their God, and My servant David a prince among them; I the Lord have spoken." This cannot refer to the restoration from Babylon because David did not then become shepherd over them; there is a day coming when David will again be a prince of Israel, but he will be the resurrected David, just as we shall have a resurrected and glorified Lord and Savior. David will be a *prince*, but Jesus will be the *King*, of whom David was but a type. Remember David as king conquered all the enemies of Israel, and laid tribute on every nation to help supply the means wherewith to build the great temple of Solomon. Solomon who built the temple was not a man of war, but of peace. David will come back in the days of the Millennium and organize Israel again into a great nation of the earth; every people will be subdued under Israel again, and Jesus Christ, the antitype of Solomon, will reign in peace and righteousness, simultaneously over the *celestial* bride, the raptured portion of the church, and over the *terrestrial* bride, Israel, and David shall be prince in the earth. The mouth of the Lord hath spoken it. It is here in this scripture.

"And I will make them a covenant of peace, and will cause the evil beasts to cease out of the land; and they shall dwell safely in the wilderness, and sleep in the woods." That means they will not be afraid. The children will go all over the land, as Isaiah tells us in the latter part of his prophecy, "they shall not hurt nor destroy in all My holy mountain," and again comes that declaration, "for the mouth of the Lord of hosts hath spoken it," and when His mouth speaks a thing it shall come to pass. There will be no ravenous beasts in that day; a little child can play on the hole of an asp and it will never sting, for there is no stinger, the lion and the lamb will be of the same spirit and the bear and the ox shall feed together. There will be no carnivorous animals in the earth in the millennium, and as men and women come into that state now they cease their carnivorous life and appetites largely. We are supposed to be a type in microcosm now, a little world of that which the whole world will be in the millennium. God is out after types now.

"And I will make them and the places round about my hill a blessing." Here is the latter rain connection, it is relative teaching because the latter rain has come and produced this. "I will cause the shower to come down in his season; there shall be showers of blessings," that is, latter rain blessings. That is what it literally means. The land will have its latter rain constantly; never to be interrupted again.

"And the tree of the field shall yield her fruit, and the earth shall yield her increase," a rule under the latter rain, "and they shall be safe in their land, and know that I am the Lord, when I have broken the bands of their yoke, and delivered them out of the hand of those that served themselves of them. And they shall no more be a prey to the heathen, neither shall the beast of the land devour them; but they shall dwell safely, and none shall make them afraid." Literally, they shall sit under their own vine and fig tree, as Isaiah says in another place. You will be just as safe in the wilderness and as safe in the woods in the middle of the night as in your own parlor. That is where God is going to bring this earth. These are tremendous truths. Do you think this earth is always to be trodden down by Satan, "the god of this world?" Do you think it is always to lie in the lap of the wicked one? No. The days are being numbered, and his time is very short. Hallelujah! Look up! your redemption draweth nigh, and following that, the redemption of this whole earth.

"And I will raise up for them a plant of renown, and they shall be no more consumed with hunger in the land, neither bear the shame of the heathen any more. Thus shall they know that I the Lord their God am with them, and that they, even the house of Israel"—that is united Israel—"are My people, saith the Lord God. And ye My flock (that is Judah— the Jews of today) the flock of My pasture, are men, and I am your God, saith the Lord God." It is men, the people of Israel, He is talking about. He is going to gather the men, then form them into a nation and deliver them from the nations of the earth.

Now I have read this in connection with the latter rain references because this Latter Rain Movement is the great sign that these things are speedily to be brought to pass. If you were members of the Zionistic Society instead of Christians, and I told you about this, your hearts would be very glad. Baron de Hirsch when he died left forty-five million dollars in a bank here in Chicago, and put it in the hands of Mr.

Zangwill, the head of the Jewish Territorialist Organization, and Mr. Schiff, one of the great bankers of this country, for the purpose of bringing Israel back to their land. These two have that fund in their hands. Mr. Schiff is now in Europe and they are appointing a committee to go and look over the land of Mesopotamia, which is capable of sustaining ten times the population of the land of Egypt, for it is more fertile than any other land in the world, except Palestine. Palestine has the advantage of receiving the rain from heaven, both early and latter, while Mesopotamia has to be irrigated. Mesopotamia is not a land of the latter rain any more than Egypt, but Palestine is. Palestine is again getting "the days of heaven," and so is this Convention; we have been getting a little of "the days of heaven;" we have sought that, and God has been true to the spiritual aspect of the Latter Rain Covenant just as much as He is to the literal aspect. Glory be to His Name, He has been giving to us a little of the warmth and light, the liberty and love, the joy and peace of "the days of heaven on the earth." You wouldn't know you were in wicked Chicago, for we are breathing the atmosphere of heaven. We are in Beulah land.

And so they are turning their attention to the land. The Ica Society, which is the special inner half of the great Zionistic Movement is the beneficiary of this will of Baron de Hirsch. They have at least five million dollars more from other societies, making fifty million in all. The new prime minister in Turkey has just told the Jewish Rabbi that Israel might return to Mesopotamia and that Turkey would give her a free grant to that land and she could have her own home government. They have accepted this and now all they require is to have the old irrigation opened up. It was irrigated once but has been stopped up. Bagdad, the leading city of Mesopotamia, has now not more than one hundred thousand inhabitants, but the whole land could support fifty million easily. They expect to put in there one hundred thousand agricultural Jews at once; they are going to take all those persecuted Jews from Russia and nearly a half million from Roumania, and put them back in Mesopotamia, and up from that country like Father Abraham they will come into the land of Palestine in due time. Now the Lord said by the mouth of His prophet they would return, but in their own way, not in His way. They are going around in their own way and by and by Mesopotamia will not be able to keep them any longer, and they will go into Palestine. Now while we have been holding this Convention in Chicago, these very things have been transpiring. Those Jews have been working out the literal phase of the Latter Rain Covenant while we in this Convention have been working out the spiritual side, and when the *literal* and the *spiritual* come together, then is brought about a third phase, the *dispensational* aspect. That is why I traced this covenant historically, spiritually and dispensationally. We have literal Israel returning to their land at the same time that the literal latter rain is coming to its normal fall upon that land. This together with the spiritual latter rain falling upon God's spiritual Israel today, betokens in a remarkable way that the closing days of the Dispensation are upon us.

I esteem it one of my greatest privileges as I near the end of thirty years of studying the Gospel and teaching it, that I am here during this twenty-five-day Convention, to enjoy the *spiritual* phase of the latter rain, and see the *literal* aspect of it confirming every thing we do, thus proving the *dispensational* order and fulfilment. We will never forget these days, and after we have gotten home to heaven and walk the golden streets of the New Jerusalem we will talk about them and praise our Lord forever. "Why," you say, "you talk like a man that had some authority." Of course, I have the best authority in the world. I have read to you three times in this passage today, "FOR THE MOUTH OF THE LORD HATH SPOKEN IT." Oh yes, I believe I know the line I am running on, and I have no fear of collisions or side-tracks. I think this line will lead into the Great Union Depot of the Lamb's glory.

IMMINENCY OF CHRIST'S RETURN.

The last division of this great subject is: *The evidence of Christ's near return and the gathering of His people unto Him.* Now we come to two passages that have the very words "latter rain" in them. The first is in Hosea 6:1-3. Here is a passage of scripture that all Bible exegetes and commentators have had a good deal of trouble about. You can go to all the commentaries you can find and read the first three verses of this chapter and you will find very little light on them. I never got any until God baptized me in the Holy Spirit, and I began to go through the Word on the Latter Rain subject, and when I came to this place it was all illuminated by the Holy Spirit. Every scripture must be interpreted by scripture, under the illumination of the Holy Spirit, to get its deeper sense.

"Come, and let us return unto the Lord." Now the Lord is not saying that, but the people—the Zionistic Society, so to speak, are saying, "Come let us return to our land," and the many Jews that are being afflicted and being made spiritual, are saying, "Come, let us return to the Lord," because God is getting a remnant according to election and grace. They are really returning to the Lord, although they

do not know it. "Come," they say, "and let us return unto the Lord, for He hath torn, and He will
heal us;" the Spirit is saying this, telling what will
happen to the people in the time of the latter rain,
and it is happening now; it is a sign of the near-coming
of the Lord. "He hath torn, and He will heal us;
He hath smitten, and He will bind us up." Well, how
will He do it? "After two days will He revive us;
in the third He will raise us up, and we shall live in
His sight."

"Well," they say, "that is prophecy concerning
the death, burial and resurrection of Jesus." That
is what some commentators tell you. It has no reference to that. It doesn't sound like that at all. I
never knew a preacher to use that as a text for a sermon on the resurrection. Of course, resurrection is
expressed in it, but listen: "After two days will He
revive us; in the third day He will raise us up, and
we shall live in His sight. THEN SHALL WE KNOW
IF WE FOLLOW ON TO KNOW THE LORD." Now
resurrected people do not do that, they do not follow
on to know the Lord because they will see Him as He
is. We shall be like Him.

This passage first of all has application to literal
Israel, and then to the spiritual aspect of the Lord's
coming. "Then shall we know if we follow on to
know the Lord." How will we know? What is

this realization, this diffusion of knowledge about the Lord? Why the Lord begins to come forth, to return. "His coming forth is prepared like the morning." How is the morning prepared? By the dark night. In the twenty-first chapter of Isaiah we read, they called to the watchman on Mount Seir and said: "Watchman, what of the night?" And what does he say: "The morning comes," but before the morning, he says, "cometh the night." God prepares for the morning through the night. God is preparing Israel for her morning through this long night, but thank God the night is nearly passed, which is evidenced by the latter rain coming on the land, the people turning back to the land, and the latter rain falling on God's spiritual people. I tell you the night is nearly passed, the day is at hand. The morning star has arisen, and the day star will soon be seen. Jesus will soon come back. Yes, "prepared as the morning and He shall come unto us as the rain, as the latter and former rain unto the earth." He shall come in His *epiphany*, visible, "as the rain;" that is the way He will come to Israel. He will come to spiritual Israel, the Bride, in the *parousia*, secretly, to catch them away. Spiritual Israel won't know much about the dark part of the night, that will come in the time of Jacob's trouble, the seven years, but Christ will come at the end of the seven years in His epiphany, forth-shining according to Revelation 1:7. They will look on Him whom they pierced, they will see Him, they will mourn, they will wail because of Him. They will say as in the ninth verse of the twenty-fifth of Isaiah, "This is the Lord; we have waited for Him, we will be glad and rejoice in His salvation." We will accept Him now. "He shall come unto us as the rain, as the latter and former rain." "After two days will He revive us." After the two captivities God will revive them once for all. Both Judah and Israel had a captivity, one the Babylonian, the other the Assyrian captivity. Then Judah fell into the greater Roman captivity (their second captivity) when their temple was destroyed and their nation disorganized, and they were scattered up and down through the earth, until they are no longer a *nation*, only a *race*, but distinct even as God called them to be. In the Covenant with Abraham He called the "Hebrews" as a *race;* the Davidic Covenant as a *nation*, "Israel;" the Latter Rain or Mosaic Covenant as a *people* and *land*, "Jews." So we may say: "Hebrew" *race*, "Jewish" *people*, and "Israelitish" *nation*.

God's Covenant with Abraham cannot be broken, therefore He has kept them a distinct *race*, though *politically* they are lost; as a nation they forfeited their rights, but politically they are connected with the land. The land lost its blessing because it broke the Latter

Rain Covenant, and because Israel broke the Davidic Covenant she has lost her position *nationally.* God said to Abraham He never would break that Covenant, and it has to hold. That is what makes it the greatest Covenant in the Bible, because in Abraham both the *literal* and *spiritual* seeds were called, and if God allowed the literal to break, the spiritual also would break. We are all the children of Abraham *spiritually* through faith in Jesus Christ. The *literal* seed of Abraham is symbolized by the *sands on the seashore,* an *earthly* type, but the *spiritual* seed is symbolized by a *heavenly* type, the *stars of heaven,* and so type and antitype correspond.

Now God is holding His two brides together just as Abraham held his two, just as Jacob held his two and served for them; one is *terrestrial* and the other is *celestial;* the last comes first and the first last. Israel, the natural branch, is cut off, and we are grafted in spiritually into the olive tree. Since He was able to graft you in where you did not belong naturally, how much more shall the natural branches which were cut off through unbelief, be grafted in, that both the natural and the spiritual olive branches shall be grafted into the old tree, the *Abrahamic Covenant* and thus God will be glorified.

Now we come to the closing passage, the one passage referring to The Latter Rain Covenant in the

ITS DISPENSATIONAL SETTING.

New Testament, James 5:7. The Greek word *opsimos* means, "the rain in the latter day, the *second or latter growth*," and it covers only the second-growth Christians. It will not cover and remain upon people who are simply saved or justified; it will not cover simply the *ekklesia*, the called-out ones, but it is for the *eklektoi*, the second-growth people, the people in whom God has wrought a *second* work of grace. Those who have gone into the crucified life, the sanctified life, the spirit-filled life, into the life of self-renouncement, the life that has laid down the self-life, the life that has lived the sacrificial life; it is for those.

"Do not those who are just saved and merely justified get the baptism?" you ask. Yes, they may, but in a *mixed*, extreme way, and usually if they do not immediately go on into the "crucified" life, it becomes perverted, and they fail. Get the "normal" order the scriptural way, if you want to *stand*. The only *abiding* life is the *crucified*, the *overcoming* life. The priestly life had not only the blood upon it but the oil also, and not only the oil, but also had the "residue" of the oil poured on it. How can anybody conceive that we have none of the Spirit till we are baptized in the Spirit? If you study the type a moment you will see that after the application of the blood in the thirtieth of Exodus the oil followed, three applications of each, corresponding to the work of the Father, the Son and the Holy Spirit, all united. The blood was put on the tip of the right ear, upon the thumb of the right hand, and the great toe of the right foot, following that the priest applied the oil to the same places; then he took the "residue" of the oil and poured it on the head of the sanctified one, as well as cleansed one, and he became in a peculiar sense, a priest unto God. God's anointing oil was placed upon my brow in Pentecost, bringing everything into captivity and obedience to Christ, and oh how smooth within my soul the wheels are turning now. Pentecost does that. It is one thing to have rest in your *spirit* but it is another thing to have the *mind* of Christ, and live in mental obedience to Him, so your mind is not questioning or doubting all the time. God will control your intellect so it will move along quietly in obedience to Him, without any strain at all; that is what Pentecost will do for you. This is *"homo-thumadon,"* the "one-accordness," all minding the same thing. It is not hard to get *hearts* to desire the same thing, but it is awful hard to get *minds* to think and speak the same thing. It is blessed to be saved from the wear and worry of thinking. What a restful life that is! God can so anoint your mind that the machinery of your whole being runs so smoothly that it calls no attention to itself.

ITS DISPENSATIONAL SETTING.

"GO TO YE RICH."

The thirteenth verse of the fourth chapter of James is where the apostle really begins to deal with this subject. People say they are going to have their own will. It were better to say, "If the Lord will, we will do this or that." The first kind of people in the thirteenth verse are the people that are going to have their own will, and the second kind are the ones who are going to have all the world they want. God says to the one, "You don't know what shall be on the morrow, your life is likely to be snuffed out in a moment," and to the other He says, "You rich men, go to now, weep and howl." The rich man is having his own way now, but things are going to change around. God's word says, they can get their own way just now, and heap up riches, but by and by the gold will rust on their hands. They are heaping treasures together for the last days; not *in* the last days, but *for* the last days. Then James mentions a third class and says, "Behold the hire of the laborers who have reaped down your fields which is of you kept back by fraud, crieth," as though this heaped-up treasure were the hire of laborers, and it is, for that is the curse of this generation; the larger portion of wealth today is the accumulation of undivided profits that do not belong where they are heaped. These heaps of gold, these stocks and bonds are making prayers to heaven, because the owners are not praying and the laborers are not praying. We cannot get the poor man into church much easier than the rich man. We are handicapped on either side in the Gospel. The rich man has gone one way and the poor man the other, but the Word of God stands between and cries to each. This heaped-up wealth that is gotten by fraud is praying to the God of justice and of battles, "and the cries of them which have reaped have entered into the ears of the Lord of Sabaoth. Ye have lived in pleasure on the earth, and been wanton; ye have nourished your hearts, as in a day of slaughter;" that is, become fat as swine that are fattened for butchering day. I was going to liken them to calves, but such a comparison would be too good, because some rich people really do live like swine. I do not say that critically or harshly, I say it because it is truth. Many of the places where they live, though gilded, are like the pig-sty, filled with rottenness and corruption of the flesh. The scenes in high life are the worse for they have hedges about them. The poor fellow in the brothel or the saloon cannot help himself, and will tell you right away he is a miserable sinner, but we poor preachers cannot enter the gilded palaces. God said it would be so. It is not the iniquity of the low dives and dens that is crying out so much today as the iniquity of the boulevards; that is what is making the tribulation of the last days. Don't forget it. James, the Lord's brother, is talking about it by the mouth of the Holy Spirit, and he knew.

"BE PATIENT UNTO THE COMING."

Then he says to these poor laborers, the down-trodden people, "Be patient," and calls them "brethren." Be patient, you that are workers, be patient, laborers, it won't help your case to strike. I say it with all soberness of thought; I have followed and studied the effect of strikes. There never was a strike on the earth that paid. History proves it. John Mitchell, the President of the Labor Union, has said it more than once; I heard him say it myself. He said, "Men and brethren, strikes do not pay," but he also said this when they were so desperate during the anthracite coal strike, "but under the circumstances what else can we do?" Well there is something else *we* can do. John Mitchell with his organization doesn't live in the Bible. God has appointed an arbitration committee; it is composed of the Father, Son and Holy Ghost, and they are going to fix things exactly right; and after strikes have come and strikes have gone, and combines and leaders of the great organizations, industrial and capital, have passed away, we are going to live under a new *regime*, we are going to live in another kingdom and another world.

It is the people that reckon with the future that

come out right. Some people say, "Oh I don't care,
I'll just do the best I can now, and the future will
take care of itself." Nobody ever adjusted himself
properly to the conditions of the present except in the
light of the future. If the future, and faith in the
future, do not govern the present, we would have a
poor present and no future at all. And so it is with
God. He tells us that we are to look beyond and set
our affections on things above, and that will glorify
the present and make it right.

"Be patient, therefore, brethren, unto the coming
of the Lord. That is the *parousia*, not the *epiphany*.
Four Greek words are rendered "coming" but they
are different events. This one is *parousia*, which occurs seven years before the *epiphany*. The epiphany is
sometimes rendered the *forth-shining*, every eye shall
see Him; but the *parousia* is a secret coming; nobody
knows it but those who are ready; they hear the voice,
and they hear the blast of the trumpet. They that
hear shall live; so says Paul in the fourth chapter of
first Thessalonians, and also in the fifteenth chapter of
first Corinthians. God says, "Be patient unto that
time." It is coming! It is near! When the latter
rain is on it is very near. Why? Because the latter
rain is to ripen the *spiritual crop*, the Bride, as well
as ripen the fruit of the land, and ripen God's literal
people. "Behold the husbandman waiteth for the

precious fruit of the earth, and hath long patience for it, until He receive the early and the *latter* rain. Be ye also patient;" the word "also" ties our patience together with the patience of the Husbandman. Turn back to the fifteenth chapter of John; this tells you that the "Husbandman" is the Father, and He wants to get all the branches put on this vine, that the great tree of God's purpose, the body of Christ, may be complete. Be patient unto the *parousia* of the Lord, the secret coming of Jesus, the catching away of the branches, living and dead, asleep or awake. Now the Father who is the Husbandman of this is "waiting"—the Pentecostal word. What for? Till the earth receive the early and the latter rain. The early rain started it, and the latter rain shall complete it, just as it does the crop in Palestine, just as it did the Jewish nation, so it is going to complete the body of Christ, and why any student of the Word with any spiritual-mindedness does not observe the signs of the times, is a mystery, but it is due to a lack of spiritual-mindedness; that is the trouble.

"THE PRECIOUS FRUIT."

For what *kind* of fruit is the Husbandman waiting? "The precious fruit," the fruit that ripens *first*. Out of this fruit comes the Bride of the Lamb. Turn back to Malachi 3:16 and you get a hint of it there: "Then they that feared the Lord spake often one to another;" they came together often, ten days won't be enough; they will extend it, and that won't be enough, they will extend it again until the ten days run on to twenty-five. "They spake often one to another," and it was so good that the Lord came down and listened to it; and He has been harkening today here, and that was not enough. He said to the great stenographer of heaven, "Get out your book and put it down; I must have a book of rememberance written about these things for them that fear the Lord, reverence Him, worship Him." Why does He want a record kept about them that fear the Lord and that reverence or esteem His Name?—"thought upon His Name;" the literal translation is, had reverence, or highly esteem His Name, the Name of our coming Lord. Why does He want a record? Because He says, "they are mine;" that kind of people are mine, they are a special enrollment, they are put down in a special book; it is the book that contains the list of invitations of the guests to the Marriage Supper of the Lamb, and we are helping to send out the marriage invitations; we are little messengers sending out the invitations to the Marriage Supper of the Lamb. "And they shall be mine, saith the Lord of hosts, in that day when I make up my jewels," my *special treasures*, my crown of glory in heaven. "I will spare them as a father spares his first-born." He is "waiting for the precious fruit of the earth, and hath long patience for it, until He receive the early and latter rain. Be ye also patient," He says; "stablish your hearts," get your hearts fixed on this thing above everything else, that you may be ready for the *parousia* of the Lord; "for the coming draweth nigh." The latter rain is on. "The *parousia* of the Lord draweth nigh." Twice it occurs here, preceding and succeeding the passage about the Husbandman waiting until the latter rain comes. God is gathering a spiritual people and establishing our hearts. Why? Because as Paul says to Titus, we are *looking* for that blessed hope, the glorious appearing of our God and Savior. Again, Paul says writing to Timothy in the last moments of his life, "I am now ready to be offered, and the time of my departure is at hand. I have fought a good fight, I have finished my course, I have kept the faith: Henceforth there is laid up for me a crown of righteousness, which the Lord the righteous Judge shall give me at that day; and not to me only, but unto all them also that *love His appearing.*" You must not only *look* for it, but you must *love* it. I do love to go home and see my two boys, I love to go home to see my flock, but I love one thing more than anything else; I love the coming of Jesus. I left home with that in view. I haven't a thing that would trouble me if Jesus would come. I keep all

143

things settled. I don't owe anybody anything but love. I have lived for twenty years with respect to the coming of the Lord.

A brother said to me two years ago at Findlay, Ohio, "Brother Myland, are you here? what are you doing? still preaching four-fold Gospel? "Yes, more than that," I said, "I have something more on top of it now. How is it with you?" I saw right away he had backslidden. He said, "Oh when I first heard about the Lord's coming I thought it was a wonderful thing, but the Lord has not come. I thought He was going to come right away." I said, "Got tired?" "Yes, got tired." "Now let us see, how long have you waited? The Lord says in the third chapter of second Peter, 'one day is with the Lord as a thousand years, and a thousand years as one day.' According to that you have waited these thirteen years about nineteen minutes, and you got tired." "The Lord is not slack concerning His promise, as some men count slackness; but is long suffering to usward, not willing that any should perish, but that all should come to repentance." He had been waiting according to the way the Lord is working, nineteen minutes and got tired. Is he worthy of a place in the Kingdom of God? The Lord will come at a time when you think not. "When the Son of man cometh, will He find faith on the earth?" Oh

heart that has been weary, that waited and He did
not come, and thought that it was too long, what is
a few years in the working out of the great dispensation
of God?   Jacob served seven years and missed it,
served seven more to get his wife, and they were as
but a day to him.   Why? Because of the *love* he had
for that dear woman. And do you love your Lord and
cannot wait fourteen years, twenty-one years, fifty, a
life-time?   Oh bless God, I'd be of the same mind
if He tarried and I lived, another hundred years.   My
heart is not tired because the nearer it comes the bigger the pull, like the boy said about his kite.   A man
said, "What is that you are holding on to?"   He
said, "A kite." "I don't see any kite. How do you
know there is a kite up there at the end of the string?"
He said, "I know it is there by the way it pulls."
The kite had gone so high he could not see it, but because it was up high the "pull" was greater than
ever.   I love Jesus and He pulls on my affections.
"He that hath this *hope;*" that is a mighty incentive;
"He that hath this hope in him purifieth himself even
as He is pure," and beloved, "now are we the sons of
God," therefore the world doesn't know us, "and
when He shall appear, we shall be like Him."

As Jesus Himself said in the twenty-fourth of
Matthew, we shall see men's hearts waxing cold, men's
hearts failing them for fear; watch and pray that ye

may be counted worthy to escape all these things that are coming on the earth, and to stand before the Son of Man. "When ye see, He says, "these things beginning to come to pass," the beginnings of sorrows, "lift up your heads, your redemption draweth nigh." Praise God the time is so near.

You see what it all means and why these things are coming to pass in these days, for while men are saying in amazement, "What is this Latter Rain Movement? I do not understand it," we are saying, with the Bible in our hands, with the light of the Holy Spirit shining on it, with the love of Jesus constraining our hearts: "This is that which was spoken by the prophet Joel: And it shall come to pass in the last days, saith God, I will pour out of My Spirit upon all flesh; and your sons and your daughters shall prophesy, and your young men shall see visions, and your old men shall dream dreams. And on My servants and on My handmaidens I will pour out in those days of My Spirit; and they shall prophesy. And I will show wonders in heaven above; and signs in the earth beneath; blood, and fire, and vapour of smoke. The sun shall be turned into darkness, and the moon into blood, before that great and notable day of the Lord come. And it shall come to pass, that whosoever shall call on the name of the Lord shall be saved."

CHAPTER VI.

The Pentecostal Psalm

AM led to the Twenty-ninth Psalm. The Psalm of The Yielded Life and of *The Seven Voices of God*. Have you heard them? the perfect, complete voice of God; the Psalm of the Sovereign God, the seven voices of Jehovah. It is also the Psalm of *giving*.

"Give unto the Lord, O *ye sons of God*." This is the literal rendering. Give unto the Jehovah—that is, unto the Jesus of the Old Testament, the Covenant One—the one in whom the Covenant is vested.

"O ye sons of God, give unto Jehovah *glory* and *power;*" that means Pentecost. Pentecost is not *power* alone; nor glory alone, but Pentecost is the glory of God's power and the power of His glory. These two things are always manifest where there is the true Pentecost, for when the power strikes you, you begin to shout "glory" for fear you will die, and

147

many would die if they could not say it. When you
cannot say it well enough in your *mother* tongue, God
gives you another tongue. Indeed, the ordinary
tongue never could bring the highest glory to God.
So says the Sixteenth Psalm, and Peter in his Pentecostal sermon, quoting from that Psalm, tells us
distinctly that the tongue of man is his highest glory,
and that it brings the highest glory to God. I cannot amplify that, but do not say I do not give you
scripture. Read the Sixteenth Psalm, and read Peter's sermon, and you will see in a short time more
than I can tell you in an hour, if the Spirit is with you.

"Give unto Jehovah, O ye sons of God; give unto
Jehovah *glory* and *strength*."

"Give unto Jehovah the glory *due* unto His name."

How many are in deep debt tonight because you
have not rendered to God the glory due Him? There
is not a soul in this house who has fully paid up that
account.

We used to sing that good old Methodist hymn:

"Oh for a thousand tongues to sing
My great Redeemer's praise,
The glory of my God and King,
The triumphs of His grace,"

but now that God is loosening the tongue and putting a little extra touch of His power into it, the

people are backing out. They do not mean half what they have been singing, nor have we meant a quarter of what we have prayed. Be careful how you pray, for God is in heaven and you are on earth; therefore let your words be few.

"Give unto Jehovah the glory due unto His name; *worship the Lord in the beauty of holiness.*" How many are paid up? We have worshipped the Lord in holiness; thought we made a pretty good start at it, but who has worshipped the Lord in the *beauty* of holiness? No soul that has not known his Pentecost. Is that scriptural? I think so. Experimentally, I never did, and now I have only just made a little start at worshipping Him.

The Pentecostal blessing brings to the soul, among other blessings, *true worship.* God is beginning to get worship in a small degree commensurate with His greatness, and if Pentecost did not bring anything else, it is bringing to God a glorious worship, such as they who worship Him in spirit and in truth and in the beauty of holiness must render. The Latter Rain ends with this worship, for it is expressed in the Latter Rain Covenant, as "the days of heaven on the earth." Deut. 11 : 21.

"Well," you say, "we are to *serve* the Lord." Yes, but we are to *worship* first and then *serve.* "Thou shalt worship the Lord thy God and Him only shalt thou serve." If you want to give a perfect service, learn a perfect worship. We have never learned to worship perfectly, and because the coming of Jesus is so near, and we are soon to be ushered into the great temple of the skies, we must have more knowledge of true worship; we must be in training now. This is an important phase of this Pentecostal Movement, for even if the Bride was perfect, she must have a real spirit of worship before she enters into the marriage feast.

God is asking for three offerings; He is not satisfied with one. He had five in the old types, but they are really summed up in three. Three times in this Pentecostal Psalm He says give. "Give!" "Yes, Lord, I have given." "Give!" Yes, Lord, I will give again." "Give!" "Yes, Lord, take everything!" Hallelujah! That is Pentecost. Why *three* times? Because man is a three-fold being— spirit, soul and body.

"Give me thy *spirit!*" "Yes, Lord," and many stop there and live along in a half-dying way. They give one-third of their being, and less than one-third of their service. Again He comes: "Give unto the Lord thy *soul!*" "Yes, Lord." He will sanctify it. Sanctification has to do largely with the *soul;* regeneration with the *spirit.* What is He going to sanctify? The soul. That is where you find the "old man."

THE PENTECOSTAL PSALM.

Sanctification is the negative. Regeneration is the positive—it's getting the life of God into the spirit. Sanctification is a big negative to start with—the crucifixion of the "old man," but it is also a positive, the infilling of the Spirit, the enthroning of Christ in the soul. People generally want to begin with the positive side, but the death of the "old man" comes first. He must be put out of the way of the new man. (Romans 7.)

Everybody wants the positive side of Pentecost first also, but God takes "the things that are not." He has to reduce you to the "not" condition first; to the *nothing* state. Nine out of every ten questions asked me about Pentecost are about the positive side. "How can I get it?" It is what you are *not* to be, and only God can understand that; only God can empty this mortal and reduce it to nothing. *Let go and let God*. Resist Satan and all that hinders; surrender, rest in God and wait and Pentecost will come.

Again Jehovah says, "Give!" Anything left? What? Oh, the big "*no thing*"; your body, give that, a living sacrifice, holy and acceptable. "Lord, that is unreasonable!" No, the very opposite; it is "your reasonable service." It is your intelligent service. God anticipated what you would say. He knew it centuries before you were born. He knew you would say "unreasonable"; He knew you would say,

"The body is physical, belongs to the earth, and we must have a dual life; the body must have this, that and the other. I worship the Lord in my spirit occasionally." Such talk is prevalent even in the churches today; the elders and deacons will argue on the street corner, "the body must have so and so," but friends, the Lord is over the body, too. "He is also the Savior of the body." That is the way my New Testament reads, according to Ephesians and Corinthians.

Give your spirit, give your soul, give your body, that the Lord may get the glory due unto His name, and that you may be brought to worship the Lord in the beauty of holiness. Can you do that with one-third or two-thirds of your being? No, sir! You must give your whole being in worship. No wonder God shakes the whole thing down and builds a new temple for Himself.

Well, what then? Then we shall hear *The Seven Voices of God*. It is *His* temple now, is'nt it? *He* has the right to the sanctuary. We shall hear His voice. Shall we? Why, of course we shall. Now I guess we have actually been reduced, for when God is in the spirit and soul and body, every passion, appetite and propensity is subdued.

See what that marvelous word means in the Greek that is rendered "one accord' in Acts 2 : 1. It is *homo-thumadon*, which means to bring into *oneness*

152

every passion of soul, and that *one holy* affection or
desire shall dominate where the seat of anger is—the
"strong room" of the soul.   That is what it means,
because the place where anger dwells is the place from
which perfect love emanates, either in God or in His
creature.   If I had time to trace that word I would
show you, and there is nothing that will cast out ten-
dencies to anger or fear but "*perfect love*," which is
always divine love.   When we say perfect love, we
mean divine love, and when it is in the dominant
place in the soul, then it is located where it subdues
all the evil passions and propensities of the soul.   It
means the soul has been brought under one desire,
one purpose, one all-controlling passion—*the love of
God*.   That means the love of souls and the love of
the Christ that we read of in the third chapter of
Ephesians.

Now you will never get victory over some of these
subtle passions and weaknesses in your life until you
get that tap-root—evil—out of your soul, and then
everything will tend toward your perfection.   To a
dear soul in whose face I looked today, talking on
this line, I said, "After God has given you the Pentecostal preparation, the Pentecostal touch, you will
forget you had such passions," and that is the truth
of God in experience.

A man told me today that the day he talked to

the boys in the Sunday School about bad habits, he tried to get all around the tobacco habit and not touch on that subject, for he had two twenty-five cent cigars in his pocket at the time. His wife was sitting there in front of him. He turned and looked at her, and finally he had to come out with it, and said, "I will have to tell you now, boys, that you must follow my precept and not my example." But the next Sunday he came back and said, "Boys, there are no cigars in my pocket, and I can open my coat now. I put them back into the box. My wife suggested I destroy them; I said 'No. I have tried to quit the thing before. I am going to leave those cigars in that box for six months, and I am going to walk in and out and eat three meals a day (he had smoked as high as twenty-five cigars a day), because,' I said, 'I have had a healing; God has touched that spot and I do not feel as though I ever smoked a cigar.' "

Now when God Himself touches a thing it is at an end. It is like the fig tree, "withered from the root." When there is any failure, God has not yet fully touched that spot, that is all. You have not come in actual contact with God for it. God has not done His complete work. That is Pentecostal work; it is God's dynamite. Dynamite is not only an *explosive*, but also an *expulsive*. When it goes off,

nothing remains.   This is the way with the perfect
Pentecostal work of the Holy Ghost; there is nothing left but Pentecost.   The thing that hindered is
not there, for God has struck it.

Now you can "worship the Lord in the beauty
of holiness."   Give thy spirit, thy soul and thy body.
Give! Give! Give!   You attend to that side of the
question.   Give some attention to what God is talking about.   Yield! Yield! Yield!   When we come
to the Sixth of Romans the proposition is, How shall
we quit sinning?   All our sins have been forgiven
and shall we sin more because it says where sin
abounded grace did much more abound?   No, sir.
God proposes to put us in a "state," sometime, somewhere, of full deliverance; the *effect* and *outcome* of
our standing in Christ; hence Paul says, "God forbid! How shall we who want to identify ourselves
with Christ, and die to sin, live any longer in sin?"
How are you going to help it?   Well, that word
"*yield*" follows a Christian all his life.   Yield your
spirit, soul and body.   Give! Give! Give! and keep
giving!   Or say it in another way, if you please:
"Take! Take me! Take all there is of me! Take
me! Shake me! Break me! Make me! Only get
me, O Lord Jesus, for Thyself!' If you do not do
this the devil, and sin, or self, will get you.   There
are any amount of bidders for you; there are any

amount of solicitors at the door of your heart, knock-
ing every day. "Who is there?" "Whom do you
want?" "Jesus lives here." That is what Billy
Bray would say, "Jesus lives here; do you want to
see Him?" Yes, Jesus is enthroned now. He
keeps the heart that is yielded and obedient. He
garrisons the heart that trusts Him.

After we have yielded our lives to him we then
need to hear the voice of God; that is the most important thing for you and me, in these days of so
much speaking and so many voices. Paul says in
I. Cor. 14:10: "There are many kinds of voices in
the world, and none of them is without signification." But above and beyond them all, we need to
hear the VOICE OF GOD. The Lord speaks SEVEN
distinct times in this Psalm and we need to hear all
of these voices—hear what the Lord says; for "He
will speak peace to His people, but let them not turn
again to folly."

FIRST VOICE.

"The voice of the LORD is upon the WATERS."
That means upon the *people*—water stands for people here, as in the book of the Revelation, and other
places in the Scriptures; and was there any time in
all the history of the world when the voice of God
was upon the people as now. And His voice is becoming strong and clear; clear enough for all. "The

voice of God is upon the waters." Another thing: water stands for the *troubles* of the people. Brother, sister, are you here tonight saying, "Where did I hear for the first time the voice of God?" Listen! When did the *world* first hear the voice of God? In trouble: "And the earth was without form and void —chaos, and the Spirit of the Lord—the Mother-God—fluttered over the face of the *waters*, and the voice of God said, "Let there be light, and there *was* light." You hear it tonight; the voice of God is over the waters; waters of people; waters of sorrow; waters of your troubles. Yes, tonight, down there wherever you are, the voice of God is over that trouble of yours to set it right—to shed light and life into it. The voice of God is there; do not run around peddling your troubles everywhere, to everybody— take them to God; get His voice, His word, on it.

Better sit down in the midst of your grief, like poor old Hagar out in the wilderness; she cried herself to sleep, and by and by the voice of God woke her up, and a great light flooded her soul, she saw a well of water, and her boy's life was saved. God had revealed Himself to her—the voice of the Lord had visited her. Brother, sister, do not take a trouble out of this room tonight that has not been spoken to by the voice of God.

And when the voice of God is upon the waters,

what happens? "The God of glory thundereth." Who thundereth? The God of GLORY. Give Him yourselves, people, and God will get His glory out of your lives; give God your troubles and He will get His highest glory out of your deepest troubles, and turn them into joys—Hallelujah! Oh man, woman, you remember those awful troubles and trials you have had; those losses and crosses; those financial distresses. They are all gone now; God's voice spoke, the God of glory thundered and shook them all away, and instead of the trouble, His glory came on you, and now you bless God, for the "curse was turned into a blessing." And "the Lord is upon MANY waters." You see there is no end to what He will do, if you will but listen to His voice and trust Him. You say, "I have *many* troubles." Well, He says, "upon *many* waters." And again, "I will be with you in six troubles," and what will He do in the seventh, that is, the fulness of troubles? "Not forsake you." He reverses the order, you see, and stays with us. Oh praise Him, what a good God He is! A sister said, "Surely He is past finding out.' I said, "Yes, you will always find Him IN, ready to help you in time of need"—Hallelujah!

THE PENTECOSTAL PSALM.

SECOND VOICE.

"The voice of the Lord is POWERFUL." Shall we hear God speak again? (People: "Yes, yes!") You are not like the children of Israel, when they complained to Aaron about Moses. They said, "Do not let that man speak any more to us, we cannot stand it."

The first voice spoke to the *people*, and to the *troubled* hearts. Well, we will hear the *second* voice of God. "The voice of the Lord is full of *dynamite*." That is what the word "powerful" means. Now you see, you are liable to get hurt; for dynamite is explosive. Yes, we must be careful, for the voice of the Lord is powerful—dynamical; and the "hidings of His power" (Hab. 3 : 4) are beginning to be manifested in these days of "Pentcostal" operations.

THIRD VOICE.

"The voice of the Lord is full of MAJESTY." These two seem to be linked together in their effects. So, it seems the voice of power (dynamite) is the voice of a King (majesty). We see by this that He is building the things concerning a Kingdom, and so the voice is full of *majesty;* it is kingly. There is a potentiality back of Him. He is preparing a Kingdom. He is organizing a new set of subjects for the new Kingdom; you cannot have a Kingdom without subjects.   God begins in the right way; most men do not.   God gets His subjects first, and He is going to get a handful of subjects as a "first fruits" to set up a Kingdom that cannot be moved.

"The voice of the Lord is powerful; the voice of the Lord is full of majesty."   That is His working power, and His majesty is Christ enthroned in the heart as our King, making us His willing and obedient subjects.   Have we heard the voice of God as our King?

FOURTH VOICE.

"The voice of the Lord breaketh the cedars," and down they go; the people go down.   What did it?   Why, Pentecost has come, and it has broken down all their strong religiousness and self-will; a good deal of their strong theology, and a good deal of their strong, "powerful" works.   When the voice of the Lord breaks the cedars, many of the churches will be turning their *kitchens* into rooms for Pentecostal waiting meetings.   They call their kitchens "power houses," so one pastor told me, and I said, "I thought power came from above."   This is the power that comes from beneath; from the outer man, the self-life, the man who gives to the church, to have the worth of it in oysters or ice cream.   Oh, we are a million miles from Pentecost in that kind of thing. There is one place you can go and get the *spiritual*

160

sandwiches; First Corinthians, twelfth, thirteenth and fourteenth chapters; *power* on one side, *wisdom* on the other and *love* in the middle. Those are "Pentecostal" sandwiches; you can get those and improve in worship and service. I think the Lord will be pleased with that, and the people will say, "See how those people love one another." Oh, yes, the world is not blind to love, and it is the cure for "hardness of heart and unbelief." Yes, I thank God that He breaketh the cedars of Lebanon, the big cedars of the high mountains; these you know stand for the great people, who are so self-sufficient and high up.

But you say, "Mr. Myland, some think this scripture describes the scene of God's operations in nature, and that it is the effects of a great storm breaking down over the mountains of Lebanon, cutting its way through the forest in cyclonic fury." Just so; so I think. I suppose the Lord let the prophet see just such a sight; but what for? Just to see the power and majesty of God in outward nature? Nay; more than that. The Bible need not have given us the history of the storm described in this Psalm simply from a *natural* standpoint; we can see the real thing here in the United States every year. God was illustrating SPIRITUAL things by the symbols of nature, as is so frequent in the teaching of scripture. This Psalm is grandly symbolic of nature being subordinated to the presence and power of God, and manifests the effect of His omnipotent voice as He works on and in His creature man, to subdue and purify, and bring him back to His glory. So what you see God doing here in the natural world, is but a symbol of what He will do morally and spiritually in man. This story, therefore, illustrates God's spiritual and moral working in man; or it has no business in the Bible.

He breaks the cedars of Lebanon. I have seen Him break many big ones, that had many branches. There is one thing remarkable about this symbol, because in cedar trees all the branches grow downward and the roots spread out in shallow ground—just like the natural man; and so the symbol is true to the truth to be taught. Now God wants just the reverse of this; He wants our roots to go down deep in love; "rooted and grounded in love"; and He wants the branches to grow out laterally and upward. The branches that grow upward develop the tree; those that grow out laterally bear the fruit. That is a law of horticulture, and so it is in the spiritual kingdom. So the law of the moral "cedar tree" is that it must be thrown down, and when it is down, if you want to trim the branches, you must begin at the *top*, for the branches grow down; that is the way God does in the "Pentecostal" work; He begins to trim you at the head, and He "casts down imaginations, and the high things which exalt themselves against the knowledge of God, and brings every thought into captivity to the obedience of Christ ."—II. Cor. 10 : 5. And thus He "trims the big cedars" which He has thrown down.

I never knew the full meaning of Calvary until I had an earnest of Pentecost seventeen years ago. After "waiting on God" for three nights, down on my face, I began to feel that I was "trimmed" indeed, and there seemed to be nothing left but the bare "trunk" of my "humanity." I said then, "this is Golgotha," literally the place of the skull—that is crucifixion of the head. Have you been crucified at the place of a "*skull*"? There is something in that when one applies it to his own experience, and proves II. Cor. 10:5. When you get to that point, you are going faster than an express train on toward Pentecostal Mount. Yes, the cedars of Lebanon must be broken.

FIFTH VOICE.

"The voice of the Lord divideth the tongues of fire." Why does that come after the cedars are broken? Is that Pentecostal order? Yes, indeed; that is exactly Pentecostal, and you could not make the Bible read any other way. "Divideth the flames of FIRE"; and they saw flames of fire divided and sitting on each of them, at Pentecost. I have seen them on people's heads and on the ends of the fingers. I have seen them on my own hands; couldn't see them on my own head. Well, who sees them? *Those who have spiritual eyes.* Who saw them in the upper room? The one hundred and twenty. Those on the outside did not see this, nor hear the noise of the wind, only the noise of the "tongues" afterwards; *the effect of Pentecost.*

If you have no internal evidence of an experience with God in His saving and working grace, you have no business with the Pentecost. "The gifts and callings of God are apart from repentance." They are sovereign. There is no choice about it. He may bestow a gift on one that you least thought of, and may keep it back from one you thought would get it first; you cannot tell about these things, and one ought not to be jealous of another nor boast against another, or he may lose its operation before he has it long.

Yes, He divideth the flames and gifts of Pentecost as it pleaseth Him, and He worketh all in the one and selfsame Spirit, and when you do not let Him work, the *spiritual* gift will not operate; Satan may give you psychical "working" that looks like it, but it will never bear fruit for God, and one who has the "discerning of spirit" can detect both its operation and its fruitlessness.

THE PENTECOSTAL PSALM.

Let us here differentiate between man's triple being—spirit, soul and body. *Pneuma* means the spirit,
Psyche means the soul. A human being is a pneumatical, psychical and physical creature. You say,
"Why do you use strange terms?" No stranger than
"physical," that is also a Greek word, but we have
become accustomed to that; it means body, the others mean spirit and soul.

The spirit is the highest part of man's nature,
that part that was "depraved" in the "fall," it is the
seat of the moral sensibilities—the conscience and
affections. Spiritual things are always regarded as
equivalent to "holy things," consequently there is no
such thing as *spiritualism;* it is *"spiritism."* Spiritual, in the Bible, means holy; you say a church is not
a spiritual church; you mean not godly, not holy;
such a man is not spiritual; not godly, not holy—
that is, he is worldly. Therefore Satan cannot do
anything spiritual; it would be death to him. He
was cast out of the spiritual realm once, and has
no business back in it, but he can deceive you in the
psychical (soul), and he is building more "psychical"
characters (Christians, so-called) today, than God
is getting of true "pneumatical" (spiritual) Christians.

What is it that keeps our preachers replenishing
their libraries? What keeps our printing presses

running almost day and night? Psychical literature; and the deep spiritual books and papers go begging, save for the few Pentecostal people who want something of that kind. Listen! We need to have new Pentecostal literature as well as preaching and testimony, and God is making it.

Now, while we have Pentecostal fire, and power, and gifts in the psychical—for that is where it operates—in all their fulness; do not let us forget the "balance wheel" of love, and the "governor" of a sound mind. We may go on, proving that God can do the supernatural all the time, and that is all right; but let us keep within reasonable bounds, and thus be saved from the presumptuous sins. Let us remember that the "spirit of a sound mind" or, as the better rendering is, "wise discretion" is third and last in the order of Pentecostal operations. See II. Tim. 1 : 7. And while you may have the *"power" in the gifts of the twelfth chapter of I. Corinthians, you need also to have the "love" of the thirteenth that will enable you to "bear all things"; and then, above all, the "wisdom" of the fourteenth chapter, in order rightly to use and understand the operation of "tongues"*; and as "wisdom is the principal thing, therefore with all thy getting, get understanding."— Prov. 4 : 7. There is danger of becoming too free because we have the spirit of power, and so run away with ourselves and give up to everything; but the spirit of a sound mind must control everything. Let us be *free*, but let us be also *real*, and wise as serpents (wise as the old serpent), and show to the world that God has not only given us the "*fulness*," the exuberance, but He has given us also the *soundest, best thing,* that must take hold of and subdue the best and brightest intellects of these days, and give God some adequate instruments through which to do His work.

One soul is worth just as much as another, as far as the redeeming blood and salvation is concerned, but one instrument or worker is not as efficient as another in the hands of God, and He wants the best He can get. There is no comparison as to the question of salvation, but there is comparison when you come to the question of whom God sets in His church as laborers. Your father or my father would never take a piece of basswood to make an axe handle; he would select a piece of good, well-seasoned hickory, and God is as wise, and is selecting the "*second-blessing*" *people for his instruments; a well defined sanctified life is one whose grain runs all the one way. God can make something out of that kind of a character.* God is looking for "second growth" timber Christians out of which to make His Pentecostal church—the church of the Advent.

I would not give much for a baptism of power on

a life that knew nothing of the sanctifying grace of God and the crucifixion of self. Suppose you get it all in one meeting. I admit you may have the work of the Holy Spirit "with," and "in," and "upon" in one night, but you cannot live a whole experience in an hour; the heavenly side, by faith, can be accomplished "instanter," but the practical experience and administration will take you years and years to prove; and some of you are not through proving it yet.

"God breaketh the cedars" and "divideth the flames of fire." Yes, God has the right tree for His symbol; God makes no mistake, for when the *cedar starts to burn you have a hard time putting it out.* I have seen people trying to get the thing stopped some way, and they got on fire themselves; nobody that has ever been through the "burning" ever touches them when the fire falls; they know enough to keep their hands off. I saw a dear brother get his Pentecost while he was trying to extinguish the fire on a young cedar—his wife. He fussed around there awhile, and by and by he "caught fire" and got his "baptism." I said to him "served you right!" Oh, it was fine to see a man and wife getting baptized into the Holy Spirit and fire together. Oh, praise God! If only men and women would get their Pentecost together, and then the boys and girls, until God gets whole families! Brother, be patient with your wife; wife, be patient with your husband. Keep sweet; God will do His work. Wait in patience; "thou shalt be saved and thy house."

God's fire will burn up the cedars. He sends the fire to burn up all that is combustible of the "flesh," and leaves nothing but the pure asbestos, which is just a basis (material) for fire to work on and warm others. It cannot be destroyed even by fire; and so God makes his people "asbestos"—fireproof material. God gives us a new outfit for the old one He destroyed. He did not promise to insure the old and give you "damages" if it was injured; no, He is not in the insurance business, insuring the "flesh," the "carnal mind, which is enmity against Him," but He *is* in the fire *baptizing* business, destroying the "flesh." *The blood cannot take out the "self-life." The blood was to be the answer for the "sin question"; it will cleanse from all sin; that is sanctification. But the destruction of the "self-life" is preparatory to the "sacrificial-life," where God has to "burn out the dross," hence an "offering of fire"—a burnt offering.* That is no type of the blood at all; it is *"an offering made by* FIRE," "a whole offering, where God gets the whole thing and you see a little "ash-heap," and for that he gives you beauty (glory). He makes out of the "ashes" the "asbestos," which glows in the fire—asbestos looks like ashes, does it not? "God

169

divides the flames of fire;" He burns up the combustible, but there is something left yet. What is that?

"The voice of the Lord shaketh the wilderness of Kadesh." While He is breaking the cedars and burning them up by dividing the flames of fire, He is also "shaking the wilderness of Kadesh." What wilderness is that? The wilderness of "holiness." You will have to surrender to Him all your holiness. If I ever saw people die hard, it was those who tried to hold on to their experience of holiness. They say, "I had the blessing of holiness, I lost it; I regained it, I lost it again." Well, God wants you to get out of that wilderness some time, and so He shakes the wilderness of your holiness—that is, your *experience of* holiness. Nearly everybody knows that Kadesh means holiness. God wanted to take Israel into the promised land at Kadesh, but they refused through unbelief. Pentecost is after you get into the land; beyond Gilgal, and Jericho, and Ai and Gideon; it's away up at old Hebron, *which means full friendship with God;* and at Timnath-serah, which means the eternal light of His glory. Yes, God will shake the wilderness of Kadesh (holiness) ; He will shake all the "blessings" out of you, till you seem to lose everything you had, even your dearest experience. After God has fully "subdued all things to Himself"

He will give you the "new things" and everything that "could not be shaken" He will give back, intensified and beautified a hundred-fold. It will remain then, and work for Him and bear fruit to His glory. Have you had the wilderness of your holiness shaken out? That *may* be the reason why many have not received their Pentecost, because they are trusting in a stale holiness.

SEVENTH VOICE.

Here is the *last* voice: "The voice of the Lord maketh the hinds to calve." Yes, when He gets His way He brings forth NEW things. I cannot speak of this in a mixed audience as plainly as I should! I want to be as full of grace and propriety as possible; but God speaks in His Word about things coming "out of the womb of the morning in the beauty of holiness"—Psa. 110 : 3. Here is something born out of the womb of Pentecost. "He maketh the hinds to calve"—the *hinds*. Those animals that are sure-footed, speedy and untiring, and can go over rough, steep places. See how those hinds get over the hills and the mountains? And so God's great Pentecostal work in your soul will make you like the hinds. Here is a hill of difficulty, there is a mountain of obstacle; you go right on over them all. Oh, God will bring the spiritual hinds out of this Pentecost, and they will skip as those did on old Her-mon. They will run over mountain and plain, to the ends of the earth, taking the last Pentecostal witness of the Gospel to the nations, and preparing the people for the coming of the Lord.

And now, what follows? Why, when you have heard the last voice of God speak, and you have the whole seven-fold, perfect, complete voice and work of God wrought out in all your being—then "everything in HIS Temple saith GLORY!" Is that Pentecost? Well, I think so. You can say scarcely anything else when God brings you through. He knows how to get glory to His name. "And in His temple everything saith, Glory." You find that *phrase nowhere else in the Bible—in no other Psalm;* and it is just in the right place in this Psalm. When God gets through speaking and His work in you is accomplished, then His glory is manifested. It was so in the temple of old; when everything had been *offered* and all obedience was complete, then the glory of God filled the house so that the priests could minister no more, it was *glory, glory, glory!*

Well, what further? The first voice of God began to deal with the "water" (people), then with "*many waters*" (much trouble); now here is a different thing. "The Lord sitteth on the FLOODS." God is the best one to keep the "lid" on your life and mine. After Pentecost, the Lord sits down and

presides over your life; the administration is God's
now, and "the government is (at last) on His shoulders"; mine are rested now, and because of the love
of it, and the ease of it all, I could serve Him forever. O blessed be His Name for that day and
hour when He, the Pentecostal God "sat upon the
floods." My friends, what an overflow there would
be if God did not sit on the flood of our thoughts,
and keep them subdued. Oh, the awful imaginations
that pass through the minds of the people who have
not yet been subdued and chained by Pentecostal
power. Oh, the confessions that have come to me
this summer from people who professed holiness; such
confessions I never thought I could hear from sanctified people—so mighty, so subtle, so deceivable are
the operations of Satan in the psychical nature—the
soul of man.

God sitting on the flood of your thoughts, on the
lid of your imagination and reason, holds it in subjection to the "obedience of Christ." That is what
God wants. Oh, beloved, this is the most marvelous
work of the salvation of Jesus yet wrought; the "renewing of your MIND," getting the "MIND OF
CHRIST." This is the great consummation of the
sanctified life, that sets people free for the exercise
of the "gifts" and to do business for God unhindered,
and unmingled with evil. Well, some people are

saying these days, "How will folks stand this; they will surely go too far, they will go all to pieces; this is on the line of fanaticism, this must be the work of the devil."

Listen! Forever and ever will I praise God for the vast scope and completeness of this Psalm; for the "Te Deum" that is put in here at the close as a farewell assurance, like the fourteenth of John. We turn to a verse in the fourteenth of first Corinthians, about which we are having so much trouble as to "tongues," and we find what the Lord said through Paul in the thirty-third verse: "For God is not of confusion, but of PEACE, as in all churches of the saints." If ultimate, abiding peace is not the product of Pentecostal reception, experience and operation, there is something wrong with the kind of Pentecost; some spurious things somewhere, be assured of that. And so the last word of this blessed "Pentecostal" Psalm is: "The Lord will give strength (*power*) to His people," but also, "the Lord will bless His people with PEACE." Thus, in all your Pentecostal experiences and manifestations—"The PEACE of God shall rule in your heart" and "the PEACE of God that passeth all understanding shall keep your hearts and minds through Christ Jesus." Amen!—Col. 3:15; Phil. 4:7.

CHAPTER VII.

"In Deaths Oft"

HE song that came into my heart after my first healing at the hands of the Lord, has been a kind of holy chant in my soul ever since and has been the keynote of my ministry these twenty years and more:

Walking with Jesus alone,
Held by the arms of his love,
Shielded from sin and the world,
Walking with Jesus alone.

Learning each day in the strife,
Dying to self and to sin,
Rising in newness of life,
Jesus abiding within.

Striving for riches untold,
Seeking for souls gone astray,
Leading them back to the fold,
This is my work day by day.

You will find the text of my story in II. Cor. 11:23, the last three words, "In deaths oft." How

I came out of these deaths you will find in the twentieth verse of the one hundred and seventh Psalm, "He sent His word and healed them, and delivered them from their destruction."

A man who had been "in deaths oft" you would hardly expect to be living, but he is living because of that scripture I just quoted. Another foundation fact in these experiences of healing is found in Romans 8:11, "But if the Spirit of Him that raised up Jesus from the dead dwell in you, He that raised up Christ from the dead shall also quicken (or add life to) your mortal bodies by His Spirit that dwelleth in you." In a sense, two persons were raised from the dead; Jesus the human, and Christ the divine, and because Jesus was the Christ and now lives on the throne as our human brother, we may have His resurrection life in our mortal bodies, healing and preserving them.

Seven times have I realized what it is to have the quickening, resurrection life of Jesus bring me back from death. It is these seven events and experiences I desire to relate to you tonight, for the honor and glory of God.

I. HEALED OF PARALYSIS.

Twenty-one years ago I was stricken down and became a poor, dumb paralytic. I had a serious accident two years before that time. My brother and I were engaged in business together; our store burned,

and while it was burning I tried to save some books
and papers by entering through an upper window. It
was in December, and the water the firemen were
throwing on the building was freezing. I slipped and
fell, striking my back on the edge of a six-foot board
fence that ran out along the side of the store. I
fractured my spine and broke the three small ribs
loose from the spine. I lay six months, helpless most
of the time, but the Lord was merciful to me. I was
then a local minister in the Methodist church, and was
studying to enter conference, for the Lord had called
me to preach His Gospel. My mother on her dying
bed had put her hands on my head and dedicated me
to the ministry. I didn't want to preach, and tried to
continue in business, and God had to let this happen
that I might become willing to quit making money and
seek to save souls for Him. God will have His way
with you, brother, sister, and you had better let Him
have it quickly. It will cost you more the longer you
put it off, and besides, you will get less blessing and
God less glory by your not yielding at once.

The effects of that injury, in the opinion of various
eminent physicians, resulted in paralysis. The paralysis, however, was superinduced by two years of zealous
and strenuous work in the ministry, which, I am sorry
to say, was not always according to knowledge. Then,
too, at that time I did not know the rest that comes

through faith for I had not been crucified with Christ fully. I was like a great many people who come and go in this Convention, I had not passed from the death of the self-life, the carnal mind, and my life was not hid with Christ in God. That old physical weakness in my spine began to manifest itself in neuralgia of the heart, and toward the latter part of the second year of my ministry I fell to the floor several times while preaching; my officers would carry me out, put me in my buggy and take me home.

That condition continued until one day, twenty-one years ago, I was traveling on the Big Four train out of Cleveland, destined for Wellington, Ohio, and was reading Dr. Talmage's Sunday sermon in the Monday morning paper, when I found my body getting very heavy. I managed to get out on the rear platform, but could scarcely get back. The train-guard told me I could not ride there, and when I tried to tell him I could not get back I found I was unable to speak. I became paralyzed on that Big Four train, the paralysis covering the entire left side, and the whole of the right side of my head—paralysis of the cerebro-spinal nerves, which manifested itself on the right side. My tongue was drawn into my right cheek. I had a little scratch-pad in my pocket, and wrote what had befallen me, that I was getting worse and wanted to get across to Elyria and to Amherst, where my wife and little boy were. My wife at that time was recovering from a terrible tumor and had been attended for three weeks by three physicians.

With the help of the train officers and others I was carried into a depot, changed trains and taken over to Elyria. A dear old friend of mine had come to the depot to meet a party who did not come, and instead he took care of me. He got a special rig at the livery stable, drove me eight miles to the old home at Amherst, and there I lay, attended by three physicians, one the best physician in the town, another a specialist from Chicago and the third a celebrated doctor from Cleveland of world-wide fame. They treated me for weeks and at last came to the conclusion that I must die.

One night, lying helpless in my bed, thinking it over as best I could, my soul went out to God, and I said, "Lord, is this the best you have for people on this earth?" And the answer came back, "Why, no, I am a wonder-working God."

Here I must step aside for a moment to say that for a year I had been following this new development of divine healing, and I had been speaking in pretty strong terms against it as one of the fanaticisms of the last days. Among the last sermons I preached at the appointment I was filling was one in defense of old, orthodox Methodism, wherein I warned my peo-

ple not to go to a certain convention that was to stand
for this teaching, and I mentioned especially the leader
who was to preside at that convention, dear old Major
Brown.   That beloved brother is still living, and for
a number of years after that I was associated with him
in the Lord's work even more closely than I have
been with any other man.

After denouncing that movement I went home to
be sick two or three days, and it served me right. But
as I lay there that night I said, "Lord, is this the best
you have?"   I was thinking of what would become
of my dear wife and little two-year-old boy, and of
the ministry that lay ahead of me, for I was then just
thirty.   God answered, "Why, no, it is not the best.
I am a wonder-working God."   I did not know what
to say then, but seemed to listen in the depths of my
soul.   Then I said, "Lord, if you have something for
me, for Jesus' sake reveal it to me right here.   They
have said I must die tomorrow and I have only about
a day to live."   Then the Lord took me over this
matter I have just related, and I saw the whole thing.
I saw the outline of that sermon I had preached
against divine healing, and I said, "God, if I ever
get up from this bed I will hunt it up and burn it."   I
saw Major Brown; his face came up before me, and
I said, "Lord, if I ever see that man I will confess
and ask him to forgive me."   I began to feel better.

Then I thought of those people I considered fanatical, the Christian Alliance people, and I said, "Lord, if I ever get into one of their meetings I will confess and tell them I am sorry," and I felt still better.

Now, if there is anybody here who has anything to do in that line, do it, beloved, but don't confess to the minister; go to the party you have wronged. It is utter nonsense to have children's meetings, young men's and young women's meetings for the purpose of confessing to some leader. Go and confess where it belongs. If it has touched anybody's life and ruined it, go to that life and confess it. If it is a thing that has not touched any other life, go to God with it. There has been a lot of harm done both in the heathen world and in the Christian world by multiplying these confessions. I have had to stop people and say, "Now we will pray God to give you grace to take that where it belongs." Confess, first to God, and then to the one you have wronged. Satan has come in at this point and wrought a great deal of havoc even in this precious Pentecostal Movement, because people have not obeyed the Word of God. We are not expected to set up a Pentecostal confessional; that would not be much better than a Roman Catholic confessional.

In every one of these seven healings *I went through to victory on some portion of God's Word.* This

181

time it was II. Kings 20:5, where Hezekiah was lying sick and Isaiah came to him to pray, and "the word of the Lord came to him, saying, Turn again and tell Hezekiah, the captain of My people, "Thus saith the Lord, the God of David thy father." I could hear the Lord speaking my name, "David;" that is my first name, my mother gave it to me—"I have heard thy prayer, I have seen thy tears; behold, I will heal thee: on the third day thou shalt go up into the house of the Lord." Now I didn't know where that is in the Bible. I knew God was speaking from the Bible, but I didn't know where. I had read it, undoubtedly, but I hadn't much scripture in my heart. "Well," I thought, "this is Thursday night; Friday, Saturday, Sunday; Sunday will be the third day. Lord, you are going to have me healed, and I will go up into the Methodist church Sunday morning and tell the whole thing." That is the way it looked, and maybe God would have done it that way, but there were many hindrances. I could use my right hand, and I wrote, "I am going to be healed."

Then they held another consultation of physicians. I could not hear all they said, I was blind in one eye and deaf in one ear, but they were saying that the paralysis had seriously affected my brain and I was deranged about these things. I was never saner in my life. That day they began to make arrangements for the

182

funeral. The little pastor of the Methodist church came down to see me. He and my wife's grandmother got down there by my bed and prayed. I remember now the prayer that he made. He said, "God, we know that you are even able to raise the dead," and held God's promises up before Him. He was a godly man; we had labored together in evangelistic work. My wife's grandmother was one of the best saints I ever saw walk this earth, and when she talked to God it meant something. I was just as sure I was going to be healed then as I am this minute that I am healed, but do you know they stopped the praying and sent the Methodist preacher away. I held on and the next night, Friday night, the Lord began to encourage me. He came and revealed Himself a little more fully to me. "Now," He said, "you are going up where these Alliance people are, and where Major Brown is, and you are going to be anointed according to James 5:14-16, and I am going to raise you up. You are going to meet all you promised Me last night." And I said, "Lord, is it possible I ever can be raised up?" He took me over to the Seventy-third Psalm that night, to two verses that I would not trade for Chicago, the twenty-fifth and twenty-sixth verses: "Whom have I in heaven but Thee? and there is none upon earth that I desire beside Thee. My flesh and my heart faileth: but God is the strength of my heart, and my portion forever."

There was the paralysis, my flesh had failed, my heart had failed, but "God is the strength of my heart, and" shall be "my portion forever." Then the enemy came around at that critical moment, just as he will with you, darkness came over me and I went through my own death. The Lord let me see my own funeral, the cemetery was within sight of the old homestead where I was lying. I could see the monument where grandfather lay, and saw the newly-made grave and the bearers putting me down. I heard the minister close the service and saw the mourners go away, and after everyone was gone the grave opened and I came up. I could see myself sitting on the nice green grass on the top of the grave, and I called after my wife and her grandmother as they were leading my little boy, Dayton, with them from the grave, and said, "Come back, you have buried the wrong man. I am alive." The Lord let me see that to "quench the fiery darts of the devil." I did die, thank God, to everything but God and Christ and the Holy Spirit. The next day they came around again and I began to write some more. I said, "The Lord has shown me some more. I am going up to the Alliance Convention; I am to be anointed and I shall be healed." They said, "He is getting crazy. There is no Alliance Convention. They will not let them hold a convention this year at Linnwood." However, they did have a convention, but not until all the other meetings were over, and thus, in the providence of God, the time was later than usual, because God knew about me.

The next thing was for me to be taken those eight miles to the Convention. My uncle said he would come and take me in his carriage, but they exhorted him and threatened him, declaring they would have him arrested if he did, and he backed out. There was nobody to fall back on at the last minute but the little Methodist preacher, and he said Saturday night, "If you will wait until Monday I will go up with you," but they threatened him. My wife's own mother declared she would arrest him if anything happened, but the little fellow didn't flinch. Monday morning came; my wife and grandmother stood by me. They took me to the depot and I suppose there were from three hunderd to four hundred people there to see me put on the train, and there were great threatenings and murmurings, but they put me on and there was no stop until we arrived at our destination. They took me into the depot and then to the hack, which was filled, but they made room for me and laid me on the cushioned side seat. All the way over they talked about what awful cases were brought to the Convention, expecting God to heal them, and I had to listen to all kinds of unbelieving and discouraging remarks. For Jesus' sake, where there is anybody trusting God to be delivered, no matter how bad the case, don't talk any unbelief. If you have any doubts or fears have them to yourself. I almost died going over there. It was only the mercy of God and the prayers of one or two dear sisters and the little Methodist preacher that sustained me. But for these prayers I would have died in the presence of that unbelief.

I arrived there just at the breakfast hour. The next meeting was a Bible-reading by Miss Sisson, from that very Psalm, the one hundred and seventh; Divine Healing was her subject that morning. They put me on a bench overlooking the lake. I sat there on my blanket and pillow while they looked for some one to pray for me. They saw a man walking along the beach, Bible in hand, who seemed to be communing with God. The Methodist minister hailed him and said, "I am looking for somebody that can anoint people for healing." "Well," he said, "I am one." God told me in that second vision that I would meet a man of my own country who would tell me wonderful things. I thought that was just a mere dream, but it proved to be the voice of God. This man was John Salmon, a good old Scotchman from Toronto, Canada, where I was born.

"IN DEATHS OFT."

They brought him to me and he asked me three questions. He said, "Are you converted?" "Oh," said my preacher friend, "he is a Methodist minister." "Well," he said, "it won't hurt to ask if he is converted. I met a bishop that doesn't know whether he is converted or not. Let him answer." I wrote on my tablet, "Yes, I am saved by the grace of God. I am regenerated and have the witness of the Spirit." He said in his Scotch way, "Very good, but now, mark you," and he put up his index finger, "do you believe that God can and will heal you if we obey Him in this ordinance?" I wrote "Yes, I do," but there was a little struggle before I could get the three words written. Something kept thumping my heart just like a man fighting me, but after I had written it I felt a great uplift in my spirit. You know it is just as Jesus said to the blind man, "Believest thou I am able to do this?" and he said, "Yea, Lord;" then, "According to your faith be it unto you." "One more question," said Mr. Salmon, "What do you want to be healed for?" I had to take a little time on that. I thought of my wife and boy, my friends, about the enjoyment of life and of preaching; finally I summed it all up: God gave me a little revelation and I wrote, "I want to be healed that I may glorify God in my body and spirit, which are His." And he said, "That is all right. He is ready to be anointed. I will get somebody to help take him over." They took me into a cottage, which I learned afterwards belonged to the President, Major Brown. There were five people around me beside the minister and myself, seven in all, the perfect, complete number. Everybody prayed, and they prayed the prayer of faith. Mr. Salmon took a few drops of oil and put it on my forehead, and said, "In the Name of the Father, Son and Holy Spirit I anoint this man to be perfectly healed from this paralysis and from other troubles. May he glorify God in his body and spirit, which are Thine." Then he said, "Brother, in the Name of the Lord Jesus Christ rise up and walk," and then came a hard test. Darkness came over me, the blackness of hell. It seemed I was sinking away. Somebody called out to praise God for my healing, and I got into worse darkness. I said in myself, "They have been telling me these people lie; that they say they are healed when they are not." Oh, how black it was! I was out in the middle of the room down on the carpet. That was the fight of my life, and I didn't know anything else to do but *trust*, and bless God, I did trust. I just said, "Jesus!" four or five times, and was thrilled right through from head to foot, and that warm, thrilling, life-giving, animating, quickening, reviving, stimulating breath of Almighty God went all through me, and I began to get up on

my right hand; the swelling began to go out of the
arm and limb that were three times their normal size.
Life and warmth went through the arm and leg, cir-
ulation came back, and I rose up in the name of Jesus:
instead of extending my right hand, I put out my left
hand and shook hands with the whole six people. My
tongue fell back in my mouth, and I found it small
and limber. I began to say like a baby beginning to
talk, "Praise the Lord." I walked along like a
drunken man trying to walk and talk, but nobody
touched me. All the way the devil was saying,
"You will fall, you will break your neck and die
here." The Methodist preacher said, "I will have
to steady him." "No, sir," Brother Salmon said,
"don't touch him; leave him with Jesus." I went
into the Tabernacle. Miss Sisson was on the rostrum
just beginning the Bible-reading. The leader said,
"We will have to interrupt the service; here is a man
marvelously healed who will soon have to take his
train home. He came here a dumb paralytic a little
over an hour ago, and now he can walk and talk."
Miss Sisson stopped, and then Satan said to me, "You
cannot get up." I was sitting on a seat and the
ground was thickly covered with rye-straw. Satan
said, "If you get up you will get tangled in the rye-
straw and fall," and then I had another struggle. I
am made to tell all this that it may help somebody who

may be tested after God has met him. The Methodist preacher said, "I will help you up," but God said to me, "No, no," and I drew away from him. Just as soon as they were ready for me I put out my hand and rose up. Then Satan met me and said, "You take a step and down you will go." I lifted my left foot high and stepped a long step. God made me do that for a sign. Then the enemy said, "You will never raise the other one." I raised that high, and the next thing I was up on the platform. My voice was weak but clear. I spoke slowly, for it seemed I had to learn to talk, but I gave God public praise. I recited the passage of scripture in II. Kings 20:5, and in Psalms 73:25, 26; also the Twenty-seventh Psalm. I related the little story of God's revelation to me, and that I had come to that meeting to confess; that I wanted to know where Major Brown was and could not go away before I confessed to him and before that great audience of nearly three thousand people that I, too, had joined the fanatics. I walked back to the depot, a mile and a quarter. The train was a little late and I lay down under a shade tree while the Methodist preacher went to a restaurant to get a little refreshment. I had been taking nothing but a little liquid food all this time through rice-straws. Lying there I fell asleep and slept as Jacob did at Bethel; my pillow was just as soft. The angels of God came to me. I dreamed I was in heaven and had a wonderful time. When the preacher came back he thought I was dead. He got the depot agent to come out and said to him, "I brought this man up here to be healed; the Lord did touch him, but I am afraid he died while I was gone." He put his hand on my heart. "No, sir," he said, "he is alive; he is all right." I opened my eyes and I thought they were angels. I was just in the place of glory, so restful, so happy. As I ate that little lunch I felt just as Elijah did when the angels brought him his supper under the juniper tree. How good that glass of milk and biscuit, and a little bit of sponge cake did taste! I ate all he brought me. "Now," I said, "when we get off the train, you go to your home; I am going home alone." I believe it was nine or ten ordinary blocks I had to walk. Do you wonder I sang that song tonight, "Walking with Jesus?" I tell you I began right there, walking with Jesus and talking with Jesus. When I got home I walked around to the back door, and just then my wife's mother stepped out at the rear. They were expecting to hear word any time that I was dead, and just as she stepped out she met me. She threw up her hands and said, "My God, he walks and talks," for I had just said, "Hello, mother, how are you?" We went in and had a praise meeting. Eight days after

that I was up at conference, and passed the hardest
year's study in the four years' course. Up to the
time of my healing I had read very little of the course
of study for that year, but I went through it all in
eight days. Scores of people came to see me, but I
never gave anybody more than five minutes. I went
up to the conference and stood second in a class of
nine. I tell this for the glory of God. The doctor
said I would never have a memory, but Jesus said
concerning the Spirit of truth, "He shall teach you all
things, and bring all things to your remembrance,
whatsoever I have said unto you." It has been no
trouble at all from that day to this for me to remember anything in God's Word, or anything pertaining
to God in any wise, glory be to His Name! At one
point in the oral examination the names of the judges
and of the minor prophets were to be given in their
order. The whole class failed on it, but I ran them
off so rapidly they suspected I had a book somewhere.
One of the examiners said to me, "How is this?"
and I told him my story to the glory of God, just as
I am telling it to you. They called my presiding
elder. He said, "Oh, I know all about this healing;
it is true." I was to go that year into a new district,
and the presiding elder said, "We will fix him. I
have the hardest place in the whole conference," and
to that they sent me. They were behind sixty-five

dollars on the former preacher's salary; there had been four appointments, one of them was closed and the church rented for a sheep-barn; another was closed because they could not support a minister. They had given but little for missionaries, and none of the other benevolences were touched at all. Soon after I took charge of this uninviting field there was brought to my attention a woman with a very malignant trouble, the most difficult case in that country; all the doctors had given her up and the people wanted me to go to see her because she was a member of the church. I prayed with her as any minister should, my wife was with me and we sang a song or two, and the Lord healed the woman. Then the work broke out and I was in trouble with the Methodist church right away. "Well," I said, "the Methodist discipline commands us to visit the sick and pray for them, and if God heals them it is not my fault." Thus God began to work in answer to prayer. I began a two weeks' meeting in the old sheep-barn, which was turned over to me by the party who held the lease, and in those two weeks thirty-five to forty souls were converted. I organized a class, went to the planing mill and made an altar and a pulpit with my own hands; God sanctified these with the birth of forty souls, and that little sheep-barn band itself gave more to missions than the whole circuit had before. The second year they had to give me an assistant preacher, divided the work and the offering for missions was four times as much as it was in its run-down condition. I gave fifty dollars myself to the mission fund, and God gave me three hundred and fifty dollars for doctors' bills for treatment for my wife and myself before the Lord healed us. I have had no salary from that time to this.

Six times since that first healing God has delivered me from death. There have been a multitude of lesser healings; time would fail me if I were to try to tell about them all, but there are six remarkable instances. The healing I have just related took place in August, 1888.

II. HEALED OF ARSENIC POISONING.

August 25, 1892, occurred my *second* healing, after I had been located in Cleveland, Ohio, one year. I continued two years in the Methodist church after my first healing, but the Lord led me out because of the pressure, though it came about in a very sweet way and with no reflection on anyone.

Our first Convention at Beulah Park, Cleveland, was held in a large tent. God did a marvelous work of healing there, the blind received sight, the lame were made to walk, consumption and cancer were healed; it was a marvelous time of healing. We have been at Beulah Park Conventions for nineteen years, but none has ever surpassed the first one in healings.

"IN DEATHS OFT."

A little weekly paper was being published in Collin-
wood, the editor of which came down and interviewed
me. I told him plainly all about it; he went back and
published the facts in his paper, and said, "This is all
right; this is according to the Gospel." But the people around Beulah Park became very bitter, and made
great threats as to what they would do. I went to
the store to pay my bill, as we were about to move
back into the city. I agreed to watch the car my
people took at the lower end of the line and get on
the same one. I was standing in the grocery where
I paid the last bill, reading my mail, when a young
man said, "Reverend, you must be hungry. Won't
you have a banana or two?" They often gave us
something like that when we paid the bill. It was
about twelve o'clock; I noticed they were soft at the
end, but bananas are frequently like that. I thanked
him; I was very hungry, and I ate them rather rapidly; the car was coming and I got on. Before I got
half way into the city, which was about eight miles
from our starting point, I was deathly sick. Everything began to look strange to me; perspiration came
out on my body, and the Lord confirmed me in the
belief that I had been poisoned. It was about half
past two o'clock when I reached home, and I grew
worse and worse until after supper, when I began to
have convulsions, which continued until eleven o'clock.

THE LATTER RAIN PENTECOST.

Then they sent to our weekly meeting, which was in progress, for my elders to come and pray for me. Elder Brown was not there; the other elder came, but he was fearful, he could not pray the prayer of faith. He thought they had to locate this trouble, so he sent to the drug store for some lobelia, but, said he, "If he knows anything about it, he won't take it." As they brought it to me I rallied out of one of those convulsive strains, and I remember as I looked up I saw his face and knew him; I seemed to know my wife was there also. I said, "What is this?" "Just a little something to quiet you." I said, "Don't give me that; it always pays to wait on God." Immediately I went off into another convulsion, and as I rallied out of it, the thought, "It pays to wait on God," came back to me, and with that I began to see light, and I said, "Lord, is this your time for me? If you want to take me home take me quickly." I saw Jesus come up to the foot of the bed with His hands up, and I thought, of course, He had come to take me. My eyes were not open. It was a spiritual vision I had of Him, and I said in my soul, "Oh, blessed Lord, take me quickly." He put up His hands and waved me back, saying, "I have not come but for victory." That was the first vision I ever had of the Lord. "Thanks be unto God who giveth us the victory through our Lord Jesus Christ." I. Cor. 15:57.

But I went off into worse convulsions after that. My brother-in-law had to get up into the bed and hold me. The poisonous substance poured out of me at every avenue; a chemical analysis afterwards revealed that I had been poisoned by arsenic. I was completely delivered. They laid me on a bed in another room, and early in the morning my parishioners came to see me. I could not lift one of my little fingers, I was so weak and exhausted, but the life of God was thrilling my mortal body, glory be to His Name!

III. DELIVERED FROM PLEURO-PNEUMONIA.

In February, 1895, I was stricken down with pleuro-pneumonia, from exposure at Akron, Ohio, while attending a Convention there. We were exposed in a drizzling cold rain and sleet as we stood waiting for an hour and a half for a street car, which could not run on schedule time because of the sleet. A number of people became sick through that exposure, but I seemed to be struck worse than the others because I had been using my voice. The elders came and prayed, but they didn't get hold of God for me; one elder wanted medicine, another wanted this thing and another that, and they could not pray the prayer of faith. Finally, one of my little deacons, God bless him, came and said, "I am not an elder, but God sent me to pray for you." They let him in, but said he must not talk to me because they did not expect me to live. I was just in the very last stages, could scarcely breathe, and the dear little deacon came and got down beside my bed, and put his hands on my head—I can feel them now—and whispered a few words, saying, "Jesus, You know You spoke to me over there in my home, told me to come over here and put my hands on my pastor's head, and that You would raise him up. I don't know what to say, but I put my hands on his head, and I believe You will raise him up." At once I felt as though a great, heavy, wet cloth had been pulled off me, my body relaxed and became warm. The deacon broke out in weeping, and so did I. The accumulated matter came out of my throat, and I got hold of his hands and we praised God together. Before he left they put me into a Morris chair, and I was at the table eating supper with them. This is the word God gave me in my heart while the deacon was praying: "Behold, I will bring it health and cure, and I will cure them, and will reveal unto them the abundance of peace and truth." Jer. 33:6. God wonderfully revealed it to that whole congregation. The elders thought God could not heal; they thought He would have to have a doctor and some medicine to help Him, but here was

God's rebuke. I went out to preach healing as I
never had preached it before.

IV. DELIVERED FROM LARYNGITIS.

Again in February, 1900, I had a very bad exposure, and a cold settled in my throat. I had been
using my voice in varous meetings and had returned
to El-Shaddai, which is the name the Lord gave me
for our home in Cleveland, for rest and healing. I
was soon to start for Columbus, Ohio, with Mr.
Simpson and Mr. LeLacheur; the Ohio Quartette
was to be there, too. I was stricken down with
laryngitis, which is one of the worst forms of throat
trouble there is. My throat was closed and I could
not breathe without struggling. The Sabbath service
was being held in the large double room below my
bedroom. After the service was over, an elder, a
deacon and several sisters came up to have special
prayer; it seemed I was dying. While they were
praying a convulsion came on and the deacon got on
the bed to hold me, for I was in the throes of death.
I had been lying there for a week, and Mr. LeLacheur said, "I do not think Brother Myland will ever
work with us again." Of course, that didn't help
me any. I was being strangled to death, and would
have died in five minutes I know. Finally, the deacon
got me by the back of my head, by my hair with a
death grip, and he said, "God, in the Name of Jesus,

deliver this man," and a great membrane as large as a small finger, burst out of my throat and flew across the large room, adhering to the wall, and I was relieved. That deacon has since received the baptism in the Holy Spirit and gone as a missionary to South Africa, taking his whole family with him.

They gave me a drink of hot water and I began to sing praises to God. I had some supper that night and God was glorified again. This time my verse was Phil. 1:28. "And in nothing be terrified by your adversaries: which is to them an evident token of perdition, but to you of salvation, and that of God. For unto you it is given in the behalf of Christ, not only to believe in Him, but also to *suffer* for His sake." God delivered me, and afterwards we found the application of the text, for right there while I was sick in bed Satan was planning to frustrate the work in Cleveland by those who professed to be its friends.

V. TYPHOID-PNEUMONIA HEALED.

In the year 1902, from overwork and exposure, and of hatred of the devil, I was taken down with typhoid-pneumonia, much worse than the other time. Prayer went up for me all over this continent. In every center of Alliance work known to us, people were praying; the people around Cleveland came both day and night to pray; all night they gathered for prayer, but I went down, down, down. I could take no more food, not even liquid; I could not get food into my mouth, for my whole face was one great scab. The poison had come up and out until my face was hideous; for five weeks I had lain in that bed and the hour had come when I was sinking away and dying. The best, the nearest and dearest friends had prayed for me; my own dear son in the faith, my own Timothy, F. W. Davis, now in South China, was down in the corner of the room, his face buried in his hands, saying, "Oh, God, must he go?" They called the children, my two boys, in from school to see their father die. I had set my house in order; the day before I had whispered to my dear personal friend, this young man Davis, and told him what I wanted done about the work. I sent for my wife to kiss me if she could, but there was no place, for my face was one solid scab. She came in, got up on the bed and refused to let me die. She said, "God, he shall not die." She held on and those who were there in prayer rallied. I was dying, but she held on. Then there broke on my soul this text in Hebrews 10:23, "Let us hold fast the profession of our faith without wavering," *confession* of the *hope* (R. V.) it really is, "for He is faithful that promised." He showed me by that text, "*confession* of *hope*" that in my weakened physical state He didn't hold me to hard, fast lines of *faith,* and took me over to the other verse, "Though WE believe not, yet HE abideth faithful. He cannot deny Himself." II. Tim. 2:13. God said to me, "You know you have a little sum of money in the bank on which to transact business; you check that out, you *draw* out that which is DEPOSITED. Now you have deposited faith with me in heaven, *and* YOU *cannot do anything, but* YOUR FAITH DEPOSITED IN DAYS PAST IN HEAVEN, IS DRAWING INTEREST, YOU CAN LIVE ON THAT; you can go through to your healing on that faith." My wife was there crying to God and saying, "He shall not die, Lord, I claim life for him." Suddenly I began to shake until the whole bed shook—it was the Spirit of God shaking the disease out of my body. My wife got me in her arms and pulled me up in the bed, and a poisonous diseased matter poured itself out of my mouth until there was more than a glass would contain. I was perfectly relieved. A great reaction went over my body; I fell back on the pillow as one dead. They praised God around my bed, and my strength came back as I lay there; that was about four o'clock in the afternoon. They gave me a little liquid nourishment that night, and the next morning I took some solid food. In a few days I was downstairs; inside of a week I was walking out on the street. I had been lying in that room five weeks, nothing scarcely but a shadow of my former self, and God delivered me from death the fifth time. This occurred May 8, 1902.

VI. FRACTURED RIBS, TORN PLEURA HEALED.

Then in 1905, February again, I was in Akron preaching on the Sabbath. I started home from the service after ten P. M. It was cold and snowing, the street cars were not running regularly. I was warm from preaching and said I would walk home; Mrs. Myland and a friend waited on the corner for the car. It was very slippery, and before me there was a sharp down-grade into a "cut." I didn't see it and slipped and fell on a large lump of hard, frozen earth, larger than a man's head. I thought it was a stone. I struck right on that place in my back that is a little weak where I was injured before I was paralyzed. It affected my whole nervous system until I shook like an aspen leaf. I could not help myself. I was injured severely; I chilled, shook, and became unconscious. It must have been three-quarters of an hour that I lay there, for they were an hour coming home. Finally some noise brought me to consciousness again. It seemed I was in heaven; the snow was falling and there was an electric light some distance from me, and it just looked like glory itself. I appeared to be dying, and had no life left in me scarcely at all. Just then I heard footfalls; I tried to turn but could not lift myself. I was covered with snow, I suppose to a depth of three inches. A form approached, looked down at me and said, "What are you doing here?" He was the son of the lady where I was stopping and was on his way home. I lifted my hand and then he saw my Bible lying in the snow, and he said, "My God, it is Mr. Myland!" He tried to help me up, but he couldn't and I couldn't bear his touch. Just then a tall, strong man was coming up the street and he hailed him. It proved to be a man he knew, who had served in the Red Cross work in the Cuban war, and he knew how to raise me up. They carried me into the house, which was only a few steps away, and telephoned for the best surgeon in Akron. He examined me and found two ribs fractured, the spine injured at the old place, the whole of the pleura torn loose and the spleen displaced, and from my chilled condition he said pneumonia was setting in and I could not possibly live. He bandaged up my side the best he could with straps and said, "If he does live he will not move from this place short of a month. He will never do any more work in this line." He was a Methodist Bible-class teacher and a very fine man. He wanted to give me an opiate, but I declined to take anything. The next morning when he came they told him I had lain in that one position all night and hadn't slept at all. I

had sweet communion with the Lord that night, although I hadn't slept at all and suffered intensely.
I knew then the truth of the old verse, "Labor is rest
and pain is sweet, while I am in communion with
Thee." The surgeon wanted to give me an opiate
in the morning. I said, "No, doctor, God is my
opiate." "Well," he said, "I admire your faith,
I would not interfere with it for the world, but, dear
man, you never can do anything any more." The
elders left their work that day at noon and came to
pray and sing for me. God had given me Romans
8:28, "For we know that all things work together
for good to them that love God, to them who are the
called according to His purpose." I said, "Why,
Lord, what does this mean? How will this ever
work for good and glorify You?" There was at
that time a series of fifteen conventions projected in
Ohio, and I was to leave the next day for the first at
Youngstown. The elders prayed and anointed me,
and it felt as though a great hand smoothed me all
over and just seemed to iron me out. That is the
only way I can express it. I got up out of that bed;
I was pretty stiff because of those straps that were
fastened around me to hold me together; I walked
around the bed with my hand on the posts to steady
me, and praised the Lord. I lay down, had a good
sleep, and all my suffering was gone. I was sore and

lame when I moved, but I didn't suffer from pain.   I
slept every night and began to eat, and the fifth day I
took the train for Cleveland.   It was an accommoda-
tion train, made many stops and shook me up con-
siderably; something developed in my kidneys from
that injury.   Mrs. Myland went home with me, but
the next day went on to the convention.   I became
rapidly worse, a great abscess formed in the descending colon, and I again went down to the very gates
of death.   On Sabbath they sent a special message
to the Convention telling them to pray, that Mr. Myland was dying.   While they prayed at the Convention three or four gathered round my bed in prayer
and God brought Romans 8:28 back to me, and immediately God touched me and that abscess passed
away; I was perfectly delivered.

I sat up in bed and wrote that song that has since
been incorporated in my song-book, entitled, "All
Things Work Together for Good." I wrote both
words and music, and sang it to the friends in the
house, although the surgeon had said I would never
be able to speak or sing again. God brought my
voice back. I went next day to the Convention in
Cleveland, preached the following Sabbath in the
morning, went to Akron and preached in the afternoon, continued the triangle to Youngstown and
preached in the evening, and came back home that

same night. Of course, it was too much, but the meetings were on and workers scarce. I suffered a little afterwards, but I went on from strength to strength, went to the rest of the meetings, singing, speaking, praising God with as good a voice as I have tonight. I have met that surgeon twice since, and he said, "Do you mean to say you keep at this work as you did before?" I said, "Yes." He said, "It is simply supernatural that you can either talk or sing." This was my sixth deliverance from death.

I moved to Columbus, Ohio, in April, 1905. The next Spring Pentecost broke out in Los Angeles, and I began to look into it. God talked to me about water and fire, and took me through the Word of God on those lines. I began studying and setting myself for this thing; I was engaged every night in teaching my Bible-classes and preaching, yet all the time I was expecting God to meet me in some wonderful way.

VII. BURNS AND BLOOD POISONING HEALED.

October, 1906, I opened our first Convention in Columbus, with the assistance of Dr. Watson. It was chilly and I lighted the big gas magazine, which was located almost in the middle of the chapel. Then I went up street on a business errand. When I came back some of the old ladies near the stove looked up to me and moved their shoulders as though

they were chilly. I looked at the heater and saw
there was no fire in it. I thought some one had
turned it off and I would have to light it again. I
threw open the door and with a lighted taper in my
hand reached down to turn the key to light it, when
there was a great explosion—the magazine was full
of gas and had evidently in some way been tampered
with. It threw me from fifteen to twenty feet against
the vestibule doors, burned the flesh off my right hand
almost entirely, and very badly burned the left hand
and my face; my clothes were burned until they
just dropped apart. Two of the sisters, who were
near, saw the burning gas coming right out of my
mouth. I would have fallen, but a brother coming
in just then, caught me as the doors flew open, and
began to call on the Lord. Two sisters came with
him, and they began to pray. He took me up in his
arms, and with other assistance, carried me into the
home of one of my deacons, next to the chapel. I
could not lie there. I got on my knees and held my
hands up to heaven, but I could not speak.

My wife was on the west side of the city. Dr.
Watson prayed, and I seemed to rally a little. They
laid me down but I swooned away again. My pulse
ceased to beat three different times, and three different times they thought I was dead. Finally they got
all the deacons and elders together, seven in all, who

prayed and anointed me. While they were praying I rallied, and God spoke these words to me as I lay there: "Always bearing about in the body the dying of the Lord Jesus, that the life also of Jesus might be made manifest in our body. For we which live are always delivered unto death for Jesus' sake, that the life also of Jesus might be made manifest in our mortal flesh. So then death worketh in us, but life in you, according as it is written, I believed, and therefore have I spoken; we also believe, and therefore speak; knowing that He which raised up the Lord Jesus shall raise up us also by Jesus, and shall present us with you." II. Cor. 4:10-14.

God presented me back again to those deacons and elders, and to my flock and the work of God, and as these words came, spoken in my soul by the Holy Spirit, I raised up on my couch, and although blind from the burns, I began to sing:

> "Grace as fathomless as the sea,
> Grace is flowing from Calvary,
> Grace for time and eternity,
> Grace enough for me."

They led me home. I could not see the way and they held their hands on my shoulders. I walked five blocks with my hands up. My wife came home. I began to see a little out of the right eye, but I was totally blind in the left for three days. God began His work of healing and He kept at it and gave me strength. With those awful burns on my hands, which with my face were covered with medicated cotton, I went to the Convention, held my hands up and stood with the Quartette and sang the songs each day for a week, and God wonderfully blessed us in that Convention. What a wonderful time I had! But it was cold weather. On a Thursday night I caught cold and blood-poisoning began to develop in my right hand. I was on my face before God during those days, going through the prophecy of Daniel: "And I set my face unto the Lord God, to seek by prayer and supplications with fasting, and sackcloth and ashes; And I prayed unto the Lord my God, and made my confession, and said, Oh, Lord, the great and dreadful God, keeping the covenant and mercy to them that love Him, and to them that keep His commandments;" Dan. 9:3, 4. Then He took me to Daniel 9:20-23 and Daniel 10:5-12.

I was in the attitude Daniel was during those days described by these verses. They came to me again and again during that time and I read them often. I was earnestly seeking Pentecost. Twenty-one days after the burning I was alone in my room on a Saturday night with no arrangements for Sunday. I knew unless God came to my rescue I would soon be dead.

"IN DEATHS OFT."

They were praying for me, but the blood-poisoning was rising and had now reached my brain, and I was almost wild. I knew my wife had gone upstairs to pray and I was desperate. Again Daniel 10:5-12 came to me, and I said, "Lord, unless you interpose I shall be dead before morning. I want to know what You are going to do, and I give You an hour to do it." Seventeen years before that in my library I had received an anointing of the Spirit and said and sang things in a way I didn't understand. So on that eventful night I asked of the Lord three things: First, if that experience seventeen years before was the beginning of this Pentecost, to give me the "*residue*" of it now; second, heal me instantly and thoroughly; third, enlighten me concerning this subject of Pentecost so I might answer the questions that had been coming to me for months both verbally and by letter concerning it. And then this came to pass literally: "I lifted up mine eyes, and looked, and behold a certain man" just as John had at Patmos.

In that hour I saw the Lord Jesus. He wasn't down here exactly as Daniel saw Him, but away up in glory and in the midst of a great multitude. A great orchestra was before me and a great chorus of singers, and they were singing wonderful music. I could see Him on a glorious pedestal with a beautiful baton that looked like gold and pearl, beating time,

and as I looked upon Him I wished He would turn
around so I could see His face. Presently as they
seemed to come to a pause in the singing, at the end
of a strain, He turned around so gracefully to me, and
looked at me and said, "Well, My child, what would
you like to have?" And I said, "Oh, Lord, I would
like to join Your choir," and then I seemed to tremble
at what I had said, "*join that choir!*" He turned
and looked toward the choir, and then at me and said,
"My child, you may," and then all the strength left
me, and I said, "Well, I can't now, I wouldn't
dare." But He made a motion to me with
His baton, and it seemed I was lifted right up and
was set down in the choir. I began to sing with them
a little and what do you suppose? I was singing
the "latter rain" song in "tongues," which I afterwards interpreted, and wrote into English. They all
seemed to join in with me and after it was all over
they sang another great chorus. I listened, and the
great Leader, my glorified Christ, motioned to me and
I sat down, and I thought, Oh, what singing! The
old Ohio Quartette never could sing like that, and
I found myself singing also. The glory died away
and I came to myself singing in "tongues." It
passed away and immediately I began to reach for my
Bible. I took out a piece of blank paper and began
to write with my left hand, tried to write with my

pencil between the first and second finger. I could not get along very fast and involuntarily took it over into my right hand, the hand that had been so badly swollen, and I found I was healed; the sores were there but I was healed. There wasn't a particle of pain or stiffness, and I wrote the words of the Latter Rain Song, word for word, as fast as I could write; never changed a word, wrote the melody, tried it on the piano, and found it a beautiful melody.

I went upstairs to bed, and slept. There on the third of November, 1906, I had the full measure of my Pentecostal Baptism and healing, *just twenty-one days*, as God had shown me, after the terrible gas explosion. Oh, what glory I was in for an hour. I took out my watch and saw that for just an hour I was lost to this world. Oh, what a vision of Jesus and of heaven! Indescribable! I have just sketched the outline. Oh, what glory there was in my soul. I got up the next morning like a new creature, and I wondered, "Lord, what will I do? go over to the church? but what will I say?" I seemed to be not of this world. Mrs. Myland took up the morning reading, which was in the thirty-seventh chapter of Ezekiel. I was struck with the first verse, for God had already given me that verse. I thought, "Lord, do you want me to preach on that?" In addition to that verse,

THE LATTER RAIN PENTECOST.

God gave me the twelfth to the fourteenth verses of the third chapter.

After breakfast I went upstairs and put these verses together, then went to the Tabernacle and preached. That was my first Pentecostal message. I tell you it wasn't I that spoke. It was God. "The hand of the Lord was strong upon me." When the Spirit of the Lord gets you, the hand of the Lord is upon you. Your spirit may shrink, but the hand of the Lord is upon you. He carried me away. First He carried me *up*, then He carried me *out*—out into service to other people, and that is why I am here tonight.

This was the *seventh* and last of my deliverances from "deaths oft." This was a death "by fire;" and resulted in my "Pentecostal baptism." I had, it seems, arrived at the completion (seventh) the *"fulness."* Many "fiery trials" have followed, but, like the *asbestos*, which is made to display fire, we, whose faith has been tried by fire, may be formed unto praise and honor and glory at the appearing of Christ.

My closing word is a prayer that this story may encourage you to trust God, to yield unquestioning obedience to Him, and He will cause you too to know that "all things work together for good to them that love God, to those who are the called according to His purpose." Blessed be His holy Name forever.

"IN DEATHS OFT."

And now I close my story by reciting two passages of Scripture:

"Worthy is the Lamb that was slain to receive power, and riches, and wisdom, and strength, and honor, and glory, and blessing."

"Unto Him that loved us, and washed us from our sins in His own blood. And hath made us kings and priests unto God and His Father; to Him be glory and dominion forever. Amen." Rev. 5:12, 1:5.

All Things Work for Good *

There's a sweet and wondrous message written in God's book divine,
'Tis a comfort to God's pilgrim and by faith I make it mine;
Hear this precious promise of God's grace which every truth has stood:
"And we know that all things work together for our good."

CHORUS.

Yes, we know, where'er we go
Come to pass what may, still in faith we say:
When we're in God's purpose, love Him as we should.
He will work all things together for our good.

In our pressing daily duties there are trials to be borne,
There are ministries of sufferings when our hearts are faint and torn;
Let us all these life "necessities" esteem as grateful food,
Knowing this that all things work together for our good.

Tho' we're hindered in our service by some circumstantial test,
Then be still to see God's providence, and "enter into rest,"
Never question, doubt or worry, when we've done the best we could,
Wait, and God will work all things together for our good.

I believe this blessed promise, and I rest upon the Word,
When I cannot fully understand I simply trust the Lord;
If we walk in true obedience, doing as our Master would,
We shall prove that "all things work together for our good."

---

*See page 206.

Pentecost Has Come *

There's a Pentecost for all the sanctified,
Heaven's witness true, which cannot be denied,
And the Spirit's gifts are being multiplied
In God's holy church today.

CHORUS.

Oh, I'm glad the promised Pentecost has come,
And the "Latter Rain" is falling now on some;
Pour it out in floods, Lord, on the parched ground,
Till it reaches all the earth around.

There's a Pentecost for every trusting soul,
Of your life the Spirit now will take control,
Filling, sealing, quickening, healing, making whole,
By God's holy pow'r today.

There's a Pentecost for every yielded heart,
And the "holy fire" God's Spirit will impart;
To obey His will you gladly then will start
In God's holy work today.

There's a Pentecost for those who wait and pray
With surrendered will, O seek it then today;
Christ will baptize all His saints who will obey
With the Spirit's tongues of fire.

---

*Tongues interpreted. See page 213.

A Letter From Palestine

The following letter sent to us with the accompanying rain chart will be of interest to the readers of these lectures:

JERUSALEM, JAN. 12, 1909.

WM. HAMNER PIPER,
Dear Sir:

Your communication to the Weather Bureau, which in that sense does not exist, was handed to us in the American Colony, we being interested in the question of rain, the water supply for the city, etc.

The accompanying chart, compiled by us from the only observations existing over such length of period, very nearly meets all the questions your letter raises. The increase in the rainfall that the chart shows has impressed us as very significant, seeing that the reverse would be expected to take place as year by year the country is being denuded of its trees for firewood, and particularly because the rain is so often used by God to be a mark or evidence of His good or ill-pleasure; the references that bear on the rain would soon make that apparent.

It is particularly in the aspect of the *latter rain* that from the prophecies' point of view the increase in the rainfall is remarkable, and yet people cavil at that. "Since the days the fathers fell asleep until now all things continue the same," is a favorite theme.

Joel 2:23 is a pretty clear indication of when to expect the latter rain, and Amos 4:7 is a clear indication of the withholding of the rain and at what time, in order to bring them to their senses.

The harvest commences in the Jericho plain in April, and in June the grain is ripe in the mountains.

With cordial greetings for the New Year,

Yours truly,   JACOB ELIAHU.

Under date of April 8, 1909, the writer further says:

I may have failed to tell in my former letter that the conditions of the rainfall here were such as evidently provided for a hot, dry spell after copious rains in the beginning of the season, during which time on account of the heat, the crops were prematurely forced forward to maturity in a few weeks; hence the withholding of the latter rain was fatal and the crops would miscarry. This seems so suggestive of God's work.

If and though there has been an early outpouring of His Spirit, there must be a latter rain to insure its benefits and blessings. Hence it is that in so many of the prophecies the *latter rain* is what is referred to, the promise of its return is linked with God's promises of spiritual prosperity and the restoration of Israel.

From Joel's prophecy it is evident that the time of the latter rain was in the "first month," the passover month, just at this time between March and April.

Again, when God says "I withheld the rain, the latter rain when there were yet three months to the harvest," we have the time set, for in Jericho the harvest commences in June; hence from this place the first sheaf was taken up to the temple for presentation to invoke and secure God's blessing on the entire harvest at Passover time, just at the time when the "first sheaf" ("first born of an entire creation") rent the vail and opened a way into the presence of God, for mankind, for all time. In May and June, then, the harvest all over the country takes place.

No hard and fast rule can be laid down; from the fall of rain in the various months during the season, as seen in the bottom of the chart sent you, it will become evident that there is no uniformity. This year is a notable example. The rains commenced several weeks later than last season, then fell abundantly, till we were many inches in advance of last season, but with the new year a dry spell came on, so I imagine we have not had five inches since the beginning of the year, and not one inch since the middle of February, with the result that in districts in Beersheba the crops have been fed green to the cattle for fear of their withering away entirely. Today, thank God, we are having a good downpour, which will abundantly satisfy and fructify the standing crops and cause a good yield, and a fall in the already fearfully inflated prices of foodstuffs.

Some other observations taken in detail show that there has been latterly a very marked, though not uniform, change in the matter of dew and cloudy days.

CHART SHOWING RAINFALL

ISSUED BY THE AMERICAN COLONY, JERUSALEM.

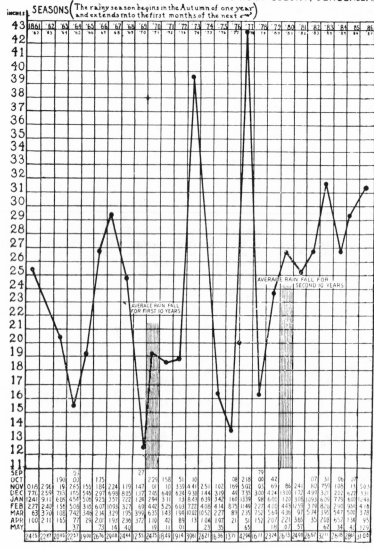

inches SEASONS (The rainy season begins in the Autumn of one year and extends into the first months of the next ⟶)

AVERAGE RAIN FALL FOR FIRST 10 YEARS

AVERAGE RAIN FALL FOR SECOND 10 YEARS

IN PALESTINE FROM 1861 TO 1907
REPRODUCED BY THE EVANGEL PUBLISHING HOUSE, CHICAGO.

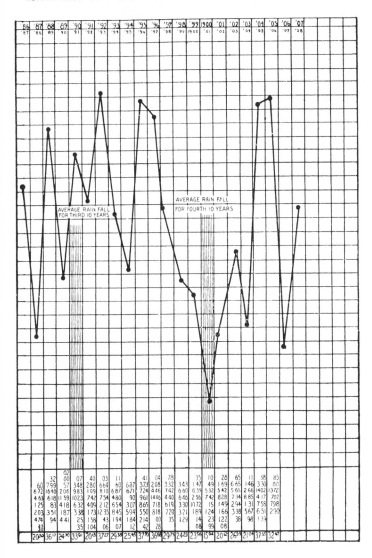

The Latter Rain Evangel

IS an International Monthly Magazine of 24 pages, published by Wm. Hamner Piper at $1.00 (4s-2d) per year.

This paper stands for the fulness of the Gospel, and gives details of the marvelous workings of the Spirit of God in all parts of the world at this time.

Today God is pouring out His Spirit as He did on the day of Pentecost, with the same miraculous signs following. If you want to read interesting accounts of Salvation, Divine Healing, Cleansing and the Baptism in the Holy Spirit with Speaking in Tongues, together with other remarkable manifestations of the Spirit, subscribe for this paper. Each issue also contains helpful teaching on these subjects and on the Signs of the Times. Send ten cents for sample copy.

These lectures by Brother Myland were first published in The Evangel, and are an illustration of the high-class literature you may expect to find in its pages.

We have an interesting and growing list of Tracts from 6 to 32 pages, which tell of the works of God. Send stamps for samples.

Address, THE LATTER RAIN EVANGEL

Chicago, Ill., U. S. A.

REV. G. F. TAYLOR

THE SPIRIT AND THE BRIDE:

A Scriptural Presentation of the Operations, Manifestation, Gifts and Fruit

OF

THE HOLY SPIRIT
IN HIS RELATION TO THE BRIDE

with special reference to

THE "LATTER RAIN" REVIVAL

BY

REV. G. F. TAYLOR,

PRINCIPAL OF FALCON HOLINESS SCHOOL

Author of a treatise on "The Devil"

"The Spirit and the bride say, Come."—Rev. 22 : 17.

PRICE, FIFTY CENTS

"Beloved, when I gave all diligence to write unto you of the common salvation, it was needful for me to write unto you, and exhort you that ye should earnestly contend for the faith once delivered unto the saints.

Jude 1:3.

PREFACE.

THE subject discussed in this book is one of grave importance just at this time. The world is stirred from centre to circumference over the great subject of Pentecost. There are but few souls in America who have not been affected more or less by the present movement, and the public mind is deeply concerned as to many features thereof. Some are uniting and identifying themselves with it, some are rejecting, some are mocking, all are agitated more or less. Realizing that upon their attitude toward the present movement depends the eternal destiny of thousands, the writer deems this subject one of the greatest importance.

He has been a close observer of the movement from the time he saw the first report of the same. Special effort has been made by him to secure all the information possible, both for and against the movement. This has been done in order that he might be able to view the question properly from all sides. Realizing that these are perilous times, we have had a great desire to know the truth and walk in it.

In this book we have made an effort to view the many questions connected with this movement from a Scriptural standpoint, and have taken especial pains to answer the question, *Do all who receive the Baptism of the Spirit speak with other tongues?* One whole chapter is devoted to answering objections offered by our brethren of the opposite school. Lest we should be accused of misrepresenting their position, we quote many of them exact.

The book has been written in much prayer and after much forethought, and we beg of all who read its pages to do so with mind and heart open to truth and to God. Accept all that is Scriptural; reject all that is erroneous.

Praying God's blessings upon all who read or circulate this book, I am,

Yours in Pentecostal glory,

G. F. TAYLOR.

DUNN, N. C., September, 1907.

INTRODUCTION.

BY REV. J. H. KING.

THE history of Christianity demonstrates that every great spiritual epoch has been productive of a literature peculiar to itself. The Holy Spirit not only moves powerfully upon human hearts, moving to intense activity on soul-saving work, but moves upon their minds simultaneously, inspiring to deeper thinking and investigation, bringing to light new truth, hitherto unknown. Divine revelation was progressive in its unfoldment, and the discovery of the meaning of the truth thus revealed is of necessity progressive in the understanding of enlightened Christendom. This progressive discovery of the meaning of truth, as we approach the ultimate completeness, implies limitation individually and dispensationally. No literature belonging to any particular epoch of the Christian Church bears the stamp of perfection. Revealed truth peculiar to each dispensation may to its adherents embrace all there is of truth, and thus present completeness in scope, but subsequent discoveries prove this to be a serious, as well as injurious, mistake. The great Protestant Reformation, and also the world-wide Methodistic movements, were mighty literature-producing epochs, setting forth precious and glorious truth, which deluged the world with blessings inestimable, but there is much that is imperfect in this literature; imperfect in nature and extent. The modern holiness movement has produced a vast volume of

literature, presenting truth beyond the range of former discoveries, which has blessed the world with its fruit, not-
withstanding its imperfection as well as unscripturalness in
many of its aspects.   It bears upon its face the claim of
completeness, but further research is bringing to light the
fact that it only brings its adherents into the vestibule of
Pentecostal power and fulness, and not into its possession.
The reducing within the range of justification and sanctification all that pertains to the fulness of grace, which is so
apparent in all this literature, is positively injurious to honest
souls, and serves as a barrier to their entrance into the
Pentecostal experience.   The second blessing does not and
can not include the Baptism of the Holy Ghost, and the
light of this truth, which has been gradually unfolding for
a number of years, culminating in the present world-wide
Pentecostal movement, is meeting with determined and desperate opposition, because it sinks the walls of limitation
erected by the above literature, leading the people out into
larger fields of truth, which enrich and empower the soul
for better service.   This movement will, like all previous
ones, produce a literature peculiarly its own.   This book
is the first to appear on this line, and fills a very unique
place in Christian literature, being the first to be written by
one who has the Baptism of the Holy Ghost according to
its bestowment in the Book of Acts, which characterizes
the present movement.   It labors to place the Baptism of
the Holy Spirit in its Scriptural setting, and to show forth
its peculiar accompaniment, the speaking in other tongues
as evidencing its unmistakable reception.   It is not an ex-

haustive treatise on this subject, but rather suggestive in its presentation of truth. Indeed, it does not claim to be anything but a primary discussion of the work of the Holy Ghost in His relation to the bridehood of Jesus, presenting the baptism as an initial preparation for membership in the same. This gives to the book an aspect of vast importance. In these closing days of gospel history, it is of momentous importance to those who are awake to the near advent of Christ to know what is the real preparation for membership in His bridehood, and a sincere perusal of this book will throw light on the question. It clearly shows that preparation to meet Christ is not ample qualification for membership in the bridehood, and the apprehension of this fact will doubtless stimulate deeper effort on the part of some to prepare for this high privilege and honor. If such efforts follow its careful reading, we are sure the author's hopes will be realized.

TABLE OF CONTENTS

(11)

CHAPTER I.

"THERE is one God; and there is none other but He" (Mark 12:32).

We read in Psalms 14:1: "The fool hath said in his heart, There is no God." The heathen believe that there are many gods. But we know "that there is none other God but one. For though there be that are called gods, whether in heaven or in earth (as there be gods many, and lords many), but to us there is but one God" (1 Cor. 8:4-6). This one God is eternal. He says of Himself, "I AM THAT I AM" (Ex. 3:14). This is the One whom John saw, and the One of whom he speaks in Rev. 4:2, *"And one sat on the throne."* The apostle here mentions no name, and describes no figure, because he was looking upon "the unnameable, indescribable Godhead," in which Father, Son, and Holy Ghost are consubstantial and the same. God, in the most hidden absoluteness of His being, in which the whole Godhead and all things stand, is indescribable; but there are embodied in this Godhead three blessed personages, each of which is indescribable, and each of which is God; and yet the three together are still the indescribable One.

We read in John 4:24 that "God is a Spirit;" but we also read in 1 Cor. 15:44: "There is a natural body, and there is a spiritual body." So we find that the Scriptures speak of the different parts of the Father's body. "The clouds are the dust of his *feet*" (Nah. 1:3); *"Eyes* of the Lord" (Zech. 4:10); "Behold, the Lord's *hand* is not shortened, that it cannot save; neither his *ear* heavy, that it cannot hear" (Isa. 59:1).

We know that the Son has a body, for He "was made flesh, and dwelt among us" (John 1:14). "And was made in the likeness of men" (Phil. 2:7). When He ascended to heaven He took His body with Him.

There is no Scripture which seems to teach that the Holy

Spirit has a body; and yet He is the Personal God, and as much so as God the Father or God the Son; forming with the Father and the Son a unity in trinity and the Trinity in unity. He is as eternal as the Father and the Son; we read of Him from the beginning. "And the Spirit of God moved upon the face of the waters (Gen. 1:2). As He was one in the councils (Gen. 1:26) of the Trinity in the eternal past, as He is now and ever will be in the advancement of God's kingdom, so was He one with Christ during His earthly ministry. The Holy Spirit was personally at one with the Son of Man from the time of His conception throughout His whole earthly life. Listen at the wondrous annunciation made to the Virgin Mary: "The Holy Ghost shall come upon thee, and the power of the Highest shall overshadow thee: therefore also that holy thing which shall be born of thee shall be called the Son of God" (Luke 1:35). At His baptism, the Holy Spirit in form like a dove came upon Him. Jesus said, "If I cast out devils by the Spirit of God, then the kingdom of God is come unto you" (Matt. 12:28). Thus He clearly sets forth their entire co-operation. Jesus said again, "I and my Father are one" (John 10:30). So these three persons, Father, Son and Holy Ghost, form the Trinity in unity. The Father has a body and the Son has a body, but the Holy Spirit dwells in the body of the Father and in the body of the Son, thus uniting the Father and the Son and making One of the three.

The Spirit is not a vapor or an influence, as many suppose, but a real Person going forth from the Father and Son, and serving in their behalf. He is God himself imparted to work in His children the good pleasure of His own will, making His grace availing in them and for them, helping their infirmities, witnessing to their salvation, and carrying into effect all the divine administrations of the kingdom of grace.

Since the Holy Spirit has no body, God has to reveal Him and His work to us through material emblems, and of these we shall treat in the following chapter.

CHAPTER II.

In the Scriptures the personal work of the Holy Spirit with reference to our salvation is represented to our intellectual conception by means of symbols with which our physical senses are familiar. These symbols are God's chosen illustrations from natural things by which He seeks to help us to understand the work of the Spirit and get a proper conception, through the physical senses, of important spiritual truths. Our intellects, accustomed to deal with material things, can by means of divinely-designated symbols more easily comprehend the real import and character of the operations of the Spirit of God in our hearts. And since the following symbols are taken from Scripture, and are therefore divinely designated, we are sure that we shall not err in the application thus made by the Holy Spirit himself.

1. Wind. "The wind bloweth where it listeth, and thou hearest the sound thereof, but canst not tell whence it cometh, nor whither it goeth: so is every one that is born of the Spirit" (John 3:8). Other Scriptures bearing on this line are: Gen. 1:2; 2:7; Ezek. 37:9, 10; Acts 2:2.

2. Water. "In the last day, that great day of the feast, Jesus stood and cried, saying, If any man thirst, let him come unto Me, and drink. He that believeth on Me, as the Scripture hath said, Out of his belly shall flow rivers of living water. But this spake He of the Spirit, which they that believe on Him should receive: for the Holy Ghost was not yet given; because that Jesus was not yet glorified" (John 7:37-39). Other Scriptures: Ps. 1:3; Isa. 44:3, 4; Ezek. 36:25-30; 47:1-5; Eph. 5:26.

3. Wine. On the day of Pentecost it was said of those who had received the Holy Ghost, "These men are full of new wine" (Acts 2:13). The figure here lies in the effect produced.

"And be not drunk with wine, wherein is excess; but be filled with the Spirit" (Eph. 5:18). (See Matt. 9:17).

4. Oil. "How God anointed Jesus of Nazareth with the Holy Ghost and with power" (Acts 10:38). "But the anointing which ye have received of Him abideth in you, and ye need not that any man teach you: but as the same anointing teacheth you of all things, and is truth, and is no lie, and even as it hath taught you, ye shall abide in Him" (1 John 2:27). (See Ps. 23:5; 92:10; 105:15; Matt. 25:1-3.)

5. Milk and Honey. The land of Canaan is said to be a land that flowed with milk and honey, thus making them a twofold symbol of the Holy Spirit. (See Ex. 3:8; 33:3; Num. 13:27.)

6. Seal and Pledge. This twofold symbol may be found in the following Scriptures: "Ye were sealed with that Holy Spirit of promise, which is the earnest of our inheritance until the redemption of the purchased possession, unto the praise of His glory" (Eph. 1:13, 14). "Grieve not the Holy Spirit of God, whereby ye are sealed unto the day of redemption" (Eph. 4:30). "Who hath also sealed us, and given the earnest of the Spirit in our hearts" (2 Cor. 1:22). "A seal is the impress of the government by the placing of the chosen design so as to secure the object sealed from any antagonism." It means that the object upon which it is placed has the authority and protection of the government. "An earnest is that which makes the promise secure, the forfeiture which stands for the promise until the promise is fulfilled." Thus the operation of the Holy Spirit in our hearts is presented to us under the twofold symbol of seal and pledge.

7. Tongues of Fire. "And there appeared unto them cloven tongues like as of fire" (Acts 2:3). Here we have another symbol of the Holy Ghost. Fire alone is never a symbol of the Spirit, but only in its connection with tongues. The principal means of communicating thought among men is by the human voice, of which the tongue is the chief instrument. The gospel is God's communication to men, and, as we have seen, is made efficient by the direct power of the Holy Ghost. So

then, when the disciples were waiting for the enduement of power, it was a most fitting symbolism that the Holy Ghost should take the form of visible tongues *like as of* fire resting upon them. The Holy Spirit is not the tongue, but His power is to be felt through tongues speaking in every direction. In other words, He is to make the tongue of the divinely-chosen messenger efficient in preaching the gospel unto the uttermost parts of the earth. His power upon the disciples is then the voice of God speaking to a sinning world.

Some think that each symbol represents a particular operation of the Spirit, but I do not so understand it. The words of Jesus in John 3:8 would lead us to believe that the Spirit regenerates under the symbol of wind; and Acts 2:2 shows that He came as wind on the day of Pentecost. He also appeared on that occasion as tongues of fire, and as wine. Jesus, in speaking of the Baptism of the Spirit, used the symbol of water (John 7:37-39). The symbol of oil applies to the Baptism sometimes (Matt. 25:1-13), and so does the seal and pledge. Milk and honey can be thus applied. All these symbols are used in representing the Baptism; but any symbol which represents an operation other than the baptism is interchangeable among all other operations. To map out a plan through which the Spirit uses each symbol for one particular operation would be nothing more nor less than to build theory, since such a plan would be without a Scriptural foundation. In this book we propose to build no theory, but to stand upon the Word.

At the baptism of the Lord, the Holy Spirit assumed the form of a dove and descended upon Him. This symbol was not used at any other time nor did the Spirit assume this form other than in His visible descension upon the Son of God. The reason for this may be seen in many ways. The offering of the poor was a dove. The Spirit of Christ was gentle like a dove. Thus the character and sacrifice of Christ could most fittingly be represented by the Holy Spirit in the form of a dove. After the Master had rendered obedience in the fulfilling of right-

eousness, there descended upon Him the Holy Spirit, choosing
as the fitting form in which to appear before men and to their
natural vision, a dove—the emblem of peace—and the fitting
sacrifice for peace between God and the sinning world. It is
only then in the Spirit's relationship to Christ that the symbol
of the dove is used. It is never a symbol of His relationship
to men either as saints or sinners. Since we propose in this
book to deal with the offices of the Spirit in His relation to men,
we omit this symbol from the enumeration above.

We have thus mentioned seven symbols which the Holy
Ghost has chosen to represent to us His manifold operations in
our hearts. There may be other symbols, but it seems to us
that these cover the ground. No one type of nature is sufficient to embody His whole ministry, therefore it is only natural
that there should be just seven types setting forth His manifold operations. But let no one think for a moment that all or
any of these symbols thus used are the Holy Ghost, or that the
Holy Ghost is the symbol. Neither the wind, the water, the
wine, the oil, the milk and honey, the seal and pledge, nor the
tongues of fire, are the Holy Ghost, but each is simply a repre-
sentation of the operation of the Spirit in our hearts. Just as
soon as we reach the place that we can comprehend the operation without the symbol, God removes the symbol, but the
reality abides.

"Living as we do in a material world, and encompassed with
material senses, God speaks to us through material emblems.
But the time is coming when He will not speak to us in parables, but will bring our spirits into immediate vision and communion with the Father. Then the soul will be able to dispense
with all secondary terms and types, and having lost itself in the
ocean of divine nature, and being one with the Father and the
Son and the Holy Spirit, it will not need to be taught any more,
but will see and know all things in the cloudless comprehension
which the Spirit will constantly give to the glorified soul."—
Dr. Watson.

CHAPTER III.

In Revelation 1:4; 3:1, and 4:5, we read of the seven Spirits of God; while in Ephesians 4:4 we are told that there is but one Spirit. Harmony exists between these Scriptures in the fact that there is but one Spirit, yet the Holy Spirit, as sent forth for the illumination, comfort and edification of all the subjects of God's redeeming grace, is represented to our finite minds by sevens. This does not infer that the Spirit is divided, but He is the one Spirit in whatever way He may operate in us.

Doctor Seiss says, "There is a sacred significance in numbers: not cabalistic, not fanciful; but proceeding from the very nature of things, well settled in the Scriptures, and universally acknowledged in all the highest and deepest systems of human thought and religion."

Three represents the Trinity—Father, Son and Holy Ghost.

Four represents humanity.

Seven is the union of three and four, hence it represents salvation, or the Christ-life in His saints. It is connected with whatever touches the covenant between God and man. It also signifies dispensational fulness. It is complete in that which is temporal. Thus we are not surprised to find that the Holy Spirit, in His offices, administrations, operations, and in whatever way He may deal with man, is presented to our minds in the number seven.

We have already seen that there are seven symbols which the Spirit uses to present to our finite minds the different ways He operates in our hearts, and now we are to see that there are seven operations of the Spirit. May the Holy Spirit help us to a proper understanding of these mighty things.

1. The Spirit Strives (Gen. 6:3). It is the office of the Spirit to convict of sin, both actual and inbred. The Holy

Ghost often strives with careless Christians to move them out into active service for God.

2. The Spirit Regenerates (John 3 : 5-8). To be born again or from above is to receive a new heart. This change in the heart and life is wrought by and through the power of the Holy Ghost.

3. The Spirit Sanctifies (1 Pet. 1 : 2). Sanctification is the destruction of the old man—the taking away of the old heart—the eradication of the carnal mind. "Jesus, that He might sanctify the people with His own blood, suffered without the gate." The Holy Ghost applies the blood of Jesus to the heart, and the heart is sanctified. The blood is the means by which we are sanctified, while the Holy Ghost is the Agent.

4. The Spirit Witnesses (1 John 5 : 6). He witnesses to our justification (Rom. 8: 16), to our sanctification (Heb. 10: 15), to divine healing, to answer to prayer, etc.

5. The Spirit Teaches (John 14: 26). The Spirit must teach the sinner how to be saved. Every saved soul realizes his need of divine guidance, of divine illumination, of that wisdom which is from above, and to every such soul there comes the blessed assurance that he will be so guided and lead. The Spirit enables him to understand the Scriptures, to perceive spiritual things, to know God's will, and to receive divine wisdom. "For we know not what we should pray for as we ought: but the Spirit himself maketh intercession for us with groanings which cannot be uttered" (Rom. 8: 26). Into all the details of the ministry of the gospel the Holy Spirit enters. It was by the direction of the Spirit that Philip was sent into the desert to preach to and baptize the Ethiopian eunuch (Acts 8: 29-39). The Spirit suffered not Paul and Silas to go into Bithynia when they desired of themselves to do so (Acts 16: 7). And it was the Spirit that sent Peter to preach to Cornelius (Acts 10: 19 and 11: 12). And so all through the ministry of the apostles they were directed by the Holy Spirit.

6. The Spirit Anoints (Ps. 23: 5, and Acts 4: 31). The purpose of these anointings is to prepare us for service, or to

enable us to undergo some particular trial. Many miss all the sweetness of a trial by failing to tarry before God until He anoints them for that trial.

7. The Spirit Baptizes (Matt. 3 : 11). This is the culmination of the offices of the Spirit; it is the grand climax. This is the seal of the Spirit of promise, by which seal we are designated as the Bride of the Lamb.

Thus I have given the seven offices of the Holy Spirit with reference to man's salvation. There may be others, but it seems to me that they can be enumerated under these seven. It may be that "the anointing" spoken of in 1 John 2 : 27 is the same as the Baptism, but there is no doubt that we may several times, either before or after our Baptism, receive "an anointing" of the Spirit to prepare us for special service or trial (Acts 4 : 29-31). But be all this as it may—consider that there are seven, less than seven, or more than seven operations of the Spirit, or explain "The Seven Spirits of God" as you may—it still remains a fact that the Spirit does operate in man's behalf, and that "there are diversities of operations, . . . but the manifestation of the Spirit is given to every man to profit withal." So any arrangement you may wish to make of the operations or offices of the Spirit with reference to man's salvation, any theory you may wish to build, will not at all affect the main truth upon which we take our position in this book.

"For He whom God hath sent speaketh the words of God: for God giveth not the Spirit by measure unto Him" (John 3 : 34). I draw from this that the Spirit is given to no man in His full embodiment, but always by measure. I mean to say that Jesus had the Holy Ghost in all of His operations, in all of His administrations, in all of His gifts, and in all of His power as far as the relation between them existed; and therefore the symbol chosen in the case of Jesus was that of a dove: but that our capacities are too small to receive Him rather than by measure, though we may be filled with Him; hence He never comes upon us as a dove. Just as one drop of water contains all the fulness of water, and as much so as a barrel, and yet the barrel cannot contain all water; even so we may have all the fulness of God, or we may be filled with all the fulness of God; and yet we can receive Him only by measure.

Realizing then that we receive the Spirit by measure, it is easy to see that not every one who knows the Holy Ghost has received the Baptism; and that not every one who has the Holy Ghost in him is filled with the Spirit. I met the Holy Ghost in conviction, I learned to know Him in justification, and I have been acquainted with Him ever since.

Before the sinner will either desire or seek after salvation, he must realize his true condition and seek for divine help. Both the knowledge of this need and the power to seek for salvation are wrought in his soul by the agency of the Holy Spirit. Our Lord set before His disciples the truth that the power to receive Him as Saviour, and the efficiency of the Word itself, were dependent upon the direct influences of the Holy Spirit (John 6: 32-64). Salvation, however, is something more than being a member of God's kingdom; it is the pledge, through the indwelling Spirit, of joint-heirship with Christ to all the glorious inheritance of God. We read in the Word, "Now if any man have not the Spirit of Christ, he is none of his" (Rom. 8:9). But this does not argue in the least degree that all who have the Spirit have the Baptism of the Spirit; in fact, it proves the opposite. To have the Baptism of the Spirit, is to hold God's pledge of resurrection "out from among the dead" and the entrance into the full enjoyment of being the Bride of Christ. Jesus said to His disciples, "But ye know Him; for He dwelleth with you, and shall be in you." So you see that all who have the Spirit are not baptized with the Spirit.

In passing let us call to mind the fact that some have greater capacities for containing God than others. One may have a greater measure of the Spirit than another, and yet his capacity may not be as near filled as the other's. The Baptism of the Spirit includes or implies all other operations of the Spirit

mentioned above, fills the spirit and soul and body of the recipient, and completely envelops the entire being with power
and glory.

So having taken this survey of the operations of God's Spirit
in our hearts, let us now pass on to the manifestation. But
this we must leave for the following chapter.

CHAPTER IV.

"AND there are diversities of operations, but it is the same God which worketh all in all. But the manifestation of the Spirit is given to every man to profit withal" (1 Cor. 12:6, 7).

It appears to me from the above Scripture that there is a manifestation which follows each operation of the Spirit in our hearts. I also gather from other Scriptures that each operation of the Spirit includes two kinds or phases of manifestation. First, there are the invisible and internal influences or manifestation; and second, the visible and external manifestation: and since there is profit in the manifestation, it is given to every man in whom the Spirit operates.

1. We know that when the Spirit strives with a man, there is an uneasiness in his soul, and a troubled look on his face (Dan. 5:6; Acts 24:25; Ps. 42:5).

2. Justification brings the invisible manifestation of peace (Rom. 5:1), and the visible manifestation of a new life (Eph. 2:1-5; Gal. 5:22, 23; 2 Cor. 5:17).

3. Sanctification brings the invisible manifestation of joy (Luke 24:50-52), and the visible manifestation of fruit unto holiness (Rom. 6:22).

4. The witness of the Spirit brings an internal manifestation of confidence towards God (1 John 3:20-22), and an external manifestation of testimony to the world (Rom. 10:10).

5. A person who is taught by the Spirit has an internal manifestation of an insight into the words of Jesus (John 14:26), and an external manifestation of wisdom, especially in regard to the Christ-life, and the hidden things of God (Gen. 41:37-40; Dan. 1:19, 20; Acts 4:13; 18:24-26).

6. A person who receives an anointing of the Spirit has an internal manifestation of an insight into God's dealings with

His children (Ps. 23 : 5, 6), and an external manifestation of boldness and liberty (Acts 4 : 29-31).

7. The Baptism of the Spirit brings an invisible manifestation of living water (John 7 : 37-39), and a visible or external manifestation of tongues (Acts 2 : 3, 4).

There are other manifestations of the Spirit which I have not mentioned, but as far as I have gone I have tried to build upon the Word. It is possible that I have made some error in giving the manifestation following each of the first six operations; for in regard to these the Word is not so clear. I will therefore give my readers the liberty to rearrange these manifestations if they choose; but you must remember, "the manifestation of the Spirit is given to every man" in whom He operates, and also your manifestation must be Scriptural. But when we come to the manifestation following the Baptism of the Spirit, we have a "thus saith the Lord." We may think for many years that we have the manifestation of the Spirit following any or all of the first six operations, and then find out that we have been mistaken; but not so in regard to the visible manifestation of the seventh.

In proof of the above, in regard to the visible manifestation, we quote from the words of Jesus: "But when the Comforter is come, whom I will send unto you from the Father, even the Spirit of truth, which proceedeth from the Father, He shall testify of Me: and ye also shall bear witness, because ye have been with Me from the beginning" (John 15 : 26, 27). How people do twist this Scripture to keep from admitting that the manifestation following the Baptism is speaking with tongues! One man, for example, after quoting the Scripture above, writes: "Now Jesus was not speaking here of the Baptism of the Holy Ghost for individual believers.

"The apostles collectively, represented the Church as a body: and the promise was that He would send the Comforter, not into them, but unto them; and that He should abide, not in them, but with them forever.

"The baptism of the Holy Ghost, and the reception of the

Spirit by individual Christians, is not in question here at all. If it were, the language would be, I will send Him upon you; and He shall dwell in you forever. But instead it reads, 'unto you,' and 'shall dwell with you.'

"So this evidently refers to the Holy Spirit coming to the church to take up His office work; and to convict, save, sanctify and fill each individual soul that will let Him."

The writer then makes a few comments and quotes: "He shall testify of me." Then he interrogates: "What will He say of me?" As an answer to his own question he quotes 1 John 5 : 6-10, and continues:

"So we see that the Comforter's testimony, when He came to the Church, and to any heart, is to testify to that heart of the divine Sonship of Jesus, and every Christian has this testimony in his soul: 'For no man can say that Jesus is the Lord, but by the Holy Ghost' (1 Cor. 12 : 3).

"So much for the beautiful promise that when the Comforter is come, whom I will send unto you from the Father, even the Spirit of truth, which proceedeth from the Father, he shall testify of me. Amen!"

On the same page of the same paper the writer, after quoting John 14 : 15-17, says:

"The phrase, 'He dwelleth with you,' had no reference to their personal salvation, but simply to their work.

"The Holy Spirit is both with and in all regenerated people. The blessed Holy Spirit dwells with, and among all God's people, whatever may be their degree of grace; and to say that the Holy Ghost is with regenerated people, but not in them, is a mistake."

Again, he writes: "So the words of Jesus to the apostles: 'For He dwelleth with you and shall be in you,' does not deny that the Spirit is in a truly regenerated heart; but they can only mean that the apostles had not received the blessed Comforter in His glorious fulness."

And again: "So when Jesus said to his apostles, 'and he shall be in you,' he no doubt referred to the baptism of the

Holy Ghost in Matt. 3 : 11, 12; which baptism was to thoroughly 'purge his floor' and 'burn up the chaff,' so they could be filled with the Holy Ghost. And all this was accomplished in the disciples on the day of Pentecost."

The best I can understand the above quotation the writer is teaching that of all that is said in the fourteenth, fifteenth, and sixteenth chapters of John concerning the Holy Ghost, nothing refers to the Baptism of the Spirit except the expression, "And shall be in you." That in all other cases Jesus was speaking, not of the "Baptism of the Holy Ghost for individual believers"; but He "evidently refers to the Holy Spirit coming to the Church to take up His office work; and to convict, save, sanctify"—and then he adds, "Fill each individual soul that will let Him."

Listen with care: "The Holy Spirit is both with and in all regenerated people. . . So when Jesus said to his apostles, 'And he shall be in you,' he no doubt referred to the Baptism of the Holy Ghost in Matt. 3: 11, 12." Thus he teaches that all regenerated people have the Baptism of the Holy Ghost referred to in Matt. 3: 11, 12. From the words of Jesus, *"Shall be* in you," we must infer that the in-coming and in-dwelling of the Holy Ghost in His relation to the disciples was still an act of the future, and since "The Holy Spirit is . . . in all regenerated people," according to the above writer, the only logical conclusion is that the disciples at this time were not regenerated. Still, they had the Holy Ghost with them (John 15 : 17), and their names were written in heaven (Luke 10 : 20). When a man tries to support an unscriptural theory, he gets in a tangle.

We quote again his own words: "So when Jesus said to his apostles, 'And he shall be in you,' he no doubt referred to the Baptism of the Holy Ghost in Matt. 3 : 11, 12"; and then commenting on John 15 : 25-27, he says: "The Baptism of the Holy Ghost and the reception of the Spirit by individual Christians, is not in question here at all. . . So this evidently refers to the Holy Spirit coming to . . . fill each individual soul that will let Him." "Which baptism was to thoroughly 'purge His floor' and 'burn up the chaff,' so they could be filled with the Holy Ghost." He says that the "filling" and the "baptism" are the same, and that they had to be baptized so they could be filled. Strange statements, indeed!

Again let us notice: "So this (John 15 : 25-27) evidently refers to the Holy Spirit coming to the Church to take up His office work; and to convict, save, sanctify, etc." If this be true, then the Holy Spirit never came to the Church to convict, save, and sanctify until the promise of John 15 : 25-27 was fulfilled; and this (John 15 : 25-27), the writer says, was a promise to "fill each individual soul that will let Him"; and that "when Jesus said to his apostles, 'And he shall be in you,' he no doubt referred to the Baptism of the Holy Ghost in Matt. 3: 11, 12," thus making John 15:25-27 and Matt. 3 : 11, 12 one and the same. But he had just said that they had no connection.

The same writer, in another article, commenting on John 15: 26, says: "I want to warn my reader against twisting the blessed Scriptures to support certain theories and then adding what he thinks they lack." I would advise him to take warning from his own signal!

If it is true that the Holy Spirit never had any office work in the world until Pentecost, please explain the following Scriptures: "My Spirit shall not always strive with man" (Gen. 6:3). "I will take of the Spirit which is upon thee, and put it upon them" (Num. 11 : 17). "The Spirit entered into me when He spake unto me" (Ezek. 2 : 2). "The Spirit took me up" (Ezek. 3 : 12). "The Spirit of the Lord fell upon me" (Ezek. 11 : 5). "I am full of power by the Spirit of the Lord" (Micah 3 : 8). "And he shall be filled with the Holy Ghost, even from his mother's womb" (Luke 1 : 15). And then the words of Jesus: "But ye know Him; for He dwelleth with you." Listen: "This is the word of the Lord unto Zerubbabel, saying, Not by might, nor by power, but by My Spirit, saith the Lord of hosts" (Zech. 4 : 6). "Ye do always resist the Holy Ghost: *as your fathers did,* so do ye" (Acts 7 : 51).

So the Scriptures seem to teach that all through the ages the Spirit has been at work in the hearts of men, but no one ever received the baptism until Pentecost. "For the Holy Ghost was not yet given; because that Jesus was not yet glorified" (John 7 : 39). This verse certainly refers to the Baptism, and not to the Spirit's work in convicting, saving, and sanctifying; for "this spake He of the Spirit, which they that believe on him *should* receive." There can be no reasonable doubt that the disciples, prior to Pentecost, received a measure of the Spirit, as had been true of others in previous periods. Some measure of spiritual light and some measure of spiritual power was theirs, as had been of holy men who lived before them; but Jesus taught them to pray for the Holy Ghost, and to seek the Baptism which had been promised by John. So we read when they came, saying. "Teach us to pray," He, after giving to them the ideal form of prayer, taught them that the Holy Spirit Himself would come in answer to prayer. From the analogy of the earthly parent He draws the lesson: "If ye, then, being evil, know how to give good gifts unto your children: how much more shall your heavenly Father give the Holy Spirit to them that ask Him" (Luke 11 : 13).

I believe that the expression, "He dwelleth with you," means that the disciples had the Holy Ghost in the same manner in which holy men had had Him in the ages past; and yet Jesus said, "I *will* pray the Father, and he *shall* give you another Comforter." "For if I go not away, the Comforter will not come unto you; but if I depart, I will send Him unto you." Here Jesus clearly teaches that the coming of the Comforter unto the disciples was yet a future event; and since the Spirit had all through the ages been with them, "His coming" must refer to the Baptism. Indeed, it would be strange that Jesus should say, "The Comforter dwelleth *with* you"—now, at the present time—and mean exactly the same blessing as He does in the preceding verse, when He says, "I will pray the Father, and he shall give you another Comforter, that he may abide *with* you forever." I mean, it would be strange that Jesus should promise them a blessing in one verse and then tell them in the next verse that they already had that blessing. But this is exactly what the above quotation teaches. The same writer, commenting on John 15 : 25-27, says:

"The Baptism of the Holy Ghost, and the reception of the Spirit by individual Christians is not in question here at all. If it were, the language would be, I will send Him upon you; and He shall dwell in you forever. But instead it reads, 'unto you,' and 'shall dwell with you.'" Now, the phrase, "Shall dwell with you," I have been unable to find in this connection. I think he must refer to John 14: 16, where it is said, "Abide with you forever." He clearly states that the promise of the Comforter to abide with them forever does not refer to the Baptism of the Spirit, but refers to the Holy Spirit coming to the Church to take up His office work; and that the phrase, "He dwelleth with you," had no reference to their personal salvation, but to their work. Since they already had the Comforter dwelling with them, the promise in John 14: 16 was the promise of nothing more than they already had, and nothing more than the people of God had always possessed. This is certainly the teaching of the above quotation.

But we do not think that Jesus would tell His disciples that He was going to pray the Father to send them the Comforter in a certain measure, and then tell them they already had Him in that measure.

But He says to them, "I *will* pray the Father, and He *shall* give you another Comforter; that He may abide with you forever; even the Spirit of truth, whom the world cannot receive, because it seeth Him not, neither knoweth Him: but ye know Him, for He dwelleth with you, and shall be in you. I will not leave you comfortless: I will come to you." "But the Comforter, which is the Holy Ghost, whom the Father will send in My name, He shall teach you all things, and bring all things to your remembrance, whatsoever I have said unto you." "But when the Comforter is come, whom I will send unto you from the Father, even the Spirit of truth, which proceedeth from the Father, He shall testify of Me; and ye also shall bear witness, because ye have been with Me from the beginning." "But now I go my way to Him that sent Me; and none of you asketh Me, Whither goeth thou? But because I have said these things unto you, sorrow hath filled your heart. Nevertheless, I tell you the truth; it is expedient for you that I go away: for if I go not away, the Comforter will not come unto you; but if I depart, I will send Him unto you. And when He is come, He will reprove the world of sin, and of righteousness, and of judgment: of sin, because they believe not on Me; of righteousness, because I go to my Father, and ye see Me no more; of judgment, because the prince of this world is judged. I have yet many things to say unto you, but ye cannot bear them now. Howbeit when He, the Spirit of truth, is come, He will guide you into all truth: for He shall not speak of Himself; but whatsoever He shall hear, that shall He speak: and He will show you things to come. He shall glorify me: for He shall receive of Mine, and shall shew it unto you."

I can see no reason for saying that none of these words refer to the Baptism of the Spirit for individuals, except the expression, "Shall be in you." According to my understanding, all the above promises concerning the coming of the Comforter refer to the same thing. If we take the words of Jesus just as they stand, they are very simple. He, in the midst of His disciples, seems to say quietly, but positively, I am going away. Because I said this, you are sad. But it is best for you that I go away; for I cannot stay with you alway; and after I am gone I will send you a Comforter, with whom you are already acquainted, for He dwelleth with you; but I am going to send Him in a greater measure; and He shall be with you for ever. There are many things I have to tell you, but you cannot understand them now. But remember, when the Comforter comes, He shall testify of Me and reprove the world of sin, and of righteousness, and of judgment. Then He will begin to teach you about Me, and to bring to your remembrance the things I have said to you, and enable you to understand them. The above quotation teaches that these words referred, not to the Baptism, but simply to the coming of the Comforter to dwell with the Church; but Jesus said that the Comforter already "dwelleth with you," but I am going to send Him unto you in a fuller measure, and when He comes He will testify, teach, etc.

Let us again note some things Jesus said the Comforter would do when He came: "He shall testify of Me; He shall glorify Me; He will reprove the world; He shall teach you; and He shall shew you things to come."

Now, to testify and to bear witness is one and the same thing; but to testify and to teach are two different things. The above quotation says: "So we see that the *Comforter's* testimony, when he came to the Church, and to any heart, is to testify to that heart of the divine Sonship of Jesus, and every Christian has this testimony in his soul: 'For no man can say that Jesus is the Lord, but by the Holy Ghost' (1 Cor. 12:3).

Here the writer clearly teaches that the promise of the Comforter to come and testify of Jesus meant no more than to enable the disciples to say by the Holy Ghost that Jesus is the Lord. It shows wisdom on the part of the writer that he adds, "Every Christian has this testimony in his soul." It is evident that Peter had this testimony in his soul before this occasion, for when Jesus asked His disciples, "Whom say ye that I am?" "Simon Peter answered and said, Thou art the Christ, the Son of the living God. And Jesus answered and said unto him, Blessed art thou, Simon Barjona: for flesh and blood hath not revealed it unto thee, but My Father which is in heaven" (Matt. 16:15-17). Here we see from the words of Christ that it is the testimony of the *Father* that reveals the divine Sonship of Jesus; and this accords exactly with the Scripture on which the writer was commenting above, viz.: "For this (the witness to the divine Sonship of Jesus) is the witness of God (the Father) which He (the Father) hath testified of His (the Father's) Son" (1 John 5:9). And all this accords with other Scriptures. (See Matt. 3:17 and 17:5.) But our brother says that the witness of the divine Sonship of Jesus is the *Comforter's* testimony. And since

Peter had this witness already, we may imagine Jesus saying
to His apostles: "I will pray the Father, and He shall give you
another Comforter. But when the Comforter is come, He
shall testify of Me"—and then turning to Peter and saying,
"Simon, this promise does not include you; the Comforter has
already come to you and testified of Me, since you have the
witness that I am the Son of God." STRANGE! STRANGE!

We cannot believe that Jesus would so mock His disciples;
but that in all His words concerning the coming of the Comforter, He was promising them a blessing which none of them
at that time had.

Again we say, to testify and to bear witness is one and the
same. Jesus said, "He shall testify of Me: and ye also shall
bear witness." Two facts here are clearly seen: First, that the
two testimonies should be of the same nature; and second, that
the testimony of the Comforter should precede the testimony
of the recipient.

Now, have all these promises of Jesus concerning the coming of the Comforter and what He would do when He came
ever been fulfilled, and if so, where, when, and under what
circumstances?

There can be no reasonable doubt that the beginning of the
fulfillment of these promises is recorded in the second chapter
of the Acts of the Apostles. Jesus had said, "I will send the
Comforter, and He shall be in you, and when He comes He
shall testify of Me." "And suddenly there came a sound from
heaven as of a rushing mighty wind, and it filled all the house
where they were sitting. And there appeared unto them cloven
tongues like as of fire, and it sat upon each of them." (I
will send Him *unto* you.) "And they were all filled with the
Holy Ghost." (He shall be *in* you), and began to speak with
other tongues, as the *Spirit* gave them utterance." ("When
the Comforter is come, whom I will send *unto* you from the
Father, even the Spirit of truth, which proceedeth from the
Father, he shall testify of Me.") The speaking with other
tongues was not the testimony of the disciples—it was without
an effort on their part—but the Holy Ghost, having come into

them and having taken possession of their entire being, was giving the utterance. So instead of looking here for the fulfillment of the promise, "He shall be in you," and then turning over to 1 John for the fulfillment of the promise, "He shall testify of Me," we find it all right here in the second chapter of the Acts.

It was while the disciples were speaking with other tongues that the world rushed up and was reproved, *i. e.,* convicted of sin, and of righteousness, and of judgment. Hence, there was a great stir among them and many of them added to the Church. "But," objects some one, "hold on, brother; it was not the speaking with tongues that convicted that crowd; it was *Peter's* sermon." Wise suggestion! The text says that Peter stood up with the eleven and preached. To whom were they preaching? "Jews, devout men, out of every nation under heaven." Were they all of the same tongue? "How hear we every man in his own tongue, wherein we were born?" Did the twelve preach to all of them, or to just that part of them who could understand the native language of the apostles? "Peter, standing up with the eleven, lifted up his voice, and said unto them, Ye men of Judea, and all ye that dwell at Jerusalem." In what college had the apostles been to learn all these languages? Let the one who suggested that it was not the speaking with tongues, but *Peter's* sermon, that convicted the crowd, answer. While waiting a reply, I remain silent on the question.

"But," says another, "I do not think that any one preached on that occasion except Peter." Very well. Whether one, twelve, or one hundred and twenty did the preaching, the fact that they were all preached to remains true. "How do you know," says another, "but that the whole one hundred and twenty preached, and that in this number there was a representative of each nation, and that, after all, all the preaching that was done was done by each one in his own tongue? A Parthian preaching to Parthians; a Mede preaching to Medes, etc.?" "Behold, are not all these which speak Galilaeans?"

There is not a single Galilaean mentioned in their congregation (Acts 2:9-11).

So, dear reader, we leave it to you to say who preached or who did not preach on this occasion; with our Bible open before us, it clearly appears from the text that conviction was brought upon that crowd by the Spirit giving utterance. How some preachers do dislike to hear this! "Tongues are no good," they cry; "they cause confusion; it was *Peter's* sermon that did the work." May the Lord bless you, brother. You may theorize, you may preach your biggest sermon, you may sweat; but after you finish, the facts stand just as they have ever stood.

But from the words of Jesus we are taught that after the Comforter's testimony, the disciples were to bear witness also. This, of course, refers to their testimony in their own language. After Pentecost, when they met people of their own tongue they themselves bore witness; when they met people of other tongues the Spirit gave the utterance.

Some one objects: "The disciples never spake with tongues after the day of Pentecost." How did Peter, a Jew, ignorant and unlearned, preach to Cornelius, a man in Caesarea, a centurion of the band called the Italian band? What are you going to do with Stephen, the deacon, for talking to the Libertines, and Cyrenians, and Alexandrians, and to them of Cilicia and of Asia after Pentecost? (Acts 6:9.) Better call Stephen up before the Church I trow, and inform him that Pentecost is a thing of the past. Now, there goes Philip down there to preach to that Ethiopian, and he will have to talk with tongues when he gets there (Acts 8 : 26-39). It seems that we just can't keep these holiness preachers straight. "Why, I thought Philip knew that talking with tongues would tear up the Church. There was our great church at Jerusalem, and we were getting on so nicely; but some of them kept speaking with tongues, until the authorities took steps against it; and now you see our Church is scattered. I told you so (Acts 8: 1-4). Philip, he started out like He might do some good; he went down to the city of Samaria and preached Christ to the people, and some of them were saved and sanctified, and he organized a church, and they are getting on nicely (Acts 8: 5-13). I do not know how he managed to preach there so the people could understand him, but they tell me he is speaking with tongues now, and I fear he will hurt the cause."

"Well," says another, "we grant you that some of those who were among the one hundred and twenty spake with tongues afterward, but no one ever spake with tongues when they received the Holy Ghost after Pentecost." As a reply, we refer you to the case of Cornelius (Acts 10 : 46), and to the case of the disciples at Ephesus (Acts 19 : 6).

So, dismissing all theories and taking the Scriptures just as they are: the promise of Jesus that He would send the Comforter, that the Comforter would testify when He came; and then turning and finding in three different places in the Acts of the Apostles that the Comforter came, and that in each case, immediately after his arrival, those who received Him spoke with tongues; and then searching in vain to find that any other manifestation ever followed the Baptism of the Spirit; and remembering that "the manifestation of the Spirit is given to every man to profit withal;" we are fully persuaded that the Comforter's testimony is the Holy Ghost taking the tongue of that one whose entire being He has filled and speaking with it a language of which the recipient of the Holy Ghost knows nothing. If the Holy Ghost should use a person's tongue to speak a language with which that person is familiar, it would appear to be the testimony of the recipient; but since the Spirit always does His talking in another language, we must admit that it is the testimony of the Comforter. And besides, if this is not what Jesus meant when He said, "When the Comforter is come, He shall testify of Me," there is no Scripture to prove that this promise has ever been fulfilled; for there is no case on record in which any other manifestation that can be regarded as the Comforter's testimony ever followed the reception of the Spirit. Jesus said, *"When* He comes, He *shall* testify."* It may be that the testimony of the Comforter includes more than this, but beyond a reasonable doubt it certainly includes this as its primary basis.

Thus I am persuaded that by the expression, "He shall baptize you with the Holy Ghost and fire," much more is implied than either the witness to our sanctification, or the filling of the Spirit, or even both. In fact, it becomes apparent from our Lord's own association of thought in the teaching (of John, fourteenth, fifteenth, and sixteenth chapters, with the record in the second chapter of Acts, that He included in the promise of the Baptism of the Holy Ghost not only the filling of the Spirit, but the miraculous manifestation and enduement of power which came with the filling. And the Apostle Peter evidently so understood the teaching, when in Acts 2:39 he affirms that the blessing is continuative, abiding, and permanent. The conclusion, then, from the Master's teaching and Peter's statement is that the work of the Holy Spirit that was inaugurated on the day of Pentecost, and to continue unto the end of time, including both the external and internal manifestations, is the real Baptism of the Holy Ghost and fire.

When we remember that the Baptism of the Spirit must precede the preaching of the gospel in all nations, and that He was to be the active Agent with the apostles and the subsequent ministry in thus proclaimng the gospel to all nations, we can see a striking significance in these external manifestations as they appeared and formed part of the Baptism of the Holy Ghost. The disciples and the Church should ever realize the importance of the filling of the Spirit, but the world of unsaved would behold the external manifestation as a testimony to the physical senses that spiritual power had been given.

Here let me say that there is quite a difference between "the manifestation of the Spirit" and emotions. A person may have emotions without "the manifestation," or he may have "the manifestation" without emotions. An emotion is caused by the spiritual overcoming the physical. But such is not the case with regard to speaking with tongues. Of course, a person may be emotional while speaking with tongues, but neither is the other, nor does either cause the other. Leaping, shouting, dancing, etc., are emotions, while speaking with tongues is "the manifestation.

Many people to-day are claiming the Baptism of the Spirit without the manifestation, and are advancing every theory and argument they can to convince the world that they really are baptized with the Holy Ghost; and these theories are, no doubt, satisfying thousands of people who otherwise would be seeking for and obtaining the Baptism of the Spirit. In the following chapter we wish to point out the weakness, the unscriptural teachings, of the theories with which we have come in contact on this line.

CHAPTER V.

JULY 3, 1902, I received a definite witness that I was wholly sanctified. Being taught in that way, I accepted this as being the Baptism of the Holy Ghost. Fourteen months later I heard Dr. G. D. Watson preach at Falcon, N. C., through a ten-days' camp-meeting, during which time he made it clear to me that there was a difference between the "emptying" and the "filling." Still, I believed that I had the "filling," and while I have spoken often since then of both being included in sanctification, yet in instructing seekers I have been careful to tell them that the blood cleansed and then the Holy Ghost filled. I did not yet understand, however, that we had to tarry for the Holy Ghost after we were sanctified. I have scores of times testified to the Baptism of the Holy Ghost, stating that I would doubt the coat on my back before I would doubt that I was baptized with the Spirit. In this I was honest, for I do yet believe that nothing could have made me doubt it but light on the Word to the contrary.

Early last autumn (1906) there appeared in the "Way of Faith" an editorial on the revival in California. My heart said, Amen. Soon other accounts appeared. My heart became hungry, and I began to beg God to send the same revival into my own soul. I became hungry, not because I doubted what God had already done for me, but because I saw that there was more land ahead yet to be possessed. As but little teaching concerning the blessing or how to obtain it appeared, I was kept in the shade, and continued to beg God to baptize me with Pentecostal power. In five minutes after meeting the first person who had his Pentecost (January 15, 1907), the Holy Ghost was talking with my tongue. Three days later a certain brother said to me that he believed all who received the Baptism of the Holy Ghost would speak with tongues.

This was a surprise to me, as it was the first time that I had ever thought on this line. I replied that I had had the Baptism of the Spirit for years, but this was Pentecostal power. He told me that I had had the witness to my sanctification, but had not had the Baptism of the Spirit. So I decided that I would find out, and at once began to pray God to teach me. The Spirit seemed to confirm what the brother had told me. But fearing lest I should be mistaken, I took my Bible, and, with my heart open to God, I began to search the Word; and to the surprise of my heart I found it the teaching of the Word that all who receive the Baptism of the Holy Ghost speak with other tongues as the Spirit gives utterance. So I gladly yielded my former views and accepted new light on the Word. Soon I found that there was a great discussion among the people as to the evidence of Pentecost, and so it continues. The question stands: *Do all who receive the Baptism of the Holy Ghost speak with other tongues?*

I have noticed with care the argument presented on both sides of this question, but most especially that brought forward by the supporters of the negative. I have listened with patience and a heart open to truth to those I have met who wished to give me their views on the subject. I have argued with no one. I have read every article on the negative that I have been able to find. In all such arguments with which I have so far come in contact I have detected unscriptural doctrine. Many prominent writers are crying out, "Debates are unprofitable; they confuse the people"; and yet they keep right on flooding the papers with argument on the negative. It is easy to see that it is not so much the fear which these writers have that argument will confuse the people as it is the fear that they themselves will get "whipped." Since God, in His mercy, has enabled me to see the unscriptural teachings which are at this time appearing in the prominent holiness papers, and which are being advanced from the pulpits, and since there are thousands who are being kept in darkness and out of the Baptism of the Holy Ghost by these articles, I feel it my duty to God and to my brethren to point out the weakness, the unscriptural foundations of the teachings of which I have any knowledge. Such objections as I have personally met, and also those which have become prominent in these teachings, I give in my own words; but there are many objections which I have seen given only by individual writers, and in such cases, lest I should be accused of misrepresenting the writer, I give his exact words. I shall not personate any of my brethren of the opposite school. I desire not to defame the experience of any one, but to point out the error of the teachings of the supporters of the negative of the above question.

The first theory I mention is that Pentecost was intended only for the early disciples. This is without Scriptural foundation or a shadow of reason. From the fact that the Church has been practically without Pentecost for many centuries, people conclude that it was only for the early Church, and then to be withdrawn. Brother, God never withdrew Pentecost or any of its power from the Church; but the Church withdrew from Pentecost and lost its power. But, thank God, Pentecost in all its fulness is for each of us to-day. The words of Peter prove this (Acts 2: 39).

One objection advanced by the negative is the fault they can find in the lives of those who profess the Baptism of the Spirit with Pentecostal evidence. This has always been one of Satan's great points. HYPOCRITES! HYPOCRITES! This is the Devil's signal. By it he has ever kept thousands out of the experiences of justification and sanctification. He sounds the same note of warning against the present movement. We give as the foundation of the affirmative, not the lives of people, but the Word. We point you, not to our good deeds, but to Pentecost. There is not a man on earth but who is found fault with by others. If you see a fault in a man, it does not prove that God sees a fault in him. If we should count all with whom fault can be found out of the household of God, we would have none left. HYPOCRITES! That is no argument on the negative! We find them in every walk of life.

Another objection: All who speak with tongues seem to be so fixed in their way that no one can change them. Thank you for this point! They have become established (1 Cor. 15:58). I notice, however, that those who are accusing the Pentecostal people of being unteachable are those who have been leaders or those who are still desirous of leadership, and since this movement has no leader, they are much disturbed, and are lamenting the fact that the people will not follow them as they used to do.

"Well, I think it is time," says another, "for them to become established. Many of them have claimed the Baptism of the Holy Ghost for years, and some of them the baptism of fire, and now here they go after this 'tongue movement.'" Yes, thousands have claimed the Baptism of the Holy Ghost for years, and were honest in their profession. Honest, because they have been walking in the light which these leaders have been instrumental in giving; but now greater light has come, and it is clearly showing who have been honest and who are willing to sacrifice theory in order to go every step of the way. A person without the light may honestly profess the Baptism of the Spirit without Pentecostal evidence for years, and then find that he is mistaken; but we have met something now which makes its own profession, and which men do not profess under a mistake very long. But after a person is thoroughly established in Pentecost, the Spirit having manifested Himself with His tongue, you cannot make him doubt it.

Many are hung up on such men as John Fletcher, William Bramwell, Charles G. Finney, Jonathan Edwards, and Hudson Taylor. "How can you say that they did not have the Baptism of the Holy Ghost?" That sounds just like anti-holiness doctrine. So many people were hung up on this same peg a few years ago in regard to sanctification. "What has become of those who never heard of holiness?" has been asked by thousands. We would say, however, in regard to the above that they, with many others, were great and good men, and were wonderfully used of God in their day; but unless they had the Bible evidence of Pentecost, we can not Scripturally say that they had the Baptism of the Holy Ghost. Besides, I want to say, Fletcher, Bramwell, nor no other man is my

standard; I am building on the Word. When God gives light,
I have no right to ask if others walked in it or are walking in
it until I walk in it myself.

Again the negative speaks: "Many of the great holiness
preachers and leaders are on our side." Of course, the ideas
of great and good men have their weight; but it is a fact the
greatest teachers we have differ among themselves concerning
the Baptism of the Holy Ghost. One of the greatest teachers
on the Holy Ghost that I have ever seen did not claim to be
sanctified. He did not teach sanctification as a second work
of grace, and yet he claimed the Baptism of the Spirit. I
heard him preach through a week's meeting, and he preached
on the Holy Ghost each time. I never came near him without
feeling the power of God. What are you going to do with
that? Some claim that all of us receive the Baptism at conversion; some say after we are converted; some at the time
we are sanctified; others after we are sanctified; some say that
all who receive the Baptism speak with tongues; others say
that they do not. All believe that they can prove their position
by the Word. Now, who among this crowd has the Bible
evidence of Pentecost separate and distinct from the evidence
of any and all other degrees of grace?

Some say that those who are now obtaining their Petecost
and speaking with tongues are for the most part those who
have never before been settled in their religious experiences.
No doubt those who say this are honest, but they are surely
mistaken. On the other hand, I know it to be a fact that the
most pious and deeply spiritual people of the land, who have
been true to God for years, have been the first to receive their
Pentecost; while all Masonic and tobacco-chewing preachers
of whom I have any knowledge have so far fought the present
movement.

We are referred to those who have received their Pentecost,
spoke with tongues, and yet say that all who receive the
Baptism will not speak with tongues. Let me ask a question:
How many people have been led into the light of Pentecost,
made hungry for the Baptism, sought for and obtained the

Holy Ghost with Pentecostal evidence under such teaching? Very few, I trow. Those who do, as a rule, are those who have heard of the revival and been made hungry from another source. The majority of people are prejudiced against "tongues" anyway, and when they hear such teaching as that they are consoled and say, "Oh, well, I have the Baptism of the Holy Ghost, and I have no need of the 'tongue.'" And so they get farther away from the present revival than ever. I have met many who firmly believed that they had the Baptism, but after hearing the truth preached, decided that they were mistaken, sought and obtained the Baptism with Pentecostal evidence. If the negative of the above question had been preached to them, they never would have been convinced that they did not have the baptism. I know some who received their Pentecost and spoke with tongues, but took their stand on the negative, and they have so far been failures in getting others into the experience. Oh, how we should present the truth in such a way as to make the people hungry for Pentecost!

We are told that the presentation of the affirmative is calculated to hurt the cause, but facts prove the contrary. Bro. G. B. Cashwell tells me that while the Pentecostal meeting was going on at Dunn, N. C. (January, 1907), he received an urgent letter to go to High Point, N. C., at once. On reaching the place, he found that Pentecost had struck there, and people had been receiving the Baptism of the Spirit with Bible evidence; but certain ones had crept in and began to teach thus: "Brethren, this movement is of God, but you are making a great mistake to teach that speaking with other tongues is the evidence of the Baptism of the Spirit." Those who had been made hungry and had been seeking the Baptism ceased to come to the altar, confusion followed. The meeting was given over to Brother Cashwell. He presented the affirmative, and confusion was cleared away and the people came back into the unity of the Spirit. While here, Brother Cashwell received a telegram to go to Danville, Va., at once. On reaching the place, he found the same condition of affairs that he had found at High Point. He took charge and began to preach the truth.

The result was the same as that at High Point, N. C. Many other similar cases could be mentioned. So I am persuaded that if all of us should preach the negative, the revival would stop. There are but few who preach the negative except those who in their hearts want it to stop.

A preacher tells me that a sister with whom I am acquainted came to his meeting and seemed to be hungry for Pentecost, and so expressed herself to him; but in a few days she heard a sermon on the negative of the question; and when through, the preacher asked all who had the Baptism of the Holy Ghost to stand up, and among others who stood was this same woman.

I am well acquainted with the people in a certain small town in which a Pentecostal meeting was held soon after this revival first came to the Atlantic coast. A few received the Holy Ghost in this meeting, and the close of it left others seeking and the town somewhat stirred. Soon afterwards a holiness preacher came to this town and preached to a full congregation, in which were represented all the denominations of the town—Methodist, Baptist, Universalist, and Holiness. Writing of the service, he himself says: "Here we had a fine congregation in which all denominations were well represented; and all seemed to enjoy the services equally well." After this I visited the town, and learned that the preacher's own statement is about correct. I was told that a certain man in the town, whom I know to be bitter against holiness, gave the preacher five dollars, and told some one the next day that that was the best sermon he ever heard. Another, whom I am told is almost an infidel, said that he would not have taken five dollars for that sermon. The Universalist seemed to have enjoyed it equally well. But what could he have preached about to create such widespread approval? The burden of his message was that all who receive the Baptism of the Holy Ghost do not speak with tongues. Did any one receive the baptism that day? I await a reply.

We are told that we exalt the "gifts" above the "Giver." This is entirely a misrepresentation of the present revival. We tell people to seek for the Holy Ghost, and that when He comes He will testify; and therefore to tarry until the Spirit manifests Himself with their tongue. And then to covet earnestly the best gifts, and God will add them as He sees proper.

Some say that the evidence of Pentecost is the fruit of the Spirit, quoting for proof Matt. 7:20: "Wherefore by their fruits ye shall know them." Shall know who? Those who are baptized with the Holy Ghost? Not at all. Nothing is said here of the Baptism of the Spirit. Fruit is the evidence of justification, and every justified man bears fruit. This fruit is made perfect in sanctification. It is no evidence of Pentecost. Nowhere do we read: "And they were all filled with the Holy Ghost, and began to bear fruit."

Many ask: Is not some other Pentecostal manifestation as much an evidence of the Baptism as that of speaking with tongues? What other manifestation did they have on the day of Pentecost? Not a word is said about the impartation of the gift of wisdom, knowledge, faith, etc. Look up all the accounts given in Scripture of any receiving the Baptism, and you will not find any other manifestation mentioned on that occasion without the manifestation of tongues. One man says that he knows he has the Baptism, because God has enabled him to believe His Word. Evidently he has forgotten that the devils do more than that, for they believe and tremble (James 2:19).

One says: "About two years ago He sanctified me, giving me the witness of it weeks later. I have gone on in this life from one degree of grace to another, and have found the way glorious, testifying to being saved, sanctified and filled with the Spirit." She then tells that she heard of the California revival and became hungry. She found out that she never had the Baptism of the Spirit, and so began to seek for Him. On a certain date, while pouring out her prayers to God, she began to laugh, which, she says, was a new experience to her, and she laughed and laughed till she finished. She says when she ceased to laugh she realized that her hunger was gone, and thanked God then and there for the abiding Holy Ghost. The only manifestation she gives is that of laughing. Is laughing a Bible evidence of Pentecost? Show us that Scripture that says, "They were all filled with the Holy Ghost, and began to laugh, or to cry, or to believe the Word." Show us any other Scriptural manifestation, and we will accept it. Show us one account of an apostolic service of which the Book says, "They were filled with the Holy Ghost, but did not speak with tongues," and we will show you a dozen such reports which have recently appeared in the holiness papers. If we claim the Baptism one time without the Bible evidence, and find that we are mistaken, are we not likely to be mistaken if we claim Him the second time without the Bible evidence?

"Suppose a man has the gift of wisdom, or faith, or interpretation, can we say that he has not the Baptism?" Bring up your man, and then we will talk about it. I leave the discussion of the gifts for the next chapter. However, I suppose if some one should receive one of the best gifts they would be greatly persecuted by the majority of holiness people.

One says: "Seven years ago I received definitely the Baptism of the Holy Ghost. But I am now eagerly, yea, hourly, expecting another baptism." The Word says there is but one Baptism.

Some advise: "When you speak with tongues in service, never let more than two or three speak at a time; it causes confusion." If such people had been present on the day of Pentecost they would have accused the Spirit for talking through too many at one time.

One writes: "In the Epistles, tongues are not once mentioned as a distinctive evidence of the filling of the Spirit. This is the more suggestive when we remember that the Epistles, above all other portions of the Word, are given to guide the Church during this dispensation. Hundreds of times is the gracious Holy Spirit mentioned in these Epistles. If the tongues were a necessary evidence of the Baptism of the Spirit, surely that fact would be frequently stated. It is not mentioned once."

Taking the above just as it stands, we must conclude that there is no evidence of Pentecost; for nowhere in the Epistles can we find any evidence given. I never knew before that it would not do for the Church to follow any Scripture unless it could be found in the Epistles.

But the same writer, who thinks that we should follow the Epistles more than any other portion of the Word, continues: "If this gift is necessary as an evidence of the Baptism of the Holy Ghost, how do we know that Jesus had the Holy Ghost, for we search in vain for any evidence of His ever having exercised this gift. We have joy in believing that all that is really essential for us was in Christ, our Pattern. The absence of any record of the gift of tongues manifested in Christ is therefore very significant."

As a reply to the above, we give a quotation from S. D. Kinne, in "The Apostolic Evangel." "Even Jesus, who never went among the Gentiles to need their tongues, or went to school, knew letters, and could read the Hebrew law (John 7:15; Luke 4:17). This book of the law was written in Hebrew, but Jesus' native language was Syriac. There were no books in the houses of the common people, no printing press, no opportunity to learn to read the Hebrew, except among the rich and the priests and the scribes. Jesus talked to the ignorant fallen Samaritan woman at the well, doubtless in her own dialect. So, too, of the Syrophenician woman and the Gadarenes. True, the Scriptures do not have the word 'tongues' in these incidents. They were not written to satisfy curiosity, else John supposes the world would not contain books enough to record the things Jesus did. Nor are they written to meet the reasoning of the learned, or the cavils of the unbelieving, but they are written for the poor, the unlearned, the simple, child-like believer who seeks to know the mystery which is hidden from the wise and prudent and revealed unto babes."

Somebody says that John the Baptist never spake with tongues, though he was filled with the Holy Ghost from birth. Is this true? It was said of him, "He shall be filled with the Holy Ghost, even from his mother's womb"; but he did not have the Baptism of Pentecost, "for the Holy Ghost was not yet given."

We have before us an article headed: HE FOLLOWETH NOT "US"! In it the writer laments the fact that there is such great division among the holiness people, and then continues:

"The tongue's movement, from its lofty pinnacle, thanks God for the real Bible evidence of the baptism with the Holy Ghost; others have only a theoretical evidence. Jesus prayed for the sanctification and unity of all His disciples, so that the world might behold and know God had sent Him as its Saviour.

"Time was when the holiness people lamented the lack of unity and brotherly love in the nominal churches and exhorted to holiness as the panacea for these ills; but alas, among us, brethren, is clearly seen zeal for our movement, our church, or our shibboleth, which transcends zeal for God."

In the above the spirit of the promoters of the present revival is compared to the Spirit manifested in James and John concerning the one they saw casting out demons (Mark 9: 38). He teaches that it would be better to lay aside the light we have received rather than to cause a division among the holiness people. So, rather than divide the crowd, the wise virgins had better not get oil in their vessels, but do all they can to keep in unity with the foolish. Brethren, shall we who have received a share in the benefits of the revival now sweeping the world, for the tender feeling which we have for our brethren of the opposite school, try to preserve unity in the holiness ranks by failing to present the whole truth? Or shall we, for the love which we have for Christ, do all in our power to carry on this revival and publish the gospel to every creature? It appears to me that our brother has taken the position of James and John, while the Pentecostal people are casting out devils.

I have read after several speaking about this way: "It is all right for my neighbor to have to speak with tongues as the evidence of *his* Pentecost. The people never did believe he had the Baptism of the Spirit. As for me, thank the Lord, I did not have to speak with tongues." Stopping here, but clearly implying that *their works* prove that they have Him.   Thus counting their works greater than the testimony of the Spirit.

One writes: "One of our most intelligent contributors, a successful revival worker, who believes in the Pentecostal revival and the gift of tongues, informs us of some deaf mutes who have recently received the Pentecostal baptism, but spake in no tongue at all.   And yet no one present questioned the reality of their experience."

These people, no doubt, received a measure of the Spirit, but there is nothing to prove that they received the Baptism. I believe that when any mute receives the Baptism of the Holy Ghost, the Spirit will manifest Himself with the tongue.   Some one says, "Do you dare to discount the experience of these poor mute creatures?"   I reply, I had rather discount any one's experience than to discount the Holy Ghost by saying He came to a heart and failed to do what Jesus said He would do, viz., testify.

Some one quotes an account of a service in Topeka, Kan., January 4, 1900, in which it is said there occurred not only the speaking with tongues, but the cloven tongues of fire were seen.   Then the writer comments thus: "If outward signs are to be in all cases the evidence of the Pentecostal baptism, then many of us who have spoken in tongues are yet short of the full blessing of Pentecost."

Now listen.   Jesus said, "Go ye into *all* the world, and preach the gospel to *every* creature" (Mark 16: 15).   This, from a human standpoint, is a great undertaking, even impossible.   Jesus said again, "But ye shall receive the power of the Holy Ghost coming upon you: and ye shall be witnesses unto me both in Jerusalem, and in all Judea, and in Samaria, and unto the uttermost part of the earth" (Acts 1: 8, margin). It is clear that the "power" which Jesus said would accompany the Baptism of the Spirit is the power to preach the gospel to every creature; and this power the one hundred and twenty received, not at college, but on the day of Pentecost, symbolized by the tongues of fire sitting upon them.   As we have said before, as soon as we can grasp the reality, God removes the symbol. The tongues of fire on this occasion, symbolizing power imparted by the Holy Ghost to preach the gospel to every creature, proves to my mind, beyond a doubt, that whosoever afterwards should receive the Baptism of the Spirit would also receive power to witness in any part of the earth to which God should call him. The tongues of fire which sat upon them was the symbol of the power of the Spirit; the speaking with tongues is the abiding reality.

I have heard some say that the speaking with other tongues meant the disciples stopped cursing and began to praise God. This needs no reply. With the facts before us, nothing but ignorance will cause an honest man to make such a statement.

Now we come to Mark 16: 17, 18. Dean Alford and other noted commentators say, "There is doubt of its genuineness as a work of the evangelist Mark." Very well. If you wish to leave it out, we have an abundance of other Scriptures to prove our position. If you wish to take it in, it is in perfect accord with our teaching and the other Scriptures. Somebody says that this teaches that converted people—all who believe— as well as any, shall speak with tongues. Jesus said, "He that believeth on Me, as the Scripture hath said, out of his belly shall flow rivers of living water. (But this spake He of the Spirit, which they that believe on Him should receive: for the Holy Ghost was not yet given; because that Jesus was not yet glorified") (John 7: 38, 39). Here it is stated that *they who believe* shall receive the Holy Ghost, and Mark states that *they who believe* shall speak with new tongues. Do you see any connection? A word to the wise is sufficient!

Some say that many claim to talk with tongues, but to them it is only a babble. They seem to forget that "there are, it may be, so many kinds of voices in the world" (said to be about four thousand), "and none of them is without signification" (1 Cor. 14: 10). There are few refined languages, but there are thousands of languages in the jungles of the dark lands and upon the islands of the sea, which, if you were to hear, would be only a babble to you; and yet these are languages spoken by branches of the human family.

"There is an intense hatred exhibited towards this work of God on the part of the unbelievers generally. At Whittier, a near-by town, the leader, while at family worship, praised the Lord too loudly to suit a neighbor, who brought him before the magistrate, who gave him thirty days at hard labor on a chain-gang with twelve Mexicans. God gave him the tongue, so that he could pray for them and speak in their own language."— W. C. Dumble, in "Way of Faith," November 1, 1906.

Here is a booklet written by a man in Ohio, in which he says: "Evidences of genuine tongues are lacking. At this point I shall confine my positive statements to local conditions which have been within observation. Reports which come to us concerning tongues in the literature which is being circulated dare not be credited in full, for we have positive knowledge that any strange sounds produced by the vocal organs are without hesitancy pronounced genuine tongues, and frequently such tongues are named."

This man says it will not do to trust reports which come to us through literature. If this be true, why did he write his book? If we can't trust others, how shall we trust him? He tries to convey the impression that he and those who agree with him only can be trusted on this question. After saying that he cannot trust reports and will confine his positive statements to local conditions which have come under his observation, he says: "We are told, however, upon good authority that of a goodly number of cases in Los Angeles, none proved to be a real language. Doctor Godbey also tells of several cases which he tested without finding evidences of genuine language." You see he can trust reports as long as they accord with his own views; it is only those reports which contradict his statements which he cannot afford to trust.

On our table lie several well-authenticated letters giving accounts of those who spake with other tongues and were understood by men of those tongues. But such accounts can be found from time to time in the apostolic papers, so I will not give space to them here.

Here is an article headed, "THE GIFT OF TONGUES—AND

WHY?" The writer speaks of the disciples on the day of
Pentecost, of Cornelius and his household, and of the disciples
at Ephesus, and says the reason that all these spake with
tongues when they received the Holy Ghost was that people
of other tongues were present. He clearly implies that when
no one of other tongues is present the person receiving the
Holy Ghost according to Scripture does not speak with tongues,
and that the "gift of tongues" is of little value even when
people of other tongues are present. On the same page he
admits that this present movement is of God, and says, "Some
are receiving the Holy Ghost, and speaking in tongues." Remembering that all of us here (especially in the rural districts
where this revival is greatly spreading) speak the same language, he leaves us in the dark as to why some are speaking
with tongues when they receive the Holy Ghost here. Later,
the same writer says that he, while praying alone in the woods,
spake in an unknown language. He says that this was no
special evidence, to him of the Baptism of the Holy Ghost, as
he had received Him a few weeks before. Then He adds:
"Just why God dealt wth me thus is not clearly revealed to
me yet." Now, he gave what he called a Bible reason for the
speaking with tongues on the day of Pentecost, at the house
of Cornelius, at Ephesus; and so, if he did give a Bible reason
in these three cases, he ought to be able to give a Bible reason
in his own case. In the first article he teaches that there is
no Scriptural reason for tongues except in the presence of
people of other tongues, or as a sign to unbelievers; and
since he spake with tongues while alone in the woods, we wait
patiently for the Bible reason which applies to his own case.

Now we come to the Corinthian Church. Many are saying
that here was a church that had tongues in abundance; and
yet they all were carnal, even babes in Christ. Many a poor,
unlearned man will stumble over this argument and decide,
Surely, to speak with tongues is no evidence of Pentecost.
But those who are acquainted with the Scriptures know that
part of the truth concerning the condition of this church is
here kept back. If the whole truth was told, it would prove

a strong point in favor of the affirmative. Five facts, if properly considered, will throw great light on the condition of this church.

1. They had been converted from heathenism, and therefore needed teaching. Doctor Godbey says: "You must remember that the larger per cent. of the Corinthian membership were Gentiles, having been so recently converted out of heathenism, that the material was somewhat gross and crude. There were also many Jews in the Corinthian church. It was really a mammoth mongrel of all nationalities, who, as well as the Jews, had concentrated at this great Grecian metropolis. They were, with few exceptions, very poor, belonging to the lower classes of society and converted out of the slums."

2. "It is reported commonly that there is fornication among you, and such fornication as is not so much as named among the Gentiles, that one should have his father's wife" (1 Cor. 5: 1). These were surely sinners. Paul says they were worse than the unconverted heathen.

3. "And I, brethren, could not speak unto you as unto spiritual, but as unto carnal, even as unto babes in Christ" (1 Cor. 3: 1).

4. "Paul, . . . unto the church of God which is at Corinth, to them that are sanctified in Christ Jesus" (1 Cor. 1: 1, 2). "And such were some of you: but ye are washed, but ye are sanctified" (1 Cor. 6: 11).

5. "What? know ye not that your body is the temple of the Holy Ghost which is in you, which ye have of God, and ye are not your own" (1 Cor. 6: 19)?

A statement before us reads thus: "Surely, the gift of tongues could not have been the evidence of Pentecost among these people, who were not even sanctified, to say nothing about the incoming and indwelling of the Holy Ghost."

Why did he not say that they were not even converted? He had just as much proof that they were all sinners as he did that those who spoke with tongues were not sanctified and filled with the Holy Ghost.

Some think that the thirteenth chapter of 1 Corinthians denies the above statement. We will study this in our next chapter.

Now we come to an account of Pentecost which a great many rest upon as settling the question. I speak of the case of the Samaritans (Acts 8: 5-25). When we look at this record we find that it is not stated that they spake with tongues; neither can we find any statement that they did not speak with tongues. Looking at the record honestly as it stands, two theories may be drawn; and either as reasonably and as legitimately as the other:

1. *They did not speak with tongues.*
2. *They did speak with tongues.*

If by a careful search we can find a Scriptural foundation for one of these theories, then that one is no longer a theory, but an established Bible truth; and since the two theories contradict each other, the other theory must be pronounced unscriptural. If you are honest, you must agree with me so far.

Now read: "Then laid they their hands on them, and they received the Holy Ghost. And when Simon saw that through the laying on of the apostles' hands the Holy Ghost was given, he offered them money, saying, Give me also this power, that on whomsoever I lay hands, he may receive the Holy Ghost" (Acts 8: 17-19).

The Greek which expresses Simon's act of seeing is "Idon de ho Simon." The Greek "Idon" literally means to know, to perceive through any of the senses. It is a stronger word than our word "see." It indicates that Simon not only saw, but heard some miraculous power of a peculiar nature. Simon perceived, was made to know that Pentecost had been repeated in the case of these Samaritans. He saw that this miraculous power followed the laying on of the apostles' hands, therefore he offered them his money that he might also have this power. In the wonderful revival which Philip had conducted there was miraculous power manifested (ver. 7), and also great joy (ver. 8); but Simon did not offer his money for these things. Here Simon saw something for which he was willing to give his money. What was it? The following is from Dean Alford. I copy it from J. H. King in "The Apostolic Evangel:"

"The only analogous chapter is 19: 5, 6, in which we must observe that there it is distinctly asserted that the miraculous gifts of the Spirit followed the laying on of Paul's hands, and that by the expression 'idon,' in verse 18, which must be taken literally, the same is implied here. Its effects were therefore visible, and consequently the effect of the laying on of the apostles' hands was not the inward but the outward miraculous gifts of the Spirit."

Now why should Dean Alford write in this way? He was not trying to prove that "All who receive the Baptism of the Holy Ghost speak with other tongues." Yet he says that from the Greek we must conclude that the same manifestation which came with the Baptism of the Ephesians, also came with the Baptism of the Samaritans. In the case of the Ephesians, we must remember that it is distinctly stated, "they spake with tongues" (Acts 19: 6).

Looking back to Pentecost, we find Peter said, "This is that" (Acts 2: 16). The word "that" refers to the prophecy which Peter then quotes. In verse 33, we have the word "this" explained: "This which ye now see and hear." Verse 7 tells us what they saw, "Behold, are not all these which speak Galilaeans?" Verse 11 tells us what they heard, "We do hear them speak in our tongues the wonderful works of God." Then according to Peter's explanation, it takes just this to fulfill the prophecy of Joel. "This which ye now *see and hear* is that." Simon was convinced that the Samaritans had received the Holy Ghost, because he (*idon*) saw and heard. Have you reached the Samaritans' experience?

Now we come to Paul's case. We are told that nothing is said of "tongues" in connection with his Pentecost. Neither can we find it anywhere stated that he received the Holy Ghost. He never testified that he received the Holy Ghost in relating the narrative recorded in Acts 9: 1-19. "But," you say, "it is implied from the statement of Ananias in verse 17, that he did receive the Baptism of the Holy Ghost." And since we have to infer that he received the Holy Ghost, we may just as legitimately infer that he received Him with the full manifestations of Pentecost; and especially so, since Paul himself says, "I speak with tongues more than ye all" (1 Cor. 14:18).

Much has been written trying to prove that all do not receive the same gift. This no one that we have seen denies. We do not teach that all will receive the gift of tongues, but we do teach that "the manifestation of the Spirit is given to every man to profit withal," and that, if the Scriptures are to be our guide, the manifestation following Pentecost always is the speaking with other tongues. So all that has been written trying to prove that we all do not receive the gift of tongues' does not effect our position at all, and therefore needs no reply from us here.

We are accused of teaching that to speak with tongues is an infallible evidence of Pentecost. If by "infallible evidence" you mean that the devil can never imitate it, I say we do not teach it; but if you mean that when the Holy Ghost takes a person's tongue beyond his control and speaks with it a language of which that person knows nothing, I say that it is an unmistakable evidence that that person has received the Baptism of the Holy Ghost.

We have before us on our table a great number of articles written by various ones stating that they know that all who receive the Baptism of the Spirit do not speak with tongues; but they fail to give any argument, reason, Scripture, or any foundation for their statement, except their own knowledge. Of course such ungrounded statements need no reply.

Here are a number of articles in which the writers, trying to bend different Scriptures to prove their theory, clearly contradict themselves several times. But I need not enter into details on this line here. I believe I have fairly considered and answered about all points that are being advanced against the teaching of the present movement except a few which I withhold for subsequent chapters. If I have omitted any prominent points advanced by the negative, it is either because

I have failed so far to see or hear them, or have unintentionally lost the reference. It has not been my purpose, in giving a whole chapter to answering objections, to simply mention a few of the less important objections to our teaching, and then leave the reader in the dark as to the main teaching of my brethren of the opposite school; but I have searched carefully for the foundation of their objections, and endeavored to bring before the reader their true position, by quoting many of their own statements.

Now let us take a little review of the present situation, and then I want to ask my brethren of the negative one question.

Here are the principal things resulting to-day from the presentation of the affirmative:

1. Many sanctified Christians are becoming hungry, seeking and obtaining the Baptism of the Holy Ghost, and speaking with other tongues.

2. Many who have been claiming sanctification for years are becoming hungry, seeking for Him, but, finding that either they never were sanctified or have backslidden, going down before God and getting pure in His sight, and then receiving the Holy Ghost, and speaking with other tongues.

3. Many who have been claiming sanctification for years are being convicted and beginning to seek for Him, finding that they will have to make right many wrongs in their lives before they receive Him, and, being unwilling to do so, they cease to seek and take a firm stand against the present revival, claiming that they already have the Baptism of the Spirit.

4. Some who claim to be holiness preachers are being located and quitting the business.

5. A few sinners are being converted, a few more sanctified; and most all of those who are being converted or sanctified are receiving the Baptism of the Holy Ghost and speaking with other tongues.

6. The world is amazed, and wondering saith, "What meaneth this?" Others, mocking, say, "These people are gone into fanaticism, they are insane, they are false teachers, they are

being used of the devil, they should be stopped by the authorities."

Some things resulting from the presentation of the negative, the best we have been able to learn, are:

1. Many sanctified Christians are concluding that they have the Baptism of the Spirit, though they have never spoken with other tongues.

2. Many are claiming to receive the Baptism of the Holy Ghost without the Pentecostal manifestation, the very thing which the most of them have been doing for years.

3. Many who have been claiming to be sanctified for years with wrongs in their lives, chewing tobacco, members of Masonic lodges, etc., greatly rejoice to hear such preaching.

4. Many good people of the country are becoming disgusted at holiness papers and preachers who advocate the negative.

5. Nobody is being saved or sanctified under sermons of this kind. Very few are receiving the Holy Ghost and speaking with tongues.

6. The world is being pleased, infidels are rejoicing, many under conviction are becoming satisfied with their present condition, and hypocrites are saying, "That is the kind of preaching I like."

Now, brother, with these facts before us, if you still believe that all who receive the Baptism of the Holy Ghost do not speak with tongues, why do you not preach as you did before this revival started, and let this question alone? I advise you to read Acts 5: 34-40, and act accordingly.

CHAPTER VI.

"Now, concerning spiritual gifts, brethren, I would not have you ignorant."

"Now there are diversities of gifts, . . . differences of administrations, . . . diversities of operations, . . . but the manifestation of the Spirit is given to every man to profit withal" (1 Cor. 12: 1, 4-7).

Here we count: "gifts," "administrations," "operations," and "the manifestation," each of which is different, separate, and distinct from the others. We are told that there are diversities of the first three, but the fourth is in the singular number —"the manifestation." While the Spirit distributes the first three, He always gives with each gift, with each administration, with each operation, not manifestations, but "the manifestation," to profit withal. God has given all these things to work together in the salvation of man. The Spirit divides these among us, not with respect to persons, but as we prepare ourselves for them.. He will perform the same operation in each heart, if each will prepare for that operation. He will impart to each heart the same administration, when He sees each heart prepared for that administration. He will bestow upon any of us any gift we desire, when He sees we have reached the degree of grace where we can use that gift for the glory of God.

In a preceding chapter we spoke of seven operations of the Spirit; perhaps there are many more. We will not here give you our ideas of the administrations, but pass on to consider the gifts. I am persuaded that much more is implied by these gifts than most sanctified people ever dreamed of. Let us approach the subject with an open heart, longing to understand the Scriptures.

Let us notice that what is said in verses 8, 9 and 10 (1 Cor.

12), rests upon the conjunction *"for,"* which connects these verses—not with verse 7, but with verse 4.

"Now there are diversities of gifts, but the same Spirit. . . . For to one is given by the Spirit the word of wisdom; to another the word of knowledge by the same Spirit; to another faith by the same Spirit; to another the gifts of healing by the same Spirit; to another the working of miracles; to another prophecy; to another discerning of spirits; to another divers kinds of tongues; to another the interpretation of tongues."

1. Wisdom. James says, "If any of you lack wisdom, let him ask of God, that giveth to all men liberally, and upbraideth not; and it shall be given him" (Jas. 1 : 5). All Christians have wisdom, some in a greater degree than others. Who has reached that degree as that it may be said of him, he has "the gift of wisdom?" Solomon had "a gift," but not "the gift." I am persuaded that the manifestation of "the gift of wisdom" should far exceed Solomon's wisdom.

2. Knowledge. This is insight into divine truth. Therefore this is the gift which we all need to understand the Bible. All have knowledge, some more than others; but who has the gift? Methodist, Baptist, Holiness, Universalist, etc., all claim it, but who has it?

3. Faith. All Christians have faith, but all have not the gift. To the one who has the gift "nothing shall be impossible."

4. Healings. "Both of these nouns (gifts of healings) are in the plural number, because there is a diversity of gifts, as well as an infinite multiplicity of diseases to be healed."—*Godbey.* The Word says, "To another"—one person—"is given the gifts of healings." So a person who has received this should be able to heal any disease or affliction unless the healing would be contrary to God's will. The gifts of healings are quite different from the "prayer of faith." A person to whom has been intrusted the gifts of healings, need never pray for the sick. The power is in him (not his own power, but the power of God imparted), and he simply bids the sick, "Be whole." Examples of the manifestation of this may be seen

in the following Scriptures: "Silver and gold have I none: but such as I have give I thee: In the name of Jesus Christ of Nazareth rise and walk" (Acts 3:6). "Insomuch that they brought forth the sick into the streets" (in every street, margin), "and laid them on beds and couches, that at the least the shadow of Peter passing by might overshadow some of them. There came also a multitude out of the cities round about unto Jerusalem, bringing sick folks, and them which were vexed with unclean spirits: and they were healed EVERY ONE" (Acts 5:15, 16). "So that from his (Paul's) body were brought unto the sick handkerchiefs or aprons, and the diseases departed from them, and the evil spirits went out of them" (Acts 19:12).

5. Miracles. Doctor Godbey says the Greek here is *"energemata dunameon,"* which means the inward workings of dynamites. He says that a more literal translation would be MANIPULATIONS OF DYNAMITES. He concludes that it refers to spiritual miracles, and not to physical. I do not know, however, but that both may be included. If it does refer only to spiritual, or only physical, or to both, it does not affect our position in this book. One thing is clear, it is a gift added after the Baptism of the Spirit; for in Acts 1:8, the literal reading is, "You shall receive dynamite of the Holy Ghost having come on you." So you see we receive *dynamite* when we receive the Holy Ghost, but the gift is *manipulations of dynamites.* Momentus conception!

6. Prophecy. This word originally meant to bubble up like a boiling spring or an artesian well. The application seems to be that of speaking under the immediate inspiration of the Holy Ghost, unfolding to men the counsels of God, especially as contained in the way of salvation through Christ, and at times unfolding future events.

7. Discerning of Spirits. This gift, I doubt not, will put us to the place where neither men nor devils can deceive us.

8. Tongues. On the day of Pentecost the one hundred and twenty spoke in other languages as the Spirit gave utterance. A person who has only the manifestation of tongues can speak

in another language only as the Spirit gives utterance, but a person who has the gift of tongues can speak other languages at will, and, no doubt, several different languages. Neither has that person who has learned them in college the gift of languages, but the gift is imparted by the Holy Ghost independently of the human intellect.

9. Interpretation. This is quite different from translation. Translation from one language to another is accomplished by a knowledge of the vocabularies and syntax of those languages; but interpretation is accomplished, while we listen to an unknown tongue, by the Holy Ghost speaking the same in our heart in a known tongue: thus we are enabled to give it out to others. All who have this gift, I doubt not, are able to understand any language which they may hear spoken under the power of the Holy Ghost, and also recognize its nativity.

I am sure that people have been claiming these gifts for years, while the manifestations have fallen far short of the Bible standard. I do not believe that anyone has ever received any of these gifts in their normal state until he received the Baptism of the Holy Spirit; neither do I believe that all or any of them often come with the Baptism, but must be sought for and obtained afterwards. It is one thing to say, I have the gift of wisdom, or of knowledge, or of faith, or of prophecy; but it is another thing to really possess it. I believe when a person receives any of these gifts that he will know it that moment, and that it will so manifest itself that others will soon find it out. The Spirit has these gifts, and He has them for us. He imparts them to those whom He sees can use them for the glory of God. I believe that it is the will of God that each of us should have all these gifts, but because all of us are unable to use all or any of them properly, they are withheld; otherwise God would be a respecter of persons. Then each one is exhorted to covet earnestly these gifts, and every exhortation of God to seek carries with it a promise to bestow.

At the present many are receiving the Baptism of the Spirit with Pentecostal evidence. Some are then receiving the gifts of the Spirit. This is meeting with great opposition. Eccle-

siastical leaders are getting uneasy, and setting about to prove
that they have had the Baptism of the Spirit for years. "Don't
discount your brother because he has not received the same
gift that you have," they cry.   Brother, nobody is doing this;
very few of us have any of these gifts; we are just getting the
evidence of Pentecost. "But," you say, "is not one gift as
much an evidence as another?"   Certainly.   And I believe that
any of these nine gifts in their normal bestowment is an evidence of Pentecost; yet no one of them is to be taken as the
testimony of the Comforter, and hence is not the first evidence
to be expected. "But," says one, "suppose a person has the gift
of wisdom or of faith or of healings, but has never spoken with
tongues, can we say that he has not Pentecost?"   Bring up your
man and we will talk about it.

But still some insist that the manifestation of tongues and
the gift of tongues are both the same, that the gift of tongues
is the least among the nine, and that they possess far greater
and more important gifts than that of tongues.   You say, "I
have the gift of knowledge, because I understand the Scriptures."   The Universalists and Roman Catholics claim the same
gift.

Yes, I have known some to claim the gifts of healings, and
pray for the sick, and yet they were not healed.   They excuse
themselves by saying, It wasn't God's will.   How different
from apostolic scenes! for we read, "They were healed EVERY
ONE."   I have known some to claim the gift of discernment,
and yet be greatly deceived by both men and demons.   Some
claim the gift of faith, and yet they meet with discouragements
and many impossibilities.   It is easy to claim the gift of wisdom
or knowledge, but why don't some of you claim the gift of interpretation?   I have yet to hear of the first one interpreting
a message spoken by the Holy Ghost who had not himself had
a manifestation of tongues.

When greater light comes, it always meets with opposition.
Those who opened the truth of justification by faith were
greatly opposed.   The truth of holiness had a struggle.   Divine
healing and the premillennial coming of the Lord have been

denounced from the pulpit and derided by thousands of writers. The Scriptural evidence of the Pentecostal Baptism receives a greater opposition than any of the former; and now when the gifts are added, this opposition is going to ripen into Pentecostal persecution. The first man who passes through healing the sick as Peter did, will likely be treated with contempt by one-half the holiness people, and soon jailed by the authorities (Acts 5: 15-18).

Now let us approach and carefully study the thirteenth chapter of 1 Corinthians.

The word which rings through this chapter from beginning to end is *charity*. This word *"charity"* in the Greek is *"agapee,"* which means Divine love, not *perfect* love, as many suppose. The same word is used in John 5: 42, "Ye have not the *love* of God in you." So also in 1 John 2: 15, "The *love* of the Father is not in him." "The *love* of God . . . be with you all" (2 Cor. 13: 14). Not one time does the word *"agapee"* alone mean *perfect* love. In 1 John 4: 18 the Greek is *"teleia agapee."* This word *"teleia,"* which means *"perfect,"* occurs but one time in the thirteenth chapter of 1 Corinthians, and that is in the tenth verse.

"Though I speak with the tongues of men and of angels, and have not Divine love, I am become as sounding brass, or a tinkling cymbal."

Some say that this verse teaches that those in the Corinthian church who were speaking with tongues were carnal Christians; and since they did not have perfect *love,* their speaking with tongues was of no profit. If this is the proper explanation, the same truth will hold good in the next two verses. So, then, we must conclude that there were those in this church who could speak with tongues of angels, who had the gift of prophecy, who understood ALL mysteries and ALL knowledge, who had the faith to remove mountains; that there were those who were giving ALL their goods to feed the poor, who were giving their bodies to be burned; and yet because they were *unsanctified Christians*, they were of no good to themselves nor to anyone else. This being true, it is impossible for those who are only converted to be of any service in the vineyard of the Lord. So all work done by the disciples before they were sanctified was no good. Don't you see where we will go if we follow this teaching. The conclusions I have here drawn from verses 2 and 3, are just as legitimate as the one you have drawn from the first verse.

I cannot believe that the above conclusions are correct. With our Bible open, let us study it for the purpose of learning the truth.

It is clear that these people were looking too much at the gifts; they were magnifying them more than they were Divine love; and in all such cases the devil would be sure to take the advantage, and palm off a counterfeit upon them. For my part, I do not believe that God will bestow any gift of the Spirit upon us until we have Divine love. The gifts are distributed according as the Spirit wills, and I do not think that He wills to bestow any of these gifts upon a person who has no Divine love. If I can understand correctly, we must not only have Divine love, a thing which every Christian has, but this love must be made perfect in us, and then we must be baptized with the Holy Ghost, and covet earnestly these gifts, before God will give us any of them. However, Satan would be pleased if we should seek the gifts before we seek Divine love; and then he could impart to us the gifts of tongues, prophecy, knowledge, faith, etc. In many places in the Scripture do we read of false prophets, teachers, etc., working many signs and wonders. So Paul told the church at Corinth to covet earnestly the best gifts; and yet there was a more excellent way. This more excellent way includes not only what is spoken of in the thirteenth chapter, but the fourteenth as well. He shows them that they should first seek Divine love, and then desire the gifts. He clearly teaches that the gifts without Divine love are of no value. Since all gifts from God are valuable, if a gift is imparted before we reach Divine love, we may know it comes from the devil; and so with a manifestation. So the more excellent way is to follow after Divine love, and then desire spiritual gifts (1 Cor. 14: 1).

When Paul says for us to covet earnestly the "best gifts," he means all the nine mentioned above. There are many other gifts of the Spirit, but these nine are designated as the "best gifts."

Many to-day are preaching about this way: God is in the present revival, but there is a great deal being taught that is calculated to hurt the cause. I see no difference between the manifestation and the gift. To teach that all who are baptized with the Spirit have the gift of tongues is a great mistake. All Christians should have at least one gift, but all have not the same gift. Many of us have much greater gifts than that of tongues. The gift of tongues is the least one of the nine, and of very little value. Where it is bestowed it generally does more harm than good. Paul did not mean for us to covet this gift, but the greater ones. If you get the gift of tongues, you will be likely to backslide and become bitter in your experience and harsh in your words.

Now please tell me what there is in the above teaching to cause any one to join the present movement. Most people are prejudiced against tongues anyway, and when they hear such preaching as the above they get farther away than before. And yet, people who are preaching this way, admit that there is a revival among the church, and claim to be friends to it. If it be true that the church has been all the while receiving greater gifts, and is now receiving the least gift of all, I can't see where there is much revival. It would seem that we are retreating instead of advancing.

Those who preach that the gift of tongues is the least of the nine gifts, do so without any Scriptural foundation—they are building upon the sand. I have before me an article in which the writer says: "The most prominent objection to the present revival is the 'gift of tongues.' This one feature eliminated, we can scarcely see any other cause of complaint." Another says: "We are never told to pray for the gift of tongues, although we are told to seek some of the higher gifts." Note he says, *"some* of the higher gifts." God forbid that I should ever so minify and depreciate any gift which the Holy Spirit sees proper to bestow upon any of God's elect.

The only argument I have seen trying to prove that the gift of tongues is the least, and therefore not to be coveted, is that in the list above it comes next to last. Now isn't that a point! What proof have you that this is a descending climax, and that the climax comes at number eight? Paul seems to put prophecy ahead of all the rest, and prophecy is neither at the first, nor at the last, nor in the middle, but number six. You have made a point here that is calculated to mislead thousands of poor unlearned people, but anyone who has any knowledge of debate knows that this is a snake in the grass. I am not the one to say that the gift of tongues is the least, or is not the least, since the Bible gives it neither way. Paul teaches that if one interprets what he says he is up with the one who prophesies.

As I have ready said, I do not believe that anyone has any of these gifts normally until they are baptized with the Holy Ghost.

"But what are you going to do with the prophets and men of old, who were so wonderfully used of God?" I reply, They had many of these gifts abnormally, as did the disciples before Pentecost. The prophets of old prophesied by vision, dreams, etc. (Isa. 1:1; 8:1; Jer. 13:1-8; Ezek. 1:1; Dan. 2:19), but a person who has the gift of prophecy, I believe, will be able to prophesy any time under the immediate power of the Holy Ghost. And so with the other gifts. Before Pentecost the disciples cast out devils, though one time they tried and failed (Mark 9:18); but we read of no failures after Pentecost, and the bestowment of the gifts.

However, one thing is worthy of notice here: While we see the gifts of wisdom, knowledge, faith, healings, miracles, prophecy, and discerning of spirits manifested to a great extent before Pentecost, yet the speaking with tongues marks the Baptism of the Holy Ghost, and stands out separate and distinct from all the rest, as a lofty mountain above a plain.

But be sure to get your heart full of Divine love before you seek any gift.

"Though I speak with the tongues of men and of angels, and have not *agapee*, I am become as sounding brass, or a tinkling cymbal. And though I have the gift of prophecy, and understand all mysteries, and all knowledge; and though I have all faith, so that I could remove mountains, and have not *agapee*, I am nothing. And though I bestow all my goods to feed the poor, and though I give my body to be burned, and have not *agapee*, it profiteth me nothing." Why? Because without Divine love it cannot be of God. But what is this *agapee*, or Divine love? Verses 4-7 tell us.

"Love never falleth" (verse 8, Godbey's translation). "Whether there be prophecies, they shall be done away." Why? Prophecy is a spiritual gift qualifying us to help save the world. When we get to heaven we will find no lost souls to be saved, hence there will be no need of prophecy. "Whether there be tongues, they shall cease." Why? In heaven there will be but one language, hence no need of the gift of languages. "Whether there be knowledge, it shall vanish away." This does not mean that we will lose all the knowledge we have acquired in this world, and pass out into a sea of forgetfulness. The topic under discussion here is the gift of knowledge. This gift means insight into God's revealed Word, to enable you to understand the Bible. This will be done away because we will not take our Bible to heaven. The Bible is the way-bill from earth to heaven, and when we get there we will need it no more. Doubtless we shall learn more in one hour after we get to heaven than we have learned before in all our lives.

"For we know in part, and we prophesy in part. But when that which is perfect is come, then that which is in part shall be done away." Many holiness preachers proclaim these two verses as teaching regeneration and sanctification, saying that after we are sanctified we have no need of the gifts. This is a mistake, and calculated to do harm. If verse ten is sanctification, then none of us are sanctified; for none of us have reached the point where we know it all. Verse nine refers to this life, while verse ten refers to the glorified state.

"When I was a child, I spake as a child, I understood as a child, I thought as a child: but when I became a man, I put away childish things." Here we are taught that the glorified state will exceed this life as far as manhood exceeds childhood. The same contrast continues in verse twelve.

"And now abideth faith, hope, Divine love, these three; but the greatest of these is Divine love." The poet says, "Faith is lost in sight, and hope in full fruition dies;" but I had rather believe Paul, who here certifies the eternal survival of faith and hope, as well as love. Prophecy, tongues, and knowledge pass away with this life, but faith, hope, and Divine love abide forever. Heaven is not a place of inactivity, but of infinite and illimitable progress. Hope will be the pioneer and faith the engine of power in conception and execution of heavenly enterprises.

Remember that the members of the Corinthian church had been recently converted from heathenism, and therefore they had great need of teaching. So Paul devotes the fourteenth chapter to teaching. Forasmuch as they were zealous of spiritual gifts, he tells them to seek to excel to the edifying of the church (ver. 12). He teaches that prophecy is the greatest gift, because it edifies the church. He gives three ways in which the gift of tongues is profitable. First, "He that speaketh in an unknown tongue speaketh . . . unto God" (ver. 2). Second, "He that speaketh in an unknown tongue edifieth himself" (ver. 4). Third, "Wherefore tongues are for a sign, not to them that believe, but to them that believe not" (ver. 22). He tells them that when the church is come together into one place, and all speak with tongues, and the idiots or infidels come in, they will begin to criticise, and say that the church has gone crazy. Then if all begin to prophesy, these unbelievers will fall down on their faces and worship God (ver. 23-25). But if they prophesy first, it "serveth not for them which believe not, but for them which believe" (ver. 22). So when Paul wanted to *teach* the Christians, he had rather speak five words in a tongue which they could understand, then ten thousand words in an unknown tongue (ver. 19).

God was wonderfully blessing these people, as He was imparting to them the gifts of the Spirit and preparing them for missionary work. Every time they came together a great host of them had something special to deliver: a new tongue had been given; to another the gift of interpretation; another has a special burning message to deliver; another a thrilling exhortation which he can carry no longer; another a sweet, new and inspiring song to sing (ver. 26). The result was their meetings were too long, wearing out the people. So Paul forbids that more than two or three should prophesy or speak in unknown tongues at one time. While one or more was speaking in another language, another was to interpret; and if there be no one to interpret, they were to keep silent. Of course, he was speaking to those who had the gift of tongues, and could talk at will. When the Spirit takes the tongue beyond our control, one hundred and twenty speaking at once will cause no confusion. We read of a meeting in which Paul laid his hands on a company, and twelve received the Holy Ghost, and spake with tongues, and prophesied (Acts 19: 6, 7). Do you think Paul jumped up and said, "Look out, brethren, that will never do, you will get confusion in the church?" Nay, verily. Paul says, "Quench not the Spirit," and "Despise not prophesyings."

"Let the prophets speak two or three." If anything be revealed to another sitting by, the order is for the leader to keep silent till the party delivers the message revealed, and so on, one giving place to another, until all prophesy.

The speaking with tongues and prophesying were not the only disorder in this church. Paul also had to correct the women for talking to their husbands during service.

Many anti-pentecostal holiness preachers are having much to say at this time about having everything done in a way to avoid confusion. They will allow as many as wish to do so to testify at one time in their testimony meetings. They will call on three or four to lead in prayer at one time. They call on the congregation to crowd about the altar and shake hands. But if one or two speaks with tongues, they cry out, "Avoid confusion, brethren."

In conclusion, I advise all my readers never to depreciate any gift which the Spirit sees proper to confer on any child of God, however humble. Seek first that Divine love that never faileth; then have that love perfected in your own heart; then seek and obtain the Baptism of the Holy Ghost, with Pentecostal evidence; and then covet earnestly the best gifts: and the Spirit will give you such as He sees you can use for the glory of God.

CHAPTER VII.

POUNDS AND TALENTS.

THE purpose of this chapter is to study a few general thoughts in the parable of the talents, recorded in Matt. 25, and the parable of the pounds in Luke 19. That the parables are not the same is clear from the context. Neither one of them refer to the gifts of the Spirit treated in the preceding chapter, and this we wish to show clearly.

Open your Bible at these parables (Matt. 25: 14-30, and Luke 19: 11-27). The traveling man or the nobleman is Christ himself; the far country is heaven; the kingdom is this world; the servants are the preachers and Christian workers; the return of the nobleman is the second coming of Christ; the pounds and talents is capital. So far these two parables are alike. In fact, the main point of difference lies in the quality and distribution of the capital. In the parable of the talents, one servant receives more capital than another; in the parable of the pounds, each servant receives the same amount of capital.

You will notice in the parable of the talents that the capital is given to each one according to his ability. This ability is capacity. The talent is a special gift of God to qualify us to do His service. Some have greater capacities than others, hence God gives them more talents. The talent is natural ability. To possess a talent is to have the genius to do a certain thing; e. g., to sing, to speak in public, to write a theme or a song.

Every sinner has the ability, and therefore a talent for something, but his talent is used in the service of the devil. After he is saved, we see him with the same talent as before, but it is used by him in quite a different way. When Jesus comes, He will reckon with His servants as to how they have used the talents given them.

You will notice in the parable of the pounds that the capital is given to each one, not according to his ability, but to each one alike. The pound is God's Word and the Holy Ghost. A person who has a talent for a certain work, and this talent intensified by the Holy Ghost, and then co-operated with the Word of God, will be able to accomplish something in the Master's vineyard, provided he sets to work. The Nobleman will one day return and require interest on the capital.

A great many people think that they have one or more of the special gifts of the Spirit, when in reality they have only a natural talent—as a talent for singing, speaking in public, teaching, writing, etc.—intensified by the Spirit, and perhaps accompanied by some knowledge of the Word. All Christians have this; but the nine gifts are bestowed normally after the Baptism of the Spirit.

Let us be careful to distinguish between talents, pounds, and the gifts of the Spirit.

CHAPTER VIII.

SANCTIFICATION is the eradication of the carnal mind; while
the Baptism of the Holy Ghost is a filling: the one takes place
at Calvary; while the other occurs at Pentecost. They are
distinct and separate the one from the other, and never take
place at the same time. The heart must be cleansed from all
sin before the Holy Ghost will come in to abide forever. He
may come in shortly after the heart is purified, or it may be
many years afterwards, or He may never come in. The Baptism of the Holy Ghost does not naturally follow the crucifixion of the old man, but He must be sought after the Spirit
has borne witness to sanctification.

We shall now undertake to prove the above statements from
Scripture.

Let us first study the case of the apostles and disciples. In
Luke 10: 20 we learn that their names were written in heaven.
Afterwards Jesus said, "All ye shall be offended because of me
this night." "Peter answered and said unto him, Though all
men shall be offended because of thee, yet will I never be offended, . . . Though I should die with thee, yet will I not
deny thee. Likewise also said all the disciples" (Matt. 26: 31-
35). But Jesus told him that he would deny Him, and that
he would have to be converted again (Luke 22: 32). When
the crisis came, "They all forsook Him, and fled" (Mark
14: 50). After His resurrection He appeared unto them, and
"breathed on them, and saith unto them, Receive ye the Holy
Ghost" (John 20: 22). This established them in the justified
experience. After this we read, "And he led them out as far
as to Bethany, and he lifted up his hands, and blessed them"
(Luke 24: 50). How do we know what this blessing included?
The result of it was, "They worshiped him, and returned to

Jerusalem with great joy: and were continually in the temple, praising and blessing God" (ver. 52, 53). That sounds like a sanctified crowd. That is the exact grounds upon which sanctification put me. And this accords with Hebrews 13: 12-15. "Wherefore Jesus also, that he might sanctify the people with his own blood, suffered without the gate. Let us go forth therefore unto him without the camp, bearing his reproach. (He led them out.) For here we have no continuing city, but we seek one to come. By him therefore let us offer the sacrifice of praise to God continually, that is, the fruit of our lips giving thanks to his name. (They were continually in the temple praising and blessing God.)" See!

Once more. In the fourteenth, fifteenth and sixteenth chapters of John, Jesus promised to send the Comforter. Before they could receive Him they must become of one accord. So in the seventeenth chapter He prayed, "Sanctify them through thy truth. . . . That they all may be one; as thou, Father, art in me, and I in thee, that they also may be one in us. . . . I in them, and thou in me, that they may be made perfect in one." Here we are clearly taught that it requires the blessing of sanctification to make us perfect in one. So we read in Acts 1: 12-15: "Then (after the blessing at Bethany) returned they unto Jerusalem from the mount called Olivet, which is from Jerusalem a sabbath day's journey. And when they were come in, they went up into an upper room, where abode both Peter and James, and John, and Andrew, Philip, and Thomas, Bartholomew, and Matthew, James the son of Alphaeus, and Simon Zelotes, and Judas the brother of James.. These all continued with one accord in prayer and supplication, with the women, and Mary the mother of Jesus, and with his brethren. And in those days Peter stood up in the midst of the disciples, and said, (the number of names together were about an hundred and twenty)." Think of it! An hundred and twenty of one accord! How different from the apostles at the passover supper (Luke 22: 24). Something must have taken place. What could have brought them in one accord? Jesus, after seeing such discord among them at supper, went out and prayed,

Sanctify them that they all may be one. Therefore, they must have been sanctified before Pentecost. Praise the Lord!

Luke says at the supper, "There was also strife among them, which of them should be accounted the greatest." This is just like conferences, conventions, etc., held by carnal Christians to-day. Each one wants to preach the biggest sermon, or get the best appointment. But sanctification brings us of one accord, and puts us to praising God continually. Not only did the disciples come together of one accord, but they continued of one accord: "And when the day of Pentecost was fully come, they were all of one accord in one place." I must conclude then that they were sanctified before the Holy Ghost came; and especially, since we find Mary, the mother of Jesus, in the crowd seeking for her Pentecost.

If we claim that conversion puts people of one accord, and therefore the disciples were only converted before Pentecost, we put the standard higher than Jesus puts it, for He prayed that they might be sanctified to make them one. Paul addressed a certain class as "Brethren," and yet there was division among them because they were carnal. If we say that it takes the Baptism of the Holy Ghost to purify the heart and bring us of one accord, we minify the efficacy of the blood and lower the standard of Pentecost.

There is no Scripture to teach that the disciples were sanctified on the day of Pentecost. There is not a word said about cleansing, purifying, nor sanctifying in the whole account. We know that it takes consecration to put us in order for sanctification. Not a word here that would seem to even intimate consecration.

To consecrate means to set apart for a sacred use. When we instruct people to consecrate to be sanctified, we mean for them to lay themselves, together with all that they possess, with all that they are or expect ever to possess or be, unreservedly on God's altar, to be used of Him for His glory at His own discretion. Did the disciples ever consecrate? and if so, when?

"He breathed on them, and saith unto them, Receive ye the

Holy Ghost" (John 20:22). This established them in the justified experience. Still they were not consecrated, for we see them afterwards going back to their fishing nets (John 21:3). If they had been consecrated they would not have gone a fishing while Jerusalem was in such a stir over their Lord. After this Jesus appeared: "Then opened he their understanding, that they might understand the Scriptures, and said unto them, Thus it is written, and thus it behooved Christ to suffer, and to rise from the dead the third day: and that repentance and remission of sins should be preached in his name among all nations, beginning at Jerusalem" (Luke 24:45-47).

"Wherefore Jesus also, that he might sanctify the people with his own blood, suffered without the gate. Let us go forth therefore unto him without the camp, bearing his reproach." Our going forth unto Him without the camp, bearing His reproach, is our consecration. There never has been a time when there was more reproach to following Jesus without the camp than at the time Jerusalem was in such a stir over His resurrection.

Remembering this, let us return to the twenty-fourth chapter of Luke, and continue our study. "And he led them out as far as to Bethany." Their willingness to go with Jesus out to Bethany at this particular time, thus bearing His reproach, signifies their consecration. They left their nets, their friends, their reputation, and laying their all upon God's altar, they were ready to follow Jesus anywhere. Hence, "He lifted up His hands"—His hands that were torn and pierced by the nails. Why were His hands so torn? "Wherefore Jesus also, that He might sanctify the people with His own blood." When He lifted up His hands, the disciples were put under the blood. Hence, they were blessed—sanctified. This blessing brought to them great joy.

In this connection Jesus said, "And, behold, I send the promise of my Father upon you: but tarry ye in the city of Jerusalem, until ye be endued with power from on high." "But ye shall receive the power of the Holy Ghost coming upon you: and ye shall be witnesses unto me both in Jerusalem, and in Samaria, and unto the uttermost part of the earth (Luke 24:49 and Acts 1:8). So the disciples were not to stay in one place long at a time (for here we have no continuing city), but were to scatter and witness in all Judea, and in Samaria, and unto the uttermost part of the earth. However, "He commanded them that they should not depart from Jerusalem, but wait for the promise of the Father." "But tarry ye in the city of Jerusalem, until ye be endued with power from on high." "By him therefore let us offer the sacrifice of praise to God continually, that is, the fruit of our lips giving thanks to his name." "And they worshipped him, and returned to Jerusalem (not to their fishing nets, as they did before,) with great joy: and were continually in the temple, praising and blessing God." How wonderfully the Scriptures do harmonize! Do you see?

In the upper room they continued of one accord, praising and blessing God, in prayer and supplication, until the day of Pentecost was fully come. Not one word is said here to intimate consecration. We are not told that they were praying for sanctification. Why do preachers contend that they were, when not a word is said to intimate such a thing? Jesus put them under the blood at Bethany, and then told them to go to Jerusalem and tarry, not until they were sanctified, but until they were endued with power from on high. "And suddenly there came a sound from heaven as of a rushing mighty wind, and it filled all the house where they were sitting. And there appeared unto them cloven tongues like as of fire, and it sat upon each of them. And they were all filled with the Holy Ghost, and began to speak with other tongues, as the Spirit gave them utterance." Not one word to intimate sanctification!

Some holiness preachers teach that one prong of the cloven tongue represented regeneration, one prong sanctification, while the fire represented the purifying power of the Holy Ghost. If this be correct, then these hundred and twenty were all regenerated, sanctified, and filled with the Holy Ghost at one and the same time; for it is clear that the cloven tongues of fire were symbolic of the real blessing that God was pouring upon them. Others teach that one prong represented the fire of heaven, while the other represented the fire of hell. If this be true, this crowd was baptized with heavenly fire and hell fire at the same time. Now, the fire is not symbolic of "the sanctifying Baptism of the Holy Ghost," for fire alone is never a symbol of the Holy Spirit, but only as it is connected with cloven tongues. When we speak of "the sanctifying Baptism of the Holy Ghost," we use a term entirely unscriptural.

Some connect Matt. 3: 11 with Mal. 3: 1-3, to try to prove that the Baptism of the Spirit purifies. There is absolutely no connection between them, as I can see. Let us take our Bible and read, not to support theory, but to understand the Scripture.

"Behold, I will send my messenger, and he shall prepare the way before me: and the Lord, whom ye seek, shall suddenly come to his temple, even the messenger of the covenant, whom ye delight in: behold, he shall come, saith the Lord of hosts." Not one word said here about the Baptism of the Holy Ghost; but the reference is to the coming of Christ himself. He is called "The Messenger of the Covenant." Neither does it refer to Christ's first advent into the world. It says, He shall SUD-DENLY come to His TEMPLE. Was this fulfilled when Jesus came the first time? Nay. He was incarnated, then born in a manger, and never began any work in the temple till He was twelve years old. Let us continue: "But who may abide the day of his coming? and who shall stand when he appeareth?" Do you think this refers either to the Baptism of the Holy Ghost or to the first coming of Christ? Then read on: "For he (Christ) is like a refiner's fire, and like fullers' soap: and he (Christ) shall sit as a refiner and purifier of silver: and he (Christ) shall purify the sons of Levi, and purge them as gold and silver, that they may offer unto the Lord an offering in righteousness. Then (immediately afterwards) shall the offering of Judah and Jerusalem be pleasant unto the Lord, as in the days of old, and as in former years. And I will come near to you to judgment, etc." It is clear that this refers neither to the Baptism of the Holy Ghost nor to Christ's first advent, but entirely to the second coming of the Lord. "But does not the messenger coming before Christ refer to John the Baptist?" Not at all (John 1 : 21-23). "To whom then?" To Elijah the prophet (Mal. 4 : 5, 6).

Now turn to Matt. 3 : 11. "I indeed baptize you with water unto repentance: but he that cometh after me is mightier than I, whose shoes I am not worthy to bear: he shall baptize you with the Holy Ghost and fire" (R. V.).

Some teach that the baptism of fire is separate from the Baptism of the Holy Ghost. This is an error. I notice that Matthew and Luke use the word "fire," while Mark omits it, clearly involving the conclusion that the fire normally inheres in the Holy Ghost, *i. e.*, is inseparable from Him. Therefore, when you receive the Baptism of the Holy Ghost, you receive the baptism of fire. To teach two baptisms is to antagonize Eph. 4 : 5, where Paul certifies that there is but one Baptism in the gracious economy. The ordinance with water is not intrinsically a baptism, but symbolically typifies the real Baptism of the Holy Ghost.

Now, does this fire purify? If so, then there must be no difference between the cleansing and the filling, that is, the filling is the cleansing and the cleansing is the filling, for there is but one baptism. But if both—the cleansing and the filling—are included in the phrase, "Baptism of the Holy Ghost and fire," and the "fire" does the cleansing, and the Holy Ghost does the filling, then according to the statement, "Holy Ghost and fire," the filling must take place before the cleansing. And this would accord exactly with the day of Pentecost; for we read, "And suddenly there came a sound from heaven as of a rushing mighty wind, and it filled all the house where they were sitting. (Symbolical of the filling.) And there appeared unto them cloven tongues like as of fire, and it sat upon each of them. (Symbolical of the cleansing.)" So I hope you can see where this explanation of the fire will lead to.

Now, I do not believe that the cleansing and the filling are one and the same; neither can I see from the Scriptures that the filling takes place before the cleansing; neither do I see that the "fire" is symbolic of "the sanctifying Baptism of the Holy Ghost." For my part, I can see no difference between those who teach the "fire" to purify and the Holy Ghost to fill, and those who teach the Baptism of the Spirit and the baptism of fire as separate and distinct the one from the other, except the latter follow the Bible order more closely than the former. And especially so, since the former say, that one prong of the cloven tongue represents regeneration and the other sanctification. And if this be true, the "fire" not only purifies, but regenerates; and so we may invent another new phrase, viz., "The regenerating Baptism of the Holy Ghost." I trust you can see the great error in these unscriptural theories. Let us not build theories, and then try to make the Scriptures support them; but let us take the Scriptures as they are, and then draw conclusions.

"And suddenly there came a sound from heaven as of a rushing mighty wind, and it (the sound) filled all the house where they were sitting."

Since nothing is said in the whole account about regeneration nor sanctification; since we have seen from Scripture that they had already been established in regeneration, and put under the blood—sanctified; since Jesus never gave them any instructions to go up to Jerusalem to seek regeneration or sanctification, but to wait for the Holy Ghost; and since they seem to have been waiting for the very blessing which had been promised them: I take this sound filling all the house where they were sitting, as a symbol of the Holy Ghost filling them who were sitting in the house.

"And there appeared unto them cloven tongues like as of fire, and it sat upon each of them."

Since Jesus not only promised the Comforter, but said, "Ye shall receive the power of the Holy Ghost coming upon you," and since this power was to enable them, without any farther education or training, to witness for Jesus unto the uttermost part of the earth: I conclude that the cloven tongues like as of fire which came upon them was symbolical of the power given by the Holy Ghost to witness to every creature.

The above conclusions accord exactly with the next verse, which gives us the reality symbolized in verses two and three. "And they were all filled with the Holy Ghost, and began to speak with other tongues, as the Spirit gave them utterance." "He shall baptize you with the Holy Ghost and fire." Or, connecting Matt. 3 : 11 with Acts 1 : 8, we might say, He shall baptize you with the Holy Ghost and power (Luke 24 : 49). The phrase, "baptize you with the Holy Ghost and fire," seems to me to include, not both the cleansing and filling, but both the internal and external manifestations.

"But what about the next verse? Does it not teach that the Baptism of the Holy Ghost purges the floor?"

Now notice. Here are three verses together, each ending with the word "fire" (ver. 10, 11 and 12). It is obvious that it is not the same fire in every case. John was preaching repentance and baptizing the people in Jordan. A momentous crisis had come to the Jews with the ministry of John. Hitherto they could be saved by the excarnate Christ, under the ministry of the law and the prophets. Now that He has come in human flesh, they must receive Him, or grieve away the Holy Ghost and take the fatal plunge into reprobacy and damnation. "And now also the axe is laid unto the root of the trees." It was a judgment come to the house of God—the Jewish church. The axe symbolizes Divine retribution; the tree, each member of the church, including all Jews. "Therefore every tree which bringeth not forth good fruit is hewn down, and cast into the fire." What fire? The answer can only be hell fire.

"I indeed baptize you (all who repent) with water unto repentance (this brings judgment to your door): but he that cometh after me is mightier than I, WHOSE shoes- I am not worthy to bear: he shall baptized you (those who have repented) with the Holy Ghost and fire." What fire? Not hell fire as above. "He shall baptize *you* with the Holy Ghost and fire." The word "you" in this statement is the second person, plural number, and absolutely inseparable. Therefore the very same, identical people, whom John had baptized with water, should be baptized with the Holy Ghost and fire. The Saviour's disciples were in this crowd, coming to Him through John's ministry, who actually received the Baptism of the Holy Ghost and fire on the day of Pentecost.

"WHOSE fan is in his hand, and he will thoroughly purge his floor, and gather his wheat into the garner; but he will burn up the chaff with unquenchable fire." The pronouns "whose," "his," and "he" do not refer to the Holy Ghost, but to Christ himself. The Spirit does not hold *His* fan in *His* hand and thoroughly purge *His* floor, and gather *His* wheat into the garner; neither does *He* burn up the chaff with unquenchable fire. This work is all assigned to Christ himself. John says, I indeed do this, but "He" (Christ) shall not only baptize "you" with the Holy Ghost and fire, but with "His" fan in "His" hand, "He" shall thoroughly purge "His" floor, and gather "His" wheat into the garner; but "He" will burn up the chaff with unquenchable fire. The "threshing-floor" is the visible church; at the time John spoke, the Jewish church. The fan separates the chaff from the wheat while both are on the floor; the wheat is then gathered into the "garner"—the kingdom of God on earth, ready for the Lord's mill, and a grand festival among angels and archangels; the chaff is blown out and burned with unquenchable fire. The visible Jewish church underwent a thorough purgation in the ministry of Christ, the Omnipotent Fan coming like a tornado from heaven, and blowing out of it the multitudes of weak, easy-going, compromising chaff, the leading clergy and officials, cutting down the membership to the pure wheat, who were gathered into the "garner," and baptized with the Holy Ghost and fire; while the chaff was blown out of the church and cast into the lake of unquenchable fire.

In verse 10, the symbol is an orchard representing the church, in which each tree is a member; in verse 12, the symbol is a threshing-floor representing the church, in which the good and bad, the fruitful and the unfruitful, comprising the entire membership, are represented by the wheat and the chaff. Some holiness preachers think that the chaff is depravity in the individual heart; but if this be true, then the unfruitful tree in verse 10 refers to it. Each is no good, and each is cast into the fire. I can't see that either verse 10 or 12 refers to the Baptism of the Holy Ghost for individual believers; but rather to the judgment of the visible church. The judgment was brought to the Jewish church—the axe was laid at the root of the trees—by the preaching of John; the floor was purged— the wheat separated from the chaff—through the ministry of Christ; the wheat was gathered into the "garner," and baptized with the Holy Ghost and fire; the chaff—the bon ton church members—was purged out and burned. The judgment of verse 10 is brought to the visible church to-day through the present movement; the judgment of verse 12, which is only a continuation of the judgment of verse 10, will occur at the second coming of Christ. Some say that the phrase, "burn up," proves that the chaff is depravity, and not the ungodly church members; but in Mal. 4:1 we have the same phrase, and here it is plainly stated that it refers to the wicked; and yet it is clearly brought out in either passage that the wicked are not annihilated. From Mal. 4:3, we learn that after the wicked are "burned up," they will be ashes under the feet of the righteous. Matt. 3:12, says the chaff will be burned with unquenchable fire—fire that will never go out.

Someone wants to know if verse 11 does not teach repentance and the Baptism of the Holy Spirit are the only two works of grace. I reply, sin has but two phases, actual and inbred. Hence there are two and only two distinct works of grace; or in other words, two works of grace do away with the sin question: but neither repentance nor the Baptism of the Spirit is a work of grace. Besides, the two works of grace are not in the question here at all. John is simply contrasting his baptism with water with Christ's Baptism with the Holy Spirit.

So having by a careful and prolonged study investigated the Scriptures concerning the Baptism promised by John and corroborated by Jesus, and also the fulfillment of that promise in the case of the apostles and disciples on the day of Pentecost, let us now proceed to make farther investigations. We will take the case of Cornelius (Acts 10).

The Word says that Cornelius was "A devout man, and one that feared God with all his house, which gave much alms to the people, and prayed to God alway." There are not many sanctified people living above this man. In Peter's vision, he "saw heaven opened, and a certain vessel descending unto him, as it had been a great sheet knit at the four corners, and let down to the earth: wherein were all manner of fourfooted beasts of the earth, and wild beasts, and creeping things, and fowls of the air. And there came a voice to him, Rise, Peter; kill, and eat. But Peter said, Not so, Lord; for I have never eaten anything that is common or unclean." What did these "fourfooted beasts of the earth, and wild beasts, and creeping things, and fowls of the air" represent? Surely it was Cornelius and his household. If God had told Peter to go to Cornelius's before he had this vision, Peter would have said, I can't do that, Lord, he is a Gentile, he is unclean. But God had told Peter not to call that man common for He had cleansed him. "What God hath cleansed, that call not thou common." So Cornelius and his household were cleansed—sanctified—before Peter ever went down there.

"But what are you going to do with that Scripture in which Peter declares that he and the rest of the apostles were sanctified on the day of Pentecost, and that Cornelius and his household were sanctified while he was preaching to them?" Well, bring it up, and we will see about it. "Very well, here it is in Acts 15 : 7-9." Read it please. "I will do so with pleasure." "And when there had been much disputing, Peter rose up, and said unto them, Men and brethren, ye know how that a good while ago, God made choice among us, that the Gentiles by my mouth should hear the word of the gospel, and believe. And God, which knoweth the hearts, bare them witness, giving them the Holy Ghost, even as he did unto us; and put no difference between us and them, *purifying* their hearts by faith." The Greek here rendered *"purifying"* is not the present participle *"katharion,"* but the aorist participle *"katharisas,"* which, when correctly rendered, is *"having purified."* So we read: "And put no difference between us and them, having purified their hearts by faith." This establishes forever the fact that Cornelius and his household were sanctified before Peter went there; and since it is plainly stated that their case was parallel with that of the disciples on the day of Pentecost, we are thus brought face to face with the fact that the disciples were sanctified before Pentecost. Thank you for this Scripture.

We are told that Acts 2 : 38 teaches that the Baptism of the Spirit and sanctification are the same. Let us read: "Repent and be baptized every one of you in the name of Jesus Christ for the remission of sins, and ye shall receive the gift of the Holy Ghost." Now, if we take this verse of Scripture as involving the whole plan of salvation, then all one needs to do to be sanctified and receive the Baptism of the Spirit is to repent, for not one word is said about consecration. "But we have to infer that Peter meant for them to consecrate in order to be sanctified." Certainly. And since we have to infer that consecration is understood, we may just as legitimately infer that sanctification is understood.

Taking the disciples at Ephesus (Acts 19: 1-6), we find nothing is said of their sanctification neither before nor at the time of their Baptism. There is no proof that they were sanctified on this occasion. If this was the time when they were sanctified, then the evidence of sanctification is speaking with tongues. "And they spake with other tongues and prophesied."

The Baptism of the Spirit has nothing to do with the sin question, but is an enduement of power for service. We are sanctified at Calvary. Where did Jesus suffer to sanctify the people? Outside the gate—at Calvary. In Eph. 2: 16, we learn that enmity—carnality—was slain at the cross, and not at Pentecost. Jesus that He might sanctify the people suffered without the gate—"He led them out" (Luke 24: 50). He went to His Father that He might send the Comforter. The disciples received the Holy Spirit within the gate. We are sanctified with the blood. "If we walk in the light, as he is in the light, we have fellowship one with another, and the blood of Jesus Christ his Son cleanses us from all sin" (1 John 1 : 7). There are many passages which teach this, but not a single passage teaches that we are sanctified at Pentecost. Sanctification is just as separate from the Baptism of the Holy Spirit as Calvary is from Pentecost—as subtraction is from addition. At Calvary the old man dies; at Pentecost you are filled with the Holy Spirit.

Jesus had no sin, and yet He had to receive the Baptism of the Holy Spirit before He entered upon His ministry. This Baptism is for service. Jesus needed it to heal the sick, to raise the dead; He needed it in Gethsemane, and at Calvary. If Jesus, who had no sin, needed the Baptism, surely you need it also.

I believe nearly all forms of religion teach sanctification in some way, *i. e.,* they all teach that we must be sanctified to get to heaven. But the teachings of different ones differ as to when and where the cleansing takes place. The Presbyterians and Baptists teach that we are sanctified at death; the Roman Catholics in purgatory; many Holiness churches at Pentecost. Where does God say that we are sanctified? "Wherefore Jesus also, that he might sanctify the people with his own blood, suffered without the gate." Where did He suffer? On Calvary. What did He do for the people? Sanctified them with His own blood. "Yes, but hold up; the Presbyterians, the Baptists, the Roman Catholics, the great Holiness churches, teach differently." Now, who will you believe, God or these churches? The reason many holiness people teach that the Baptism of the Holy Spirit is sanctification, is they have made salvation two blessings, first and second, and thus far will they go and no farther; and they twist the Scripture to fit their doctrine.

Now, if the Baptism of the Holy Spirit sanctifies, no one was ever sanctified until Pentecost, for no one was ever baptized with the Spirit until then. That no one was ever sanctified until Pentecost, we know to be untrue. Read David's experience in the twenty-third Psalm. Note the command to Abraham, "Walk before me, and be thou perfect" (Gen. 17:1). Listen: "And ye shall be holy men unto me" (Ex. 22:31). "Ye shall be holy: for I the Lord your God am holy" (Lev.

19:2). So holiness or sanctification was required of the Jews long before the era of Christianity was ushered in.

Observe the real experience of a true Hebrew: He possessed clean hands and a pure heart;" was "an Israelite in whom is no guile." Listen at David: "Wash me thoroughly from mine iniquity, and cleanse me from my sin." "Purge me with hyssop, and I shall be clean: wash me, and I shall be whiter than snow" (Ps. 51:2, 7).

"There was a man in the land of Uz, whose name was Job; and that man was perfect and upright, and one that feared God, and eschewed evil" (Job 1:1). "And they were both righteous before God, walking in all the commandments and ordinances of the Lord blameless" (Luke 1:6).

Sanctification is a dedication; the Baptism of the Holy Spirit is an empowerment. The one is entirely (as to its second phase) a subtraction; the other is wholly an addition. Sanctification has to do with sin; the Baptism of the Holy Spirit has to do only with the saint.

We hope that all who read these lines will be able to distinguish between sanctification and the Baptism of the Spirit. To count them as one and the same is to mix up the Scriptures.

CHAPTER IX.

God fashioned the land of Palestine to be the model land of all lands, to contain the products of all zones and climes, to be a miniature world in itself, and so He arranged the coming and going of its rain clouds on a spiritual pattern, to beautifully adumbrate the movements of the Holy Spirit. So just what rain is to the earth, the Holy Spirit is to the soul. God arranged the showers of rain in the land of Canaan, as a type of the operations of grace. Many Scriptures allude to the early and the latter rain, and these rains are used as types of the Holy Spirit (Deut. 11:14; Jer. 5:24; Hos. 6:3; Joel 2:23, and Jas. 5:7).

The land of Canaan received two special rains each year. One in the early spring to give the earth a good soaking, and cause the seed, just planted, to sprout. The soil of that land is very fine and heavy, and so a rain will last three times as long as in land of which the soil is lighter. After the early rain, there came a dry spell of several weeks, allowing ample time of bright clear weather for the cultivation of the crops. Then there came another copious rain, the latter rain, just in time to re-enforce the exhausted forces of the grains and fruits with abundance of sap. The latter rain then passed away, leaving the bright warm sunshine to mature and mellow all the grain, and giving beautiful cloudless days for the reapers to work in.

Now let us make a spiritual application of these rains as they concern the church at large. The early rain came at Pentecost, and immediately the seed which Jesus and His disciples had sown sprang up. This early rain continued for more than a hundred years, during which time the church was kept inundated with mighty floods of salvation. But when the church became popular and was formed into a great hierarchy, the long drought began, interspersed with a local shower of gra-

cious revival now and then through the middle ages. Under
the reformations, the latter rain began to be foreshadowed.
The holiness revivals which have been going on in our land for
the last few years are the preliminary showers of this rain.
They have been glorious and wonderful: so much so that many
have taken them for the latter rain itself. But we know that
these revivals, though gracious, have fallen far short of the
apostolic revivals—the early rain. The Scriptures seem to
teach that the latter rain is to be far greater than the former.
The most of Old Testament prophecy is two-fold, *i. e.*, it has
two fulfillments, the first being the shadow of the second. Joel's
prophecy quoted by Peter (Joel 2:28-32 and Acts 2:17-20)
was partially fulfilled on the day of Pentecost, but that its
greater fulfillment is still future appears from Joel 2:30-32.
So we may expect the latter rain to be much greater and more
powerful than the apostolic revivals.

The early rain began on the day of Pentecost, and the first
manifestation was speaking with other tongues as the Spirit
gave utterance, and then followed the healing of the sick, casting out devils, etc. So it would only be natural to expect that
in the latter rain Pentecost should be repeated and followed
by the same manifestation.

Let us not forget that the Spirit has always been in the world.
It requires only a careful study of the world's moral and spiritual development to see that it was the Holy Spirit that led
the world by successive stages, through patriarch, law-giver,
priest, judge, and prophet up to Christ, who prepared His
people for the Baptism of the Spirit—the early rain. It required four thousand years to do this work, but under the
Spirit's direction the soil was finally prepared, the seed sown,
and then the early rain came.

From the tenor of the Scriptures it becomes evident that
there were in the Old Testament times limitations to the efficiency of the Holy Spirit. Limitations, not made by any difference in His nature, but in the conditions of men themselves.
Special emphasis is laid in the Old Testament prophecies upon
the blessings to follow the Saviour's advent in the enlarged

and intensified presence and power of the Holy Spirit. That which had been in measure, was then to be in abundance. That which had been limited, was then to become unlimited. New and glorious blessings were to follow the coming of the Christ, because of the increased activity of the Holy Spirit in the world. Joel's prophecy reveals that neither race, age, nor condition are to be unblessed by its fulfillment. John, filled as the prophets of old, by the Holy Spirit, and yet in a greater degree than any of them, stood and declared: "But he that cometh *after me* is mightier than I, whose shoes I am not worthy to bear: he *shall baptize* you with the Holy Ghost and fire." It is the *Baptism* of the Holy Spirit upon the church at large that was typified by the annual rains in Canaan.

During the long drought of the middle ages a few saints received the Baptism of the Holy Spirit, and spake with other tongues, as the Spirit gave them utterance. Over two hundred years ago, the Huguenots, in France, who were so persecuted by the Roman church, had quite a number among them that received the Holy Spirit, and spake with other tongues. About one hundred years ago, when Irving, of London, was preaching on the pre-millennial coming of the Lord, a number of persons spake with other tongues. We read of a number of people in Topeka, Kansas, who spake with tongues about the beginning of the year 1900. There were a number of people at West Union, S. C., who were baptized with the Holy Spirit, and spake with tongues a few years ago. I am personally acquainted with a certain sister, living near Magnolia, N. C., who has had the Bible evidence of Pentecost for some time before she came in contact with the present revival. While in Birmingham, Alabama, in May of this year (1907), I met two brothers, Smith and Dixion, who had their Pentecost. After talking with them a short while, I interrogated: "How long have you had your Pentecost?" "Four years last December," replied Brother Smith. "We had been sanctified for a number of years when we met a man who had his Pentecost. We saw the light, and went down and received the Baptism of the Spirit and spake with tongues." They were still enjoying the Baptism with Pentecostal evidence. I left Birmingham and came to Greenville, S. C., and here I found others who had been in the experience two years. So you see there have been some scattered along all the while who have had the real Pentecostal evidence to the Baptism of the Holy Spirit. But they have been few in number, and the latter rain has been withheld until now. It seems to have had its starting point in the year 1906. I here give a few sketches as to the opening of the present revival, and its starting point in Los Angeles, Cal.

"As my home is in Los Angeles, I am impressed to write to you concerning our Lord's workings in marked ways. . . . Early in this year (1906) God sent three humble saints from Texas to Los Angeles, and on their arrival, with a very few others, they met to seek for the Baptism of the Holy Spirit. They sought earnestly to know God's will by daily searching His Word, yielding themselves up to Him for His fulness for service. But few were favorable to what they called new teaching, so this little band had to move their place of meeting; but with one purpose in view, they unceasingly sought the Lord for the promise of the Father. So earnest became this little band that, with much fasting, they almost continued day and night for some days, till, indeed, their day had fully come, and as suddenly as on the day of Pentecost, the Spirit fell upon them and filled them, and all began to speak in other tongues as the Spirit gave utterance. But this speaking in other languages was not all, for, indeed, they were filled with all the fulness of God, and all the characteristics of the first Pentecost was manifest. Can any unbiased man doubt as to the source of this strange power, when these humble children of God were waiting only upon Him, seeking for Himself. This was, indeed, the day of small things, and only so in comparison to the promise, that the latter rain is to be much more abundant than the former. . . . In these few months from the time the praying, fasting few received the long-sought-for rending of the heavens, and Jesus did baptize them with His Spirit, up till now (October 15, 1906), this work has spread till its influence has reached half around the world. Many of all ages and races, from varied conditions and abilities, from the very young to the octogenarian, those learned and of no education, each alike has received a definite Baptism of the Spirit. From here God has sent those living witnesses for Him up the coast for hundreds of miles across the continent; into China, India, Africa and Jerusalem—each able to speak in any language to whom God sends, using the language thus given of God with absolute perfection."—A. H. Post, in "Way of Faith," November 8, 1906.

"The center of this work is an old wooden Methodist church, marked for sale, partly burned out, recovered by a flat roof and made into two flats by a floor. It is unplastered, simply whitewashed on the rough boarding. Up stairs is a long room, furnished with chairs and three California redwood planks, laid end to end on backless chairs. This is the Pentecostal 'upper room,' where sanctified souls seek Pentecostal fulness, and go out speaking in new tongues and calling for the old-time references to 'new wine.' There are smaller rooms where hands are laid on the sick and 'they recover' as of old. Below is a room 40 x 60 feet, filled with odds and ends of chairs, benches, and backless seats, where the curious and the eager sit for hours listening to strange sounds and songs and exhortations from the skies. In the center of the big room is a box on end, covered with cotton, which a junk man would value at about 15 cents. This is the pulpit from which is sounded forth what the leader, Brother Seymour, calls old-time repentance, old-time pardon, old-time sanctification, old-time power over devils and diseases, and the old-time 'Baptism with the Holy Ghost and fire.'

"Meetings begin at 10 o'clock every morning and are continued until near midnight. There are three altar services daily. The altar is a plank on two chairs in the center of the room, and here the Holy Ghost falls on men and women and children in old Pentecostal fashion as soon as they have a clear experience of heart purity. Proud preachers and laymen with great heads, filled and inflated with all kinds of theories and beliefs, have come here from all parts, have humbled themselves and got down, not 'in the straw, but 'on' the straw matting, and have thrown away their notions, and have wept in conscious emptiness before God and begged to be 'endued with power from on high,' and every honest believer has received the wonderful incoming of the Holy Spirit to fill and thrill and melt and energise his physical frame and faculties, and the Spirit has witnessed to His presence by using the vocal organs in the speaking forth of a 'new tongue.' "—Article in "Way of Faith, October 11, 1906.

In this way, and in this humble place this movement had its beginning. Every great epoch in the history of the church has been brought about through humble instrumentality. The great preachers are always set aside when a reformation sets in. Indeed, it has been true through the history of the ages, that the leaders always reject greater light. I know but very few great holiness leaders who have accepted this revival. How they do dislike to give up the lines to others! They would gladly hail this movement if they could continue to hold the reins, but, oh, how they dislike to recognize a movement so humble! But do what they may, they are loosing their hold on the people. Those who reject light must go down. This movement has no leader except the Holy Spirit. It started with a few saints in Los Angeles, but they are not recognized as the leaders. Some have tried to make themselves leaders, but the movement will not be led by them. Every one whom I have known to try to take the lead of the movement in a prayer meeting, church, community, or country has been defeated. It will not be led by man. Thank God! The Spirit attends to His work. It is true, there are many who are being greatly used of God to spread this revival, but none of them are leaders; we are following the Holy Spirit. Last November (1906), Rev. G. B. Cashwell, of Dunn, N. C., went across the continent to California to seek his Pentecost. He received Him, and came back to his home at Dunn and began a meeting in this town December 29, 1906, which continued near a month, during which time scores of people in the South received their

Pentecost. From here they scattered in every direction, and began to spread the fire. And so it still continues to spread up to date. Praise God! Praise Him! Praise Him!

So a great revival is now upon us, and it is sweeping the world. This is the latter rain. Many missionaries have already gone from this movement to foreign fields. Never did any movement spread so fast and so wide. Not many sinners are being saved at this time. The latter rain is, not to bring up seed, but to ripen the fruit. So we need not expect many sinners saved in Christendom these days. "Be glad, then, ye children of Zion, and rejoice in the Lord your God: for he hath given you the former rain moderately, and he will cause to come down for you the rain, the former rain, and the latter rain in the first month" (Joel 2:23). This Scripture teaches that lands upon which the early rain has never fallen, *i. e.*, the heathen fields will receive both the early and latter rain during this revival. So I am expecting millions of souls saved, sanctified, and filled with Holy Spirit on foreign fields.

After the latter rain there was a dry spell, during which the grain matured and mellowed, and then came the harvest, and then the winter. So it will be at the end of this revival. After this great outpouring of Pentecost, there will come another dry spell, in which severe trials will mellow the saints and mature them for the harvest, and then will set in the wintry storms of the Great Tribulation, to be ended only by the millennial spring morning, when Christ and His glorified saints shall "return from the wedding to take charge of the world."

Jesus said, "When the Comforter comes He shall testify of me." During the early rain the Holy Spirit, when giving utterance through a person, spake of the sufferings, death, and resurrection of the Lord; in these days of the latter rain the burden of the messages is the second coming of the Lord, the marriage and the marriage supper of the Lamb.

The holiness people have been for years praying for a general revival. God has sent it. But because it has brought greater light on the Word, and different from the old theory, and not exactly through the same old channels and leaders, and not in exact accord with the numerous holiness books scattered over our land, one-half the holiness people have turned their backs upon it.

The higher you climb, the harder the devil will fight you. The faster you run, the more dust you will raise, the more noise you will make, the more stock you will kill; and still it is wonderfully true, the more passengers you will haul. The other railroad men who cannot make the same schedule time will talk of danger and disaster that must overtake those who patronize the lightning express, and thus help advertise to the world that there is a lightning express—and thus keep her cars packed. Yet the slow-scheduled trains get a great many passengers. Some people like to ride all day for a dollar, even though they pay regular car fare.

I believe in progressive theology, in aggressive effort, in agitation, in conflict, in conquest, and in crowns. There can be no movement without friction, no battle without issue, no issue without the drawing of lines. The devil has rights in this world, but they are the rights of conquest; and only by that right does he hold it, and never will he surrender an inch of his ground until it is covered with blood. The lines have never been drawn at any time that those who were loyal to God did not take a stand for truth and right; and God fought with them, and through Him they did valiantly, for He himself said: "One can chase a thousand, and two can put ten thousand to flight."

The greatest triumphs of the cross ever witnessed by man have been when the roar of cannon and the rattle of musketry and smoke of guns almost drowned the voice of God and hid His face; and yet when the din and smoke of battle blew away, we saw that God was with us and the angels had pitched their tents about us. The Scriptures have much to say of warfare, and we sing of "soldiers of the cross." We are truly in a warfare now, and while victory means crowns and palms and harps, it also means scars and hardships, but the command is: "Earnestly contend for the faith which was once delivered unto the saints," "Fight the good fight of faith," and "Lay hold on eternal life."

The apostles had a great fight in preaching Jesus and putting forth the plan of salvation. Then came the long drought of the Middle Ages, during which the whole truth was lost sight of. A few centuries ago God raised up Martin Luther to lay the foundation of the gospel which is justification by faith; and you remember what a revolution it produced, and how he was opposed in preaching this wonderful truth. How he did stir Europe and shake the world! Why so? Because he brought new light on God's truth, and God's Spirit was behind it.

After this truth was accepted, God raised up John Wesley to turn on more light by presenting the great doctrine of entire sanctification by faith. He, like Luther, was opposed, but the world received another great shaking, the Holy Spirit confirming the truth proclaimed in signs and wonders.

Then came the truths of Divine healing and the pre-millennial coming of the Lord. Each of these were fought by the powers of darkness. Now since the truths of justification, sanctification, Divine healing, and the pre-millennial coming of the Lord have been accepted by many, God is turning on more light, and the fight is now on the Baptism of the Holy Spirit and the evidence of Pentecost.

All things are culminating—coming to a head. Shall not the children of God be as wise? Has not God the right to impart new light to His children from time to time as He may choose? General principles remain the same, but there are sovereign principles at work, not so clearly defined even in the Scriptures, though always in harmony with them. We have in mind the fact that since the days of the apostasy of the early church we have been groping our way slowly back to God as faith could grasp the thought, as we could receive the light. Up through the restoration, justification sighted and re-established, though greatly fought at the time. It was fought by the professed church, as is always the case. It seems in general to be her quarrel, a quarrel within herself, her own worst enemy every time. Then sanctification came, another long lost blessing. Fagots and stones and dogs and howling mobs and criticisms have been the price. The synagogues have always blindly led in this resistance of their own best good.

Now light has come; the latter rain is falling; the command to go forward is upon us. What shall we do? If we have been "satisfied wholly" under the best light we have had, shall that hinder us from receiving greater light and inspiration of God to-day? When a person is first converted, he is "satisfied wholly" for the time being; but if he means to go all the way with God, as soon as he sees God wants to eradicate the carnal mind he becomes hungry for sanctification: and so on from one degree of grace to another. So many are afraid and ashamed to confess that they have been in the dark, and preached in the dark. Oh, brethren, break away from this bondage, limitations of men to God. We must move forward. We are coming back to God, to the theory of the Spirit dispensation. The Bible has been our chart for direction, but by the Spirit it is unfolding, returning to apostolic light. We are drawing out of the woods, objects become clearer as we approach them. Before they were hazy, telescoped. Now we can see them differently and understand.

CHAPTER X.

OUR Lord in talking to His disciples just before His death, insisted upon the necessity of a vital union between Himself and the believer or disciple. The relationship between Christ and His disciples was not to be a mechanical, conditional, temporary, nor an optional union, but was to be as vital as exists between the vine and the branches. Indeed, such is the illustration He uses and by which He also enforces this truth. And so He argues that the branch without the vitality of the vine is dead and no value, except to be burned; but that with this vital life communicated and used, fruit will be borne that will become an evidence of the internal nature in due season; so that the fruit borne by the disciples becomes, not an evidence of a certain degree of grace, but an evidence of their discipleship (John 15: 1-8).

The important truth we wish to consider now is, what is the fruit of the spiritual life which becomes the test of real discipleship? Two results are secured by fruit, viz., nourishment and increase, or food and seed. The natural primary purpose of fruit is the sustenance of the seed, and to maintain and secure the perpetuation and development of the seed in its future life. It is only a secondary purpose that it ever contributes to the sustenance of other life than its own. We do not purpose now to study the nature of the stem, nor the need of the branch, nor to enquire as to its ability to endure the various vicissitudes of climate, weather, storm, frost, heat or drought. We are not even to consider the form of leaf with which it is outwardly adorned. But we come now to enquire after results growing therefrom that perpetuate the spiritual life in the soul and secure its nourishment and growth when the seed having died that it may live again. In other words, we come now to enquire what are the spiritual characteristics given to a soul by the Spirit, which will endure the shock of death, and which will form a basis of the eternal glory of the believer.

Of course, we know that richly developed Christian character is the surest means of imparting spiritual nourishment to other souls; but let us not mistake the effect for the cause, nor the blessings which flow from fruit bearing for the fruit itself. So let us ever remember that developed Christian graces in the believer, is the fruit of the Spirit and the evidence of discipleship.

Paul says: "The fruit of the Spirit is love, joy, peace, long suffering, gentleness, goodness, faith, meekness, temperance" (Gal. 5:22, 23). This is not the enumeration of so many kinds of fruit. There are diversities of gifts, but there is only one fruit. These are the different characteristics of the one common result of union with Christ, and so, taken as a whole, constitute the fruit of the Spirit. Every Christian bears this fruit, whatever may be his degree of grace; not simply one or more of the characteristics, but all of them—the fruit of the Spirit—at one and the same time, and at all times.

These characteristics of fruit, while begotten by the Holy Spirit, are developed in the soul, not naturally, but spiritually. Hence there devolves upon the Christian the responsibility to seek their development, using such means as may be granted by the Spirit to make them to abound more and more. Sometimes the development may be dwarfed and imperfect, sometimes the development is hindered, but if we will remove all obstacles and let the Holy Spirit take up His abiding place in our soul, then in greater or less power of development will this fruit be found. It is our Christian duty to see that nothing hinders the growth of these characteristics, since the world so much needs to feel the power of their highest development.

Nor can we fail to recognize the blessed state of that soul in which these characteristics abound. It is the heavenly state. Oh, may we all seek to abound more and more in these graces.

CHAPTER XI.

IT is wonderful to note how everything in the Bible, every line of truth, every development of error, every phase of natural and church history, has its beginning in the book of Genesis. Here we have the account of the creation of heaven and earth, with all that in them is. The whole world must have been an Eden, while the garden was a select spot for the habitation of the first pair in their innocence. This was a pure, holy, happy, sinless, and unsuffering world. Here we see how sin entered the world; and here we have the first promise of the Redeemer. In Genesis we see how step by step man wandered farther and farther away from God; in Revelation we see all things brought back to God and renewed. Each step which man has taken away from God has brought a great gulf between him and God, and between man and man, which man has been able to bridge and recross only by the redeeming grace and salvation of our Lord and Saviour Jesus Christ.

If you will read in Genesis the eleventh chapter, you will find the account of the first organization on earth for the purpose of opposing the church of God. Although man had strayed far away from God, and sin had divided the families of the earth into nations, yet the whole earth was of one language, and of one speech. The children of men said, "Go to, let us build us a city and a tower, whose top may reach unto heaven; and let us make us a name, lest we be scattered abroad upon the face of the whole earth." This city was called *Babel*, which, in the language of the time, means *The Gate of God;* of course, not the God of Noah, for the whole proceeding was in known and intended antagonism to the true God and His will and commands. God came down and there confounded their language, that they could not understand one another's speech. "So the Lord scattered them abroad from thence upon the face of the earth: and they left off to build the city." On account of this confounding of language, the word *Babel* or *Babylon* now means "confusion" or the "city of misunderstanding."

Great and deep was the gulf that Babylon, or the confusion of languages, excavated between man and man. Rivers can be bridged, oceans can be crossed; but after we are on the other shore, the lines which Babylon drew are still between us and our fellow-man. Grammars and rhetorics may be mastered and dictionaries wore out by study; but after putting all our intellectual powers to the task for a lifetime, man can hope to bridge only a few chasms, and to speak imperfectly only a few dialects.

The question of sin, as far as our relationship to God is concerned, is completely done away at Calvary; but all the effects of sin, as far as the world as a whole is concerned, will never be removed—the chasms will never be completely filled—until the earth is renewed. In the renewed earth, as all vestiges of Babylon will have been destroyed, the whole human race will be of one language. The Saviour, who was promised to the world after its fall into sin, was not only to save His people from farther sin, but the primary purpose of His advent into the world was to undo that which sin had already done. While, as we have said, the question of sin as far as individuals are concerned, was not simply bridged over, but completely done away at Calvary; yet many of the effects of sin, many chasms, will continue until the complete redemption of the earth,

If, after our heart is cleansed from all sin at Calvary, we go on in the grace and power of God, He will bridge and enable us to cross many chasms into which others fall. While the "confusion of language" will never be completely done away until the "restoration of all things," yet this chasm was bridged at Pentecost. The bridging of Babylon is contained in the promise of Jesus himself: "But ye shall receive the power of the Holy Ghost coming upon you: and ye shall be witnesses unto me both in Jerusalem, and in all Judea, and in Samaria, and unto the uttermost part of the earth." Jesus had just said,

"Go ye into all the world, and preach the gospel to every creature" (Mark 16:15). What a task! From a human standpoint impossible. The chasms are too many and too great to
cross. When can we learn all the different languages? Why,
says He, the power of the Holy Ghost coming upon you will
build bridges from you in Jerusalem unto all Judea, and unto
Samaria, and unto the uttermost part of the earth. Whatever
may be his degree of grace, to whatever heights he may have
attained, whatever work he may have accomplished for God,
that person who receives his Pentecost will cross a bridge over
which he has never passed before. That person who has received the gift of tongues has a bridge from him across Babylon to every creature on earth.

Why do men minify the gift of tongues? The other eight
special gifts are grand, and are numerated among "the best,"
but not one of them will bridge Babylon. Is it a great thing
to be able to preach the gospel to every creature with whom
we meet? Then the gift of tongues is just that great.

Oft and anon assemble here and there great convocations of
scholarly clergymen and high-steeple officials, with tall plug
hats, sleek coats, toothpick shoes and golden-headed canes, with
long faces and lugubrious countenances and deep sighs, con-
sulting one with another, "How to reach the masses" They
are nineteen centuries behind the times. That problem was
solved at Pentecost. Come down from your "lofty pinnacles"
and tarry at Jerusalem until you receive the Baptism of the
Holy Ghost and fire, and immediately you can cross over to
the other shore, and the masses will reach you.

For centuries we have been trying to preach the gospel in
all nations and reach every creature with the glad proclamation of salvation. God has blessed the means used and the
efforts put forth as best He could. The progress has been
slow. God is now augmenting the spread of the gospel by
bridging and enabling His children to cross at once the chasms
which they hitherto have had to cross by years of study and
practise. I believe as soon as many receive the gifts of the
Spirit, persecutions will arise that will scatter us to every

corner of the earth, and thus the gospel will be preached to every creature.

The manifestation of writing which many are having in these days is, no doubt, a means by which God is going to augment the spread of the gospel among the heathen. Scores of pages are often written in another language with one hand under the power of the Spirit in a short time. The manifestation of singing and instrumental music in foreign dialects and tunes will also, no doubt, be greatly used of God in spreading the gospel.

Thus we see that the great inanity brought between the nations of the earth by the "confusion of tongues" is spanned over, and is spanned over only by Pentecost.

CHAPTER XII.

THE JUDGMENT.

"For the time is come that judgment must begin at the house of God: and if it first begin at us, what shall the end be of them that obey not the gospel of God? And if the righteous scarcely be saved, where shall the ungodly and the sinner appear?" (1 Pet. 4: 17, 18.)

There are some things in the Bible which we may not understand; but there are many things which are too plain to be misunderstood. And one among others is the fact that "God hath appointed a day, in the which he will judge the world in righteousness by that man whom he hath ordained" (Acts 17: 31). As to just how, or the circumstances under which this judgment is to take place, however, there is a diversity of opinion, and may be room for discussion.

I used to think of heaven as one great auditorium with a platform on one side, while just before the door was a stand. I thought at the judgment Christ would sit in the door, while upon this platform would be gathered all nations and peoples: an angel would call the roll, beginning with the first man that ever lived, and continuing throughout Adam's race; each one as his name was called taking his place upon the stand, and, bowing his knee, would give an account of his life to God; the Judge setting the one on His right hand and the other on His left, according as his works had been. Then He would say to those on the right hand, "Come," and to those on the left, "Depart." I had this idea of the judgment, not because my heart was not open to the truth, but because to me the truth had never been presented; and I was unable from a mere study of the Word, to get hold of the facts in the case. Later I saw the light, and found that these ideas of the judgment are erroneous. While I may not have given above your exact ideas of the judgment, yet the majority of Christians do think of it just about as I did.

An erroneous idea arises from the fact that many misunderstand the purpose of the Resurrection and Translation. They are not something which precedes nor introduces the judgment, but they are a part of the judgment, or, better still, they are a result of the judgment already past.

The Word declares "that judgment must begin at the house of God," and that Christ "is ready to judge the quick and the dead" (1 Pet. 4:5). Now, if words have any meaning, "quick" means *quick,* and "dead" means *dead;* "quick" cannot mean *dead,* neither can "dead" mean *quick.* Christ is ready to judge the "quick" as *quick, i. e.,* men in this life; He is also ready to judge the "dead" as *dead, i. e.,* men who have passed out of this life. If, as some teach, at the close of this age all the dead are to be resurrected and brought, together with all the quick, upon one common platform to judgment, then Christ is the judge of the quick and not of the dead; and if, as others teach, all the quick are to be "struck dead" and brought, together with all the dead upon one common platform to judgment, then He is the judge of the dead, and not of the quick; and so this Scripture, which we have woven into our creeds for centuries, and upon which we base our hope, falls to pieces. But God's Word must stand; in the face of opposition, contrary to the ideas and theories of men, "One jot or one title shall in no wise pass from the law, till all be fulfilled" (Matt. 5:18).

So let us lay down all erroneous theories, and with an open heart ask God to help us to harmonize and understand the Scriptures.

The fact is, the judgment sets in before Jesus comes to catch away His own. In the twenty-fourth chapter of Matthew we learn the circumstances under which the Resurrection and Translation will take place. "Then shall two be in the field; the one shall be taken, and the other left. Two women shall be grinding at the mill; the one shall be taken, and the other left." Luke says, "In that night there shall be two men in one

bed; the one shall be taken, and the other left" (Ch. 17:34).
These two in the field, at the mill, and in bed are both Christians. They are both occupied alike; but the one is taken, and
the other is left. These are caught away, not to be judged, but
to receive the rewards of the judgment ready past. How could
there be a discrimination without a judgment? Here we see
the dividing line has already been drawn—the judgment has
already taken place with these two; and as a result of this
judgment, the one is taken, and the other is left.

Immediately after the bride is gone, The Great Tribulation
will set in, during which many of the "left ones" will go up
by companies to join the band in the air (Rev. 6:9; 7:9-17;
14:1, 13-16). Just before the close of these awful days we
hear a company called to the Marriage Supper of the Lamb
(Rev. 19:9). Then Jesus comes down from the Supper, lays
hold on the devil, and binds him a thousand years, and casts
him into the bottomless pit, and shuts him up, and sets a seal
upon him. He then sets up His throne at Jerusalem, and reigns
on earth a thousand years, during which time He and His
saints are engaged in judging the nations then living on the
earth. "And when the thousand years are expired, Satan shall
be loosed out of his prison." After going out and deceiving
many Gentiles who have been saved during the millennium,
and getting them to believe if they will follow and obey him
they can capture the King and take the world for their own,
Satan compasses the camp of the saints about and the beloved
city: then fire comes down from God out of heaven, and de-
vours him and all his crowd. Then the devil that deceived
them is cast into the lake of fire and brimstone, and shall be
tormented day and night for ever and ever. From the time of
the sounding of the trump of God (1 Thes. 4:16) up till now
the saints have been gathering on the right hand of the Judge
(Matt. 25:33). Now takes place "the great white throne"
judgment, in which John says, "I saw the dead, small and
great, stand before God; and the books were opened: and
another book was opened, which is the book of life: and the
dead were judged out of those things which were written in

the books, according to their work. And the sea gave up the dead which were in it; and death and hell delivered up the dead which were in them; and they were judged every man according to their works. And death and hell were cast into the lake of fire. This is the second death. And whosoever was not found written in the book of life was cast into the lake of fire" (Rev. 20: 12-15). Thus ends the last judgment scene.

"For the time is come that judgment must begin at the house of God: and if it first begin at us, what shall the end be of them that obey not the gospel of God."

This day is this Scripture fulfilled among us. The judgment has begun. Where did it begin? At the house of God. Among the elect. It is clearly drawing the line. Many are crying aloud and lamenting the great division that judgment has brought, but still the judgment goes on. "Oh! let us get together," they cry; "how long shall this division continue? Unity is what we need." But still they continue to declare their position, and beg all of us to step back over on their side of the line. It is a true saying, "Misery loves company." Shall we recant? or shall we go forward? These are perilous times; these are judgment days. Where do you stand? Which side of the line are you on? This line is not a local affair, neither is this division temporarily; but the line is universal, and the result is eternal destiny. Every creature must meet the issue, and each soul must take his stand. No one can remain neutral long; God, men, and devils demand that we take a stand on the one side or the other. You may run from it awhile, but it will tree you before you go far. You are not compelled to take one certain side, but you must take the one side or the other. If the movement is hell-born, then take issue against it; if it is from God, then fall in line with it. All may hold themselves aloof from this movement that can afford it; all may dabble around the edge and stir snakes and leaves, trying to convey the impression that they are the great leaders and mighty factors of the revival, without the evidence that they have even drank of the fountain themselves, that wish to do so: but as for me, I do not wish to be the fly that sat on the axle of a chariot wheel, and said, "What a dust I do raise;" neither could I ever afford to hold my own poor soul from beneath the showering blessings of the latter rain, nor refrain from taking my position in full fellowship with the true promoters of the present movement.

At least every saint on earth must come face to face with the movement. Those who see the light, but wilfully resist it, will likely apostatize. God holds us to a strict account for all light given us. Many, however, who fail to get in the bridehood, will reach the shores of everlasting bliss in other companies. But judgment must begin at us, and if part of the church apostatize, so that scarcely the righteous are saved, where will the sinner and the ungodly appear?

"Let us draw near with a true heart in full assurance of faith, having our hearts sprinkled from an evil conscience, and our bodies washed with pure water. Let us hold fast the profession of our faith without wavering (for he is faithful that promised); and let us consider one another to provoke unto love and to good works: not forsaking the assembling of ourselves together, as the manner of some is; but exhorting one another; and so much the more, as ye see the day approaching. For if we sin wilfully after that we have received the knowledge of the truth, there remaineth no more sacrifice for sins, but a certain fearful looking for of judgment and fiery indignation, which shall devour the adversaries. He that despised Moses' law died without mercy under two or three witnesses; of how much sorer punishment, suppose ye, shall he be thought worthy, who hath trodden under foot the Son of God, and hath counted the blood of the covenant, wherewith he was sanctified, an unholy thing, and hath done despite to the Spirit of grace? For we know him that hath said, Vengeance belongeth unto me, I will recompense, saith the Lord. And again, The Lord shall judge his people. It is a fearful thing to fall into the hands of the living God". (Heb. 10: 22-31).

These words carry a terrible word of warning to the soul that knows his duty and will not do it; and to the soul that in the full light of Pentecost, turns by force of will away from

the blessing which God offers to all. Verse 22 tells us that this
Scripture applies to those of us who have our hearts sprinkled
from an evil conscience, and our bodies washed with pure
water. Therefore let us hold fast the profession of our faith
—hold to the ground we have—and press on, since "ye see the
day approaching." Let us not minify the blood of Jesus,
wherewith we are sanctified, by counting it an unholy thing,
and therefore cannot cleanse from sin, nor let us do despite to
the Holy Spirit in any way; "for if we sin wilfully after that
we have received a knowledge of the truth, there remaineth no
more sacrifice for sins, but a certain fearful looking for of
judgment and fiery indignation, which shall devour the adversaries." What is meant by adversaries? Those just mentioned, who count the blood wherewith they were sanctified,
an unholy thing, and do despite unto the Spirit. Therefore let
us draw nigh and tarry until we be endued with power from
on high.

God holds both Calvary and Pentecost sacred. He expects
men to hold them sacred. The soul that turns under the light
of Divine truth away from Calvary or Pentecost turns from
God's final offer of salvation and power, and turns to eternal
woe.

To sin against God the Father is grievous enough, since
such sin ruined the human race. To sin against the Son of
God who gave Himself for us is still greater, as it embodies
enmity with deepest ingratitude. But to sin against the Holy
Spirit, the Convincer, the Teacher, and the Comforter is greater
still, since it not only includes all the others, but adds to them
transgression against all truth and light. Let each soul then,
whether in the depths of sin, or in the way of life, or whatever
may be his degree of grace, learn the enormity of sinning in
any way against the Holy Ghost.

"Whosoever speaketh against the Holy Ghost, it shall not be
forgiven him, neither in this age, neither in the age to come."

CHAPTER XIII.

THE TEN VIRGINS.

THE parable of the ten virgins recorded in the twenty-fifth chapter of Matthew has long been a subject of much discussion, and greatly diversified have been the theories drawn from it. So many are the explanations offered, that he who would honestly enquire after truth hardly knows whom to follow or what to believe. I have carefully studied the parable from childhood for the sole purpose of knowing the truth. I have eagerly and with an open heart read any and all explanations on the subject that I have been able to find, and taken special pains to hear others advance their ideas and thoughts. My heart is still open for information and truth: gladly will I hear you on the subject. By all that I have seen and heard, I have been helped more or less; but still, though greatly diversified have been the explanations, none of them has satisfied me, as has the one which has come to me while praying and waiting before God.

Below I give you the thoughts which are most strikingly impressed on my mind after many years of careful study.

Let us bear in mind that this is a parable. To speak a parable is to draw a spiritual truth from an historical fact. The best way to understand the parables spoken by our Lord, is to first note the facts from which He drew them.

"The details given in this parable of the ten virgins are in full accord with the customs in the East to the present day, and form as important a part of the wedding ceremonies as they did in ancient times. The Jewish custom was for the bridegroom, accompanied by his friends, to go to the house of the bride and carry her with pomp and ceremony to his own home. She was accompanied from her father's house by her young friends and companions; while others, like the virgins of the parable, at some convenient place met and joined the procession and entered with the rest of the bridal company into the festal hall.

"Marriages in the East always take place at night, and, according to rabbinical authority, when the bride was conducted to her future home ten lamps were carried on the top of staves before the procession. Ten is the number always mentioned by the Jews in connection with public solemnities, it being considered a sacred number. Thus it was a rule that wherever there were ten Jews living in one place there was a congregation, and there a synagogue ought to be built.

"The Jewish lamp consisted of a shallow vessel filled with oil, the wick floating on the oil. . . . In the marriage procession these lamps were placed on sticks, and thus converted into torches. In separate vessels oil was carried with which to replenish the lamps."—*M. B. Chapman, D. D.*

There is no doubt that Jesus drew this parable from the common Jewish custom of weddings, as we have given in the quotation above. I have found this little sketch of their custom a great help to understand the true import of the parable. Let us study it in this light.

It is clear that whoever the virgins may be, they all go forth to meet the bridegroom, who is no other than Jesus himself. If we lay aside all our former ideas, and come with an open mind and heart to learn the truth, whether it conflict with former views or not, from the custom from which the parable was spoken, together with certain phrases in the parable, it clearly appears that none of these virgins is the bride. She is in her chamber dressing for the marriage, when these virgins are leaving their homes and going forth to await, at some point on the road, the coming of the bridegroom. When the bridegroom comes, they that are ready go in with Him to the marriage. But it seems to me that they are only attendants, and not the bride herself. "They went in with Him to the marriage," but were not married to Him themselves. This may be new, but let us go on.

I am convinced that the whole parable is a tribulation scene. In the twenty-fourth chapter of Matthew we read: "The dis-

ciples came unto him privately, saying, Tell us, when shall these
things be? and what shall be the sign of thy coming, and of
the end of the age?" Here are two questions: When shall the
temple be destroyed? (see ver. 1 and 2) and what shall be
the sign of His coming at the end of the age? Jesus then pro-
ceeds to answer both of them. He shows that the destruction
of Jerusalem is a type, a foreshadowing of The Great Tribulation. A few verses in this chapter apply wholly to the former; others, wholly to the latter; while others apply to both.
The chapter closes by saying, "Blessed is that servant, whom
his Lord when he cometh shall find so doing. Verily I say
unto you, That he shall make him ruler over all his goods."
There is the bride. But if a servant fails to watch, and thus
goes back to sin; the lord of that servant shall come in a day
when he looketh not for him, and shall cut him off, and appoint him his portion with the hypocrites: there shall be weeping and gnashing of teeth. That is, he will be left to go through
The Great Tribulation. The expression "cast into outer darkness" is not here as in Matt. 8:12, and 25:30. In the last
named verses the weeping, etc., is in "outer darkness' or hell,
of which The Great Tribulation is only a type. This evil servant is not "cast," but simply "appointed his portion."

"Then"—after the bride is gone to her chamber—"shall the
kingdom of heaven"—not the kingdom of Satan nor of the
world nor of darkness—"be likened unto ten virgins." They
were all virgins; virginity means purity. They were all sanctified. If they had had carnality, they would not have been
virgins, because sin would have made them unclean. As these
virgins were pure, free from sin, they were sanctified, for
purity and sanctification are synonymous. "Do you mean to
tell me that the sanctified people will not be in the bridehood?"
That is what this parable teaches, and I purpose to stick to the
Word, though the heavens fall; though it comes in contact with
all the man-made creeds in the world.

"For then shall be great tribulation, such as was not since
the beginning of the world to this time, no, nor ever shall be.
And except those days should be shortened, there should no

flesh be saved: but for the elect's sake those days shall be shortened" (Matt. 24: 21, 22). The Greek word for "elect" is *eklektos,* which signifies a double outness: therefore the "elect" are the sanctified. We are told, except the Tribulation days should be shortened, there should no one live through them: but for the sake of the sanctified—the virgins—those days shall be shortened. How much clearer can words be put, to teach us that the elect will be here during the Tribulation? It is comical to see the modern teachers of sanctification twist this parable to fit their theology. Let us look the Scriptures "square in the face."

All the virgins have lamps, vessels, oil, and lights. They are alike in every respect except one, viz., the supply of oil. The lamp is the heart, the wick is the mind, the vessel is the body, the oil is the Holy Spirit, the light is the love of God. Every lamp is clean; every light is perfect. The purpose of the light at this particular time is not so much to give light to other souls, but to lighten their own way through the darkness of the Tribulations. We can be a light to ourselves or to others only as our intellectual powers float on the Holy Ghost and the love of God burns in our hearts, and causes to shine forth the Holy Spirit through us. As the oil must impart itself to the fire through the wick, so the Holy Spirit must use our intellectual powers to shine through us. The Holy Spirit dwells in the heart of every sanctified soul, He uses their mental powers; but He dwells in the body of only those who have received the Baptism of the Spirit. Then the difference between the wise and the foolish virgins is, the former have received the Baptism of the Holy Spirit, the latter have not.

The ten virgins are virgins—sanctified—before the bride is called into her chamber; but they fail to obtain the Baptism of the Spirit, hence are among the "left ones." Finding to their surprise they are left out of the bridehood, and being greatly aroused and alarmed by the fact, immediately they take their lamps and go forth to live for Jesus, determined to be true, and with the hopes of going in with Him to the marriage. Five of them are wise, from the fact that, seeing on account of their negligence to receive the Baptism of the Spirit they have missed the bridehood, they now tarry until their vessels are filled with the Holy Spirit, and then go forth to meet the bridegroom. Five of them are foolish, from the fact that, although they see that it is on account of their negligence to receive the Baptism of the Spirit they have missed the bridehood, yet they believe they can go in with Him to the marriage without the Baptism and so they take their lamps, but take no oil in their vessels with their lamps.

The bridegroom tarries; the Tribulations darken; they all slumber and sleep. This refers not to literal sleep, but to a cessation from work. Why do they sleep? It is all they can do. God's judgments are in the world. No need to work now. "The night cometh, when no man can work" (John 9:4). If the judgments of God will not touch the hearts of men, nothing can. "And at midnight"—when the Tribulations have reached their climax—"there was a cry made, Behold, the bridegroom cometh; go ye out to meet him."

If you will study the different companies in the book of Revelation, you will find that our teaching is in exact accord with that book. In the fourth chapter we see the bride and a company of attendants perhaps taken into her chamber, and the saints taking their places as "beasts"—living ones—and "elders." Both of these companies remain distinct and separate throughout the book. The Great Tribulation sets in, during which several companies go up to join the band around the throne (Rev. 6:9; 7:9-17; 14:1-5, 13-16). When the last vial of wrath is poured out into the air, "There comes a great voice out of the temple of heaven, saying, It is done" (Rev. 16:17). Just before this Jesus says, "Behold, I come as a thief" (ver. 15). In what sense does He come just here as a thief? It is midnight; the Tribulations are reaching their climax; the virgins are slumbering. It is a call to them to awake, watch, and pray. "Blessed is he that watcheth, and keepeth his garments, lest he walk naked, and they see his shame."

"Then all those virgins arose, and trimmed their lamps."

"The Jewish hand lamps were quite small, and the supply of oil would not last many hours. Even the lamps used at a festival, which would be larger, needed to be replenished if kept burning long into the night. Hence the 'trimming' implied not only the removal of whatever had gathered around and was clogging the wick, but also the pouring in of fresh oil. For the purpose of removing whatever debris had gathered around the wick, a small pointed instrument often hung by a slender chain from the lamp itself."—*Chapman.*

How perfectly all this custom fits in this explanation of this parable; and how perfectly this explanation fits in the other Scriptures! This small pointed instrument, not a part of the lamp, but chained to the lamp, and with which debris was removed from the wick, corresponds to the Scriptures, which every virgin should have bound to the heart; and this each virgin should use daily, yea hourly, to remove the unscriptural debris that may clog in the mind while in "slumber and sleep," or otherwise engaged. When these ten virgins start out through the tribulations to meet the bridegroom, they each make sure to take with them a copy of the Word. No doubt, at intervals they stop and study the Scriptures, and then their lights burn brighter, and they are encouraged to wait on till He comes. But towards midnight they all slumber and sleep. Suddenly they hear the cry, "Behold, I come as a thief." They all arise and seize their Bibles; and then they pray. The wise virgins have oil in their lamps and in their vessels—they are filled with the Holy Ghost, Spirit, soul, and body. Immediately their lights burn brightly, and as they hear the "Hallelujahs" of the coming bridal party (Rev. 19 : 1-6), they begin to sing and shout. The foolish virgins at this crisis see from the Bible that they are unprepared to go in with the bridegroom to the marriage. As they hear the "Hallelujahs" of the coming bridal party, and realize that the time is short, they rush to the wise virgins and say, "Do lay your hands on us that we may receive the Baptism of the Spirit right now." "For our lamps are burning low." The phrase "are gone out" is a mistranslation. But the wise answer, "Not so." "We have no power to give you the Holy Ghost." "Lest there be not enough for us and you." "While we are praying with you we may get left ourselves. We must watch and be ready. We cannot afford to be left now. Go tarry for yourselves, until ye be endued with the Holy Ghost from on high." And while they are gone to tarry for the oil, the bridegroom comes; and they that are ready go in with him to the marriage: and the door is shut. "Let us be glad and rejoice, and give honour to him: for the marriage of the lamb is come, and his wife hath made herself ready." (Rev. 19 : 6).

The foolish virgins having neglected to seek the Baptism of the Spirit before the bride was called into her chamber to make herself ready, and after missing the bridehood, having blindly supposed that they could go into the marriage without the Baptism, now at this extreme moment go off to tarry for their Pentecost. They dare not return until they receive Him. After they are baptized, they come and say, "Lord, Lord, open to us." That is, they will beg God to take them up into the air to the marriage. But the bridegroom answers, "Verily I say unto you, I know you not." He does not say, "I never knew you, depart from me, ye workers of iniquity," as He would do if they were sinners (Matt. 7:23), but simply, "I know you not." That is, I do not recognize you as worthy to enter upon the ceremonies of the marriage.

After the marriage is over, John says, "And he saith unto me, Write, Blessed are they which are called unto the marriage supper of the lamb." (Rev. 19 : 9). Doubtless the foolish virgins will get into the marriage supper.

Thus I have given an explanation to the parable of the ten virgins as I see it. Perhaps you disagree with me. But I beg of you an honest, candid consideration of these thoughts before you set them aside. I can find no other explanation of the parable that will explain all its phrases. Every other application breaks down somewhere. In this explanation of the parable, I have not twisted the Scriptures to fit my former views, but have faced the facts open hearted, and endeavored to learn the truth.

CHAPTER XIV.

THE BRIDE.

The importance of the subject upon which we now enter cannot be too greatly emphasized. As Abraham sent Eliezer his servant into a distant land to seek a wife for his only son Isaac, so God has sent the Holy Spirit into the world to seek a wife for His only Son Jesus. Who shall be the bride? That it is left to the will and choice of every human soul to-day to become members of the bridehood of Christ is apparent from the Scriptures; though it is just as apparent from them that unless the necessary preparations are made by us we shall in no wise become members of that body. Therefore it should be a question of the highest concern to us, *what qualifications are necessary to designate us as the bride of Christ?* The general ideas that all the saved are members of the bride, that we are married to Christ in this life, are unscriptural. So diverse are the theories of men on this subject, and so furiously will our position be attacked by the enemy, that we wish to go slow and give a Scriptural foundation for each stand we take. May God help us to a proper consideration of this all important subject.

From numerous passages it appears that all saints will not receive the same reward. To one He says, "Have thou authority over ten cities"; to another, "Be thou also over five." (Luke 19 : 17, 19). "Every man in his own order." "For one star differeth from another star in glory. So also is the resurrection of the dead." (1 Cor. 15 : 23, 41, 42). There are seven distinct rewards promised to "overcomers" in the second and third chapters of Revelation. (Chap. 2 : ver. 7, 11, 17, 26. Chap. 3: ver. 5, 12, 21). "Thou hast made us unto our God *kings* and *priests*." (Rev. 5 : 10). Other passages will be given as we move on.

The Transfiguration of Christ, which is a type of His second

coming, if carefully studied, will throw much light on this subject. The persons whom Jesus gathered about Him on this
occasion were samples of that company of saints who will be
gathered to Him at His second coming. Out of the twelve
apostles and the great number of disciples, Jesus selected only
three to witness His majesty. Moses comes to represent that
class who will be raised from the dead at the coming of the
Lord, and Elijah comes to represent that class who will be
translated and glorified without passing through death. It is
easy to see that Moses and Elijah have a closer relationship to
Jesus than the others have. Yet, while Peter, James, and John
witness the Transfiguration, the great body of disciples are at
the foot of the mountain. From this we see at least three
orders of saints—those who are joined to Him, those who
witness the scene, and those who are at the foot of the mountain.

"Know ye not, brethren (for I speak to them that know the
law), how that the law hath dominion over a man as long as he
liveth? For the woman which hath an husband is bound by
the law to her husband so long as he liveth; but if the husband
be dead, she is loosed from the law of her husband. So then
if, while her husband liveth, she be married to another man,
she shall be called an adulteress: but if her husband be dead,
she is free from the law; so that she is no adulteress, though
she be married to another man. Wherefore, my brethren, ye
also are become dead to the law by the body of Christ; that ye
should be married to another, even to him who is raised from
the dead, that we should bring forth fruit unto God." (Rom.
7 : 1-4).

The husband here does not represent the law, as some think,
for he is under the law and held in bondage to the law; and is
what holds the wife under law. He is the "old man," while the
wife is the "new man." The spiritual mind is in bondage by the
law to the carnal mind as long as the carnal mind is there. We
can never be the bride of our Lord, nor designated as His bride
until the old man is dead, for that would be spiritual adultery.
The death of the old man does not marry us to Jesus, nor mark

us as His bride, but simply liberates us from the bondage of
the law, and makes us free to be married to another if we
choose. The woman whose husband has died may live single
if she chooses. After the death of the old man—after sanctification—the real courtship between Christ and the saint begins.
If that saint yields to all the wooings of the spirit, Christ will
place upon that one "the seal"—the engagement ring—which
is no other than the Baptism of the Holy Ghost. (Eph. 1 : 13,
14). Just as it is expected that a man should first make love
to the maiden whom he loves, so the Son of God begins to
court that saint whose heart has been made pure. I say not that
the justified man does never feel the love of Christ pulling the
love cords of his heart, but the real courtship and the proposals
to marriage begin after the old man is dead. The Songs of
Solomon is a love letter, in which is portrayed the mutual love
of Christ and His bride after the engagement has been made.
Just as the maiden is aware of the fact that she is engaged the
moment she says yes to her beloved, so we know the moment
when we fully decide to become the bride of Christ. Our God
is a jealous God. When we consent to become the bride of
our Lord, He wants to put upon us His mark, that all who meet
us will recognize us as one set apart, "A peculiar people." (Tit.
2 : 14). Many would like to become the bride, but they do not
want to wear the ring. They are willing to take the ring, wrap
it up in a napkin, put it in their pocket, or keep it in their
bosom; but they do not like for it to be visible. "Lord give it
to me, but let me look at it only when I am alone, do not let
anyone else see it, it will do them no good." Brother, do you
wish to be in the bridehood? Slay the old man, say yes to
Christ, receive the seal. Let the world know that you are engaged by the ring you wear. "Oh, yes, I have the seal, but I
just testify and let the people know I am engaged." Suppose
I should bring you a certain document upon the safety of which
your life depended. On looking over the instrument you failed
to see the Governor's seal and anxiously inquire why it has been
neglected. I will tell you that the seal is there, but it is invisible.
Would this satisfy you? But so many think they have the
seal of the spirit, when they have no visible evidence.

My brother, the call of God to become the bride of His Son is the highest honor ever conferred upon us. Will you treat the invitation with indifference? or think that it is a small thing to be the bride of Christ? Do you consider it but a child's play to prepare yourself for that occasion? Mere profession or church membership will not prepare you for the marriage. Neither pardon nor cleansing will designate you as the bride. You must "be filled with all the fullness of God," which is nothing short of the full Baptism of Pentecost.

"Come, my people, enter thou into thy chambers, and shut thy doors about thee: hide thyself as it were for a little moment, until the indignation be overpast." (Isa. 26 : 20). When the trump of God shall sound the bride shall be caught away into her chamber. Perhaps many of her maidens will go with her. "There are three score queens, and four score concubines, and virgins without number. My dove, my undefiled is but one; she is the only one of her mother, she is the choice of the one that bare her. The daughters saw her, and blessed her; yea, the queens and concubines, and they praised her." (Cant. 6 : 8, 9). At last when the marriage of the Lamb is come the annunciation is, "His wife hath made herself ready." (Rev. 19 : 7). This refers not so much to the preparation of this life, justification, sanctification, Baptism of the Spirit, etc. But the allusion seems rather to be to something of the same sort with the putting on of the wedding garment, of which so much is made in the parable of the marriage of the King's son. (Matt. 22 : 1-14). Thus it is said in Isaiah 61 : 10: "I will greatly rejoice in the Lord, my soul shall be joyful in my God; for he has clothed me with the garments of salvation, he hath covered me with the robe of righteousness, as a bridegroom decketh himself with ornaments, and as a bride adorneth herself with her jewels." Who knows into what grand activities the saints of God are ushered when their mortality is swallowed up of life? or with what preparations they may then be called to busy themselves for the sublime events and ceremonies that lie before them in their installment into the relations and dignities of their everlasting estate? After the bride is fully dressed and adorned, she is carried forth to the marriage.

"The forty-fifth Psalm unmistakably refers to this subject. The qualities and doings of the King, come forth from the ivory palaces, are there described with great vigor and animation. But there is also the Queen, the King's bride, standing on his right hand, in gold of Ophir, and all glorious within. It is said of her that 'she shall be brought unto the King in raiment of needlework.' But, besides the Queen, the King's bride, there is another blessed company, who are also to enter with rejoicing into the King's palace, and to share the light of his countenance. They are called 'the virgins,' the 'companions,' associates, and bosom friends of the Queen, but plainly distinct from the Queen herself. They do not go with her when she is taken, but 'follow her,'—come after her—and are 'brought unto the King' at a subsequent time, and in quite another capacity from that of the Queen and Bride. All of them belong to the general congregation of the saved. All of them are made forever happy in their Lord, the King. But the Queen is one class, and 'the virgins her companions that follow her,' are another class." —*Seiss.*

Just at this point the bridal procession is joined by the five wise virgins. There are great diversities in the portions awarded to the saints. There are some greatest and some least in the kingdom of Heaven: some who shall be first and some who shall be last, some who get crowns and some who get none. (Rev. 4 : 4 and 7 : 9-17).

"Besides, princesses and queens, above all on occasions of their marriage, always have their associates, companions, maids of honor, attendants, suites, and friends, who, in a general way, are counted with them as making one and the same company, but who in fact are very distinct in honor and privilege from those on whom they find it their happiness to attend. Just as the Bridegroom comes not alone, but with attendants, companions, and a long train of rejoicing ones who make up his party, the whole of them together are called the Bridegroom's coming, whilst, strictly speaking, there is a wide difference between him

and those with him; so it is on the side of the Bride. She has
her companions and attendants too—'virgins which follow her.'
They make up her company and train. In coming to wed her
the Bridegroom comes also into near and close relation to them.
To a blessed degree they share the Bride's honors. And in
general terms we must include them when we speak of the
Bride, although, in strict language, they are not all the Bride.
The Bride has relations to the Bridegroom which belong to her
alone, and it is only because of her and their association and
companionship with her, and not because they are the Bride in
actual fact, that the whole company of the saved Church of
God is contemplated as the Lamb's wife."—*Dr. Seiss.*

But where does the marriage occur? An answer to this is
nowhere given. Perhaps it will take place in the New Jerusalem, which Jesus has gone to prepare for His people. We
have not space just here to speak of this city. Read for yourself in Revelation 21st. chapter. "He measured the city with
the reed, twelve thousand furlongs (1500 miles). The length
and the breadth and the height of it are equal." If possible
read Dr. Seiss's lectures on the New Jerusalem. We give you
the benefit of a short sketch from him.

"It is a *new* city, one which never appeared before, one of
which all other cities are but the poor preintimations, and one
as compared with which all present cities will sing out of mind
and memory. It is new in its materials, in its size, in its
location, in its style, in its permanence, in its moral purity, and
in everything characteristic of it. It is heaven-built; jewelled
in its foundations, walls, and streets; perfected in everything
that is charming and beautiful, 'as a bride adorned for her husband;' lighting the nations with its brilliancy, its self ever lum-
inous with the glory of God and the Lamb; the true 'Eternal
City'—the imperishable palace of the immortal king's of the
ages."

Perhaps it is within this clean, and pure, and holy city that
the marriage of the Lamb takes place. Just what the marriage
includes we do not know; we are nowhere told. John, when
in the spirit did not see the marriage, neither was it explained

to him. He only heard the heavenly rejoicing that the time for it had come, and that the bride had made herself ready. "And to her was granted that she should be arrayed in fine linen, clean and white: for the fine linen is the righteousness of the saints." (Rev. 19 : 8). When we would give you an outline of the picture which presents itself to us while reading such Scripture as this, our vocabulary fails us and we have to give up in despair. Read, meditate, and think for yourself.

"Eye hath not seen, nor heard, neither have entered into the heart of man, the things which God hath prepared for them that love him." (1 Cor. 2 : 9). Many people think this refers to sanctification; others, to the Baptism of the Spirit. I can see in it no reference to either. I believe it refers more to the subject now under consideration, together with many subsequent heavenly scenes. Listen at the next verse: "But God hath revealed them unto us by his Spirit: for the spirit searcheth all things, yea, the deep things of God." Would you learn something of the marriage? Get your Pentecost, and listen to the Spirit talk. The Lord has enabled me to understand many things said by others under the power of the Spirit, that I have been unable to put into English. (See 1 Cor. 2 : 13).

After the bride has been called into her chamber for the purpose of making herself ready, together with whatever attendants may or may not go in with her at that time, after many others have gone up out of The Great Tribulation to enter into her chamber, after the bridal party has been joined by the virgins, and all have gone into the marriage, and the great and long anticipated matrimonial ceremony has taken place, the order then is to enter into the banqueting hall. Contrary to the Scriptures and all congruity many take the marriage and the marriage supper as one and the same. Marriage is the establishment of relationship and *status;* a marriage supper is the refreshment, the eating, and drinking, and general social joy on the part of those attending it. After the marriage, the bride and groom upon invitations step into the festival hall, the groom takes his place at the head of the table, at his right stands his newly-wedded bride. She is dressed in the gold of Ophir, and raiment of needle-work. "As the apple tree among the trees of the wood, so is my beloved among the sons. I sat down under his shadow with great delight, and his fruit was sweet to my taste. He brought me to the banqueting house, and his banner over me was love. Stay me with flagons, comfort me with apples: for I am sick of love" (Cant. 2:3-5). Then there goes out the last invitation to this supper that man shall ever receive: "Blessed are they which are called unto the marriage supper of the Lamb" (Rev. 19:9). So after the King and Queen have taken their places, then comes those guests who were at the marriage, together with a great number of saints out of their graves and those coming up out of The Great Tribulation. I believe all saints of all ages, of all lands, of all languages, will be present on this occasion. Everywhere in the Scriptures do we read of this feast. It is the first grand celebration in which every saint will participate together. Abraham, Isaac, Jacob, Moses, Elijah, Daniel, and every one who has heard of the promised seed of the woman, and believed in Him, and listened to the calls and promises of God, and directed his soul and pilgrim steps for that blest city, shall also be there, whether as bride or guest. It may be that on this occasion "the roll will be called." Shall you be there? shall I? I want to be there, I expect to be there, I mean to be there, and by the grace of God I shall be there.

After supper, Jesus and the bride and the guests ride down from heaven on white horses. Jesus lays hold on Satan and binds him in the pit. He then sets up his throne in Jerusalem, and together with the saints He judges the world, rules and reigns a thousand years. After the millennium all things are made new, the New Jerusalem comes down and hangs over the earth. This city is the home of the Bride, *i. e.*, it is the palace, while the earth renewed will be her kingdom forever. "Blessed are the meek: for they shall inherit the earth" (Matt. 5:5). "And hast made us unto our God kings and priests; and we shall reign on the earth" (Rev. 5:10).

CHAPTER XV.

"THE Spirit and the bride say, Come" (Rev. 22:17).

In this book we have endeavored to study from a Scriptural standpoint the relation existing between the Spirit and the Bride. We have noticed such operations of the Spirit in the heart as are necessary to designate us as the Bride of Christ. We have called special attention to the fact that each operation is attended by a Scriptural manifestation. We have seen that the Baptism of the Holy Ghost is the seal, the grand climax of the operations of the Spirit, so far as concerns our personal salvation; and that it is by this we are marked as the Bride of our Lord. We have seen that there is such an inseparable, unmistakable Scriptural manifestation of "the seal" that no honest heart can be deceived long. That it is true, that all who receive the Baptism speak with tongues, the Bible nowhere denies; that there is a difference between "a gift" and "the manifestation" the Scriptures make clear. The Bible nowhere commands a person to quench the Spirit. It would be impossible to quench the Spirit more than to stop Him from speaking through a person when He himself is giving the utterance. Not one time can we find in the Bible that any other manifestation ever followed Pentecost as an evidence of the Baptism, but we do read where the manifestation of tongues convinced others of the fact that those having such a manifestation had received their Pentecost (Acts 10:44-46). Those who came with Peter to the house of Cornelius were astonished, because that on the Gentiles also was poured out the gift of the Holy Ghost. How did they know that Cornelius and his household had received the Holy Ghost? "Because they heard them speak with tongues, and magnify God." This company certainly took the manifestation of tongues as the evidence of Pentecost. If they had been mistaken, Peter would have corrected them. We

search in vain for one other manifestation that convinced anyone that the Holy Ghost had been given. We have also seen
from the Bible that the gifts of the Spirit are added after the
Baptism. Many claim them, but they fall far short of the
Scriptural standard. We have seen that talents and pounds
are not gifts and that gifts are not fruit. We have noticed how
God is pouring out His Spirit to-day all over the world, and
that He is selecting for His Son a bride from among the elect.
We see that Christ will not take as His bride those who are
married to another. The "old man" must be slain, and then
there must be a decision on our part, before we receive the seal
that marks us as the Bride.

Jesus held before His disciples continually the importance of
one promised blessing. He taught them to pray for it, to look
for its fulfillment, to realize their need of it. That promise
was the coming and abiding presence of the Holy Ghost. The
relationship of the Spirit and the Bride is sacred, holy, and permanent. The Master uses the strongest of terms—*forever*
abides, dwells in you. These words evidently conveyed to the
minds of those hearing them, that it was a blessing never before
enjoyed and one that could only be bestowed subsequent to the
Master's earthly life. As John was the forerunner of Jesus, so
Jesus was the forerunner of the Holy Ghost. As John prepared his disciples for Jesus, so Jesus prepared his disciples for
the Holy Ghost. No wonder then that John and the apostles
came to look to this blessing as one of the most important to
come as a result of our Lord's life and work. No wonder that
our Saviour understanding better than they the need of this
blessing, should continually seek to impress upon them this
blessing, for which they were to pray and wait, even while the
world was perishing.

The Baptism of the Holy Ghost establishes a permanent relationship between the Spirit and Bride. The same Spirit that
dwells in the body of Christ comes and dwells in our body. It
is thus that we become bone of His bone and flesh of His flesh.
We are united by the same Spirit; we are one. Sanctification
makes us one in Him; the Baptism of the Spirit makes us one

with Him. "For we are members of His body, of His flesh, and of His bones. For this cause shall a man leave his father and mother and shall be joined unto his wife, and they two shall be one flesh. This is a great mystery; but I speak concerning Christ and the church" (Eph. 5: 30-32).

"And the Spirit and the bride say, Come." I am sure that the common explanation of this text is far from being correct. It is generally thought that this united cry of the Spirit and the Bride is an invitation to others to come to Christ for salvation. I do not so understand it. The whole Apocalypse points to the second coming of Christ. With the promise of the Comforter, Christ said, "He will guide you into all truth; and *He will show you things to come*" (John 16: 13). The Spirit is ever active and operative in and through the Bride. And in all these gracious operations there is a direct and constant reference to the things to come, to make them known, and to nurture faith in them. In all these operations therefore there is a constant looking and yearning for the fulfillment of what is thus to come. Jesus says, "And, behold, I come quickly; and my reward is with me, to give every man according as his work shall be" (Rev. 22: 12). No wonder then that there is an unceasing calling of the Spirit and the Bride to the bright and morning star to come, as promised and foreshown—to consummate the great work by that Apocalypse to which all prophecy, all faith, all hope, and all the operative graces of the Spirit have reference. It is the very spirit, soul, and aim of divine grace to bring the great consummation which comes along through the coming of Christ. Therefore this united cry of the Spirit and the Bride is an unceasing call for the coming of the Bridegroom.

All the great epochs of divine providence and manifestations in this world have been preceded by great prayer. Just before the flood, before the destruction of Sodom and Gormorrah, before Moses led the children of Israel out of Egypt, before the return of the Babylonian captivity, and before the birth of Jesus, in all these cases we see examples of this truth. And so it would seem that just previous to the coming of the Lord all holy saints in heaven and earth will be drawn out in vehement intercessions and longings for Christ's appearing.

The following is from Dr. G. D. Watson:

"What an era of prayer that will be when the martyred saints of all ages, in heaven are uttering one prayer, and all the blood washed hearts of earth are uttering the same prayer, when millions and millions of those who love Jesus in heaven and earth are pleading for His coming, when the very throne of God the Father is encircled with golden cords of prayer, as if to pull heaven down to earth, and, so far as we know, the myriads of sympathetic angels may be saying one grand Amen to those united prayers of all the saints; it will be in such an hour as this that the silence of the sky shall be broken with the piercing, penetrating cry, 'Behold the Bridegroom cometh.' "

Can you say, "Even So, Come, Lord Jesus"?

APPENDIX.

After having made a careful study of the operations, manifestation, gifts, and fruit of the Holy Spirit in His relation to the bride, after having presented the Scriptural qualifications essential to designate us as the bride and admit us into the Divine matrimonial relation and make us a joint-heir with Jesus Christ, the author feels that this book will be incomplete without a chapter giving instruction as to how to receive and retain the Baptism of the Spirit. While throughout the book, he has endeavored to keep before the mind of the reader the unmistakable fact that heart purity must precede the Baptism, yet no specific instruction as to how to receive has been given. When the author drew the outline for this work he expected this chapter to be written by a dear friend, who is far more capable of instructing souls into the experience than I; therefore this part of the work was omitted; but after the manuscript has been prepared, the present obligation seems to fall upon the author also; therefore he joyfully submits the following appendix, trusting that some hungry soul will read and thereby be helped to enter the blessed experience of which this book has so much to say, and be so established on the Word that all the powers of hell shall not be able to move him.

You Must Be Straight in the Scriptures. I believe the man who builds upon the sand (Matt. 7:26, 27) is he who has a desire to live right, who tries to work for God, but failing to go the Bible way, his structure is built upon the sand, and so when the storms of life assail, his building goes down, and great is the fall of it. How many cases of this kind we have seen! The greatest trials the church has had since the early centuries are still in the future perhaps, and the people need to go into the present revival the Bible way, and then they will obtain an experience that will stand the storms. Unless we go the Bible way we shall never obtain the real Baptism of the Holy Ghost. In order to go the Bible way we must be straight in the primary doctrines of the Bible. There are so many theories contrary to the plan of salvation! Before we can obtain the Baptism of the Spirit we must get willing to lay aside any erroneous theory, no matter how long we have believed or preached it. I do not here refer to church ordinances, or doctrines of non-essentials, but to the cardinal doctrines of salvation and the Christian's hope; such as, justification by faith, entire sanctification subsequent to justification, Divine healing, resurrection of the dead, second coming of Christ, *evidence of the Baptism of the Spirit*, etc. I do not mean to say that a man must understand all these, but he must have a heart open to accept any of these Bible truths when they are presented. The Holy Ghost will never come in till every door and window of the soul is open to the truth. A person may receive the Baptism with an erroneous idea concerning the truth mentioned above, but he will never receive his Pentecost while he is fighting the truth. God does not require us to understand a thing upon which we have no light, but when the light is given, He does require us to walk in it. I obtained my Pentecost before I had ever noticed that any one taught that speaking with tongues was the evidence of the Baptism of the Spirit. I thought we had to have the Baptism before we were ready for Pentecost. God soon turned on the light, and I walked in it; otherwise I should have backslid. I am personally acquainted with some who had a manifestation of tongues before they learned of the question now before the people. When this question arose among us, they took a stand on the negative, and now they are fighting the revival. God will never give us the Baptism until we surrender our ideas and let Him teach us.

You Must Be Right with God. To be straight in the Scriptures is not enough. A person may have no theory and be open to the truth, or he may be entirely straight on the Bible, and yet he may be altogether unprepared for Pentecost. You must have a straight life. You must start at repentance, and after you are clearly converted you must consecrate and be sanctified. You must be *wholly sanctified.* There are a great many people who have been claiming to be sanctified who are not. Masonic, tobacco-chewing, easy-going preachers and laymen can claim to be sanctified for years, but Pentecost is not so easy claimed. Most of such preachers fight this movement. You must get everything out of your life that is opposed to God before you are prepared to seek Pentecost. It is possible for you to work up a manifestation yourself that will very much resemble the manifestation of tongues, or the devil may give you a manifestation while your heart is impure; but you will never receive the real baptism until you are entirely cleansed from all sin.

There Is a Death Subsequent to the Death of the "Old Man." The question of death as connected with the Christian life is a great subject indeed. I am unable to say just when or into what degree of grace a person enters before he is finally dead. There is a death prior to justification, and another death before sanctification. The sin question is done away altogether at sanctification. After all roots of bitterness are gone, there remains a self life. Just what it is, I am unable to say; but I have yet to meet the first person who manifested entire freedom from it. Sometimes I think that it must be humanity in its fallen state. We see some in every degree of grace who manifest more of the self life than others, but each one must pass through a certain death to self before obtaining the Baptism of the Spirit. Please bear in mind that this is not a death unto sin, for sin must be put away at Calvary, but a death unto self. Someone may say, "When we are dead, we cannot become more dead." And so it is with regard to sin, but there are so many phases of the self life, that I am persuaded we must continue to pass through death after death. I know that I can never prevail with God in prayer until I pass through a death. There is a death through which we must pass in order to obtain the Baptism. As to its nature, we shall see as we pass on.

You Must Carefully Count the Cost. Your obtaining the

Baptism of the Holy Ghost will not make the world think any more of you. You must give up all hopes of ever being called great in the holiness movement, or ever becoming a leader in the same. This movement has no human leader, and it needs none. Here is the place where many hang up. Still we must be *entirely* willing to go anywhere to testify of Jesus. Your obtaining the Baptism may mean for you to go to some place and preach Jesus, but never be heard of by many. It may mean for you to be forsaken by the holiness people, imprisoned by the authorities, and finally carried to the block. Have you carefully counted the cost?

You Must Look to Jesus Alone. You must take your eyes off your circumstances and surroundings, and forget the things that are going on about you. This can be done only through prayer and looking to Jesus by faith. You must not depend upon others to take you through, but look to Jesus only. Pray until your intellect is lost in God. When you begin to move along this line, you will find yourself entering a death through which you never passed before. Keep looking to Jesus, He will carry you through.

You Must Praise Him. After meeting all other requirements, you must offer praises to God. If you are actually justified, sanctified, straight on the Scriptures, having passed through a real death to self, having carefully counted the cost, with an eye fixed on Jesus, trusting only in Him, there springs up in your soul wells of joy. If there is no joy, there is trouble somewhere. A very small item will stop the joy. Ask God to search you out again. Be careful, however, to let *God* search you, and not the *devil.* You must pray until you can hear only the voice of God. You must not listen to suggestions from the devil. Surely, the witness that you are accepted of God will cause the joy to bubble up in your soul. When it begins to rise, you give vent to praises. It may even then be a task to praise God aloud, but we must offer the sacrifice of praise (Heb. 13:15). Offer the praises continually. Avoid formality of any kind, but continue to praise. Never draw back, but accept any manifestation He may offer you. At this point many miss the Baptism. Never choose the language: let the Spirit attend to that part. The Spirit may offer one word to you; it may not have the sound of Greek or Latin, therefore you draw back; this grieves Him. Accept His manifestation. Continue to praise.

If these directions be followed, the soul will now realize itself sinking deep into God. Circumstances and surroundings will be forgotten, and the soul shut in with God will be able to trust Him for the baptism. Never hold up until the Spirit has manifested Himself with your tongue. He will testify when He comes. He always comes through praises, but praises is the very last step.

Having glanced at the requisites for obtaining the experience, we come now to consider what is comprehended by the real Baptism of the Holy Ghost.

"For with stammering lips and another tongue will he speak to this people. To whom he said, This is the rest wherewith ye may cause the weary to rest; and this is the refreshing: yet they would not hear" (Isa. 28: 11, 12). It is easy to see that this Scripture connects with the words of Jesus in John 7: 37-39: "If any man thirst, let him come unto me, and drink. He that believeth on me, as the scripture hath said, out of his belly shall flow rivers of living water." "This (stammering lips and another tongue) is the rest and the refreshing." ("But this spake he of the Spirit, which they that believe on him should receive: for the Holy Ghost was not yet given; because that Jesus was not yet glorified.") The first evidence of the Baptism is the manifestation of tongues. This may or may not be accompanied by emotions. We must not mistake emotions for the manifestation. When a person reaches great joy, then opens his heart and mouth and lets it flow out in praises to God, the joy as it flows washes the channel wider and wider, and as the channel enlarges, God will keep it filled by a continual increase of joy until "out of his innermost being shall flow rivers of living water," which is the Baptism of the Holy Ghost. "Open thy mouth wide, and I will fill it" (Ps. 81: 10). This stream is a perpetual flow. Not necessarily a flow of shouts and emotions, but a flow of the personal Holy Ghost. The stream seems to flow into the soul no longer, but the soul seems to contain the fountain head, and the rivers flow out in every direction. Glory! He is overflowing my soul now! Praise Him! There may be times of greater emotions than at others, but emotions do not affect the flow. Thank God!

As the Holy Ghost flows out of our innermost being in rivers, He may flow directly from the spirit, from the mind, or from the body. He sometimes flows through the arm, and manifests Himself by writing in another tongue. But this must not be confounded with the manifestation of tongues, which is the evidence of Pentecost. Oh, thank God! It is blessed.

The first time the soul stops to think after the Baptism has been received, it will find itself let down into God to a depth never realized before. Don't get the idea that you never have another trial, for the soul being now better prepared to fight, will have greater battles than ever before. Thank God for the honor! As you fight, you can count it all joy. Each battle will carry you deeper than before.

This is the real Baptism. Have you received Him? If you have, then listen to a few words of advice from your unworthy writer.

Never listen to the devil. He will try to make you doubt your Baptism. It may be that some who receive the Baptism will never have the manifestation of tongues any more. The manifestation of tongues is sure to come with the Baptism, but it may never occur again. Jesus says when the Comforter comes, He shall testify, and then He will abide forever. He testifies to the fact that He has come in, and then we have the words of Jesus that He will abide forever. Don't let the devil trouble you here. He will abide if we always follow Him.

The Greek expression translated, "to another *divers* kinds of tongues" (1 Cor. 12: 10) is, *"hetero gene glosson,"* which literally means, "to another offsprings or nations of languages." The word *"gene"* is the same word that is used in the verb form so many times in the first chapter of Matthew, and there translated "begat." Just as the male and female are brought together to produce offspring, so the "gift" and the Holy Ghost are brought in contact, and offsprings of languages are produced. The "gift of tongues" is planted in the soul by the Holy Ghost, and then He works upon this "gift," and languages are produced or borne. The Spirit gives this "gift," as He does all others, viz., to whomsoever He will.

Read the Word, and spend much time in prayer. You must pray a great deal, otherwise the devil will sidetrack you. Enter into a spirit of constant prayer while you are at your daily occupation. Beg God to teach you to pray. Humble your spirit, and stay in an humble attitude. Never speak of yourself as of any importance; nay, let no such thought enter your heart. If such thoughts are presented, resist them with all the power of your soul. Be willing to go to any place to work for Jesus, and be content in the place where He puts you. Never try to get the lead, nor to do greater things than you are able. If you can't prevail with God in prayer, you are no good in this movement.

Learn to try the Spirits. Be careful not to follow the flesh. It is easy to start emotions in the Spirit, and stop in the flesh. Take time to hear the Spirit talk. Be sure to follow only Him.

Ask God to teach you how to lead others into the Baptism. Learn to extend no human sympathy to seekers. It always hinders the Spirit. Learn to keep your hands off and let the Spirit work. When a soul is on the eve of receiving the Baptism, your finger laid upon his head may defeat him. There are cases in which it will do to lay on hands, but you be sure God leads you before you do so. There are only two cases in the Bible where apostolic hands were laid on for the receiving of the Holy Ghost (Acts 8: 17 and 19: 6). The great thing for you to do is to pray and believe. Let the Spirit attend to His own work.

Give God all the glory all the time. Never praise man for anything. If a sermon helps you, give God the glory. If the reader finds anything in these pages to help him, let him give no praise to the writer. It is due to God. Do not rob Him. Be sure to remember this on all occasions.

Now, dear reader, I commend you to God. While you may be greatly helped by following these directions, yet you must avoid all formality. You cannot bring God down to any special form in any matter. The best advice after all is, *Get in the Spirit, stay in the Spirit, and follow the Spirit at any cost.*

The Spirit is seeking a bride for Jesus. Will you yield and follow where He leads?

And now leaving this book with all of its readers in the hands of God, hoping to meet many of you at the Marriage, the writer bids you adieu.

THE END.

THE APOSTOLIC FAITH RESTORED

By B. F. Lawrence.

The Gospel Publishing House
2838 Easton Avenue
St. Louis, Mo.

INTRODUCTION.

By

Elder J. W. Welch. Chairman of the General Council of the Assemblies of God.

In this booklet, which the author, Elder B. F. Lawrence. is presenting to the public and especially to all who are interested in the Latter Rain outpouring of the Spirit, there is evidence of a conscientious, painstaking effort which is highly commendable.

Both the author and all others who have contributed to the interest and success of the articles printed in the Weekly Evangel, are to be congratulated upon the appearance of this booklet.

God has helped, showing His favor in various ways as the matter has proceeded, until we are persuaded that His hand has been in it from the beginning. Of course, all may readily see that this booklet does not contain an exhaustive account of the many wonderful events which have occurred during the past decade, and that it must be considered as but a partial mention of the glorious manifestations of divine power which have stirred the religious world from center to circumference, and which have proven beyond a doubt that God's time-piece has reached the dispensational hour in which He had promised to pour out His Spirit in *Latter Rain* significance.

The last times are ushered in. The last days have come, in very truth. The harvest is at hand; nothing can stay the onward march of God and His glorious kingdom. Many signs indicate the near approach of Christ's second advent. It is the hope of many hearts that this little book, carrying as it does the record of at least some of the mighty workings of the Eternal Spirit in these last days, may stir up many to realize the imminence of that longed for and anxiously awaited event.

If He shall tarry for a time, it is hoped and expected that this book will be followed by another in which it will be possible to give a fuller and more accurate account of the greatest revival the world has seen since the early church period.

TABLE OF CONTENTS.

THE APOSTOLIC FAITH RESTORED

CHAPTER I.

BACK TO PENTECOST.

There is, in the religious world of today, a great activity of the Lord's Spirit known as the Pentecostal or Apostolic Faith Movement. This movement of God has resulted in the salvation of hundreds of thousands of sinners, both in so-called Christian lands and in those called heathen; tens of thousands have been healed of various diseases; other hundreds of thousands have received a Pentecostal Baptism in the Holy Spirit; lunatics and demoniacs have been restored to reason and to peace; believers have been brought into a vital touch with God which has meant a tremendous increase of faith in, and knowledge of, Him; hundreds have felt the missionary zeal of the first evangelists and have gone to the uttermost parts of the earth in one of the most spontaneous and widely spread missionary efforts the world has seen since the days of Pentecost.

The honest-hearted thinking men and women of this great movement, have made it their endeavor to return to the faith and practice of our brethren who served God prior to the apostasy. They have made the New Testament their rule of life. This effort, which is so general throughout the movement, has had a peculiar effect upon those who were exercised thereby. The older denominations have a past which is their own in a peculiar sense; they can trace the beginnings of their church and the course of its history subsequent to its foundation. The time between the beginning and the present has been sufficient to establish precedent, create habit, formulate custom. In this way they have become possessed of a two-fold inheritance, a two-fold guide of action, a two-fold criterion of doctrine—the New Testament and the church position. The Pentecostal Movement has no such history; it leaps the intervening years crying, *"Back to Pentecost."* In the minds of these honest-hearted, thinking men and women, this work of God is immediately connected with the work of God in New Testament days. Built by the same hand, upon the same foundation of the apostles and prophets, after the same pattern, according to the same covenant, they too are a habitation of God through the Spirit. They do not recognize a doctrine or custom as authoritative unless it can be traced to that primal source of church instruction, the Lord and His apostles.

This reversion to the New Testament was directly responsible for the Movement, as we shall see as we continue our history. It is also responsible for another thing, viz. the absence of any serious effort on the part of the movement to trace an historical connection with the primitive church. There are those among us who believe that the phenomena of the Holy Spirit, for which we so strongly stand, never was entirely absent from the church; perhaps this is true; but to tell the truth, all of us are indifferent about it. If we can so order our lives that they shall fit the New Testament, we care no more for a lack of evidence that the majority of professors of religion did so in the past than we do for the overwhelming evidence that the majority of them are not doing so today. We shall present a few reports of the work of God down through the ages, more for the purpose of providing a ground of expectation that such a work was permanent in the church than in an effort to trace any historical connection with the primitive believers. If we can establish a fellowship of faith and practice we shall be abundantly satisfied.

And now perhaps you are asking, "In what particulars are you so earnestly striving to revert to primitive Christianity?" The answer is of course, "In every way." We recognize the fundamentals of Christianity, we do not slight them, but in addition, we are laboring to obtain that supernatural character of the religion which was so pre-eminently a mark of it in the old days. We do not mean to say that others who believe in the new birth have wholly lost this, but we desire a return to New Testament power and custom along all those lines of activity which made evident beyond controversy that the church was the living body of a living Christ. We believe that healing for the body, expulsion of demons, speaking in other tongues, were in early times the result of an activity of the Holy Spirit in direct harmony with, nay, stronger still, a direct result of the divine attitude toward the church and the world. Further, we hold that this attitude was the only one consistent with the divine nature. If this is true, then with the writer of the Letter to the Hebrews we say, "Jesus Christ is the same yesterday, today and forever," and expect the immutable nature to maintain an unchanged attitude accompanied by the same glorious results.

THE IMMUTABILITY OF GOD.

Upon this point of the immutability of God depends all the value of the Bible as a revelation of God : all the value of Christianity as a real, proper comforting form of worship of God.

First, *The Bible as a revelation of God.* The Canon of Scripture was closed some eighteen hundred years ago; there has been no "year book" issued to keep pace with heavenly developments. If God, in character, attitude, affection, purpose or power, has removed from the place in which the scripture leaves Him, we do not know where to find Him. Mormonism and Christian Science (falsely so-called) profess to have information of a later date than that contained in the Bible, but this information contradicts that which we have obtained from the Scriptures, and we are rejecting it upon that very ground. Our very rejection of these modern messages compels us to admit that we believe that the God of the Bible is the God of today. If we make this admission, why not go all the way with it and allow God to manifest Himself in the church today as He was pleased to do in the days of our predecessors in His House.

Second, *Christianity as a real, proper, comforting form of worship*. This form of worship is founded upon the Bible and upon the God of the Bible. It tells us to draw nigh to God, to love Him, to trust Him. It does this because the God with whom it was acquainted in the days of its inception was of the nature that delighted to have man do these things. If He has changed, Christianity is at fault, it does not give a real form of worship.

Again, Christianity instructs us how to draw nigh, and this instruction was founded on the character, nature, attitude, etc., of God. If He has changed, we no longer have a proper form of worship.

In bidding us draw nigh to God, Christianity tells us that He will receive us, love us, comfort us, defend us, strengthen us, supply all those various needs which only such a one can supply. If God has altered, we no longer have a comforting worship.

THESE SIGNS SHALL FOLLOW.

Mark 16:15-18 declares two things; first what will happen to a believer of the gospel; and, second, what will happen to an unbeliever. Of the believer it is declared that he will be saved and that certain signs shall follow him. The orthodox churches admit that the fifteenth and sixteenth verses contain a perpetual commission and promise. Why not admit also that the seventeenth and eighteenth present a perpetual description of the activities of the believer. *There are no special classes of believers mentioned.*

There are only three reasons why these signs do not

follow in the church today. First, God may not desire to do these things; second, God may no longer be able to do these things; third, men may not allow God to do these things.

First, *God may not desire to do these things.* If God ever did these things to edify, and bless men, and it can be proven that they would still bless and edify, then the refusal of God to do them would create serious question as to whether He might not, in time, lose all affection for us and view our eternal loss with equanimity.

It is the excuse of many that medical science has made such progress that we do not now need the help of God in Miracle working. So long as the hearses daily carry victims of the ignorance of medical science; so long as the lame, the halt, the blind, the lunatic continue to defy the most advanced methods of that vaunted science, so long do we need the kind of help which God vouchsafed to blind Bartimeous, to the lame man at the Gate Beautiful, to the demoniac in the Gaddarene tombs.

This is not an arraignment of the medical fraternity—the world owes a great deal to them—but God can still outwork the arm of flesh.

Second, *God may not be able to do these things.* If not, why longer trust a weakening, failing God to save from sin and hell? The attacks of professors upon these manifestations of God's power have bred a doubt in men along every line.

Third, *Professed believers may not allow God to do these things.* And here you have the real reason. "These signs shall follow them that believe." When men *will not* believe, the signs have no one to follow.

Lastly, every thing in creation is either changing or is subject to change. God alone can say, "I Am That I Am." He alone can say, "I contain within myself all the principles of life and being necessary to an immutable, eternal existence. Time, conditions, environments do not affect me. I created them and am independent of them." It is this immutability which makes God an object of perfect faith.

Because these things are most certainly true, we are diligent in searching the Scriptures that we may discover those conditions which made it possible for the power of God to manifest itself in the midst of our ancient brethren. We count nothing of their faith and practice too small or too difficult to imitate. inasmuch as it was practiced and believed upon such authority and with such results.

We are conscious that the pursuit of such a course, the acknowledgment of such an ambition, will attract the scorn and opposition of those who are wise in their own conceits and who are satisfied with that condition of affairs which ministers to their personal profit. But we are encouraged in the recollection that our Lord and His apostles made such a profession and endured opposition even unto blood. We are happy in following them and, by suffering with the Master of the House, prove the legitimacy of our claim to membership in that House.

CHAPTER II.

THE BAPTISM IN THE HOLY SPIRIT.

THE TIME OF RECEPTION, THE CHARACTER, AND RESULT OF THE EXPERIENCE.

THE BAPTISM AN EXPERIENCE SUBSEQUENT TO REGENERATION.

The expressions, Baptism in the Holy Spirit, Gift of the Spirit, Promise of the Father, are used to denote the different aspects of the one experience. Matt. 3:11; Acts 2:33; 2:38; 1:4, 5, etc., etc.

In this first portion of the chapter, we desire to declare that saved men and women need to receive the blessed, Pentecostal fulness of the Holy Spirit. To this end we will appeal to the Scriptures in an effort to show that it was the doctrine of the primitive church that there was a definite experience subsequent to regeneration, and that that experience was the baptism in the Holy Spirit.

In the case of the disciples of Jesus we find the following facts:

First, they knew about the new birth prior to Pentecost: stronger still, the new birth was known and experienced by many before Pentecost.

In speaking of the new birth, Jesus said to Nicodemus, "Art thou a teacher in Israel, and knowest not these things?" Our Lord, in this whole passage (John 3), used that tense in his verbs which indicated present knowledge of the subject; present ability to experience the new birth; in effect, rebuked Nicodemus for professing to be a teacher among God's people when he was ignorant along this line. Jesus certainly did not use language which would lead us to believe that he was referring to a future experience, not at that time obtainable.

In the third verse of this chapter Jesus says, "Except a man be born again, he cannot see the kingdom of God." Again, in the fifth verse, "Except a man be born of water and the Spirit, he cannot enter into the kingdom of God." In Matt. 8:11, he just as distinctly affirms that Abraham, Isaac and Jacob will sit down in the kingdom of God. How could they *sit* down in it unless they *entered* it? How would they enter except by the new birth?

Peter, upon confession of his faith that Jesus was the Christ, the Son of the living God, was blessed and Jesus testified that flesh and blood had not given him the revelation, but "my Father who is in heaven." Mat. 16:13-17. John declares in the fifth chapter and the first verse of his first epistle that, "Whosoever believeth that Jesus is the Christ is born of God." What was Peter's condition when he believed?

Jesus testifies of his disciples in John 15 that they were branches in living, vital contact with the vine, and that they had his life in sufficient measure to cause them to bear fruit; for which cause they had *been* purged, or pruned, and were *now* clean, and so in condition to bear more fruit. Present tense.

Again, he says of them in the seventeenth chapter of the same book, "They are not of the world, even as I am not of the World." What wonderful testimony. These men were born from above; they had a knowledge of, and a part in, divine things; they were partakers of a divine nature; God was their Father: the standard was set in these words, "even as." And this prior to their receiving the Holy Spirit.

Lastly, these men were eye-witnesses of the resurrection of Jesus, and for forty days were the recipients of his teachings after the resurrection. Surely, these who looked and listened with such faith that Jesus was indeed the Christ, "were born of God." Their confidence was sound, their hearts were clean, their hope was sure ; so, when one day their master left them, they returned to Jerusalem with great joy, and were continually in the temple, praising and blessing God, until the day on which the promise of the Father came.

The truth of the matter is, the baptism of the Holy Spirit is a Christian specialty, something added to the experience of God's people by this dispensation. Doubtless, the fact that the cross is now visible in history enables us who look back upon it to see more in it than did those who, through the light of prophecy, looked forward to it. Also, doubtless, the indwelling Spirit enables us to perceive more of the richness of God's love and mercy in the cross than did those who dwelt in the times before us, but the Lamb was slain in the mind of God from before the foundation of the world, and the old worthies knew something about the new birth and entrance into the kingdom thereby.

SAMARIA.

The record of the revival at Samaria under the ministry of Philip bears us out in the assertion at the head of this chapter.

Those brethren received the word of God ; had great joy in the word and work of God ; were, in testimony of their unity and fellowship with Christ, baptized in water. *Then* when the men at Jerusalem heard that these things were so, they sent Peter and John unto them that they might receive the Holy Spirit.

The fact that these brethren were baptized in water between the time of the reception of the word of God and the time of the reception of the Holy Spirit, is highly significant. There are two great schools in Christendom who differ as to the place and importance of water baptism. One teaches that baptism is a testimony of an inward work ; that it is a testimonial salvation ; that it should be administered only after the candidate has been saved through faith in Jesus. The other says that men are not completely saved until baptized ; that baptism has an actual part in the washing away of sins. Brother, *whichever side you hold with, you must admit that these Samaritans were saved prior to the visit of Peter and John.*

PAUL.

The experience of our beloved brother Paul is also corroborative of our declaration. On the road to Damascus he falls in with the glorified Christ; calls him Lord; believes that God has actually raised him from the dead; rises and in obedience to him, goes into the city. If his own testimony is worth anything, he was saved on the road, before entering the city. Hear him speak, "If thou shalt confess with thy mouth the Lord Jesus, and shalt believe in thy heart that God raised him from the dead, thou shalt be saved. For with the heart man believeth unto righteousness; and with the mouth confession is made unto salvation." Romans 10:9-10. Afterward, Ananias comes with the ministry of healing and the gift of the Spirit.

Evidently this order was, in the sight of Paul, proper. In Ephesus his question was, "Have you received the Holy Ghost since you believed?" Upon confession of their ignorance he instructs them more perfectly in the way of the Lord, and then, in testimony of their enlightened, intelligent unity with Jesus. baptizes them in water. *After* this, he lays hands upon them and they receive the blessed Spirit. Acts 19:1-7.

Brethren, let us stop our quibbling and follow the example of our predecessors in the faith, receiving an abounding, satisfying portion from the Lord our God.

THE CHARACTER OF THE BAPTISM.

First, it is a baptism. An immersion into the Spirit; an infilling of the Spirit; a saturation with the Spirit. In this baptism, Jesus Christ is the administrator, a believing, blood bought, blood washed child of God, the candidate, and the Holy Spirit the element. Glory to God! Brethren, it is the purpose of God that this immersion into the Spirit should be an abiding thing; that the Spirit should become our dwelling place.

Second, a gift, not a work. "Repent, and be baptized every one of you in the name of Jesus Christ, for the remission of sins, and you shall receive the *gift* of the Holy Ghost." Acts 2:38. "How much more will your heavenly Father *give* the Holy Spirit to them that ask Him?" Luke 11:13. God gave his Son to be the savior of the world; the Son gives the Holy Spirit to lead and guide his church. And if it is a gift, it is to be received upon the merits of him for whose sake it was promised to us, and in whose name it was sent.

"In the last day, that great day of the feast, Jesus stood and cried, saying, If any man thirst, let him come unto me and drink. He that believeth on me, as the Scripture hath said, out of his innermost parts shall flow rivers of living water. This spake he of the Spirit, which they that believe on Him should receive: for the Holy Ghost was not yet given; because Jesus was not yet glorified." John 7:37-39.

In the fourth chapter of the same Gospel he speaks of a well of living water. A well is for private or local use. Rivers water thirsty lands and peoples. The intent of the parable is plain. Rivers of salvation, righteousness, light, blessing shall flow in the wake of those who, wholly yielded to God, are filled with the blessed Spirit.

Eph. 1:13; 4:30, declare that the gift of the Spirit is a seal unto the day of redemption. That is, "God who knoweth the hearts, bare them witness, giving them the Holy Spirit." Acts 15:8. The gift of the Spirit is the seal of God's approval upon the surrendered, cleansed heart. Again, it is a seal of ownership. By it, God says to all men and devils, "This soul is mine." We may, from within, break that seal and go out from the ownership of God; but nothing can break in from without and steal our life in God.

Jesus frequently spoke of the Spirit as the Comforter, and in making the promise of the Father he used this term. In Acts 1:4 he bids them wait for it. The old Anglo-Saxon meaning of the word was "strengthener," "helper," "enabler." The truest satisfaction and comfort that can come to the true child of God is to know that the will of God is being done in his or her life. When trials come, when sorrows roll, when burdens heavy grow, that soul which desires only the will of God is rested, strengthened, encouraged, when it knows that the will of God *is* being done, and that in the midst of all its troubles it is behaving in a way to please God.

In the last place I desire to speak of the gift of the Spirit as an evidence of the resurrection of Jesus. "It I go away, I will send you another comforter." Again, "When He is come, He will reprove the world of . . . . . righteousness . . .; of righteousness, because I go to my Father." His ascent to His Father, was a proof of his righteousness, the gift of the Spirit a proof of the ascent. I *know* that Jesus Christ rose from the dead. The Spirit that came after the glorification, has come to me.

THE RESULT OF THE BAPTISM.

First, and all the other results depend on this, the abiding Spirit. John 14:16. The baptism in the Holy Spirit is not a good feeling, the sway over you of a beneficent influence. Whatever our opponents say, Jesus, in the three chapters of John which deal more particularly with the coming of the Holy Spirit, more than twenty times uses the personal pronoun—indicating personality.

For the sake of convenience, we will discuss the results of the abiding of the Spirit under two heads, the result upon the recipient, and the result through the recipient.

The very first result is the sign of other tongues. We will cover this ground in the chapter on tongues.

The guidance of the Spirit into all truth is promised to believers. Truth theoretical and truth experimental and practical. A light falls on the sacred page when the Spirit comes that was never known before. Education will not supply it. We believe in education, but the illumination of the Spirit who inspired the record will certainly aid in the understanding of it. Also, this way of life is a strange one to our feet; we have never traveled it before; how blessed it is to have the voice of the Spirit in our lives leading us into the fulness of God; into the experience of His power. We can read about many things in the Bible, but only God can make himself real to us.

Further, Jesus promised that the Spirit would show us things to come. There are many authentic instances where men of God have foretold events of individual, communal and national interest and importance; sometimes in definite language. However, the main blessing derived from this "showing" is obtained in personal guidance. I do not mean that God draws back the veil of the future and reveals to us what shall be tomorrow as we can remember what was yesterday; but if we yield ourselves, our lives, our business, to him, he will make plain his will to us. That will will be determined with a full vision of the future before him and will lead us into every good thing which is prepared for us. Thus, we who have problems daily confronting us which reach on into the future, have a way open to us by which we can determine what should be done.

We have already noticed that in speaking of the coming of the Spirit, Jesus used the expression "Comforter." We also saw what was the meaning of the term. It will suffice us here to call attention to the experience of Peter before and after Pentecost, as an illustration of the result of the presence of the Spirit. When Jesus was on trial, Peter, when accused by a damsel of fellowship with Jesus, denied it with an oath. After the day of Pentecost, he steadfastly affirmed it before the Sanhedrin. Of course, the resurrection of Jesus had a great deal to do with it; but that is the very secret of the whole matter: the baptism in the Holy Spirit is intimately connected with the resurrection. The presence of the Spirit and the revelation of the risen Lord contained in that presence made him bold in the face of great danger.

THE EFFECT THROUGH THE INDIVIDUAL.

First, It makes him a witness. Acts 1:8. The apostles were acquainted with the facts of Jesus' birth, life, teaching, work, death and resurrection, before the day of Pentecost. In spite of this, they were bidden to tarry in Jerusalem until they should receive an induement of power which was to qualify them as witnesses. All commands to teach and preach were suspended until this command was obeyed and the Spirit came. Men ought to follow God's order today. We still need that induement which John and Peter needed. Our work for God is no more important than was theirs; if, in the will of God they could afford to wait until they received the gift of the Spirit, we can afford to tarry a little also. Follow, brother, you need the same thing. Luke 24:49; Acts 1:8.

The baptism makes every one a messenger; some of course, are more definitely chosen than others; but all are to beseech the world to be reconciled to God. And, mark you, the message is simple. "Be reconciled to God"—not to all our ideas about God, all our notions as to how men ought to live—"be reconciled to God."

It will also make him or her a worker and a revival center. O, brother, get the flame, the world in darkness needs your light; the church in her formality needs your life; the God of heaven, forgotten by so many, needs your body and soul as an abiding place out of which to reveal His Majesty.

This is brief; we have touched only the high places; we have endeavored to direct your minds into profitable channels, rather than to explore the truth in detail. We have, in effect, said, "Here is a valley, here is a mountain range, here is a water course, explore them for yourself, enjoy the detail of the scenery, rejoice in the fulness of the Spirit in your own life."

CHAPTER III.

MODERN TONGUES IN BIBLE LIGHT.

IS IT POSSIBLE TO SHOW THAT MODERN TONGUES ARE IDENTICAL WITH THE SCRIPTUIAL PHENOMENA?

The following passages contain the direct scriptural utterances upon the subject of glossalalia, or speaking in tongues as the Spirit gives utterance. Other passages refer to the subject in connection with other things, for instance, John 15:26, where Jesus says that the Holy Spirit would bear witness to him. Doubtless the speaking in tongues is a part of that witness.

To avoid many parentheses we give the passages here and refer hereafter to their teaching, supposing that you will now stop and read them. Isaiah 28:9-13; Mark 16:15-18; Acts 2:4, 6-11, 16-19, 33; 10:44-47; 19:6; the 12th, 13th and 14th chapters of 1 Corinthians.

A careful examination of these passages reveals the following facts regarding the phenomena of tongues in the primitive church.

1. Jesus promised that speaking in tongues should, (with other signs) follow them that believed. That is, that these signs and salvation were dependent upon the same thing, and that they were for the same people and that as long as faith should be possible these things should be possible.

2. From Acts 2 and the experience of the Apostles we see that this one of the signs did not accompany faith in its first stages, but only when it had come to its full fruition in the baptism in the Holy Spirit. And we do earnestly believe that men are not living up to a New

Testament standard in Christian experience unless they have been baptized in the Spirit. So, inasmuch as faith in Jesus will bring the baptism in the Spirit, it is not perfect until it has done so; and we do not refer to this work of faith as we do to divine healing and growth in grace. We believe that the baptism in the Spirit will come upon every honest, surrendered soul, just as salvation will. In fact, Peter said that those who repented and were baptized, (in water) should then receive the Spirit.

THE PURPOSE OF TONGUES.

3. Upon the day of Pentecost, some who spoke in other tongues did so in languages understood by those of different nationalities who were present. This, however, *is never reported as happening again;* and in 1st Cor. Paul distinctly affirms that those who speak in another tongue do *"not speak unto men, but unto God, for no man understandeth him." The gift of Tongues was not given for the purpose of enabling the early ministry to evangelize the world.* Practically every one of the commentators agree to this. Those who hold that tongues must be understood, and used in this manner, are without scriptural warrant and at the same time afford ground for self-condemnation. If it were ever possible to reach the heathen in this way, surely now, when so many are agreed that the end of the dispensation is at hand, is the time for these who hold such opinions to prove their faith and go to the heathen in a mighty, time-saving evangelization that would hasten the return of our Lord.

4. The exercise of speaking in other tongues was intended primarily to edify and bless the speaker; in its secondary purpose it was, when combined with interpretation, used to edify the church—and is, *when so combined*, on a par with prophecy. (Except that it takes twice as much time). Those who spoke in tongues were in close communion with God, and in the exercise, were granted a satisfaction in prayer that they sometimes were

wholly unable to obtain when depending upon their own efforts.

THE GIFT OF TONGUES.

5. 1 Cor. 12:10 reads, "and to another, (individual, singular number) divers kinds of tongues, (plural number)." In the 30th verse of the same chapter Paul asks this question, "Do all speak in tongues?" and of course the answer is "No." But observe this, he speaks of "tongues," plural number, thus referring you back to the 10th verse and to the gift of tongues. We might paraphrase his question thus, "Do all have the gift of tongues?" That this paraphrase is allowable is evident by a glance at the context.

Furthermore, in the 14th chapter of this book, Paul makes it plain that those who possessed the gift of tongues might use it upon their own initiative. He would never have ventured to say to men who were directly moved by the Holy Spirit, "If there be no interpreter present, let him keep silent, (in the church) and let him speak to himself and God." They would have needed no such instructions. But because they could speak at will they sometimes carried the matter too far and abused the gift. It seems that the gifts of the Spirit were bestowed upon believers and then the use of them largely left to their discretion.

THE SIGN OF TONGUES.

6. There is record of several manifestations of the speaking in tongues that do not seem to fit the above perfectly; and we have called such manifestations "the sign of tongues." In 2nd, 10th and 19th chapters of Acts it plainly states that all who received the baptism in the Holy Spirit in the first revivals at Jerusalem, Caesarea and Ephesus spoke in other tongues. Paul testifies for himself that he spoke in tongues, and Oldhausen, Matthew Henry, Adam Clarke agree that the thing that made

Simon Magus desire power to transmit the Holy Spirit was the result of the baptism, viz., speaking in tongues. These and other commentators say that this speaking in tongues was an uncontrollable, spontaneous outburst of praise and adoration.

Peace with God is an evidence of justification; love of the brethren, of a passage from death to life; the witness of the Spirit, of Sonship; what then is the evidence of the baptism in the Holy Spirit? Not peace, joy, love, healing, casting out of demons, all these belonged to the disciples before Pentecost. One answer remains in the light of the scripture—the sign of tongues This is the sign to unbelievers, this is the sign which did not follow the apostles till after Pentecost but which did come then.

It is evident that Peter regarded it in this light. When he went to Caesarea and there preached the Gospel to the household of Cornelius he admitted that household to Christian fellowship in baptism because they had received the Spirit, and he knew that they had received the Spirit "For they heard them speak with tongues." At his defense in Jerusalem he maintained that they had received the like gift as he and the Jerusalem church had received in the beginning; it was accompanied by the same results Observe that we do not say that the speaking in other tongues is the only evidence of the baptism, it is the initial one. Further we do not say that the gift of tongues is the evidence. The scripture does not say that the men of Caesarea and Ephesus ever spoke again, though it is likely that they did so. There are many among us who do not have the gift of tongues as described in 1 Cor. 12 and 14 who did speak in tongues as the people in the Acts did.

If you are a Jew and receive the baptism in the Spirit as the Jews first received, you will speak in other tongues: if you are a Gentile and receive the baptism in the Spirit as the Gentiles received it in Bible times, you will speak in tongues.

MODERN TONGUES

as manifest in the Pentecostal Movement conform to this description in every detail. Sometimes they are understood by bystanders; more often not. Their first use today is to bless the speaker and we are willing to observe the law of the 14th chapter in our public worship, so far as the gift of tongues is manifest among us. Those who receive the baptism in the Holy Spirit in our meetings invariably speak in other tongues and we believe that a like gift with that which forever hallowed the Day of Pentecost has again been bestowed because we hear them speak in tongues and magnify God. There are abuses of the gift among us; there were in the Corinthian Church. If ours are therefore false, so were theirs.

We are sometimes condemned as heretical, but *we are the only body of Christians on earth to whom the 12th and 14th chapters of 1st Cor. are applicable; we are the only body of Christians on earth who do not forbid to speak with tongues.*

THIS AND THAT

These two words appear in Isaiah 28:11 and 12; Acts 2:12, 16, 33.

Paul quotes Isa. 28:11, 12 as referring to the speaking in other tongues.

Observe these points.

1.   Isaiah says that God will speak with men of stammering lips and other tongues, and calls *this* the rest and the refreshing.

2.   When the men of Jerusalem said, "What meaneth *this?*" they undoubtedly referred to the speaking in tongues, for the tongues of fire and sound of the rushing wind were seen and heard in the upper room, not in the place where Peter preached to them.

3.   Peter, in answering, said, *This* (speaking in other tongues) is *that* which was sjoken by Joel the Prophet. What was "that?"

4. Peter said that "Jesus being at the right hand of God exalted, and having received of the Fàther the promise of the Holy Spirit, has poured out *this* which you see and hear." What did they see and *hear?*

Does not this indicate that in the mind of the Divine Spirit there was a close unity between the baptism in the Holy Spirit and the exercise of speaking in other tongues? For while it is true that on the Day of Pentecost Peter classed what they saw and heard together, that does not hold true all through the manifestation of the out-poured Spirit. In Cesarea, Ephesus, Samaria, they did not act like drunken men so far as the record goes.

Hallelujah, I am glad that He has come. It looks like rain—it sounds like rain—it acts like rain—it must be the Latter Rain.

We add the following extract by Bro. Chamberlain, published in Weekly Evangel No. 127.

"Often it is asked what use is the speaking in tongues, what purpose do they conserve, etc.?

"A careful study of the Scriptures and the conditions obtaining at their first introduction, will, we think, clearly reveal God's purpose in them, which is two-fold. FIRST the tongues are the sign of the Son of Man— our great High Priest—in heaven.

"SECONDLY—They are the only means through which the New Executive, the Holy Ghost, who was inaugurated and took up the reins of Government on the day of Pentecost, could have issued His first proclamation of "the wonderful works of God" (Acts 2:11), understandingly to the world, embracing peoples of divers tongues, languages and dialects; this He accomplished through "the apostles whom He had chosen," (Acts 1:2), speaking to "men out of every nation under heaven," confounding the multitudes "because that every man heard them speak in his own language." It is no wonder that "they were amazed and marvelled, saying one to another, behold, are not all these which speak Galileans? and how hear we every man in our own tongue, wherein we were born?" Acts 2:6-8

"Yes, says one, we grant all this may have taken place and been necessary on the day of Pentecost when it occurred but that was more than nineteen centuries ago, and conditions then were vastly different from those of today. True, my brother, but our High Priest IS IN HEAVEN STILL.

"Paul tells us that 'the invisible things of Him (God) from the creation of the world are clearly seen being understood by the things that are,' (Rom. 1:20), i. e., the things which we can see and comprehend with our finite minds. Thus we are referred back to the type, Aaron, the first High Priest under the law or first covenant, where we find "Golden bells and pomegranates, beneath, upon the hem of the robe round about, and it, (the robe) shall be upon Aaron to minister; and his SOUND shall be heard when he GOETH IN unto the holy place before the Lord, and when he COMETH OUT. Ex. 28: 33-35.

"The bells were the signs designated by the Lord Himself to give forth the sound when Aaron went in and when he came out, the SAME SIGN, the SAME SOUND, at both the ingoing and the outcoming.

"The tongues being God's appointed sign, when Christ, our High Priest ENTERED INTO heaven (the most holy place) before the Lord, we may expect the SAME SIGN, the SAME SOUND, when He cometh out; this is why we have the tongues with us today, pealing forth the sound of His coming, for He is nearing the door. The sound thereof is increasing in volume and will increase more and more until 'the Lord·Himself shall descend from heaven with a shout, with the voice of the Archangel, and the trump of God,' (1 Thess. 4:16) to gather His loved ones unto Himself as He promised He would do. Jno. 14:3."

We close this chapter asking you to prayerfully read 1 Cor. 1:26-29. If you have pride, place, reputation, forsake them and become one of the instruments of God's choice.

CHAPTER IV.

TONGUES IN HISTORY.

Pursuant of our plan to trace a few details of the work of God from the days of Pentecost to the present outpouring of the Spirit, we present the following:

It is obvious that the preparation of a detailed chronological record covering 1500 years would involve a deal of time, labor and research; and the publication of such a record would require as much space as we are prepared to give to this whole history. The space for publication and the facilities for research we do not possess; moreover, as we declared in our first chapter, it is the Scriptural rather than the historical aspect which interests us.

Before we take up the details which we have allowed ourselves, we desire to call your attention to the following facts.

PRELIMINARY OBSERVATIONS.

First. The primitive Christians were persecuted by Rome, in the persons of her emperors, governors, magistrates and citizens, largely because of the circulation of false reports concerning them. They were said to be atheists; to offer infants in sacrifice, and then to eat their flesh; to be guilty of gross immorality, even to incest; to be enemies of the State; and to be responsible for fires, earthquakes, floods and pestilences.

Second. The greater amount of our information regarding the "heretics" who took their stand against the established (and generally corrupt) order of things in the middle ages, is derived from their enemies. And it

must be remembered that these informants were often
as destitute of righteousness, sound judgment and love
of the truth as were those who circulated such false reports about Paul and his brethren.

Third. The Protestant scholars who have investigated these records have, in the majority of cases, been
as prejudiced against the phenomena in which we believe as were the ones who wrote the derogatory accounts of the revivals. Understand, in many cases, these
investigators believed in the *doctrines* of the "heretics"
while condemning the "excitement" under which they
labored.

This disposition to slight and undervalue glossalalia,.
(speaking in tongues) is apparent, not only in their
manner of handling the reports of its appearance in history but in their criticism of the New Testament manifestations as well. This fact robs their condemnation of
mediaeval and modern tongues of much of its weight
with those who believe that God, "divided to every man
severally as He willed" and that tongues were included in
the giving.

Fourth. The stories now disseminated in many
places regarding the present work of God are of the
the same family and bear the same general characteristics of those told against the primitive and mediaeval
Christians. We are all hated by the world, and for the
same reasons.

ENCYCLOPEDIA BRITANNICA,

Vol. 27 Pages 9 to 10, 11th edition says that glossalalia, (tongues) "recurs in Christian revivals of every
age, e. g., among the mendicant friars of the thirteenth
century; among the Jansenists and early Quakers, the
converts of Wesley and Whitefield, the persecuted
Protestants of the Cevennes and the Irvingites." Along
with this phenomena came reports of healing, miracles
and prophecy.

ST. FRANCIS XAVIER.

The Catholic Encyclopedia says that St. Francis Xavier, who was born April 7, 1506 in Navarre and died Dec. 2, 1552 on the island of Sancien just off the Chinese coast, preached in tongues unknown to him. The sphere of this man's labors embraced Spain, Portugal, Japan, India, Ceylon. He is accounted one of their greatest and most successful missionaries of all time, and, of course, this manifestation of tongues is received by Catholics as a genuine work of the Spirit.

SOUTHERN FRANCE

With its mountains and valleys was a famous breeding ground for so-called "heretics" from the twelfth century on down. Indeed, some of those old congregations are still in organic existance. In this territory the Waldenses and Albigenses were nearly coexistent in point of time, beginning about 1170 and continuing until the 15th century. The Camosards appeared at a somewhat later date and held on until 1705 or later. Each of these sects had those among them who spoke in tongues.

THE JANSENISTS.

Just prior to the disappearance of the Camosards, a man by the name of Cornelius Jansen, a French Catholic, began to set forth his ideas. It was not his intention to separate himself from the Roman Church, but he did insist on personal knowledge of God and communion with Him. This contention provoked a storm among the sacramental religionists of Rome, and the Jansenist doctrines were condemned by the Pope. Those who held to the proscribed doctrines were at last unable to refute the charge of heresy and many fled to Holland. The persecution waxed fiercer. the power of God fell, and many spoke in tongues and prophesied. This occured in 1702-1705.

THE QUAKERS.

Over in England the fire was burning at the same time. Geo. Fox, the first Quaker, had begun his ministry in 1647. He insisted on personal salvation, communion with God and the leading of the Holy Spirit. He also, in opposition to the Puritans, Baptists and other nonconformists of his day, believed in present, complete deliverance from sin. He was opposed to war for any cause, would not take oath, and the people whom God raised up under his ministry were the only ones for a long time who refused to meet secretly in times of persecution. This persistence in public worship brought much suffering to them, but was one of the great factors in bringing about religious liberty in England.

For a long time the Quakers had no regular organized existence; and it was easy for any one to obtain a reputation of being a Quaker by simply attending their meetings. Many men of no principle did so attend and were the source of great reproach to the true children of God. This condition is notably true of the Pentecostal Movement.

Later, when an attempt was made to correct this and to provide an orderly worship and government, there was strong opposition on the part of some very good men who seemed to be afraid of the same things some of the Pentecostal people are afraid of today.

The Quakers further refused to set out a written creed and did not attempt to bind the consciences of their people in minor matters.

In their worship, they permitted women to preach and pray on equal terms with the men, and sometimes had great manifestations of the power of God. So great was that power at times that both saint and sinner would fall prostrate, and frequently those falling would shake, or "quake" as they called it then. Speaking in tongues was frequent among them, not only in England but in this country.

From 1647 to 1662, a period of fifteen years, four hundred of these godly persons are known to have died in prison, while another hundred died as the result of the violence of mobs. During this time a total of 4500 were imprisoned, and in 1685 when a petition was addressed to the king praying for relief and protection, there were 1460 in confinement.

This brief account shows that these people were, in many respects, our true fathers in the faith; the burden of their preaching and practice was identical with our own. This exception should be noted, however; they neither baptized nor took the Lord's Supper. Truth requires that we add that this lack was less from objection to the sacraments than to the place assigned to them by the other religious bodies of their time.

WESLEY AND WHITEFIELD.

During the 18th century both Wesley and Whitefield accomplished great works for the Lord. Whitefield was one of the most eloquent, powerful, successful preachers the church has known. His converts were numbered by the thousands, and some of them received the baptism in the Spirit and spake in other tongues.

Both the Encyclopedia Britannica and the Life and Epistles of St. Paul admit the presence of glossalalia among the early Methodists. The latter work in the People's Edition, pp, 451, 452 has the following in a foot note, "....If, however, the inarticulate utterances of ecstatic joy are followed (as they were in some of Wesley's converts) by a life of devoted holiness, we should hestitate to say that they might not bear some analogy to those of the Corinthian Christians."

It might be noted here that speaking in tongues was not always followed by a "life of devoted holiness" on the part of some in the Corinthian Church. See 1 Cor. 3rd to 6th chapters. Both from the Scriptural record and modern observation we know that tongues are not the evidence of a mature Christian character. If, as we believe, they are an evidence of the baptism in the Holy

Spirit, then they often come at an early stage of the development of that character. See Acts 8, 10, 19. Those who contend otherwise injure the truth and create an improper impression in the minds of those who are or will be in contact with the phenomena of tongues.

EDWARD IRVING.

Sometime after the revivals of Wesley and Whitefield the work broke out in Scotland. Edward Irving became acquainted with it from that source in 1830. He was a divine of the Established Scottish Church, but for some time had been dissatisfied with the condition of things in his heart and church. When he heard and saw the wonderful works of God he fell in line with them though at a considerable sacrifice. His church excommunicated him in 1832 on the charge of heresy and he was chosen pastor of the Congregation in Newton Street London, in the following year. The name chosen by the movement at that time was, "Catholic Apostolic Church." Irving was an eloquent, forceful speaker, a man of great natural ability, the friend of such men as Carlyle, Henry Drummond and Coleridge. Carlyle said of him that, "His was the bravest, freest, brotherliest human soul mine ever found in this world. or hopes to find."

About this time the great Charles G. Finney, Presbyterian, was engaged in a revival campaign which resulted in the salvation of five hundred thousand souls. He says of himself that he "literally bellowed out the unutterable gushings of his heart." Inasmuch as he taught that the baptism in the Spirit was an experience subsequent to regeneration, it is evident that he spoke in tongues. Authentic testimony from those who knew him also confirms this fact.

Though arising at different times, under different circumstances, rebuking different abuses, holding different doctrines along some lines, these all, to a greater or less extent, enjoyed the presence and power of God, and suffered for it. We follow in the steps of a goodly company.

CHAPTER V.

THE WORK OF THE SPIRIT IN RHODE ISLAND.

In this chapter we will satisfy ourselves with presenting an account of the work of God beginning in 1874. It is written for us by a present minister of the movement, R. B. Swan, Pastor of the Assembly meeting at 7 Winter St. Providence, R. I.

My own heart was made to burn within me as I read the following. It is so very like the present work of God. I want you to notice especially the dates. There is a mistaken impression that this Movement is a mushroom growth, originating in California in 1906. This is not the case. God, Who in sundry places, at diverse times poured out His Spirit with the sign of tongues, sent the outpouring at Los Angeles after He had prepared for it by smaller, but by no means less genuine, works in other places. Observe, also, how many of our present ministry received the baptism prior to that outpouring.

The letter from Brother Swan follows:

"I was converted and joined the Stewart Street Baptist Church in Providence, R. I. in 1864, and remained a member for several years; after which I left them under the following circumstances,—I providentially came in contact with a small company of believers who were looking for the soon coming of Jesus, and who were teaching the receiving of the Holy Spirit and the gifts as taught in 1 Cor. 12th Chapter. This appealed to myself and wife, and we, with them, became earnest seekers for the baptism of the Spirit.

"In the year 1875 our Lord began to pour upon us His Spirit; and wife and I, with a few others, began to utter a few words in the "unknown tongue." I recall one incident at that time, in connection with this gift, of a sister (who at present is a member of my assembly) who was wrought upon by the Spirit to speak. She did not want this gift and refused to do so. One evening at a gathering held at my home, she was again wrought upon, but she kept her lips closed. We labored with her to yield to the Spirit, and when she did, she broke forth in a volume of words in the unknown tongues which continued for quite a time. Her name is Amanda Doughty. Her husband is an Elder in my assembly. They live at 1104 S. Broadway, East Providence, R. I.

"In the year 1874-5 while we were seeking the baptism, there came among us several who had received the baptism and the gift of tongues a number of years before this and they were very helpful to us. They are now sleeping in Jesus, but at your request for names I will append them as follows: Wm. H. Doughty of Maine, father-in-law of Amanda Doughty above noted; Zina Ford of Concord, N. H.; Wm. Hawkes of East Boston, Mass.; Eliza Libby of Lawrence, Mass.; Rose Jenkins of Vermont; Rosa Childs of Hartford, Conn. (By the locations here given, it is evident that there was considerable territory reached with this light at that early day. Ed. Note.)

"I will now inform you how the unknown tongues that we had received in the year 1874-5 were brought before the public—except those who had heard them in our Assemblies.

FIRST PENTECOSTAL CONVENTION.

"In the summer of 1875, I with some others, felt that the time was due for calling the "Gift People" (as we were then called) together. How was it to be accomplished? Only a few of us, and no money in sight; certainly we must do it by faith, for did not the Lord say so? In taking account of stock, I had eight dollars and Brother Dinsmore had six. I bought 50 postal cards and had the camp-meeting call printed on them which said, "Come for all things are free, and without money and without price." They were sent into all of the states where we knew of any who were in sympathy with the Spirit's work and manifestations.

"We hired Adelaide Grove in the suburb of Providence, lumber was hired to seat it and to make frames for tents, a long frame was made for an eating tent, and, with my eight dollars and the brother's six, we bought cotton cloth enough to cover it. A big tent was hired and we were ready for the King's business. On came the saints until the camp was full. The meeting was extended to two weeks. All were fed free, with lodging, and at the close we were six hundred dollars in debt and no money in sight, as we had taken no collections.

"On the last Sunday a call was made to meet in the big tent. The bills were presented; the six hundred dollars was raised in a short time and we left the grounds free from debt.

"The point I wish to make is this, during these two weeks meetings many thousands came from the city and outlying districts and saw the marvelous works of the Holy Spirit; many messages were given in the unknown tongues; some were slain and baptized in the Holy Spirit —it was Pentecost indeed.

"In addition. some years before the outpouring at Los Angeles, Bro. T. F. Plummer, who is now connected with the Pentecostal Assembly at the Franklin Union Building, Boston, Mass. was given the gift, and so continues. Also Sister Mattie Osgood of Millbrook, Mass. received before 1906."

The following account is given by the same brother, published by Word and Work.

"In the year 1882 a great burden came upon me, and for three days I was bowed under the Holy Spirit's power. I was led to go to a chapel in West Duxbury, Mass. (a hamlet called Ashdod), which has since been described by the reporters as "being five miles from everywhere." This chapel had been closed for some years, and sin was reigning; a revival followed, the house was filled, and some conversions followed.

"In this same year above mentioned, Bro. J. C. Osgood and wife moved there from New Hampshire, C. W. Marsh and 'wife were already there, and a small company who united with us, and the work began. All the vessels were gotten together for the work that was to follow as the years went on, preparatory for the 'latter rain' that was to fall upon His people.

"The writer became pastor and leader of this work, and the others rallied around him; efforts were made to keep in touch with those who in those days were called 'gift people' who believed in all of the gifts of the Holy Spirit and God's mighty power which would follow the baptism and filling. *We knew of many who were scattered abroad in many States;* how could we bring them together and have days of Pentecost?

"We had a chapel and a few homes where we could lodge them, and not much money; but we had not forgotten God's message to Zerubbabel when he was bidden to 'finish this house....for who hath despised the day of small things?' This work of bringing the people together must be accomplished by conventions; we began this work in 1886, we sent out notices to the saints to meet in a three days assembly. Only a few came to this first gathering, for we were out in the wilderness, 'five miles from everywhere' (five miles from four depots at different points of the compass.) The few that came we entertained without money and price. All was free, and that method has continued up to the present time, but on the last day of the conventions a free-will offering is taken and in every case all bills have been met.

"As the years pass, on they come, all were hungry for the 'bread from heaven' and the 'living water.' We must enlarge our borders; an old house near the chapel was empty, the sisters cleaned it, beds were brought from our homes, what the house could not hold were taken to our homes in teams, food was cooked by the few families of our assembly. But our barns were not large enough to hold the wheat, and the work of setting up and taking down was taxing; heroic measures must be taken to meet the oncoming saints who were jumping fences of the old pastures which were eaten to the roots, and were now coming into the wilderness to get some clover that was springing up.

"Temporary measures were at an end, for a house and about two acres of land were bought near the chapel, and the work began; donations were asked for, a prompt response came from those who appreciated the situation and under the direction of Bro. C. C. Foster, who is a master builder and who had been with us from the beginning, we took our saws and hammers and erected a large building containing a large dining room capable of seating nearly ninety persons at one sitting; a nice kitchen, pantry, and sitting room below, and room above to lodge sixty. This surely will do now, and the first convention was in April, 1897. It was soon filled to its capacity, and a second lodging house was built, and in a year later a third house was built, all having nice beds that will accommodate over two hundred people.

"Saints from many States and a few from abroad have met with us, and if the Lord tarries and the 'Latter Rain' continues to fall, other precious gatherings will be held. A large number have received their baptism and fillings, and *on April 9, 1906, when the Holy Spirit fell at Los Angeles, we were holding a convention on the same day and God's blessing was present, one assembly was on the Pacific coast and the other on the Atlantic coast.*"

A WONDERFUL HEALING AMONG THE GIFT PEOPLE.

The gift people, of whom Brother Swan wrote in his account of the work in Rhode Island and Massachusetts, were a well known body before his time, as he admits. In the state of New York lived a woman who told the following story regarding her association with them; the story is vouched for by good authority.

She said that, in her youth, a body of them worshipped in her neighborhood and were despised and hated by the professors about them. It was regarded as a disgrace to attend their meetings, and the better class of persons generally refused to do so.

Her sister was at that time a confirmed invalid—a hunchback. Hearing of the healings reported to be performed by the Gift People, she desired her father to take her to one of their meetings in the hope that she might find help. This he refused to do. The woman who told the story was then a wild, high-spirited girl, on the lookout for a chance to have a lark. When her father refused to take her sister to the meeting, she promised her that she would herself take her at the first opportunity.

One Sunday morning, therefore when the old folks went to their regular place of worship, she went out and got a rig ready, carried her sister out to it and drove her to the Gift meeting. When they arrived, they saw a man who had his limb broken who was carried into the meeting. The people went to prayer, and presently one from among them arose, went to the man with the broken limb, laid hands on him, and in the name of Jesus bade him arise and walk. He did so, much to the astonishment of the visitors. (I, myself, have seen such things done in the last four years. Editor.) Then, turning to the invalid sister, he laid hands upon her, bidding her to be straight in the name of Jesus. She was instantly healed. This wrought such conviction upon the heart of the girl who had brought her there that she fell prostrate under the convicting hand of God, and when she arose she had yielded her heart to God. It was the custom of these people to pray over the new converts, and after prayer, to decide which gift they should receive. They did so with her and decided that she should have the gift of tongues. They laid hands on her according to the scripture and she spoke in other tongues. This account was given to a minister in New York State by the woman herself a few years ago, and is doubtless true.

CHAPTER VI.

INCIDENTS OF THE SPIRIT'S WORK FROM
1890 TO 1900.

DANIEL AWREY, OHIO AND TENNESSEE.

In 1889 our Brother Daniel Awrey, of blessed memory, was converted and began a life for God which has been singularly blessed and owned of his Lord. He has preached the gospel around the world and has suffered persecutions for the gospel's sake in many localities, and at many times. He left this life to be with his Lord, December 4. 1913 in Liberia, West Africa.

About nine months after his conversion, or on the last night of the year 1889, he was reading a religious book which brought his mind into a mood proper for communion with the Lord. As the bells were ringing the old year out and the new year in, the Spirit spoke to his heart, assuring him that God had for him a new and better experience. He raised his hand and said, "Then, by the grace of God I am going to have it." The next day his testimony was that he felt so clean all day. As he expressed it. he seemed to be able to look through and through himself.

That night (Jan. 1, 1890) he attended a prayer meeting where volunteer prayers were called for. He, among others, responded and as he began to pray, his faith rose, claiming an immediate fulfilment of the promise given the night before. Suddenly, the Spirit of God fell upon him and he began to pray in an unknown tongue. The Spirit, which had been working in Providence, R. I., and Duxbury, Mass., had now, in Delaware, Ohio, found another tabernacle and was furthering His effort to bring in the gracious revival which we are now enjoying. So far as we can trace, there was no human connection between this work of the Lord and that in Providence and Duxbury, though both were simultaneous.

Ten years later, Mrs. Awrey received the Spirit and spake in another tongue.

In 1899 the Awreys were living at Benah, Tennessee. About a dozen received the Spirit there with the accompaniment of other tongues. It should be stated, however, that Brother Awrey did not teach at that time that tongues were the evidence of the baptism, though he did teach (either then or shortly afterward) that the baptism was subsequent to what he knew as Sanctification. The manifestations of tongues here recorded appeared to them to be a sovereign operation of the Spirit.

Brother Awrey, when he came in contact with the present outpouring, fell in line with the people of God and was able to give them a vast amount of very beneficial counsel drawn from his sixteen years walk in the Spirit prior to 1906.

SISTER SARAH A. SMITH, N. CAROLINA AND TENNESSEE.

In the neighborhood of 1900 there was another outbreak of the Spirit's work in tongues. Mrs Sarah A. Smith, a returned missionary from Egypt, writes to the following effect. A little prior to the above date she was a member of an organization called "The Fire Baptized Association." At the time when the Spirit fell, the Association had been disbanded.

Over in North Carolina there was a body of people who had withdrawn from the Baptist Church on account of their faith in the doctrine of the second work of grace. Former members of the Association frequently went over from Tennessee (where they lived) to hold meetings for them.

At the time we speak of, two brethren were holding a meeting there. Their names were Joe Tipton and W.

B. Martin. One night, while the meetings were in progress, a woman began to pray, and presently broke out speaking in another tongue. *Those present believed at the time that it was a revival of the original Pentecostal blessing* and Bro. Tipton and others soon received the experience.

They returned to Tennessee to the place Sister Smith was staying at the time, and there she, with a number of others (perhaps 40 or 50), were baptized in the Spirit. This was about six years before the work came to Indianapolis, Indiana in December. 1906.

We insert here a few words from her own testimony.

"I remember hearing them say that nearly everyone fell under the power (that is, over in North Carolina), and the thought came to me that I had been unwilling to fall, for the Lord had been trying me by putting His power on me in a peculiar way, so that I would spin around like a top; two or three times He had done it, and every time I would back up to the wall to keep from falling. But when I heard their testimony, I told the Lord I would fall or do anything, but I wanted what He had for me.

"Of course, He tried me again, and of course, I yielded and fell and spoke at once. In a few days the power for interpretation came upon me and I interpreted every thing I spoke. It was such a wonderful thing to me that I seemed to be in a new world. The coming of Jesus seemed so near, and God revealed many things to me that have since come to pass. One of them was that I and many others would cross the ocean and tell these wonderful things in other countries."

She further says that to the best of her remembrance, Brother Tomlinson and Lemons were baptized in the Spirit at that time.

SOUTH DAKOTA.

Between 1900 and 1903, the Spirit fell in South Dakota upon a band of people, who afterward went to

Africa. I have not been able to get in touch with the man who could give me full information concerning this work, but I think that these people were Norwegians. I know that the man who accompanied them to Chicago was, and that he afterward preached in La Grange, Illinois. His name was Bakke. These people, at least Mr. Bakke, did not believe that tongues were the evidence of the baptism, but regarded them as gifts given in the sovereignty of God.

NUMEROUS OTHER INCIDENTS.

There have been numerous reports from many places regarding individuals who spoke in tongues. For instance, a woman in Nebraska, a member of the Baptist Church, was attending a Methodist protracted meeting when, during the preaching, she began to shout, and wound up by speaking in other tongues. Again, one of my friends tells me that her mother heard many of the Quakers in Canada speak in tongues sixty years or more ago.

While it is true that the most of those who received the baptism prior to 1900 did not regard tongues as the invariable accompaniment of the baptism in the Spirit, those who received in South Carolina and Tennessee did so regard them, at least to the extent that when they first heard one speak in another tongue they did what Peter did at Cesarea, viz. believed that the Gift of the Holy Spirit had been given to them as to the disciples at the beginning.

CHAPTER VII.

THE EXPERIENCE OF W. JETHRO WALTHALL.

In response to our request for information regarding the work of God in Pentecostal measure throughout the earth, I received the following from W. Jethro Walthall, a Holiness Baptist preacher.

"I was filled with the Holy Spirit in the year 1879. I sought the Pentecostal type of experience, not by any name, nor according to any theory, but I received the fulness of experience and power. I always felt that I had the experience corresponding with the records given in the Acts of the Apostles. The realization of Christ's presence was continuous and I would often fall under the mighty power when the Spirit came upon me.

"At the time I was filled with the Spirit I could not say what I did for I was carried away out of myself for the time being, but once since, under great spiritual agitation, I spoke in tongues; it did not seem to bring any deeper experience. Speaking in tongues has not been general amongst us, though many have so spoken and we have had some interpretations and many visions, with manifestations of other kinds.

"The ordinary Methodist and Baptist teaching was all that I knew, and, of course, that served to diminish my experience and to paralyze my faith rather than build me up.

"In the meantime I began preaching, a work to which I was called when the blessed Spirit filled me. I always felt that there was a lost chord in the Gospel ministry. My own ministry never measured up to my ideal, nor did the teaching of my church (Baptist) measure up to my experience.

"Finally the Holiness revival came my way. It approximated my ideal more nearly than anything else, but I could never accept its theory of sanctification; nor could I accept its abridgement of the supernatural. So we were necessarily called Holiness Baptists, in contradistinction to other Holiness people. I never appreciated the name, although it still lingers with us.

"The light of the full Gospel ministry began at this time to dawn upon me, and I had the courage to preach it. This caused me to be ostracised from the Baptist ministry. This was in the year 1895. All who acquiesced in my teaching were also disfellowshipped, and one whole church was dropped from associational connection. The revival spirit was so great, and fellowship was so free in this church, that others of the kind began to spring up here and there, and soon an annual convocation was inaugurated.

"We continued to press our way into the full Gospel ministry, looking for the restoration of the supernatural in the same, when the Spirit's downpour came in 1906. It was the expected with us; our ideal was, for the first time, realized. We did not, however, accept the second cleansing theory that so many associated with it. When the finished work agitation began, while many enthusiasts pressed it beyond true measure, it met our ideal of theology.

"Almost simultaneously with the great spiritual downpour, speaking in tongues began among us. With it came wonderful healings, among them two advanced cases of cancer, consumption, paralysis, etc., etc.

"A careful study of the Pentecostal Movement in general, and a special inquiry into the objects of the General Council, impresses me with the idea that we are, in reality, one people, with one or two discrepancies, as follows: while you maintain that speaking in other tongues is the Bible sign of the baptism in the Holy Spirit, and that physical healing is in the atonement, we have always regarded the supernatural, tongues and healing included,

to be confirmatory signs of the preached Word, in its
fulness, as in Mark 16:15-20; but we have no special contention with you on that point. We feel that the one
thing needful for the saints is the real baptism into the
Spirit, and whatever is the will of the Spirit to follow,
will be the inevitable. We feel also that technicalities
should not be a bar to the unity of the faith in the body
of Christ. *Amen.*

Yours in the blessed hope of His coming."

W. Jethro Walthall.

Brother Walthall sent us a copy of the minutes of the
Annual Convocation he mentioned in his letter, and on
page 4 we read this: "All the preaching services were interesting and highly spiritual, but Sunday noon and night
were attended with special supernatural manifestations,
such as speaking in tongues, singing in the spirit, and
falling in trances."

On page four, also, "A very interesting healing service was held, in which quite a number were anointed, with
prayer offered for healing, with some very blessed and
immediate results."

HOLINESS BAPTISTS IN THE CAROLINAS.

In subsequent letters, Brother Walthall advises that
there was a body of Holiness Baptists in Georgia which
had really come into existence before the one to which he
belonged. Also of another body of like faith in the Caro-
linas. Both of these bodies had manifestations of the
Spirit's presence, including the speaking in tongues.

His letter relative to the Carolina work follows:

"A great holiness revival was on in and around Greenville, S. C., in 1894 and 1895. A Baptist minister, Robert R. Singleton, was the prominent leader. He was excommunicated from his church, and there became such
a following that Parish Mountain Holiness Baptist
Church was formed, three miles from Greenville. In
1905 there was such a spiritual upheaval in that church
that a number spoke in tongues. The pastor told me

that one young man, who could neither read nor write, was so wrought upon by the Holy Spirit, and so filled with the Spirit of interpretation, that as the pastor would call the names of the letters in the English alphabet, the young man would give their Hebrew equivalents. It was marvelous to hear Brother Singleton tell of the manifestations in that revival. (This was before the outpouring in Azusa street.)

"The revival subsided somewhat in a year or so, and finally, just after the restoration of tongues in 1906, an extremist, who had been vacillating, came to the church and began to preach tongues as a sign of the baptism in the Holy Spirit. He rigidly enforced the idea, and denounced all others as false. If his contention was true, it was not the thing to do there, on account of their past teaching, coupled with the fact that they had tongues already, without seeking for them in that way. The pastor opposed the teaching, and so he and the church retrograded somewhat, until in 1911 they called me there for a camp-meeting. I began to preach the full Gospel, free from extremes on both sides. During the progress of this great revival the spiritual tide returned in full force with divers tongues, many visions and other manifestations of the Spirit.

"This church grew into a movement of several churches, but from what I can learn, the revival tide has, comparatively speaking, passed over and the work lags somewhat.

"There is also a large movement of Holiness Baptist churches in Southern Georgia, in which speaking in tongues and other great spiritual manifestations have played an important part in the progress of their work. Tongues were introduced there, however, after the Los Angeles downpour.

"These three movements of Holiness Baptist churches sprang up almost simultaneously, without any knowledge of each other until some years after their inception."

Here were three movements, unknown to each other, and yet each were, led by God, walking in the same light, enjoying the same measure of the Lord's Spirit.

CHAPTER VIII.

THE EARLY APOSTOLIC FAITH MOVEMENT.

We have seen that in divers places and at diverse times, God has poured out His Spirit in the time between 1875 and 1900. Indeed, we have had fragments indicating that the speaking in tongues was known prior to 1875 in a quite wide degree.

TOPEKA AND GALENA, KANSAS.

In the close of the nineteenth century the following question was propounded to the students of a Bible School in Topeka, Kansas. "What is the Bible evidence of the baptism in the Holy Spirit?" That question was at the time agitating the minds of many, and in its answer the threads we have traced through various states were tied together.

My understanding of the happenings of the occasion is as follows. The students had finished their regular studies and had some little time left before the holidays. This important question was given them to study over in these remaining days. On the first of January, 1901, Miss Agnes N. Ozman, now Mrs. La Berge of Texas, felt that she must receive the gift of the Spirit and called for some present to lay hands upon her according to Acts 19. They did so, and she was filled with the Spirit and spoke with other tongues. On the third of the month, thirteen others received a like experience.

As a result of their study and experience, they declared that the speaking in tongues was a part of the baptism in the Spirit in the sense that it invariably accompanied it. This was a bold stand for a little, unknown company of people to take, and it resulted in much persecution. However, many thousands now agree with them.

This experience naturally created considerable excitement in Topeka when it became known, and the meetings were crowded. Government linguists were brought in who testified that the people were speaking in real and intelligent languages. The Kansas City papers published this report and interest increased. Every prospect pointed to a great revival, but unwise counsels prevailed and the work was for a time hindered. However, there is now a strong assembly at Topeka.

Unsuccessful meetings were held in Kansas City, Mo., Excelsior Springs, Mo., and Nevada, Mo., under the leadership of Chas. F. Parham, who was at the head of the Bible School in Topeka where the work broke out.

In the fall of 1903 Mr. and Mrs. Arthur of Galena, Kans., opened their home and a meeting began. A tent was procured and erected about October 20, 1903, at the corner of Galena Avenue and Third Street. Here the meeting continued until Thanksgiving, when the weather forced them indoors.

The Grand Leader building on Main St. was rented and the meeting continued. This place never accommodated the crowds, though it was 50x110 in size and the doors were never closed while services were going on.

The meeting ran about three months and in the neighborhood of one hundred received the baptism in the Spirit, many being saved and healed. From this meeting the news went to many other localities, and the success of the new movement seemed assured.

The work at Galena continues under the care of the same Mrs. Arthur who first opened her house to it. They are now worshipping in the Pearl Theatre building on Main St. Our beloved brother H. A. Goss, now at Hot Springs, Ark, was converted in the meeting held here in 1903.

From Galena the work spread to Joplin, Mo., where in 1904 a successful meeting was held. Both these works have gone through bitter testings; some who promised well have fallen away when persecution threatened; ministers have come and gone; doctrines and issues have left their mark upon them; but they still stand, lights in dark places, enjoying the presence of God.

A TIME OF SEED SOWING.

From 1901 to the spring of 1905 with its struggles, persecutions, failures, few successes, seemed a long time to the toiling, faithful few who carried the spark of the holy fire. It seemed that the sodden world would not ignite, that revival fires would never catch; that labor and prayer bore small fruitage in return for the time and strength expended. But, from small beginnings God has frequently brought great endings. Sometimes, we are compelled to plant and plant until we are in despair: but "God giveth the increase."

The spring of 1905 marked the beginning of an important spiritual era for Texas. A handful of workers, carrying the blessed tidings of Pentecostal experience restored, came to Orchard and there held the first meeting of the Movement in the State.

Galena. Kans. and Joplin. Mo., had combined forces to send them forth. Bedding, eatables, money, were gathered together, and the trip to Orchard was somewhat in the nature of a pilgrimage or an invasion.

Some success attended this effort and the invaders, with renewed courage advanced upon

HOUSTON TEXAS.

Here they found a body of Holiness people who had open ears and hearts. Brother Carothers says of this Assembly that, "Being already thoroughly established in the grace of God, this congregation afforded a basis for a lasting work in the new Movement, something which it had not found up to this time."

Perhaps three hundred souls received the precious baptism in the Holy Spirit in the city of Houston alone before the work began in Los Angeles. Our Bro. W. F.

Carothers, who has served as field director for Texas, and as a member of the Presbytery of the General Council, was pastor of the Holiness Assembly mentioned above, and came into the light in the first meeting. Also Bro. D. C. O. Opperman entered the Movement a few months later.

The Movement was now truly a movement. Order and harmony prevailed. Field Directors and State Encampments helped to preserve the integrity of the movement and to repress lawlessness. Systematic attempts to evangelize were made, for the most part with success. For instance, from the Kansas State Encampment, workers were sent to Zion City, Ill. A gracious revival resulted and some of the fruits of that revival have since served God in the "ends of the earth."

It is a significant fact that all the great impulses toward Bible order and unity have emanated from the territory covered by this old "Apostolic Faith Movement," or from men trained directly or indirectly under its influence.

W. J. SEYMOUR;

an African preacher of Houston, became interested in the new Movement and its doctrines. and allied himself with it. Bro. W. F. Carothers and C. H. Parham instructed him in the doctrines held by the Movement at that time. (They are substantially the same today.) Preparations were under way to send him to those of his own color in Texas, when circumstances arose which changed the whole history of the movement.

Parties in Los Angeles, having heard of the work of God, sent money to Bro. Seymour so that he could come west with the glad tidings he had learned in Houston. They were under the impression that he had, while there, received the baptism of the Spirit. Such, however, was not the case. He did not receive, in fact, until some time after the Spirit fell in Los Angeles.

Bro. Seymour was rejected by all the Holiness bodies of Los Angeles for preaching that tongues invariably accompanied the baptism in the Spirit. Thereupon he began a series of prayer meetings in Bonnie Bray Street, and it was here that the Spirit first fell in Los Angeles. on the evening of April 9th 1906. Afterward, because of the need for more room, they moved to the famous Azusa Street Mission at 312 Azusa St. Detailed accounts of the Los Angeles revival will appear in the following chapters.

Many have made the claim that this blessed revival originated among the colored associates of Bro. Seymour. These reports, as we have seen, are unfounded in fact. The name of the movement and its doctrines were communicated to Bro. Seymour by the brethren in Houston, Texas. One of the Houston saints, Mrs. Lucy Farrow, followed Bro. Seymour to Los Angeles and became one of the most helpful of the workers there.

Following we append a selection from an article by W. F. Carothers published in the Apostolic Faith, Vol. 2. No. 2, Oct. 1908 issued in Houston, Tex.

TO ZION CITY.

"From the State encampment held in Baxter, Kansas, in the early autumn, 1906, precious workers carried the news of Pentecost, and the blessed experience with them to Zion City. They found those people in the midst of discouragements and confusions, wrought by the common enemy of us all, and the new message came as an unspeakable blessing to them. With ready consent many of the Zion people here and elsewhere have accepted the experience, and no more blessed work has been nor is being done than is going on in their midst and through their instrumentality in many parts of the globe.

THE FIRST SCHISM.

"Later in the winter of 1906, *or after nine months of unity* with the original movement, the work in Los Angeles separated from us, under circumstances which the present writer believes justified them, but about which it would be painful to write.

"They first called themselves the 'Pacific Coast Apostolic Faith Movement' *and had evangelistic and pastoral directors just as the original Movement had.*

"God continued to bless them and visions of greater service for God came before them and they changed their title to 'The Divine Apostolic Faith Movement,' but in a short while they dropped all this and with it practically all semblance of an orderly and united Movement.

"While we believe that in the end good will come from the division, yet temporarily it wrought great damage in many ways:

"1. It was an entering wedge which well nigh disrupted Christian discipline and Bible order in the whole Movement. At once certain free lances, who had before been held in check, leaped to the front and introduced great confusion and disorder. God has singularly overruled this feature, however, and has continued to bless the precious saints who have gone out from Los Angeles to the uttermost parts of the earth.

WORLD WIDE.

"From Zion City and the older Movement on the one hand and from Azusa Street, Los Angeles, on the other, by the word of mouth, and by letter, by the Spirit and by the Word, over all lands and across all seas, the tidings have been carried until they have circled the globe.

"It must be remembered that this is only a brief outline of the progress of events. Space forbids us going into the blessed details and telling of the sacrifices, the persecutions, the victories and blessings, the failures and successes that have marked the progress of the Movement. We do not deem it wise, nor have we the disposition to give the names of the actors for the simple reason that all the glory belongs to God—and all the evil that has been palmed off simultaneously belongs to the devil, whence it will ultimately return. Suffice it to say that heroes have been made, both men and women, boys and girls, whose deeds are recorded in the Lamb's book of life, and many more are rising up to carry the fully restored Gospel of our blessed Lord to the uttermost bounds of the earth—after which we look for Him to return.

POSITION OF THE OLD "MOVEMENT."

"We believe that the foregoing account of the origin and spread of the present-day Pentecostal experience, although necessarily very brief, will throw a great deal of light upon the subject to thousands of interested people over the world. At the same time we trust that it will put us of the older part of the Movement in the right light before our brethren who are not acquainted with us.

"While it is true that God has carried the message and experience clear out beyond the confines of the original Movement, and poured out of His Spirit upon thousands who have never heard of the origin of the present Movement, yet we have not been led to disband our forces and cease our labors—as some have advised us to do. There is much ground to be occupied all around us, young workers called into the vineyard need training and guidance, young congregations need building up and new territory in our very midst needs evangelizing while our united resources should be behind the missionaries who have trusted God and gone to foreign lands.

"But though we maintain our original name and united Movement, it does not mean any lack of appreciation for all of the blessed work being done by others in different branches of the great vineyard. We love them all who are in divine order and are pressing the battle on lines that honor God and earnestly covet the love and prayers of every branch of the work.

"While we preach unity and believe in it, yet we have no desire to see it come at the expense of elevating any man or combination of men above their fellows, and this is the real obstacle to unity. We believe there is a practical spirit of unity among all the various forces in the experience and perhaps that is sufficient for present purposes.

"It may be that we of the older part of the Movement place a little more emphasis upon Bible order and thoroughness in the work, and stand more for Christian discipline that will weed out the goats, than do some of the newer works, but this is only natural. Please be sure that we are as firm as ever against 'organization' as it has been practiced in the modern church movements and which saps spirituality."—W. F. Carothers.

CHAPTER IX

REMINISCENCES OF AN EYEWITNESS.

We are indebted to Brother H. A. Goss of Hot Springs, Arkansas for the following lines:

In the fall of 1903, Chas. F. Parham came to Galena, Kansas and opened a tent meeting. I was an infidel and had no concern about religious work; but this meeting was something unusual, so I went once in awhile just for curiosity, and later, when the meeting was moved to a large double store room on Main St., I went oftener with some of my fellow High School students to see the "show" as it was called.

CONVERSION OF H. A. GOSS.

The Galena Revival was a wonderful meeting; hundreds were saved and baptized in the Spirit, also there were many cases of healing.

The speaking in tongues was a marvel to me, as I did not believe in supernatural power. However, these things soon convinced me that there was an Almighty, so tongues proved a sign to me. 1 Cor. 14:22.

I remember watching a big Peoria Indian preacher receive the baptism of the Holy Spirit and begin to talk in other languages and shake as if some great machine had hold of him. His whole frame shook for more than two hours, his hands all this time being held above his head. These wonders, with many others, put me on my face seeking God, and after more than a week, God saved me. I had much unbelief to fight through, but, thank God, He brought me out victorious. At once I began to seek my baptism in the Holy Spirit and to read my Bible.

On New Year's Eve there was a watch meeting held which included foot washing and the ordination of twelve people to the ministry. Among the twelve were John James and E. Pierson, a former Quaker minister. These men are in the Pentecostal ministry today. That was a wonderful night; at six in the morning there were about four hundred people present. Wonderful altar services were held. I have seen as many as a hundred line up before the platform at a time, waiting their turn to be prayed for for healing. And hundreds found their desire.

After the great revival, the work spread to the surrounding country and to Joplin, Mo. where a great meeting was held. There are Assemblies in these places to this day.

In the spring of 1905 Mr. Parham went to Orchard, Texas to visit some friends, and while there held some meetings. Later, he returned to Galena and held a kind of camp meeting in July. Many people from nearby towns came to this camp, at the close of which Mr. Parham selected about fifteen preachers and workers to take back to Texas with him. They stopped at Orchard again and held another meeting; then with additional help moved on to Houston to open a work there.

THE WORK OPENED AT HOUSTON, TEXAS.

Bryan Hall was rented at a cost of $50 per week, and in a short time the city was stirred and much people were added to the Lord, healed and filled with the Spirit.

Among the most noteworthy cases of healing was that of a Mrs. Delaney, a woman well known in the city. About two years previous to her healing she had been injured in a street car wreck and had sued the Street Car Co. for damages.

Sometime before the meetings opened, she had a vision, in which she saw Mr. Parham, and the Lord showed her that this man would pray for her and that she would be healed.

As she was being wheeled down the street one day (paralysis and a wheel chair were the results of her accident), she came to a street meeting and saw the man that the Lord had showed to her in her vision. She stopped and listened to the preaching, enquired where the meetings were being held, and after a few days was brought to the hall. A few of the brethren carried her. chair and all, up the stairs. She was prayed for and was instantly healed, and has been walking ever since. This caused a still greater stir among the people.

THE WORK SPREADS TO BRUNNER TABER-NACLE.

As the work spread over the city, W. F. Carothers, who was pastor of a Holiness church in Brunner, a suburb of Houston, invited some of the workers out to his place. Great blessings were upon the work in those days.

After the revival, Mr. Parham left the work in charge of some of the helpers, and with some of the young Texas converts, came back to Kansas and held a great Camp meeting in Columbus, Kansas, and this city also was mightily stirred.

At this time I had not yet cut loose for the Lord's work, but I knew that God had called me, and others, who felt the same way about it, came to me and asked me to consider getting free to go to Texas, as there was another company arranging to go. I decided to do so, and on October 15, 1905, a company of twenty-two of us left Columbus on the Frisco 'Meteor' for Texas. I felt that I was really forsaking all to go and do His bidding. I had a great deal of opposition in getting out into the work, my friends telling me that I was making a great mistake in my determination; but I knew that God had called me, and I felt so good to get away from discouragements and obey the Lord.

We stopped at Orchard for a few days and had a blessed time· One of the preachers of our company received the baptism in the Spirit on the train after leaving Orchard. We had to change trains at Alvin, and while waiting for our train we held a street meeting. Many of the citizens were interested and desired us to return and hold a revival.

At Houston the brethren received us joyfully, and we had a few days conference at the Brunner Tabernacle. At the close of the conference several bands of workers were formed to go to nearby towns and hold revival services; about six being in each company.

ALVIN, TEXAS.

Oscar Jones and myself, with a few others, went back to Alvin; rented the opera house and opened fire on the enemy. Soon there was a great revival on; the power of God was falling, people were getting saved, filled with the Holy Spirit and speaking in other tongues; the sick were being healed and the town was in a stir. About two hundred were saved and one hundred and thirty-four received the baptism in the Spirit. Some very precious workers came out of this meeting, among them W. B. Jessup, Standley Bennett, Miss Milicent McClendon who became a powerful preacher, Hugh Cadwalder, later a missionary to Africa, about a year later, and my wife. Many others were launched out as result of the meeting.

We had some mighty and wonderful manifestations of the power of God in the Alvin revival and a great work was established.

From Alvin we went to Galveston where, later, we had some trouble with fanaticism, but Mr. Parham acted with great wisdom and corrected it as soon as he found it out. He was very careful to keep the work clean and free from extremes. All through the work at this time we had manifestations of the gifts of the Spirit as recorded in 1 Cor. 12.

THE HOUSTON BIBLE SCHOOL AND W. J. SEYMOUR.

The Bible School at Houston was a great blessing to all of us, as Mr. Parham was a very interesting teacher. Also a revival was carried on in the city in connection with the school and a great work was done on the streets. Many more were saved and filled with the Spirit and spake in tongues. Mr. Parham taught that all would speak in tongues when filled with the Spirit.

This school is the place where Mr. Seymour, later of Azuza St., Los Angeles, received the light about the baptism in the Spirit. I remember very clearly his coming to the classes at 9 A. M. and he and Mr. Parham preached to the colored people of the city, and some of them received the light. Mr. Seymour was already a minister, but was seeking the baptism.

He soon wanted to go to Los Angeles, but was urged not to do so until he received the Baptism. However, he did go before receiving, and later opened the Azusa St. work. Later, Mrs. Lucy Farrow, a colored baptized saint that had cooked for the company of workers while holding meetings at Bryan Hall in Houston, and who had been in Mr. Parham's family for several months, went to Los Angeles to assist Seymour in his work there. This was about Feb. 1, 1906.

February 15, 1906 a company of us went to Wallis to open a work. I stayed there two weeks and then came back to Houston to the school. Soon the school closed and all the workers were sent out to various towns around about.

Another young man and myself went to Angleton, a new field, to open up a work. Here after several weeks of bitter opposition, the power began to fall and God gave a great revival.

At the close of the Houston School there were about fifty preachers and workers in the field, and as the companies were in new fields they were having great revivals.

HE RECEIVES THE BAPTISM ON A TRAIN.

A convention was announced to be held in Orchard, Texas, April 13-15. Many of the preachers and workers came together, and we had a great time. I sought my baptism almost all night and day, as it seemed I could not go back to Angleton without the experience. On Monday, while we were all at the depot waiting for the train (which was late), Mr. Parham started services which continued until the belated train arrived. After we were on the train the power began to fall and some were singing, while others were praying and still others were seeking for the baptism in the Spirit. God answered and the Spirit was poured out and some of the seekers received the baptism and began to speak in other tongues. I saw that the power of God was mightily in the car. Brother Caywood, of Houston, came to me and told me to praise the Lord. I did not feel like doing so, but he urged me, and so I began and soon the power was coming on me stronger and stronger· Directly, my strength was about gone and I could not speak another word Another wave of glory struck me and I relaxed every muscle, fell back in the chair and said, "Lord, have Thy way." Directly another wave of the power of God which took hold of my tongue. The glory filled my soul, so that it cannot be described, while the fire of God seemed to be burning me up. Presently my tongue was loosed and I began to speak in languages I had never heard before. O, the joy of that experience is more than I can tell.

In about an hour, twelve more on this train received the baptism. Among them, P. M. Stokely and Joe Rosselli. Both are now in our ministry.

We soon had to change cars and others with me from Angleton got off. I could not speak English at all, and could only tell them what to do by motioning with my hands. On the train we now took, more of our company received the baptism.

We shortly after this heard of the power falling at Los Angeles and our hearts were made to rejoice in the blessing of God on the work.

At this time (the beginning of the Outpouring in Los Angeles) there were 60 preachers and workers in Texas, and I think I am safe in saying that there were more than a thousand who had received the baptism in the Spirit and had spoken in other tongues.

THE FIRST STATE ENCAMPMENT.

The first State Encampment was announced for Brunner (Houston) in July, 1906. We all gathered there again and the power fell mightily. Here Mrs. Farrow came and gave us a detailed account of what was happening in Los Angeles. She was endued with an unusual power to lay hands on people for the reception of the Holy Spirit. At one time I saw a row of about twenty-five lined up before her, she laid hands upon them and many began to speak in tongues at once.

Hundreds and thousands of Houston people came to hear the Gospel. From the camp-meeting the preachers scattered again with this great message, some of them going to other states.

Mr. W. F. Carothers was appointed General Field Director, and I was made field Director for Texas and Kansas. This was the first step toward church government for the general work. Heretofore, Mr. Parham had been the only general leader, and he, with the advice of others, selected us.

The work now spread to Zion City and Chicago. Mrs. Mabel Smith Hall, a woman used of God in a marvelous way in Texas in speaking in tongues, interpretation and preaching, went to Zion City with others, and later to Chicago, and was first to bring the message to that

City. She was known to have spoken and been understood by foreigners in as many as eighteen different languages; she speaking by the power of God, without previous knowledge of the languages in which she spoke.

THE WORK GREATLY HINDERED.

When we learned of Mr. Parham's failure, our hearts were almost broken, and we could hardly believe it; and then the trials began. Some took sides with Mr· Parham and some believed the charges. Mr. Carothers was some what in the lead, and tried to bring peace again, but the matter grew worse, and Mr. Carothers and myself, in an endeavor to hold the work together, announced a Bible School at Waco, Texas.

The school was a blessed one, but we had another fight along another line, viz. speaking in tongues as the evidence of the Baptism in the Spirit. Some contended that all did not speak in tongues, while we held that all should. Thank God, it came out victorious that tongues were the evidence of the baptism in the Spirit, though not the only one.

Brother D. C. O. Opperman assisted us in the school, as he was at this time seeking his baptism. Later, he, in company with A. G. Canada and workers, went to San Antonio to open the work.

After the school, the work in Texas was somewhat torn up over Parham's failure, and many of the preachers and workers were discouraged. I wrote a circular to the workers to go on and to stay in the field till Mr.. Carothers and Mr. Parham got the trouble settled. At this, I was accused of desiring leadership at the expense of others. This hurt me, so after a few weeks I resigned. The work went to pieces as far as order was concerned. Most all of the workers left the field, with the exception of my own company, and we had many discouragements.

Soon we had a meeting and disfellowshipped Mr. Parham, but this did not help matters as far as the general work was concerned. But at the camp-meeting in July, Brother A. G. Canada, who had been free from all this trouble in Texas (having gone back to North Carolina after the San Antonio meeting), was elected Director of the Texas work, and the brethren that stood with us lined up for the battle again, and our God led us out to victory. The Texas work is still the strongest state movement in the Pentecostal company.

CHAPTER X.

THE PENTECOSTAL OR "LATTER RAIN" OUT-POURING IN LOS ANGELES.

(Bro. Frank Bartleman of Los Angeles, Cal., has kindly
supplied us with the following valuable information
about the beginning of the work in that city.)

I have been requested to write briefly what I know
about the present Pentecostal outpouring of the Spirit
that has swept around the globe in the last nine years.
In doing so, I shall write from personal knowledge only.
I reached California in the spring of 1903, with my little family. We located in Sacramento. Shortly before
Christmas, 1904, we came to Los Angeles. Just after
the first of the new year our oldest daughter died. It
was a terrible blow, but it drove me to God. I had been
preaching the gospel since 1895. Had been converted
in Philadelphia, Pa.

In my sorrow at the loss of our oldest child, I threw
myself on God and consecrated myself to His service
anew. Beside the coffin of my dear one God definitely
entered into a new contract with me. He began to reveal to me a deeper, wider service than I had ever known
before. The burden of "soul travail" came upon me. I
felt I could only live by being used of Him for lost souls,
and He showed me that He would grant my desire. He
promised that it should not seem long to me until my
work was over and I should meet my darling child
again.

Then He began to open up to me a wonderful "forward" vision in faith and prayer. He showed me it was
in His purpose again, as of old, to pour out His Spirit

amongst us mightily. We had gotten quite pessimistic before this. Few people seemed to be expecting anything better for the last days.

The spirit of prophecy came upon me. I began to prophesy of mighty things from the hand of God. I seemed to receive a "gift of faith". And the travail of soul was wonderful. It consumed me. This began in January, 1905. I began meetings in a little Mission in Pasadena, Cal., at once, after the funeral of our little child. I felt I must be at work for God.

THE TRAVAIL OF SOUL.

The Lord wonderfully poured out His Spirit. A number of workers were dug out in those meetings that later received the Pentecostal baptism and are Pentecostal preachers in the field today. They caught the vision and the faith also. We began to cry, "Pasadena for God!" Meetings were started in a Methodist Church of which these workers were members. They got under the burden. About two hundred souls knelt at the altar in two weeks' time. The Lord began to stir up His people in different churches in the city. The results were directly traced to the prayers of these young men. They were on fire. Our cry was for a "Pentecost." The Lord was clearly directing.

About April, I first heard of the wonderful revival in Wales. It stirred my soul to its very depths. I laid my life in God's hands and asked Him to use me if he could to help further the same wonderful Spirit in America. A few weeks later, while reading S. B. Shaw's Book on the "Great Revival in Wales." God spoke to me and asked me to contract definitely with Him that I would never go back to the plow again, but that I would spend all my remaining years in His service only. I have never turned back since that time. I dare not. We have been tempted, but God has proven faithful.

INSPIRATION FROM THE WELSH REVIVAL.

In June, 1905, Pastor Smale, of the First Baptist

Church in Los Angeles, returned from England, where he had been attending the revival in Wales. He started prayer meetings in his church to wait on God for an outpouring of the Spirit similar to that which they were having in Wales. God wonderfully anointed him to exhort the people. He was full of faith for mighty things. I immediately began to attend his services and found them exactly in line with my own vision and aspirations for God.

These prayer meetings ran for a number of weeks, and there was much spontaneous worship, also some very wonderful healings. But the burden that gathered volume daily, and the cry, was for a "Pentecost" for Los Angeles, and for the world. "Pentecost" is the very word we all had on our lips, given by the Holy Ghost. Spiritual workers began to gather to this little company from all over the city. They came from many different denominations and missions. It was a gathering together of those to whom the Lord had spoken. Faith increased rapidly for extraordinary things. God made Pastor Smale a regular Moses to lead us toward the "promised land."

But soon the church dignitaries could tolerate the new, spontaneous order no longer. They ordered it to cease, or the Pastor to resign. The consequence was the Pastor wisely resigned to go on with God, and the Lord and the people went with him. The "cloud" moved. A "New Testament Church" was formed. Here God wonderfully led and blessed, up to the Spring of 1906.

All this year the travail of soul was heavily upon me. In fact, for at least fifteen months, day and night, almost without intermission, the hand of the Lord was upon me to "bring forth". I had no rest day or night from these "groanings that could not be uttered." My precious wife believed that I would die. Days and nights I rolled on my bed in an agony of prayer for a lost world. I seemed almost as separate from my family as though I had been in a distant country for a year. But God spared my life to "eat of the fruit" of my groans and tears. I wrote many tracts during this time, and a number of articles for the papers. God shut me off from preaching much. I could only prophesy of the "things to come." I was tired of my own preaching and that of others. We needed a reviving. We needed the "anointing."

ENCOURAGEMENTS TO FAITH.

I had a number of most wonderful visions during this year also. Mostly while in travail of soul. One night, after a specially heavy burden in prayer that seemed to almost take my life, the Lord Jesus Himself appeared to me and strengthened me. I lost all sense of time and space. When I came to I had to pinch myself to see if I was flesh and blood. For days I walked with an invisible presence at my side. Human voices sounded harsh and grating. Human contact pained me. I had been with the Lord.

Gradually the stream was rising, ready to overflow all banks as He had promised. The clouds of blessing were gathering overhead, accumulated by the prayers of many. There was great expectation. But still the situation seemed to wait for something. It would be a great mistake to attempt to attribute the Pentecostal beginning in Los Angeles to any one man, either in prayer or in preaching. Personally, for months the matter seemed to be accumulating within me. The tide of the Spirit was rising, but it could not yet burst forth. I was not abandoned for it. None of us understood fully what we were seeking or just what to expect. We wanted God to come forth; but just in what way we did not know. We never do. He could not come the same as in Wales, for conditions were very different in Los Angeles.

They did not break through at Pastor Smale's Assembly. There was too much reserve there. God had taken them as far as he could. We had marvelous meetings both there and in private prayer meetings, however, all through the year. More than once we saw and felt God's glory. At times the "cloud" was visible to the naked eye. "Pentecost" did not drop down suddenly out of heaven. God was with us in large measure for a long time before the final outpouring. It was not a mushroom of a night by any means.

PRAYED FOR SIGNS FOLLOWING.

Much that would be of interest in this connection must be omitted for lack of space. Finally in February, 1906, seven of us met after a prayer service at the New Testament Assembly, and, joining hands, agreed that God should be petitioned to pour out His Spirit speedily "with signs following." I don't think we, any of us, knew what we meant by that. But we felt something out of the ordinary was needed to awaken the people. God gave us that prayer.

HELP CAME FROM TEXAS.

Somewhere about this time, perhaps a little earlier, Bro. Seymour came to Los Angeles from Texas. He was a quiet colored man, very unassuming. He had been invited by some saints in Los Angeles, who supposed he had already received his Pentecost in Texas. They began to hold quiet meetings in cottages, waiting on God for the outpouring with signs following. Bro. Seymour felt the Lord had sent him to Los Angeles for a special purpose at that time. He was in the closest sympathy with the burden that was on all of our hearts. He himself had never spoken in "tongues", but he believed in it and had met the Apostolic Faith saints in Houston, Texas, who were already so speaking and had the teaching from them. He believed that "tongues" should accompany a real Pentecostal baptism, according to Acts 2:4. This he asserted not at all in a dogmatic way. He himself did not speak in "tongues" until weeks after others had begun to in our midst.

Finally he began to meet with a little company of white and colored people in an humble cottage in Bonnie

Brae St. They decided' to wait on God in a ten-days'
special petitioning of God and in yielding themselves to
Him. The time had come. God had found the right
company at last. The most spiritual of the saints were
among this company. Suddenly, one night in these meetings, the Spirit of God was poured out and some began
to "speak with other tongues, as the Spirit gave them
utterance." The news spread like fire naturally. The
expectant saints began to gather. They opened public
meetings in old Azusa St., in an old Methodist Church
that had been for a long time in disuse, except as a re-
ceptable for old lumber, plaster, etc. It was very dirty.
A space was cleared large enough to seat a score or two
of persons. We sat on planks resting on old nail kegs,
if I remember correctly. But God was there. The work
began in earnest. The fire had fallen.

THE SAN FRANCISCO EARTHQUAKE.

It was on the 9th of April, 1906, that the Spirit was
first poured out in Bonnie Brae. On April 18th we had
the terrible San Francisco earthquake. It had a very
close connection with the Pentecostal outpouring. God
covered the fire at old "Azusa Mission" and protected it
during the first few days of its existence until there was
no danger of its being stamped out by the enemy. Then
He let loose His judgments in California. This shook
the whole state, as well as the nation. Men began to
fear God. California was very wicked. Their consciences needed to be knocked' at. This paved the way
for the revival. Otherwise they would have mocked us.
There was "no fear of God before them."

Workers began to gather from all parts of the city,
from throughout the state, and in fact from all over the
nation, to old "Azusa Mission." Bro. Cashwell came
from North Carolina, got his "baptism," and carried
the fire back and spread it all over the Southland, especially the South Atlantic States. Sister Ivy Campbell
went back to her home in Ohio and spread the flame

throughout that whole eastern country. Others came in from different sections and carried the news and the blessing everywhere. Missionaries returned from many parts of the heathen world, sent directly and impressively by God, to tarry for their "baptism." It was a time of wonderful gathering. God alone had ordered it. "Gather My saints together unto Me." Ps. 50:5. Thousands were saved and baptized with the Spirit, all speaking in other tongues.

AZUSA BECAME THE CENTER.

God suddenly shut up many little Holiness Missions, Tent meetings, etc., that had been striving with one another a long time for the pre-eminence. It would not work any more. They had to come together. God only could tame them. There was little going on anywhere else, but at Azuza St. All the people were coming. Even Pastor Smale finally came to "Azusa Mission" to hunt his people up. Then he invited them back to let God have His way. The fire broke out at his own Assembly also. When God dries a place up it is dry. This many churches which opposed the Azusa work soon found out to their sorrow. And many are yet sorrowing over it. They would not take God's way. They were "also among the prophets," but when the Lord came He did not come through them. This killed them. They would not go to "Azusa," nor let "Azusa" come to them. "Azusa" was despised in their eyes.

SPREAD AROUND THE WORLD.

But "Joseph" has got the corn. The "seven years of plenty" have now swept round the world. Missionaries returned, by faith for bread, and for the healing of their bodies in sickness, to all parts of the world. They carried the Pentecostal message and power with them. Almost every country on the globe has been visited by them. The work is almost stronger in some other countries than it is even in America. It has been my personal privilege to "see the mighty works of God" in Pentecostal power in England, Scotland, Wales, France, Holland, Switzerland, Germany, Norway, Sweden, Finland, Russia, Egypt, Palestine, Ceylon, India, China, and in the Islands of the Sea, outside of the United States and Canada.

CHAPTER XI.

AZUSA STREET SCENES.

(We are indebted to Bro. A. W. Orwig for the following
account of the Azuza St. work.)

It was in September, 1906. I had heard of the meetings during the early part of the same year, when there
was "no small stir" concerning them. The daily papers
of the city had characterized them as scenes of wild fanaticism, enacted by ignorant and crazy people. Especially was the reputed speaking in unknown tongues bitterly denounced as a fraud, and was sacrilegiously cari-
catured. Besides this, many church-members spoke dis-
dainfully of the meetings, some declaring them to be of
the devil. This naturally influenced others to condemn
them; some, however, suspended judgment, wholly or in
part, for the time being; I was among the latter.

During the month and year above mentioned, a
large, four-page paper was issued by the mission, a copy
of which accidentally or providentially fell into my hands
on a Friday afternoon. At once I began to read it with
considerable interest, and in a very short time was convinced that God was in the work. I continued to read
nearly all day Saturday until my heart burned within me,
and I said to my wife, "I am going to Azusa Street Mission on Sunday and see and hear for myself."

I arrived at ten o'clock, and at that early hour found
the house practically full, with many more coming later,
some glad to secure standing room. I remained until
one o'clock, returned at two and stayed until five, thus
spending six solid hours on that one day. And I was
more than ever persuaded that the movement was of
God.

I will not now attempt to describe sermons, testimonies, prayers and songs, only to say that they were usually attended with divine unction to such a degree as to move and melt hearts in every direction. The altar of prayer was generally crowded and other space designated for seekers, both saint and sinner. Many of both classes who came out of curiosity, and some possibly to ridicule, were smitten to the floor by the power of God, and often wrestled in agony and prayer until they found that for which they sought,—some for pardon and others for deeper experience in God, by whatever name the latter might be called. Often it was termed sanctification, holiness, or the baptism of the Holy Ghost. Quite prominent was the teaching that the baptism in the Spirit was upon the sanctified life, and evidenced by the speaking in another tongue, however brief, as on the day of Pentecost. Not all, however, who gladly attended the meetings and derived profit thereby, fully or at all accepted this teaching. Nor did they specially identify themselves with the movement, although often endorsing it in general terms.

The subject, or doctrine, of divine healing received special attention and many cases of deliverance from various diseases and infirmities were more or less continually reported. Likewise was the doctrine of the premillenial coming of Christ ardently promulgated.

One thing that somewhat surprised me at that first meeting I attended, and also subsequently, was the presence of so many persons from the different churches, not a few of them educated and refined. Some were pastors, evangelists, foreign missionaries, and others of high position in various circles, looking on with seeming amazement and evident interest and profit. And they took part in the services in one way or another. Persons of many nationalities were also present, of which Los Angeles seems to be filled, representing all manner of religious beliefs. Sometimes these, many of them unsaved, would be siezed with deep conviction for sin under the burning testimony of one of their own nationality, and at once heartily turn to the Lord. Occasionally some foreigner, alhough somewhat understanding English, would hear a testimony or earnest exhortation in his native tongue from a person not at all acquainted with that language; thereby be pungently convicted that it was a call from God to repent of sin; often such repentance followed just as on the day of Pentecost. I could give interesting details of such instances if space permitted, and may possibly do so at some other time. (We have received another article from Bro. Orwig which appears below.—Ed.)

. Of course some persons attending the meetings in those early days of the revival, mocked and cavilled, also as on the day of Pentecost, and are doing so at the present. But this is true of every mighty work of the Holy Spirit. It would be unlike Satan not to stir up derision and opposition. By this I am not saying that there have been no indiscretions and positively no counterfeiting of the Holy Spirit's work: the devil is an expert in imitating that work. And undiscerning persons have not known the difference between the true and the false. The genuine is, therefore, sometimes doubted even by some Christians; and what is true as to unfortunate things connected with the so-called Pentecostal Movement, is just as true of some things occurring in the various Christian denominations.

FURTHER FROM LOS ANGELES ABOUT THE PENTECOSTAL WORK.

In the above I spoke of my first visit to Azuza Street Pentecostal Mission in the year 1906, and the very favorable impressions made upon me. My heart is often stirred with praise and gratitude as I think of their beneficial effect upon me at the time. Especially did the enchanting strains of the so-called "Heavenly Choir," or hymns sung under the evident *direction* of the Holy Spirit both as to words and tune, thrill my whole being. It was not a something that could be repeated at will, but supernaturally given for each special occasion and was one of the most indisputable evidences of the presence of the power of God. Perhaps nothing so greatly impressed people as this singing; at once inspiring a holy awe, or a feeling of indescribable wonder, especially if the hearers were in devout attitude.

Most vividly are other scenes recalled of the mighty power of God upon the minds and hearts of both sinner and saint. Often the hardness of heart, the levity, of the former were completely overcome by the burning truth of God, and men and women were gloriously swept into the kingdom of grace with whirlwind power. Not that the preaching was great, humanly speaking, but because mighty prayer, faith, singleness of eye and truly anointed speech were used of God for the salvation of souls, the edification of believers, and the receiving of the Holy Spirit with various manifestations. Not a few of the so-called "Holiness People," who perhaps thought they had about all there was to be obtained, found the meetings a great blessing to them. Others of this class stood aloof for different reasons; some because of not understanding the movement; some from more or less prejudice; others because the occasional speaking with other tongues proved a stumbling block to them.

INCIDENTS, WITH REMARKS.

1. *"It Will Soon Blow Over."*—Either in 1906 or 1907, a beloved brother preacher said to me, "The Lord has shown me that this movement will soon blow over." Of course he erred in two things, namely, his claim as to what the Lord had shown him, as also what he thought would happen to the movement in a year or two. But the brother was simply a representative of many others. Of course I need not specially refer to the fact that "this movement" soon spread to many parts of the country and to other lands. It is admitted that some defects were connected with it, as is natural with any enterprise or work in which fallible humanity has a part. The same is true of the various Christian churches. But the imper-

fections of the "Apostolic Pentecostal Movement," or even some of its seemingly strange features, is no evidence whatever that God was not and is not with it. But how many foolish and even pernicious things are found in some churches! And in not a few cases no effort seems to be made to eliminate them.

2. *The Invitation of a D. D.*—I now recall what I heard a prominent Baptist preacher say at one of the Sunday afternon meetings in the Azusa Street Mission in 1906. Standing in the back part of the church, perhaps for lack of room elsewhere, and while listening to the very glowing testimonies, he called out, substantially, "I wish some of you persons on that rostrum would come over to my church this evening and speak to the people who gather outside for a meeting before the services begin inside." And, he continued, "No one will lay his hand on your shoulder and say, 'Be brief, brother,' for you may continue to speak as long as you please, even though there be no service inside." That was indeed a significant endorsement of what was occurring at the Mission. He was magnanimous enough to go and see and hear for himself, instead of persistently remaining away and condemning without personal and unprejudiced investigation. I mention this as being in happy contrast with the unfair, stolid condemnation and even uncharitable and sinful derision of some professors of religion. Oh, the loss and injury often sustained by some persons because of the malignant demon of *prejudice* possessing them!

3. *A Prominent Methodist's Declaration.*—He was a high official in the principal church of the city, and at one of the meetings at old Azusa's humble, almost barnlike place of worship, he declared that he thoroughly believed the work was of God, and wished the same holy fire and marvelous work of grace would break out in his church and other churches. He seemed to be greatly captivated, although a man not given to excitement, but a prudent, influential business man. Occasionally the "holy fire," of which he spoke, did seize some persons of

social, religious and intellectual standing, besides those among the more "common people." Many, of course, did not identify themselves with the movement, as such, though frequently attending the services, but remained in their own churches as better "lights" and more efficacious "salt" than they had hitherto been. Not infrequently, however, some left their church and attended the meetings regularly, and became one with the "Pentecostal" people, or, as some persons would say, with "the tongues people," sometimes saying it with intentional derision, and sometimes with no unfriendly feeling. No ecclesiastical organization, strictly speaking, was "joined," for there was none to join, and is none to this day, although a brotherly union of spirit is usually maintained.

4. *A Daily Paper's Reporter Captured.*—It was during the early days of the meetings at Azuza Street Assembly. He had been assigned to "write up" an account of the meetings held by those supposed ignorant, fanatical, demented people. But it was to be from the standpoint of the comic or ridiculous,—the more highly sensational the better. It was doubtless supposed that this would the more freely meet the tastes of the readers of the paper. And the reporter went to the meeting with feelings in harmony with those of his employers. He was going to a "circus," as he and others would say, so far as genuine worldly amusement is concerned. But, fortunately for himself, he witnessed some very touching and solemn scenes, and heard the Gospel truth so powerfully presented in the Holy Ghost by different persons, that his frivilous feelings gave way to devout ones.

After a little while a Spirit-filled woman gave such a mighty exhortation and appeal to the sinner to turn to God that the reporter was still more greatly impressed. Suddenly she broke out, not voluntarily, but truly as the "Spirit gave utterance" (Acts 2:4), in a different language, one with which she was utterly unfamiliar. But it was in the native tongue of the foreign-born reporter, who was also proficient in the English language. Directing her earnest gaze upon him, she poured forth such a holy torrent of truth, by way of exposing his former sinful, licentious life, that he was perfectly dumbfounded, no one seemingly understanding the language but himself.

When the services were over, he at once forced his way to the woman, asking her if she knew what she had said concerning him while speaking in that particular foreign language. "Not a word," was her prompt reply. At first he could not believe her, but her evident sincerity and perfectly grammatical and fluent speech thoroughly convinced him that she absolutely knew nothing of the language. Then he told her that she had given an entirely correct statement of his wicked life, and that he now fully believed her utterances were exclusively from God in order to lead him to true repentance and the accepting of Jesus Christ as his personal Saviour. And he at once faithfully promised such a course. Going from the meeting he informed his employers that he could not give them such a report as they expected him to present. He added, however, that if they wanted a true and impartial account of the meeting he would gladly give it. But they did not want that, and also plainly told him that they did not need his services thereafter.

ADDITIONAL FROM LOS ANGELES CONCERNING THE EARLY PENTECOSTAL WORK.--A. W. ORWIG.

For a third time I write about the work in question, even though not formally identified with any of the assemblies here or elsewhere. My knowledge of the work in this city is chiefly derived from attendance at some of the various meetings and from the literature that is sometimes published. From the beginning, however, I have read different Pentecostal papers published both in this country and a few in other countries. And while I have received considerable benefit from the meetings and the periodicals, I have not always been able fully to coincide with all the doctrines taught. But it is well known that these dear people do not themselves agree in all phases of doctrine. Nor is this always essential. Love and unity of spirit are more important.

INCIDENTS, WITH COMMENTS.

1. *Not Knowing French, Yet Speaking French.*—It was during the very early Pentecostal movement in Los Angeles that a woman. who knew only the English language. actually addressed a man in the French language. He was her grocer, a Frenchman, but understood English well. While both of them were crossing the street, in opposite directions, she suddenly spoke to him in his native tongue. But it was in the form of a Gospel message, with a view to his salvation. Utterly surprised, he asked, "Since when have you been able to speak French?" To this she replied, "I do not know that I spoke French, for I don't understand a word of that language." To this the man answered, "You certainly spoke in very excellent French, warning me to repent of my sins and to give my heart and life to God." Verily "tongues are a sign" to the unbeliever.

2. *"Would Not Tolerate Speaking in Tongues."*—Years ago a brother preacher, whom I very highly esteem, came to Los Angeles from another state, and who had never been to a meeting held by the people under consideration. Discussing with him the subject of speaking in a new or unknown tongue at meetings, he said, "I would not tolerate such gibberish in any of my meetings." Knowing that he was not familiar with certain conditions, and had not specially studied the subject from a Scriptural standpoint, I told him that he would doubtless assume a grave responsibility in attempting to interfere with what might be a demonstration of the Holy Spirit. He then admitted that his language was very likely too strong. But other persons have said practically the same thing who have never been to one of those meetings; but some, on going several times, have com-

pletely changed their opinions. And sometimes some of the most hostile ones have been so mightily wrought upon by the Holy Spirit, even to their physical being, as subsequently to speak in an unknown tongue very freely, and became the most ardent defenders of this divine manifestation. That there may occasionally be counterfeit or Satanic manifestations is admitted, but this is no proof whatever that there is not an actual utterance given by the Holy Spirit through certain persons in another language. Only a *genuine* thing can be *counterfeited*.

3. *Not Opposed by Rev. Dr. Geo. D. Watson.*—On some one telling me, a number of years ago, that Dr. Watson did not allow the speaking in other tongues in his meetings, I assured the person that he was in error, for I had heard some thus speak without the slightest protest. Some of the "Pentecostal" people sometimes attend Brother Watson's meetings because of the high order of Scriptural expositions they receive on the deepest and most blessed themes of the Sacred Oracles, frequently on prophetical subjects.

4. *A Preacher Rebuked by an Interpreter.*—During the camp-meeting, in the outskirts of Los Angeles in 1907, the Lord gave a certain brother the interpretation of a number of testimonies spoken in languages unknown to the speakers. It was a great surprise to very many persons thus to witness this wonderful manifestation of the Divine Presence. A holy awe rested upon the audience. A brother who expected to preach on the occasion made some seemingly unnecessary apologies as to not being fully prepared, etc. Instantly some one arose and spoke in a strange tongue, directing his gaze at the man standing behind the pulpit who expected to preach. Then followed the interpretation which was to the effect that no apologies should be made by any one who was conscious that God wanted him to preach; also that if the preacher had truly met God in prayer and meditation He would use him to the Divine glory. The preacher was evidently moved by the solemn

interpretation and acknowledged the fault mentioned. The incident may be of value to other preachers.

"TONGUES" THE GREAT STUMBLING BLOCK.

The "tongues" feature of the Pentecostal movement has been and still is the great stumbling-block to many persons. But they forget, or have never known that it has a real *Scriptural* side to it, both pro and con. Certainly there is Scripture for the speaking in an entirely unfamiliar language, under certain circumstances, and often not understood by any one present. But the fact or importance of such speaking should not be unduly magnified, nor may it be entirely ignored. We should abide by the Word of God, whether we understand the subject or not. Generally the leaders in the movement disapprove and deplore all excesses in the matter, including all unseemly bodily demonstrations.

5. *"Don't Talk About Tongues."*—In the first year of the work in Los Angeles I heard W. J. Seymour, an acknowledged leader, say, *"Now, don't go from this meeting and talk about tongues, but try to get people saved."* Again I heard him counsel against all unbecoming or fleshly demonstrations, and everything not truly of the Holy Spirit. Wise words, indeed. There had been some extremes, and still are in other places. But these things no more represent the real Pentecostal work than do the follies in various churches represent genuine Christianity. Bro. Seymour constantly exalted the atoning work of Christ and the Word of God, and very earnestly insisted on thorough conversion, holiness of heart and life and the fulness of the Holy Spirit. And yet some uninformed persons uncharitably declare that the chief or whole thing consists in talking in tongues and is of the devil.

6. *Favorable Editorial Comment.*—Three cases, among papers outside of the movement in question, allow me briefly to quote. An editor of a holiness paper

in the East wrote thus: "If you fail to take up with the 'tongues' feature, stand with Gamaliel and wait. We know of no reason why the Lord should not send to the faithful today what He once sent to Jerusalem and Corinth."

The well-known Rev. Dr. A. B. Simpson, of New York city, declared in his paper thus: "There is no reason to believe that these special gifts were ever intended to be discontinued. Many of the most remarkable, as miracles and even the gift of tongues, have occasionally re-appeared in modern times."

The Rev. Dr. A. S. Worrell (now deceased), whom I saw at several meetings at Azusa Street Mission, wrote to his paper that he firmly believed the movement was of God. He further stated: "There are real gifts of tongues here in Los Angeles and other gifts of the Holy Spirit."

And thus I might continue to present testimony from persons of deep piety and learning as to their belief (and some from actual experience) that the speaking in unfamiliar tongues is still one of the manifestations of the Holy Spirit. But I must forbear for the present.

THE TONGUES OF PENTECOST DUPLICATED.

The following remarkable narrative was sent me by R. W. Nichols of the Galena, Kans., Assembly of God. I, myself, have met Bro. Nichols; heard him pray and seen his face shine. Also, the narrative bears the endorsement of Mrs. Mary Arthur, for many years the leader of the work in Galena.

She says, "I commend to you Bro. Nichols testimony as being worthy and true; he is a most earnest and humble Christian; one whom God can use to His glory."

Sister Arthur needs no commendation to those among us who know her; to those who have not that privilege, we say that she is a wise, level-headed, godly, Spirit-filled woman. So this story may be accepted as true.

The narrative follows:

"I thought it would glorify God to write of an experience I had shortly after receiving the Baptism in the Spirit. I was filled with the Spirit about Oct. 31, 1914.

"In the beginning of November I met a Syrian woman at my home when I returned to dinner. She had taken sick and had stopped in to wait for a friend.

"Finding that she was sick, I started to ask her if she knew Jesus could heal her. Part of the question I asked in English and then the Spirit led me off into her own native language

"The Spirit thereupon told her of Jesus and His power to save and heal and warned her of his soon coming. Presently her friend came in and heard a large measure of the warning.

"When work time came at one o'clock, I sent my brother-in-law in my place and continued talking and praying with the two for sometime. Part of the prayers I offered were in the Syriac.

"A week later, lacking one day, I met two other Syrians. My mother was acquainted with one of them and she stayed patiently while the Spirit again warned them of Jesus. She said that she had met the first two and they had told her how frightened they were when the Spirit had told of the soon coming of Jesus.

"I was ignorant of their way of worship, but while talking to the second couple the Spirit led me through many manifestations, such as counting beads, crossing myself, etc. I told them that they were deluded and that the priest was taking them to hell. They were so bound and set in their way of worship that the message had little effect upon them at the time.

"Months afterward I met a young Syrian man who spoke pretty good English. He told me that the person for whose healing I prayed in the first instance immediately recovered."

Here is a well authenticated case of glossolalia identical with the manifestation upon the day of Pentecost. The young man was, and is, ignorant of the Syriac; he spoke—as the Spirit gave utterance—of Jesus and the wonderful things of God. The fact that the message did not result in the immediate salvation of all the hearers does not take it out of the Pentecostal class; some on that day "mocked." Further, the woman for whom prayer was offered, recovered.

In spite of the learning of the wise, I believe that God is the "same yesterday, today, forever."

CHAPTER XII.

THE GLAD TIDINGS CROSSES THE MISSISSIPPI.

BEGINNING OF THE OUTPOURING OF THE HOLY SPIRIT IN THE SOUTHERN STATES.

The invasion of the Southern States with the Pentecostal message, as told by M. M. Pinson, was in this wise:

Brother G. B. Cashwell went from Dunn, N. C., to Los Angeles, Calif., to make an investigation concerning the outpouring of the Holy Spirit and found it to be real. He yielded to the Lord and received the baptism, speaking in other tongues and glorifying God. He returned to Carolina and had some wonderful meetings, many receiving the baptism.

During this time, the Way of Faith of Columbia, S. C., (a Holiness paper) was publishing some articles about the Pentecostal outpouring at Los Angeles. The good news was spread far and near. L. P. Adams of Memphis, Tenn., heard of the outpouring of the Holy Spirit and sent for Brother Cashwell to hold a meeting in Memphis. Brother Cashwell arranged to stop off at Birmingham, Ala., on his way to Memphis.

Sister Daniels, who was a strong stay in the Birmingham work, decided to write to Brother M. M. Pinson to come over to Birmingham and meet Brother Cashwell. Brother Pinson was holding a meeting at the time at Bowling Green, Ky., in the First Methodist Church. Brother Pinson says:

"I knew nothing about it at the time, but while I was walking from my room to the post office, the Lord spoke to my heart and said, 'Go to Birmingham.' I did not know that it was the Lord at first and felt I could not go as I had just commenced a revival meeting. But He kept speaking to me until I knew it was Him, and I said, 'Yes Lord, I will go anywhere for you, close the meeting, or anything,' and I did it.

"The letter from Sister Daniels arrived either that day or the following, to come and meet Brother Cashwell. At that time I was a Holiness preacher, associated with the Pentecostal Mission work, with headquarters at Nashville, Tenn., having spent twenty-one months in J. O. McClurkin's Bible School. I thought it right to stop off and see him, which I did, telling him of what I was going to do. We had prayer together in his office, and he thanked God I was going to be with the assembly, as he had confidence in me as a Bible student. I was on the General Committee of the Pentecostal Mission, and had been for three years; I was also one of those appointed by the annual convention to the committee of three to examine preachers for ordination. He had confidence that I would stand by the Word.

"When I arrived in Birmingham, G. B. Cashwell was already there, and had held one service, and, as well as I can remember, a little girl, Anna Dean Cole, a niece of Sister Anna Dean, who is now, together with her aunt, a missionary in China, had received the baptism in the Holy Ghost and had spoken in tongues.

STIR AMONG THE HOLINESS PEOPLE.

"There was quite a stir among the Holiness people. Our teaching was that the baptism of the Spirit sanctified, and we all believed we were sanctified and yet we did not talk in tongues. Cashwell was declaring that as surely as the disciples spoke in tongues on the day of Pentecost, that we would also do it when we received the baptism in the Spirit. He believed that the tongues was the evidence of the baptism of the Holy Ghost, but I did not accept it as such. I did recognize the tongues as a gift of the Spirit. The question with me was, 'Did the baptism in the Holy Spirit sanctify?' Later I found that the Holiness teaching was incorrect in regard to the baptism of the Spirit sanctifying, not because the speaking in tongues was the evidence, but because I found the Scriptures to show plainly that Calvary was the place for sanctification.

"Some of the Holiness people were so hungry and thirsty that they yielded their theology and professions and received the baptism of the Holy Spirit. Brother Cashwell only stayed about two days and passed on to his appointment at Memphis, Tenn.

"I boarded the same train and went with him to investigate further. I was fully convinced by the Word of God that I did not have the baptism, although I had been anointed with the Holy Spirit a number of times, and I believed that He dwelt in my heart, witnessing to my cleansing; and He, the Spirit, had enabled me to preach the Gospel for a number of years and had crowned my efforts with numbers of souls, for which I praise Him. But when I realized that I was not filled with the Spirit, I said, 'Lord, I want you to fill me,' and the Lord began to wonderfully bless my soul. Then the enemy would come to me and say, 'You haven't yet talked in tongues.' I would agree with him and fail to believe God for the filling, and the Spirit seemed to withdraw His presence from me. But when I began to pray again, and yield and believe, the Spirit would begin to move upon me in a blessed way.

M. M. PINSON RECEIVES THE BAPTISM.

"The third of May, 1907, early one morning, while I was communing with the Lord, the Holy Spirit came mightily and blessedly upon me while in bed. Brother H. G. Rodgers, who had begun to tarry for the baptism, was rooming with me. He was praying and he noticed the bed shaking as the Spirit moved upon my body. He hastened out to call for some more praying people to pray the Lord to baptize me with the Spirit. He meant it for good, but I needed no help—Jesus baptizes with the Holy Ghost. Matt. 3:11. They came in and prayed earnestly and fervently, but it seemed as though the Spirit withdrew His power and presence. When they left the room, I again communed with the Lord in prayer, and oh the presence and power of the Holy Spirit the Lord brought into my soul again. It was that way, off and on, for five days.

"The fifth day, after several hours prayer, the Holy Spirit came upon me and so flooded me and possessed me. Then He composed a song I had never heard and I sung it in other tongues. It seemed that Eph. 5:18-20 was surely fulfilled in my life. Blessed hours!

"Sister Daniels and numbers of others received the baptism in that meeting. Of course we saw manifestations we were sure were not of the Holy Spirit, and neither did we assign them to the Holy Spirit; but we had asked for fish and we were sure Father would not give us serpents. Hallelujah!

"Brother Cashwell left before I received my baptism, and returned home with the promise that he would meet us in Birmingham, Ala., for a meeting, which he did later.

"I returned by way of Nashville, Tenn., to notify my brethren what God had done for me. They said they could accept me, but they could not accept the general teaching, but would investigate further. However, they permitted me to go on with them from May until October, and many of the precious brethren would have been glad for me to have continued longer, but some few rose up and said, 'No!'

"I went from Nashville to Birmingham and met Brother Cashwell, Brother Taylor and numbers of others. Sister Daniels also returned from Memphis, where she had received her baptism, and we all pitched battle against sin and the devil in Birmingham, and God did come forth in a blessed way, numbers being saved, receiving the baptism, and some healed.

THE WORK SPREADS OVER THE SOUTH.

"In a few days Brother Cashwell went to Georgia, while we took a tent to North Birmingham, where God met with us in great glory, many workers and preachers coming from far and near to investigate, and finding that the work was real. A number of them received and went back to work, while others returned without it and later received.

"Brothers Tomlinson and Lemons from Cleveland, Tenn., came down, realized it was God, returned home and received their baptism; and began to spread the fire there.

"A blessed meeting was held at Atlanta, Ga. The power fell and numbers went through to the Pentecostal outpouring of the Spirit. I went down through South East Alabama with a tent and a band of workers and numbers of people were saved and baptized with the Spirit. A number of young preachers who had been saved in my meetings before that, were filled with the Spirit and began to tell the good tidings. Sister Anna Dean, who is now a missionary, and has been for several years in Hong Kong, China, received her baptism in one of these meetings. Miss Mattie Ledbetter, who has spent several years as a missionary to China, received her baptism in a later meeting at Birmingham.

"Meetings were held and the work was opened up at Anniston and Warrior, Ala.; a camp meeting was also held near Franklin, Tenn.; and H. G. Rodgers, having received his baptism, spread the fire down through Mississippi, Tennessee and Alabama.

"So the good work continues. There have been some changes in doctrinal points, but no change in regard to believing that the baptism of the Holy Spirit is for all believers. The Holy Spirit had been outpoured as God said, 'I will pour out my Spirit upon all flesh.'

"It is sad, however, that not all who receive this outpouring of the Holy Spirit are true to the leadings of the Spirit, and some, as Paul says, 'make shipwreck of their faith.' It has been reported that G. B. Cashwell, by whom the light of the Pentecostal outpouring was first brought to the Southern States, had stepped aside and left the ministry, also some others. 'Nevertheless, the foundation of God standeth sure, having this seal, the Lord knoweth them that are His.' And 'He that overcometh shall inherit all things,' and 'they overcame him by the blood of the Lamb and the Word of their testimony.' 'Ye shall be witnesses unto me * * * unto the uttermost parts of the earth' when the Holy Ghost comes upon you. Let us be true to the blood of the Lamb and the Word of our testimony and love not our lives unto the death.

"Much more could be said in regard to this outpouring in the Southern States. Have only been able to give the beginning of it in this brief article; but we want to give a testimony here to the abiding presence, power and glory of God, as we yield to Him and let Him have His way in our lives."

CHAPTER XIII.

THE WORK SPREADS TO INDIA.

(Bro. and Sister Garr were the first Pentecostal missionaries to carry the news of the Pentecostal outpouring to India and China. We are indebted to them for the following remarkable account.)

"Forasmuch as many have taken in hand to set forth in order a declaration of those things which are most surely believed among us, even as they delivered them unto us, which from the beginning were eyewitnesses and ministers of the Word." It seemed good to us also to write of those things which our eyes have seen and our hands have handled of the Word of God. Luke 1:1, 2.

We were permitted to be among the first to witness God's mighty power as poured out at Azusa Street, Los Angeles, and also were chosen of Him to be *the first Pentecostal missionaries* to cross the seas to tell to missionaries and natives of India and China that God had visited the earth and given the "Latter Rain."

For years, in the Holiness Movement, our hearts had hungered to be filled with all the fulness of God, and though told by leaders that the experience of sanctification was the same as the great infilling received by the disciples on the day of Pentecost, the blessed Spirit of God was true to our hearts and God's precious Word revealed to us that there was an experience beyond what we possessed, which would bring with its reception a power hitherto unknown.

After much prayer and fasting and very definite seeking of God's face, we were led to come to Los Angeles and take charge of the Metropolitan Holiness Church, several months before the outpouring at Azusa.

These months were very special seasons of prayer for a revival on our own souls, and the work in our charge, and although we could not state very definitely what our own hearts needed, still we followed our convictions like the Psalmist, who said, "*When* Thou saidst, Seek ye my face: my heart said unto Thee, Thy face, Lord will I seek." Psa. 27:8.

He "whose eyes run to and fro throughout the whole earth to show Himself strong in behalf of those whose hearts are perfect toward Him," found us in this waiting, hungry attitude and led us with the then small company at Azusa to enter into an experience with Himself which was more than we could have asked or thought.

WONDERFUL DAYS IN THE SPIRIT.

These were wonderful days in the Spirit.—the new worship through the manifestation of tongues and the Heavenly song, was marvelous to us, but there had been in our seeking that longing for power to win lost souls.

It was for this we tarried. It was with this prayer on our lips one night—"Oh! God, Thou hast called us to preach Thy Gospel, souls are going down, but we cannot go without the power from on high"—that the Spirit descended upon us and we felt and knew that *the promise of our Father* was fulfilled. He had come and, with Him, the power for service.

After a few days of this joy and fellowship, the blessed Spirit began to give such travail for souls and such reaching out for the nations of the earth as we had never known, though God had given much soul agony in the Holiness movement. The Spirit made us to know we were to be witnesses unto the uttermost parts of the earth.

THE FIRST PENTECOSTAL MISSIONARIES.

It was not long before we were on the seas, our hearts burning with longing to carry this glorious Gospel to India and China. We had, as it were, suffered the loss of all—all our old Holiness friends rejected us, the old doors were closed, but God was setting before us an open door which no man could shut.

It was like beginning life over, a new ministry in the power of God's Spirit, not limited to a small fraction of the Holiness people, nor to one country as before, but the "World our parish" and a message of God's outpouring for all nations. Blessed be our God, who prepared Cornelius in a vision for Peter's message, so also, He went before us into India to get ready the soil in hearts for the seed of this blessed Pentecostal Truth.

On reaching *India*, we found it was the Viceroy's season in Calcutta, when the missionaries had come in from all parts of India to make a special effort for souls. This was so truly the hand of our God.

They were much in prayer for a revival so that it could have been said of us, "I sent you to reap that whereon ye bestowed no labor; other men labored, and ye are entered into their labors."

God moved in a mysterious way before He brought us into contact with those to whom we were sent.

THE DOOR OPENED IN INDIA.

With no funds with which to open up in India, we were kept in much prayer for God's opening. One day we were directed to a prayer meeting where we found quite a body of missionaries whose testimonies revealed not only their own deep hunger of soul, but a longing for a revival in Calcutta, and there was real faith that God was going to give them their heart's desire. We were strangers among them and therefore said nothing, but our hearts kept telling us that this was our company and that God had given us a message for these hungry ones.

The next morning we went to another mission home and the way opened for us to tell of God's visitation in America. With the exception of one or two, we found the whole company very receptive, and when the Spirit spoke through us in other tongues, the reverance and deep hunger with which it was received proved to us that we had found the people to whom God had sent us.

THE FIRST PLACE OF WORSHIP.

At the night service an opportunity was given to tell of the outpouring of the Spirit at Azusa St., Los Angeles, and at the close an elderly gentleman, Bro. Hook, the Pastor of Lal Bazaar Baptist Church, Calcutta, came forward and offered his church to us for the preaching of this blessed "Truth." We had believed for a tent or a store building to open, but this fine Baptist church to which we were taken on the following Sunday morning, and such a saintly old Pastor, this was beyond our fondest dreams, but oh, so like our God who always does more than we can ask or think.

There was nothing said in our hearing of the closing of the other meeting, of which Pastor Stockmeyer of Germany and Mr. Ward of Coonoor were the leaders, but on entering Lal Bazaar Baptist Church for our first service, we found the same body of noble missionaries, who like the Bereans, "received the Word with all readiness of mind, and searched the Scriptures daily whether those things were so."

Many of them were very ripe in experience, having received very rich anointings from the Lord, but the Gift of the Holy Ghost, with the accompanying sign of speaking with other tongues, had not been received. Lal Bazaar Church proved to be an ideal place for tarrying before God.

Hours were spent in prayer each day. They were wonderful seasons! Sometimes silence would reign for a long time, but there were the deepest heart searchings after God, which He abundantly rewarded.

We had quite a cosmopolitan audience, composed of missionaries from all denominations, officers and soldiers of the English army, Englishmen and Americans in business in Calcutta, Eurasians and East Indians, but God was coming in answer to prayer to *"pour out of His Spirit upon all flesh."*

THE FIRST MAN TO RECEIVE THE BAPTISM IN INDIA.

Before any one received the Baptism in the Spirit, there was much confession and restitution and a very wonderful revival. Many were saved. The church floor looked like a battle field. "The slain of the Lord were many."

Among them were quite a number of very fine young men from the army, some of whom are today Pentecostal missionaries in India, having bought their discharge. The *first man to receive the baptism in India* was a captain in the English army.

The night he was slain under the mighty power of God was one to be remembered. It was the first witness, and there was much fear in the hearts of his loved ones when this fine soldier fell to the floor, slain by God's power. As one brother bent over him and asked, "Is it all right, Captain?" back came the answer, filled with God's anointing, *"All is well."*

His dear wife and daughter soon entered into the same experience. God granted to the wife some very marvelous visions during those days.

We could not work at the altar; in fact there seemed no need. The deep repentance, the strong cryings of those seeking salvation, the many slain on the floor, showed us the work was being carried on by the Spirit and we needed only to stand by and worship our God that we were permitted to live and see His workings.

A REMARKABLE EXPERIENCE.

One very marked case of restitution is worthy of mention. An Englishman who was attending the meeting had deserted from the English army many years before, marrying his wife under an assumed name, and had also taken supplies from the railroad company that employed him, to the amount of 1,000 Rupees (over $300.)

During the preaching of a sermon on "Hell," he was seen to fall forward on the seat in front of him and cry out bitterly. At the close of the service, he asked if he had to confess his life, and on being told that "he that covereth his sins shall not prosper, but whoso confesseth and forsaketh shall find mercy," he went home to confess to his wife and son. It was a great sorrow to the wife who felt she could not forgive, but God dealt with her and the father, mother and son fell at the altar, and the glory of God filled them, and a happier family could not have been found.

The thousand rupees was restored and we went with the brother several hundred miles to "Wellington," the headquarters of the English army, where he delivered himself up to the commission officer.

Though our brother was a man weighing over two hundred pounds, and in charge of three hundred natives, still the officer, after hearing the testimony of our brother, pronounced him unfit for service, and in answer to the prayers of God's people he was released.

MAX WOOD MOORHEAD.

Bro. Max Wood Moorhead, afterward editor of the Pentecostal Witnesses of India, the first issue of which was published during the revival at Calcutta, received his baptism very early in the meetings, and from that day until now has been used through his testimony, and pen, for the spread of this blessed "Truth."

God used Bro. Moorhead to open a large house in Calcutta, when persecutions became so fierce that it seemed impossible to go on in the church, although the Pastor stood by us nobly.

God rewarded him by giving him the blessed Spirit, and since then Lal Bazaar Baptist Church has been an open door for Pentecostal Truth. Most of the conventions since held in India have been within her sacred walls.

Bro. Moorhead threw open this home for hungry ones and they came from all parts of India, received their baptism, and went back to their stations in the power of the Spirit to tell their co-workers of God's marvelous workings at Calcutta. Hunger was created in the hearts by these living witnesses, and they, too, would come and receive.

WONDERFUL RESULTS FOLLOW THE BAPTISM.

Our services were held in the large drawing room of this "Home." Wonderful results followed the baptisms of these missionaries. Frequently the power of God would be poured out on their whole school in a short time after they received.

In the case of Miss Easton, head of the American Mission Board in Calcutta, who had charge of a large girls' school, we think there were forty of her girls entered into the baptism in a few days from the time Miss Easton received.

Miss Costello, who had charge of the Orphanage of the same missionary board, found the same power attended her ministry.

The dear Indians under her care were filled with God's power. Miss Salatti, at the head of the Salvation Army Rescue Work, experienced the same among the Rescue Women, some lay for hours under God's power, worshipping the Lord in new tongues. These are a few out of the many that proved indeed that power does come with this mighty baptism.

One missionary, after receiving her baptism, returned to her station and took her regular morning service with the school. She said nothing to the girls of what God had done for her soul, but just praised the Lord.

There was a new unction, a new power in their missionary that took hold on the hearts of those Indian girls, and that night lights were seen in the dormitory at a late hour. This was against the rule, and the missionary went to investigate. She found the girls pouring out their hearts in prayer. Confession and restitution followed and God poured out His Spirit on that whole school.

A CALL FROM PUNDITA RAMABAI.

During the Calcutta revival *Pundita Ramabai,* so well known to Pentecostal readers for the wonderful outpouring at Mukti (her school), wrote us, inviting us to come and preach to her school. We were in the midst of a mighty revival and felt we could not go, but God stirred the hearts of quite a number at Mukti to pray for a revival. When God later on permitted us to go there and preach, the power of God on the work was wonderful.

It was no uncommon sight to see hundreds in prayer at once, many of them in other tongues and mightily under the control of God's Spirit. Cases in which ignorant Indian girls prayed or praised in pure English were among them.

THE SPIRIT POURED OUT AT THE BOYS' SCHOOL.

Seventeen miles from Ramabai's, at *the boys' school* of Bro. Albert Norton, sixty of the boys were baptized in the Spirit in a short .time. Confessions and restitution and a very great spirit of prayer—in fact the supernatural spirit of prayer was beyond anything seen in America—were always followed by a mighty visitation of God's power. Results followed the outpouring of the Spirit, for which the missionaries had spent years of labor, but the Spirit accomplished it in these dear Indians in a short time.

One of the marked characteristics of the baptism, both among missionaries and native Christians, was the great burden of souls. This was most convincing to other missionaries. One missionary wrote us after returning to her work, that she knew more love and travail for souls in the few short weeks since her baptism than in all her previous years of ministry to India's needy souls. When she came to our meeting she saw some seekers under the power of God and she made this remark, "What could I do with that in my work?" (referring to the manifestation.)

That night she retired to her room to pray, and the Spirit gave her a vision of a "Christless" grave, with India's millions pouring into it. The Spirit led her out in prayer for these until at two o'clock the next morning, she received the baptism in the Spirit, and came from her room—a transformed woman—with a new power, and floods of God's love in her being.

THE WORK SPREADS ALL OVER INDIA.

And what shall we more say?, for the time would fail us to tell of the mighty works done by the Spirit at Allehabad, when days and nights the school at dear Miss Chuckerbutty's were in a mighty supernatural spirit of prayer; when cries of penitent ones were mingled with shouts of victory, victory for Jesus Messiah (in their own native tongues).

We scarcely knew when we would get a meal or rest. As we look back over the scenes there and remember how God answered by fire, baptizing many with His Spirit, we thank God we were privileged to be with these dear ones.

Then of Coonoor, in the hills, where the missionaries gather for a rest. It was here that battles were fought on our knees, and victories won. Missionaries fought thru great opposition to come to our meetings; were even met at stations along the railway and warned;—all manner of evil was said against us, but our answer was a mighty Spirit of prayer for these dear ones. God told us we were not to be "weary in well doing, for in due season we would reap if we faint not."

He came and poured waters on thirsty souls and floods upon the dry ground, making their hearts to blossom and bloom like a rose.

The missionaries became witnesses with power to the death and resurrection of Jesus. Witness after witness arose in India, who had a mouth and wisdom which all their adversaries could not gainsay nor resist. More and more they multiplied until some of India's strongest missionaries are today baptized in the blessed Spirit, with the sign of speaking in other tongues.

We could not close this article without mentioning the faithful company who stood by us in those pioneer days of Pentecost and who went with us through India and the Island of Ceylon with the flame of God's love burning in their hearts and who suffered much. It makes us to realize afresh that mighty things can yet be accom plished on our knees, through faith in Jesus' name. The husbandman waits for the precious fruit of the earth until he receive the early and latter rain.

CHAPTER XIV.

PASTOR BARRATT AND THE WORK IN EUROPE.

We have the privilege here of presenting something of the personal testimony of Pastor Barratt and a letter from him dealing with the work in Europe. Also, a letter from Miss Yunna G. Malick, now in this country, but who was born, saved and baptized in the Spirit in Palestine.

Bro. Barratt was born in Albaston, Cornwall, England, on the 22nd of July, 1862. His parents were both English and belonged to the Wesleyan Methodist Church. When he was five years old, his parents removed to Norway; he has made his home there ever since.

He was converted when twelve years old, and was, in his sixteenth year, stirred to a deeper consecration and a larger life for God. He soon entered the ministry and presently had great success in winning souls for his Master.

In 1905 he visited America to raise funds for the erection of a large hall in Christiania, intended for the center of a great mission work in that city. He was at this time a member of the Wesleyan Methodist Church.

His mission here, though supported by appeals from several bishops and other leading men, was not successful. This grieved his heart and really began a work which made room for the blessed light and truth of "Pentecost."

We here append an account of his experience in his own words. This extract is taken from "When the Fire Fell," a pamphlet containing a detailed narrative of the Lord's dealings with him.

PASTOR BARRATT'S OWN TESTIMONY.

. . . . All this time I remained 'neath the *cleansing and protecting Blood of the Atonement,* knowing that Christ alone could impart the blessing I sought. Acts 2:33; John 7:37-39.

I had not mentioned to anybody, except by correspondence, that I was seeking the full Pentecost. But at last I felt I must. A sudden tremor passed through my body when I did it. Oh, how precious those days are to me still!

Taking a nap in the afternoon, I awoke, feeling my jaws working on their own account. The physical sign of the coming blessing had therefore commenced, before anybody had prayed with me or laid their hands on my head. Calling on 'Mrs. L——, the wife of a physician. who had received her Pentecost. I conversed with her about the subject and requested her prayers. The devil taunted me by saying: "The idea of a minister going to ask a woman to pray for him!" I bade him begone. She prayed with me and sent me to meeting, conducted by a friend of hers. But it was at the meeting the next evening I first felt at liberty to tell those present what I was seeking. This was on the 15th of Nov.. 1906. About fifteen persons were present. Some seeking sanctification. others the baptism of fire.

We could not close the meeting and I determined, God helping me, to stay till the victory was won.

I requested the leader a little before 12 o'clock to pray for me with the laying on of hands. After that I had no more strength in me. I lay on the floor by the platform in a reclining postion. At about half-past twelve I asked a Norwegian brother there and Mrs. L. to lay their hands on my head and pray for me once more.

My jaws and tongue began to work, but there was no voice. The brother said, "Try to speak!" But I would not force matters myself. *There was to be no humbug in this.* The Holy Spirit was to do the speaking Himself, or rather, *make* me speak.

THE HOLY SPIRIT COMES.

Just then both of them saw a supernatural light, over my head, and in this, Mrs. L. says, she saw a crown of fire and a cloven tongue, the length of her hand.

Immediately I was filled with light and power and began to speak clearly and distinctly with a great volume of voice, in a foreign tongue. The power came so suddenly and powerfully that I lay on the floor speaking in tongues incessantly for some time. In fact I kept on, mostly speaking in tongues, singing and praying, with very little intermission, until 4 o'clock in the morning. Nine persons remained until three o'clock, and are witnesses of the whole scene. I must have spoken about eight different languages during that time. Some present believed the number was greater. All were spoken with great distinctness.

It seemed as if an iron band lay over my jaws. Both jaws and tongue were worked by this unseen power. I could very easily detect the various sounds and forms of speech, and the different position of the tongue, and at times also the vocal chords. One of the languages had a deep guttural sound, and came slowly, in one the nasal sound predominated, another rushed forth like a cataract, others came more regularly and smoothly. Once the twisting of the organs of speech, in order to produce the sounds, made the muscles of the throat ache. They were of course not used to it.

I knelt, stood or sat in a chair while this was going on. I stood erect sometimes, speaking so forcibly that several thousand persons could easily have heard all I said. I felt such strength throughout my body that I now understand, by personal experience, where David and Samson obtained their strength.

But the most wonderful moment, the most rapturous of all, was when I suddenly commenced to sing a beautiful baritone solo, using one of the most pure and delightful languages I have ever heard. The tune and words were entirely new to me, and the rhythm and cadence of the verses and chorus seemed to be perfect.

I was perfectly conscious of all that was going on, but was led by the Spirit of God, filling my whole being with His presence. I felt at times as if on fire inside. But there was no pain. It was a mighty sense of the holy purity and gracious love of God within.

Now and then I had seasons of prayer. But it was the Holy Spirit praying within me. I received an illustration of Romans.8:26, 27. I don't remember having prayed in that way before. New York and the United States, Norway and all Scandinavia and Europe, my loved ones and friends, lay like an intense burden on my soul. What power was given in prayer! Oh, the blessing of those wonderful hours! That night will never be forgotten by anyone present.

God's presence overwhelmed me completely. I then threw myself on the floor with the cry, "At last! At last!" It seemed as if the heavens would open above us and the glory of God appear before us.

LETTER FROM PASTOR BARRATT.

In answer to a letter asking him about the rise and progress of the work in Europe, he sent us the following:

"After receiving the baptism of fire in New York, I returned back to Norway and commenced meetings in Christiania; immediately the fire fell there and the revival commenced. From this center it spread all over Europe. Brother Johnson commenced shortly afterward in Schofde, Sweden, while numbers carried the fire from Christiania to other parts of Norway.

"About three months after the outbreak of the revival in Christiania I commenced to travel. Visited Stockholm and other towns in Sweden. I then went to Copenhagen and the revival began there. From there I went to Sunderland, England, and the revival commenced there.

"Two sisters, Miss Thille and Miss Dagmar Gregerson, (both are now married and are missionaries in India) took the fire to Germany and Switzerland. I did not have time to go there then, nor had I time to visit Hol-

land. But later on I visited India (by invitation), and
the Holy Land and stopped some time in Switzerland,
making the work more secure there. I also visited Germany and some years after, Holland.

"The revival spread from Sunderland, England, to
Holland. That is, Brother Pollman received his baptism in
Sunderland and the revival, which had entered Holland
from Switzerland, was brought into a purer line of influence.

"In Germany, God raised up great workers; among the
foremost might be mentioned Pastor Paul.

"Later on, I visited Finland and Russia. A great revival broke out in Finland, especially after Pastor Smidt's
work there. I have visited Finland several times since
and crowds have attended and remarkable revival scenes
have taken place.

"But in no country have I seen a deeper work than in
Norway. The revival has spread all over the country,
more or less, and God is constantly glorifying his holy
name in our midst."

How much of labor, groaning prayers, mighty preaching, fastings, trials, victories is covered by this brief letter, only the Day will declare. We hope in time, to present fuller details of the work abroad. This, however,
will take time, and we can only do the best we can.

That much of interest may be developed is evident
from the following letter from Miss Malick. Bro. Barratt covers the time spent in the Holy Land with a half
dozen words; I wish that we had side lights on all his
trips as we have this little one upon this visit to Palestine.

MISS MALICK'S LETTER.

"A friend placed in my hand a copy of the Weekly
Evangel of Jan. 22, 1916, in which I read of your desire
to acquire as much information as possible about this
Pentecostal Movement. So I thought to send you a brief
account of my experience along this line, hoping that it
will add a little to the interest in the subject, and bring

honor and glory to God for His wonderful works among the children of men.

"Away in the Holy Land, in the lower slopes of Mt. Lebanon, there is a small town, Shwifat by name, about six or seven miles from the Mediterranean coast. In this town I was born, brought up, and there I taught school for several years.

"I was saved as a child and my heart's desire was and always has been to reach every creature with the Gospel news. I tried to do so, as much as I had a chance. At one time I worked in Hebron, South of Jerusalem, for six years among the Mohammedans. I was there with Mrs. Murray, a blind lady, who died a few years ago in India. All this time there was in my heart a craving for more of the Holy Spirit and power in service.

"In the year 1909 this desire became more intense. I was at home then in Shwifat. Talking to a friend about it one day, she said, 'Let us pray definitely about it.' This suggestion settled deep in my heart and I started to wait on God for an outpouring of His Holy Spirit. I made this a regular thing at an appointed time in my room. This went on for several weeks. One day I received a Latter Rain paper from across the ocean, do not know who sent it to me. It was the first of the kind I had ever seen, and contained the first news which I had received of the outpouring of the Holy Spirit as on the day of Pentecost. I cried unto the Lord, saying, 'If this thing is going on in the world, I must have it too, for thou art no respecter of persons; it is the thing I have been praying for all this time.'

"A week after this, Pastor Barratt of Norway, on his way home, stopped in our town to spend a few days with some friends. He had been in the United States and while there had received the baptism in the Holy Spirit and spake in other tongues.

"We arranged to have prayer meetings for a week. What was supposed to be the last day of the meeting came, and no one had received their baptism as yet. That morning my younger sister and I were the only ones in the upper chamber besides the pastor and the household members. The rest of the seekers had perhaps given up, and perhaps some were busy. But, praise the Lord, he never gives up, not even the ones and the twos, for as soon as we knelt down to pray the power of God fell on my sister and she began to speak in tongues. In a few minutes, I too, lost control of my tongue and the Spirit was interceding through me with utterances unknown to me. When this was known outside, the afternoon and evening meetings were crowded with people. Some came out of curiosity, others were in earnest. The meetings were extended another week; a few received the baptism. You may be sure the devil caused no small stir over it, but the Lord held steady the faithful ones, those who were willing to suffer loss for His name's sake."

Five years later Miss Malick came to this country and spent some time in the Rochester Bible Training School. She expects, ultimately, to return to Palestine.

What hath God wrought! My soul delights in the telling of it.

CONCLUSION.

What shall I more say? Time and space alike forbid further detail at this time. We hope in the future to supplement this booklet by another, carrying the history of the work on to present day developments, at home and abroad. Both home and foreign work present many profitable lessons which will greatly encourage and bless us when we have opportunity to gather them together.

All around the world this blessed Gospel has gone bringing light and life to perishing thousands. This country is covered with large and small assemblies. Great cities have had, and are now having, testimony borne to them. Chicago, Cleveland, New York, Rochester, Buffalo, Pittsburg, Atlanta, Memphis, Washington, Newark, Baltimore, Ossinning, Indianapolis, St. Louis, Kansas City, Denver, Los Angeles, San Francisco, Portland, Seattle, Salt Lake City, Dallas and Ft. Worth, all these are hearing the glad tidings of God's power and faithfulness.

Rural communities have not been neglected. Literally hundreds of churches and school houses are now being used, and hundreds of church houses have been built by the movement, especially in the great Southwest.

Texas has a District Council embracing eighty-seven ministers and sixty-seven assemblies. Arkansas has nearly as many. The Southern Missouri Council, just formed, has between sixty-five and seventy preachers, and in the neighborhood of that many assemblies. The east and the west are dotted with them. Every state is represented in this great movement. The General Council of the Assemblies of God numbers nearly nine hundred ministers upon its roll; and they represent only about twenty-five or thirty per cent of the movement in the United States. It is true that there is no other co-operative, united body anything like as strong, but the other brethren are, in their places, doing a great and mighty work for God.

Canada has not been neglected in the visitation. Thousands there are rejoicing in the knowledge of a living God. Her ministers are, many of them, coming into fellowship with us, and are expressing their belief in, and co-operation with, the principles of fellowship and unity.

India has had a very gracious outpouring, as we saw in the account furnished by Brother and Sister Garr. The revival did not stop then, the work goes on with continued power and blessing.

A hundred and fifty missionaries in China are holding up the truth.

A great movement has developed in the South African states.

Germany, Holland, Switzerland, France, England, Russia, Finland, Norway, Sweden, Persia, Liberia, Palestine, India, China, South America, South Africa, practically every tongue and people are hearing the *witness,* soon the end shall come.

Let the prayers of God's people everywhere ascend to the throne that this great body of God's children may do the thing for which they were raised up; may not be divided and hindered by men of corrupt minds; may not lose sight of the heavenly business of preparing a people for his name, and of bearing witness to all, that the end may come. Great blessings and profits have been ours in these happy days of heaven upon earth; great responsibilities also rest upon us. "To whom much is given, of him much is required."

We desire to make this statement in closing: Many things have happened in the movement which have not truly shown the purpose or the Spirit of God. Extremes have crept in, both in doctrine and in practice; into what movement have they not intruded themselves? But with all this, I believe with all my heart that this is the best thing in the land today: that God is more truly manifest in the lives and ministry of the members of this movement than in any other body of believers: that the power and spirituality of the religion of Jesus are more appreciated by these people than by any other: that, though frequently despised by those who rank higher than they in the estimation of the world, these are true aristocrats of heaven; that their names are written in the Lamb's Book of Life: that in the case of thousands of them, God Himself knows that He can depend on them to go anywhere, do anything, bear anything for His glory and in His will.

I am delighted to go to heaven with the Pentecostal people. Their virtues outweigh their faults; their piety is greater than their ignorance: their love for God and souls broader than their prejudice; their abundance of grace more than their eccentricity. It is a goodly company; brother, come with us and we will do thee good.

APPENDIX.

THE GLOSSOLALIA IN THE EARLY CHURCH.

HISTORICAL DESCRIPTION FROM THE WRITINGS OF THE LATE DEAN OF CANTERBURY.

In these days, when by reason of the long distance both of time, and of spiritual power and experience which separates the Modern from the Ancient Church, Christian people are so sceptical of the Scriptural and Divine character of supernatural manifestations and gifts of the Holy Spirit, which are accompanying the latest movement of the Spirit of God, throughout the world, it is refreshing and reassuring to come across the following descriptive scene of a gathering of a primitive Christian assembly, and the manifestations of the Spirit which attended their worship. It is from the pen of the late Dean Farrar, in his "Darkness to Dawn."

In the preface he tells us that the whole story is "determined by the actual events of Pagan and Christian History!" and again "Even for the minutest allusions, and particulars I have contemporary authority." Once more, he assures us that his story has been decided for him "by the exigencies of fact, not by the rules of art," and that "scarcely in one incident have I touched the preachers of early Christianity with the finger of fiction."

The quotation from this remarkable book follows:

"The room in which the Christians met was a large granary in which Plantius stored the corn which came from his Sicilian estates * * * In such a community, so poor, so despised, there could be no pomp of ritual, but the lack of it was more than compensated by the reverent demeanor which made each Christian feel that, for the time being, this poor granary was the house of God, and the gate of heaven.

"Every look and gesture was happy as of those who felt that not only angels and archangels were among them, but the Invisible Presence of their Lord, Himself.

"First they prayed—and Britannicus had never before heard real prayers. But here were men, and women, the young and the old, to whom prayer evidently meant direct communion with the Infinite and the Unseen; to whom the solitude of private supplication, and the community of worship, were alike admission into the audience chamber of the Divine. Never had he heard such outpourings of the soul, in all the rapture of trust, to a Heavenly Father. How different seemed such intercession with the Eternal from the vague conventional aspirations of the stoics towards an incomprehensible soul of the universe, which had no heart for pity, and no arm to save!

"But a new and yet more powerful sensation was kindled in his mind, when at the close of the prayers they sang a hymn. Britannicus listened entranced to the mingled voices as they rose and fell in exquisite cadence. He had heard in the theatres all the most famous singers of Rome; he had heard the youths and the maidens chanting in the temple processions; he had heard the wailing over the dead, and the Thalassio-chorus of the bridal song. But he had heard nothing which distantly resembled this melody and harmony of voices wedded to holy thoughts; and, although there were no instruments, the angelic soft trembling voices seemed to him like echoes from some new and purer region of existence.

"When the hymn was over they sat down, and Linus rose to speak to them a few words of exhortation. * * * Was not the day of the Lord at hand? Would He not speedily return?

"So far had he proceeded, when a mighty answering 'Maranatha' (O Lord come) of the deeply awed assembly smote the air, and immediately afterwards Britannicus stood transfixed and thrilled to the very depths of his whole being.

"For now a voice such as he had never heard—a sound unearthly and unaccountable—seemed not only to strike his ears but to grasp his very heart. It was awful in its range, its tone, its modulation, its startling penetrating, appalling power; and although he was unable to understand its utterance, it seemed to convey the loftiest eloquence of religious transport, thrilling with rapture and conviction. And, in a moment or two, other voices joined it. The words they spoke were exalted, intense, impassioned, full of mystic significance. They did not speak in their ordinary familiar tongue, but in what seemed to be as it were the essence and idea of all languages, though none could tell whether it was Hebrew, or Greek, or Latin, or Persian. It resembled now one, and now the other, as some overpowering and unconscious impulse of the moment might direct. The burden of the thoughts of the speakers seemed to be the ejaculation of ecstasy, of amazement, of thanksgiving, or passionate dithyramb or psalm. They spoke not to each other, or to the congregation, but seemed to be addressing their inspired soliloquy to God. And among these strange sounds of many voices, all raised in sweet accord of entranced devotion, there were some which no one could rightly interpret. The other voices seemed to 'nterpret themselves. They needed no translation into significant language, but spontaneously awoke in the hearts of the hearers the echo of the impulse from which they sprang. There were others which rang on the air more sharply, more tumultously, like the clang of a cymbal, or the booming of a hollow brass, and they conveyed no meaning to any but the speakers, who, in producing these barbarous tones, felt carried out of themselves. But there was no disorderly tumult in the various voices. They were reverberations of one and the same supernatural ecstasy—echoes awakened in different consciousnesses by one and the same emotion.

"Britannicus had heard the Glossolalia—the gift of the tongue. He had been a witness of the Pentecostal marvel, a phenomenon which heathendom had never known.

"Nor had he only heard it, or witnessed it. For as the voices began to grow fainter, as the whole assembly sat listening in the hush of awful expectation, the young prince himself felt as if a Spirit passed before him, and the hair of his flesh stood up; he felt as if a Power and a Presence stronger than his own dominated his being; annihilated his inmost self; dealt with him as a player does who sweeps the strings of an instrument into concord or discord at his will. He felt ashamed of the impulse; he felt terrified by it; but it breathed all over and around and through him, like the mighty wind; it filled his soul as with ethereal fire; it seemed to inspire, to uplift, to delate his very soul; and finally it swept him onward as with numberless rushings of congregated wings. The passion within him was burning into irresistible utterance, and, in another moment, through that humble throng of Christians would have rung in impassioned music the young voice of the last of the Claudii pouring forth things unutterable had not the struggle ended by his uttering one cry, and then sinking into a faint. Before that unwonted cry from the voice of a boy the assembly sank into silence, and after two or three moments the impulse left him. Panting, unconscious, not knowing where he was, or whether he had spoken or not, or how to explain or account for the heart shaking inspiration which had seemed to carry him out of himself beyond all mountain barriers, and over unfathomable seas, the boy sank back into the arms of Pudens, who, alarmed, amazed and half ashamed, had sprung forward to catch him as he fell.

"As he seemed to be in a swoon, one of the young acolytes came to him, and gently bathed his face with cold water. And meanwhile, as the hour was late and they all had to get home in safety through the dark streets and lanes through which they had come—some of them from considerable distances—Linus rose, and with uplifted hand dismissed the congregation. * * *

"Pudens and Nereus carried back the still half-conscious boy into the house of Pomponia, where his sister awaited him   Octavia was alarmed at the wildness of his look, but the fresh air had already revived him. 'I am quite well,' he said, as the empress bent anxiously over him, 'but I am tired, and should like to be silent. Let us go home, Octavia.'

"When they had started, Claudia said, 'Oh Pomponia, while he was at the gathering the Power came upon him: he seemed scarcely able to resist it; but for his fainting I believe he would have spoken with the tongue.' Pomponia clasped her hands, and bowed her head in silent prayer."

As we read this marvelously accurate portrayal of the manifestations accompanying the Glossolalia, it is difficult to realize that Dean Farrar had never been present at one of these latter day Pentecostal gatherings having died (several years. at least) before the present Revival of the "Charismata" in the Church—C. E. D. de L., in "Victory," reprinted by "Trust" and the "Weekly Evangel."

TITLES in THIS SERIES

1. THE HIGHER CHRISTIAN LIFE; A BIBLIOGRAPHICAL OVER-
   VIEW. Donald W. Dayton, THE AMERICAN HOLINESS MOVE-
   MENT: A BIBLIOGRAPHICAL INTRODUCTION. (Wilmore, Ky.,
   1971) bound with David W. Faupel, THE AMERICAN PEN-
   TECOSTAL MOVEMENT: A BIBLIOGRAPHICAL ESSAY. (Wilmore,
   Ky., 1972) bound with David D. Bundy, Keswick: A BIBLI-
   OGRAPHIC INTRODUCTION TO THE HIGHER LIFE MOVEMENTS.
   (Wilmore, Ky., 1975)

2. ACCOUNT OF THE UNION MEETING FOR THE PROMOTION OF
   SCRIPTURAL HOLINESS, HELD AT OXFORD, AUGUST 29 TO SEP-
   TEMBER 7, 1874. (Boston, n. d.)

3. Baker, Elizabeth V., and Co-workers, CHRONICLES OF A
   FAITH LIFE.

4. THE WORK OF T. B. BARRATT. T. B. Barratt, IN THE DAYS OF
   THE LATTER RAIN. (London, 1909) WHEN THE FIRE FELL AND
   AN OUTLINE OF MY LIFE, (Oslo, 1927)

5. WITNESS TO PENTECOST: THE LIFE OF FRANK BARTLEMAN.
   Frank Bartleman, FROM PLOW TO PULPIT—FROM MAINE TO
   CALIFORNIA (Los Angeles, n. d.), HOW PENTECOST CAME TO
   LOS ANGELES (Los Angeles, 1925), AROUND THE WORLD BY
   FAITH, WITH SIX WEEKS IN THE HOLY LAND (Los Angeles, n.
   d.), TWO YEARS MISSION WORK IN EUROPE JUST BEFORE THE
   WORLD WAR, 1912-14 (Los Angeles, [1926])

6. Boardman, W. E., THE HIGHER CHRISTIAN LIFE (Boston,
   1858)

7. Girvin, E. A., PHINEAS F. BRESEE: A PRINCE IN ISRAEL (Kansas City, Mo., [1916])

8. Brooks, John P., THE DIVINE CHURCH (Columbia, Mo., 1891)

9. RUSSELL KELSO CARTER ON "FAITH HEALING." R. Kelso Carter, *THE ATONEMENT FOR SIN AND SICKNESS* (Boston, 1884) *"FAITH HEALING" REVIEWED AFTER TWENTY YEARS* (Boston, 1897)

10. Daniels, W. H., *DR. CULLIS AND HIS WORK* (Boston, [1885])

11. HOLINESS TRACTS DEFENDING THE MINISTRY OF WOMEN. Luther Lee, *"WOMAN'S RIGHT TO PREACH THE GOSPEL; A SERMON, AT THE ORDINATION OF REV. MISS ANTOINETTE L. BROWN, AT SOUTH BUTLER, WAYNE COUNTY, N. Y., SEPT. 15, 1853"* (Syracuse, 1853) *bound with* B. T. Roberts, *ORDAINING WOMEN* (Rochester, 1891) *bound with* Catherine (Mumford) Booth, *"FEMALE MINISTRY; OR, WOMAN'S RIGHT TO PREACH THE GOSPEL . . ."* (London, n. d.) *bound with* Fannie (McDowell) Hunter, *WOMEN PREACHERS* (Dallas, 1905)

12. LATE NINETEENTH CENTURY REVIVALIST TEACHINGS ON THE HOLY SPIRIT. D. L. Moody, *SECRET POWER OR THE SECRET OF SUCCESS IN CHRISTIAN LIFE AND WORK* (New York, [1881]) *bound with* J. Wilbur Chapman, *RECEIVED YE THE HOLY GHOST?* (New York, [1894]) *bound with* R. A. Torrey, *THE BAPTISM WITH THE HOLY SPIRIT* (New York, 1895 & 1897)

13. SEVEN "JESUS ONLY" TRACTS. Andrew D. Urshan, *THE DOCTRINE OF THE NEW BIRTH, OR, THE PERFECT WAY TO ETERNAL LIFE* (Cochrane, Wis., 1921) *bound with* Andrew Urshan, *THE ALMIGHTY GOD IN THE LORD JESUS CHRIST* (Los Angeles, 1919) *bound with* Frank J. Ewart, *THE REVELATION OF JESUS CHRIST* (St. Louis, n. d.) *bound with* G. T. Haywood, *THE BIRTH OF THE SPIRIT IN THE DAYS OF THE APOSTLES* (Indianapolis, n. d.) *DIVINE NAMES AND TITLES OF JEHOVAH* (Indianapolis, n. d.) *THE FINEST OF THE WHEAT* (Indianapolis, n. d.) *THE VICTIM OF THE FLAMING SWORD* (Indianapolis, n. d.)

14. THREE EARLY PENTECOSTAL TRACTS. D. Wesley Myland, *THE LATTER RAIN COVENANT AND PENTECOSTAL POWER* (Chicago, 1910) *bound with* G. F. Taylor, *THE SPIRIT AND THE BRIDE* (n. p., [1907?]) *bound with* B. F. Laurence, *THE APOSTOLIC FAITH RESTORED* (St. Louis, 1916)

15. Fairchild, James H., *OBERLIN: THE COLONY AND THE COLLEGE, 1833-1883* (Oberlin, 1883)

16. Figgis, John B., *KESWICK FROM WITHIN* (London, [1914])

17. Finney, Charles G., *LECTURES TO PROFESSING CHRISTIANS* (New York, 1837)

18. Fleisch, Paul, *DIE MODERNE GEMEINSCHAFTSBEWEGUNG IN DEUTSCHLAND* (Leipzig, 1912)

19. SIX TRACTS BY W. B. GODBEY. *SPIRITUAL GIFTS AND GRACES* (Cincinnati, [1895]) *THE RETURN OF JESUS* (Cincinnati, [1899?]) *WORK OF THE HOLY SPIRIT* (Louisville, [1902]) *CHURCH—BRIDE—KINGDOM* (Cincinnati, [1905]) *DIVINE HEALING* (Greensboro, [1909]) *TONGUE MOVEMENT, SATANIC* (Zarephath, N. J., 1918)

20. Gordon, Earnest B., *ADONIRAM JUDSON GORDON* (New York, [1896])

21. Hills, A. M., *HOLINESS AND POWER FOR THE CHURCH AND THE MINISTRY* (Cincinnati, [1897])

22. Horner, Ralph C., *FROM THE ALTAR TO THE UPPER ROOM* (Toronto, [1891])

23. McDonald, William and John E. Searles, *THE LIFE OF REV. JOHN S. INSKIP* (Boston, [1885])

24. LaBerge, Agnes N. O., *WHAT GOD HATH WROUGHT* (Chicago, n. d.)

25. Lee, Luther, *AUTOBIOGRAPHY OF THE REV. LUTHER LEE* (New York, 1882)

26. McLean, A. and J. W. Easton, *PENUEL; OR, FACE TO FACE WITH GOD* (New York, 1869)

27. McPherson, Aimee Semple, *THIS IS THAT: PERSONAL EXPERIENCES SERMONS AND WRITINGS* (Los Angeles, [1919])

28. Mahan, Asa, *OUT OF DARKNESS INTO LIGHT* (London, 1877)

29. *THE LIFE AND TEACHING OF CARRIE JUDD MONTGOMERY* Carrie Judd Montgomery, *"UNDER HIS WINGS": THE STORY OF MY LIFE* (Oakland, [1936]) Carrie F. Judd, *THE PRAYER OF FAITH* (New York, 1880)

30. *THE DEVOTIONAL WRITINGS OF PHOEBE PALMER* Phoebe Palmer, *THE WAY OF HOLINESS* (52nd ed., New York, 1867) *FAITH AND ITS EFFECTS* (27th ed., New York, n. d., orig. pub. 1854)

31. Wheatley, Richard, *The Life and Letters of Mrs. Phoebe Palmer* (New York, 1881)

32. Palmer, Phoebe, ed., *Pioneer Experiences* (New York, 1868)

33. Palmer, Phoebe, *The Promise of the Father* (Boston, 1859)

34. Pardington, G. P., *Twenty-five Wonderful Years, 1889-1914: A Popular Sketch of the Christian and Missionary Alliance* (New York, [1914])

35. Parham, Sarah E., *The Life of Charles F. Parham, Founder of the Apostolic Faith Movement* (Joplin, [1930])

36. The Sermons of Charles F. Parham. Charles F. Parham, *A Voice Crying in the Wilderness* (4th ed., Baxter Springs, Kan., 1944, orig. pub. 1902) *The Everlasting Gospel* (n.p., n.d., orig. pub. 1911)

37. Pierson, Arthur Tappan, *Forward Movements of the Last Half Century* (New York, 1905)

38. *Proceedings of Holiness Conferences, Held at Cincinnati, November 26th, 1877, and at New York, December 17th, 1877* (Philadelphia, 1878)

39. *Record of the Convention for the Promotion of Scriptural Holiness Held at Brighton, May 29th, to June 7th, 1875* (Brighton, [1896?])

40. Rees, Seth Cook, *Miracles in the Slums* (Chicago, [1905?])

41. Roberts, B. T., *Why Another Sect* (Rochester, 1879)

42. Shaw, S. B., ed., *Echoes of the General Holiness Assembly* (Chicago, [1901])

43. The Devotional Writings of Robert Pearsall Smith and Hannah Whitall Smith. [R]obert [P]earsall [S]mith, *Holiness Through Faith: Light on the Way of Holiness* (New York, [1870]) [H]annah [W]hitall [S]mith, *The Christian's Secret of a Happy Life*, (Boston and Chicago, [1885])

44. [S]mith, [H]annah [W]hitall, *THE UNSELFISHNESS OF GOD AND HOW I DISCOVERED IT* (New York, [1903])

45. Steele, Daniel, *A SUBSTITUTE FOR HOLINESS; OR, ANTINOMIANISM REVIVED* (Chicago and Boston, [1899])

46. Tomlinson, A. J., *THE LAST GREAT CONFLICT* (Cleveland, 1913)

47. Upham, Thomas C., *THE LIFE OF FAITH* (Boston, 1845)

48. Washburn, Josephine M., *HISTORY AND REMINISCENCES OF THE HOLINESS CHURCH WORK IN SOUTHERN CALIFORNIA AND ARIZONA* (South Pasadena, [1912?])

DATE DUE